The Method of Grace

HOW THE HOLY SPIRIT WORKS

JOHN FLAVEL

495

BAKER BOOK HOUSE
Grand Rapids, Michigan

Reprinted 1977 by
Baker Book House

ISBN: 0-8010-3481-7

PHOTOLITHOPRINTED BY CUSHING - MALLOY, INC.
ANN ARBOR, MICHIGAN, UNITED STATES OF AMERICA
1977

CONTENTS

CHAPTER VI

CHAPTER VII

CHAPTER VIII

CHAPTER IX

CHAPTER X

CHAPTER XI

THE LAMENTABLE STATE OF UNBELIEVERS

CHAPTER XXXIV

CHAPTER XXXV

THE AUTHOR'S PREFACE

READER—It is the one thing needful for thee to get an assured interest in Jesus Christ; which being once obtained, thou mayest with boldness say, Come, troubles and distresses, losses and trials, prisons and death, I am prepared for you; do your worst, you can do me no harm: let the winds roar, the lightnings flash, the rain and hail fall never so furiously, I have a good roof over my head, a comfortable lodging provided for me: "My place of defence is the munition of rocks, where bread shall be given me, and my water shall be sure."

The design of the ensuing treatise is to assist thee in this great work; and though it was promised to the world many years past, Providence has reserved it for the fittest season, and brought it to thy hand in a time of need.

It contains the method of grace in the *application of the great redemption to the souls of men*, as the former part* contains the method of grace *provided and accomplished* by Jesus Christ. The acceptance God has given the former part, signified by the desires of many for the publication of this, has at last prevailed with me, notwithstanding the secret consciousness of my inequality to so great an

---

* THE FOUNTAIN OF LIFE, published by the American Tract Society.

undertaking, to adventure this second part also upon the candor of the reader.

And I consent the more willingly to the publication of this, because the design I first aimed at could not be complete without it; but especially as the subject, through the blessing and concurrence of the Spirit, may be useful both to rouse the drowsy consciences of this sleepy generation, and to assist the upright in clearing the work of the Spirit upon their own souls. These considerations have prevailed with me against all discouragements.

If thou be one that hast sincerely *applied* and received Jesus Christ by faith, this book may be useful to thee, to clear and confirm thy evidences, to melt thy heart in the sense of thy mercies, and to quicken thee in the way of thy duties. Here thou wilt see what great things the Lord has done for thy soul, and how these dignities, as thou art his son or daughter by the double title of *regeneration* and *adoption*, oblige thee to yield up thyself to God entirely, and to say from thy heart, Lord, whatever I am, I am for thee; whatever I can do, I will do for thee; and whatever I can suffer, I will suffer for thee : all that I am or have, all that I can do or suffer, is nothing to what thou hast done for my soul.

If thou art a stranger to regeneration and faith, making a powerless profession of Christ; if thou hast a name to live, but art dead; here it is possible thou mayest meet with something to convince thee how dangerous it is to be an old creature in the new creature's dress and habit; and what it is that blinds thy judgment, and is likely to prove thy ruin; a seasonable and full conviction of which will be the greatest mercy that can befall thee in this world, if thereby at last God may help thee to put on Christ, as well as the name of Christ.

If thou art in darkness about the state of thy soul, and willing to have it faithfully and impartially tried by the word, which will not warp to any man's humor or interest, here thou wilt find some assistance offered thee to clear thy doubting thoughts, which, through thy prayer, and the supply of the Spirit of Jesus Christ, may lead thee to a comfortable inward peace.

If thou art a proud, presumptuous soul, who hast too little knowledge, and too much self-love, to admit any doubts of thy state towards God, there are many things in this treatise proper for thy conviction and better information; for woe to thee if thou shouldst not fear till thou begin to feel thy misery, if thy troubles do not come on till all thy hopes are gone off.

I know all these things are performed by me with much infirmity, and that the whole is quite below the dignity of the subject. But when I consider that the success of sermons and books in the world has but little relation to the elegance of language and accuracy of method, and that many may be useful who cannot be excellent, I am willing in all humility and sincerity to commit it to the direction of Providence and the blessing of the Spirit.

One thing I earnestly request of all the people of God into whose hands this book shall fall, that they will be persuaded to end all the strifes among themselves, which have wasted so much precious time and consumed the vital spirit of religion, hindered the conversion of multitudes, and increased and confirmed the atheism of the times. O put on, as the elect of God, bowels of mercy, and a spirit of charity and forbearance, if not for your own sakes, yet for the church's sake. O that you would dwell more in your closets, and be more frequently and fervently upon your knees: that you would search your hearts more narrowly and sift them more thoroughly than ever, before the Lord's fierce anger come upon you: look into your Bibles, then into your hearts, and then to heaven, for a true discovery of your condition; and if this poor mite may contribute any thing to that end, it will be a great reward of the unworthy labors of

Your servant in Christ,

JOHN FLAVEL

THE

METHOD OF GRACE

NATURE OF THE SPIRIT'S APPLICATION
OF CHRIST TO MEN

CHAPTER I.

THE GENERAL NATURE OF THE EFFECTUAL APPLI-
CATION OF CHRIST AND HIS BENEFITS

"But of him are ye in Christ Jesus, who of God is made unto us wisdom, and
righteousness, and sanctification, and redemption." 1 Cor. 1 : 30

He who inquires what is the just value and worth of
Christ, asks a question which puts all the men on earth
and angels in heaven to an everlasting nonplus.

The highest attainment of our knowledge in this life,
is to know that himself and his love pass knowledge.
Eph. 3 : 19.

But how excellent soever Christ is in himself, what
treasures of righteousness soever lie in his blood, and
whatever joy, peace, and ravishing comforts spring up to
men out of his *incarnation, humiliation,* and *exaltation,* they
all give down their distinct benefits and comforts to them,
in the way of *effectual application.*

For never was any wound healed by a prepared, but
unapplied plaster ; never any body warmed by the most
costly garment made, but not put on ; never any heart refreshed and comforted by the richest cordial compounded,

but not received ; nor from the beginning of the world was it ever known that a poor *deceived, condemned, polluted,* miserable sinner, was actually delivered out of that woful state, until of God *Christ was made unto him wisdom and righteousness, sanctification and redemption.*

For as the condemnation of the first Adam passes not to us, except as by generation we are his ; so grace and remission pass not from the second Adam to us, except as by regeneration we are his.   Adam's sin hurts none but those that are in him ; and Christ's blood profits none but those that are in him.   How great a weight therefore does there hang upon THE EFFECTUAL APPLICATION of Christ to the souls of men !   And what is there in the whole world so awfully solemn, so greatly important as this ?   Such is the strong consolation resulting from it, that the apostle, in the context, offers it to the believing Corinthians as a superabundant recompense for the meanness of their outward condition in this world, of which he had just before spoken. In the text we have,

1. An *enumeration* of the chief privileges of believers, "*wisdom, righteousness, sanctification,* and *redemption :*" mercies of inestimable value in themselves, and which respect a fourfold misery lying upon man, namely, *ignorance, guilt, pollution,* and the whole train of miserable consequences and effects let in upon him by *sin.*

Lapsed man is not only deep in misery, but grossly *ignorant,* both that he is so, and how to recover himself : sin has left him at once senseless of his state, and at a perfect loss about the true remedy.   Christ is made to men *wisdom,* not only by employing the treasures of wisdom in himself, for the benefit of souls united to him as their head ; but by *imparting* his wisdom to them by the Spirit of illumination, whereby they come to discern both their sin and danger, and the true way of their recovery from both, through the application of Christ to their souls by faith.

But alas, simple illumination does but increase our burden and exasperate our misery, as long as sin in the guilt of it is either imputed to our persons unto condemnation, or reflected by our consciences in a way of accusation.   Christ is therefore made of God unto us *righteousness*, complete and perfect righteousness, whereby our obligation to punishment is dissolved, and a solid foundation for a well-settled peace of conscience firmly established.

But though the removing of guilt from our persons and consciences be an inestimable mercy, yet alone it cannot make us completely happy; for though a man should never be damned for sin, yet what is it less than hell upon earth, to be under the dominion and pollution of every base lust? To complete the happiness of the redeemed, Christ is made of God unto them not only *wisdom* and *righteousness*, the one curing our ignorance, the other our guilt ; but he is made *sanctification* also, to relieve us against the dominion and pollution of our corruptions.   He comes both by water and by blood, not by blood only, but by water also, 1 John 5 : 6 ; purging as well as pardoning.   How complete and perfect a cure is Christ !

But yet something is required beyond all this to make our happiness perfect and entire, wanting nothing ; and that is, the removal of those doleful effects and consequences of sin which still lie upon the souls and bodies of illuminated, justified, and sanctified persons.   For even with the holiest of men what swarms of vanity, what deadness and unbelief daily appear and oppress their souls, imbittering all the comforts of life !   And how many diseases and pains oppress their bodies, which daily moulder away till they fall into the grave by death, even as the bodies of other men do who never received such privileges from Christ.   For if " Christ be in us, the body is dead, because of sin."   Rom. 8 : 10.   Sanctification exempts us not from mortality.

From all these, and whatsoever else, the fruits and consequences of sin, Christ is also *redemption* to his people. This seals up the sum of mercies ; this so completes the happiness of the saints that it leaves nothing to desire.

These four, wisdom, righteousness, sanctification, and redemption, include all that is necessary to make a soul truly and perfectly blessed.

2. We have here *the method* by which believers come to be invested with these excellent privileges : " *Who of God is made unto us;*" in which expression four things are to be observed :

(1.) Christ and his benefits are *inseparable :* we can have no saving benefit apart from the person of Christ. Many would willingly receive his *privileges* who will not receive his person ; but it cannot be : nay, we must accept his person first, and then his benefits ; as it is in the marriage covenant, so it is here.

(2.) Christ with his benefits must be *personally applied to us* before we can receive any actual, saving privilege by him ; he must be *made unto us*, as a sum of money becomes, or is made the ransom and liberty of a captive, when it is not only promised, but paid down in his name, and legally applied for that use and end. When Christ died, the ransom was prepared in his own blood ; but yet the elect continue in sin and misery, till by effectual calling it be actually *applied* to their persons, and then they are made free, reconciled by Christ's death, by whom "we have now received the atonement." Rom. 5 : 10, 11

(3.) This application of Christ is the work of God, and not of man : " *Of God* he is made unto us." The same hand that prepared it must also apply it, or else we perish, notwithstanding all that the Father has done in contriving, and all that the Son has done in executing and accomplishing the design thus far. And this actual application is the peculiar work of the Spirit.

(4.) This expression imports the suitableness of Christ

to *the necessities* of sinners : what they want he is made to them. As money answers all things, and is convertible into meat, drink, raiment, medicine, or whatever else our bodily necessities require ; so Christ is virtually and eminently *all* that the necessities of our souls require : bread to the hungry and clothing to the naked. In a word, God prepared and furnished him on purpose to answer all our wants. The sum of all is,

That the Lord Jesus Christ, with all his precious benefits, becomes ours by God's special and effectual application.

There is a twofold application of our redemption : one *primary,* the act of God the *Father,* applying it to Christ our surety, and virtually to us in him ; the latter *secondary,* the act of the *Holy Spirit,* personally and actually applying it to us in the work of conversion. This personal and *actual application of redemption* to us by the Spirit in his sanctifying work, I am engaged here to discuss.

1 The application of Christ to us, *not only comprehends our justification, but all those works of the Spirit which are known to us in Scripture by the terms regeneration, vocation, sanctification, and conversion.*

Regeneration expresses those supernatural, divine, new qualities imparted by the Spirit to the soul, which are the principle of all holy action. *Vocation* expresses the terms from which and to which the soul moves when the Spirit works savingly upon it, under the gospel call. *Sanctification* denotes a holy dedication of heart and life to God: our becoming the temples of the living God, separate from all profane and sinful practices to the Lord's only use and service. *Conversion* denotes the great change itself, which the Spirit causes upon the soul, turning it by a sweet, irresistible efficacy, from the power of sin and Satan to God in Christ.

Now all these are included in the *application of Christ to our souls;* for when once the efficacy of Christ's death and resurrection are applied to the heart of any man, he then turns from sin to God, and becomes a new creature, living and acting by new principles and rules. So the apostle says to the Thessalonians, speaking of the effect of this work of the Spirit upon that people : "Our gospel came not to you in word only, but in power, and in the Holy Ghost"—there was the effectual application of Christ to them. "And ye became followers of us, and of the Lord"—there was their effectual call. "And ye turned from dumb idols to serve the living and the true God"—there was their conversion. "So that ye were ensamples to all that believe"—there was their life of sanctification or dedication to God. 1 Thess. 1 : 5-9. So that all these are comprehended in effectual application.

2. The application of Christ to the souls of men is the great design of God for the accomplishment of which *all the ordinances and all the officers of the gospel are appointed.*

This the gospel expressly declares to be its direct end, and the great business of all its officers. "And he gave some apostles, and some prophets, and some evangelists, and some pastors and teachers ; till we all come in the unity of the faith, and the knowledge of the Son of God, to a perfect man, unto the measure of the stature of the fulness of Christ," Eph. 4 : 11, 13 ; that is, the great aim of all Christ's ordinances and officers is to bring men into union with Christ, and so build them up to perfection in him ; or to unite them to, and confirm them in Christ : and when it shall have finished this design, then shall the whole frame of gospel ordinances be taken down, and all its officers be disbanded : the kingdom, that is, this present economy, manner, and form of government, shall be delivered up. 1 Cor. 15 : 24. What are ministers but the Bridegroom's friends, ambassadors for God, to beseech men to be reconciled ? When therefore all the elect are brought home in a reconciled state in Christ, when the marriage of the Lamb is come, our work and office expire together.

3. Such is the importance of the personal application of Christ to us by the Spirit, that whatsoever the Father has done in the contrivance, or the Son in the accomplishment of our redemption, it is all *unavailable and ineffectual to our salvation without this.*

It is confessedly true, that God's good pleasure appointing us from eternity to salvation, is, in its kind, a sufficient impulsive cause of our salvation, and every way able—for so much as it is concerned—to produce its effect. And Christ's humiliation and sufferings are a most complete meritorious cause of our salvation, to which nothing can be added to make it more able to procure our salvation than it already is; yet neither the one nor the other can actually save any soul without the *Spirit's application* of Christ to it. The *Father* has elected, and the *Son* has redeemed; but until the *Spirit* has wrought his part also, we cannot be saved. For he comes in the Father's and in the Son's name and authority, to complete the work of our salvation, by bringing all the fruits of election and redemption home to our souls in this work of effectual vocation. Hence the apostle, noting the order of causes in their operations for the bringing about of our salvation, thus states it: "Elect, according to the foreknowledge of God the Father, through sanctification of the Spirit unto obedience, and sprinkling of the blood of Jesus Christ." Here you find God's election and Christ's blood the two great causes of salvation, and yet neither of these alone, nor both together, can save us: there must be added the sanctification of the Spirit, by which God's purpose is executed; and the sprinkling, that is, the personal *application* of Christ's blood, as well as the shedding of it, before we can have the saving benefit of either of the former causes.

4. The application of Christ to souls, by the regenerating work of the Spirit, makes *the first internal difference and distinction among men.*

It is very true, that in respect to God's foreknowledge and purpose, there is a distinction between one man and another; and Christ laid down his life for the sheep, he prayed for them, and not for the world ; but as to any relative change of state, or real change of temper, they are upon a level with the rest of the miserable world.   The elect themselves are "by nature the children of wrath, even as others." Eph. 2 : 3.   And to the same purpose the apostle tells the Corinthians, when he had given in that black bill, describing the most lewd, profligate, abominable wretches in the world, men whose practices might make the more sober heathen blush, "Such were some of you; but ye are washed," etc.   1 Cor. 6 : 11.   The work of the Spirit makes us new creatures.   "If any man be in Christ, he is a new creature ; old things are passed away; behold, all things are become new."   2 Cor. 5 : 17.

5. *The application of Christ, by the work of regeneration, yields to men all the refreshment and joy they have in Christ, and in all that he has done for sinners.*

An unsanctified person may relish the sweetness of nature, as well as he that is sanctified ; he may also seem to relish and taste some sweetness in the promises and discoveries of the gospel, by a *misapplication* of them to himself.   But this is like the joy of a beggar dreaming he is a king, who awakes and finds himself a beggar still. The rational, solid, and genuine delights and comforts of religion no man tastes till this work of the Spirit is wrought upon his soul : it is an enclosed pleasure, a stranger intermeddles not with it.   The white stone and the new name, denoting the pleasant results and fruits of justification and adoption, no man knows but he that receives them. Rev. 2 : 17.

The unsanctified soul does not *appropriate* Christ to itself.   Luther was wont to say, that the sweetness of the gospel lay mostly in *pronouns*, as *me, my, thy.*   "Who loved *me*, and gave himself for me ;" "Christ Jesus *my*

Lord ;" " Son, be of good cheer; *thy* sins are forgiven." The unsanctified soul has neither the *evidence* requisite to joy and comfort, nor yet the *temper* of spirit required ; for how can Christ be sweet to that man's soul whose thoughts repel so holy and pure an object ?

6. The application of Christ to the soul effectually, though it be so far wrought in the first saving work of the Spirit as truly to unite the soul to Christ, and save it from the danger of perishing, *is a work gradually advancing in the believer's soul while it abides on this side heaven and glory.*

It is true indeed, that Christ is perfectly and complete-ly applied to the soul in the first act for righteousness. " Justification being a relative change," says Ames, " prop-erly admits no degrees, but is perfected at once in one only act ; though as to its manifestation, sense, and effects, it has various degrees." But the *application* of Christ to us, for wisdom and sanctification, is not perfected in one single act, but rises by many and slow degrees to its just perfection. Though we are truly said to come to Christ when we first believe, John 6 : 35, yet the soul after that is still coming to him by further acts of faith. 1 Pet. 2 : 4. " To whom *coming*, as unto a living stone :" the expression denotes a continued motion, by which the soul gains ground, and still gets nearer and nearer to Christ ; grow-ing still more inwardly acquainted with him. The know-ledge of Christ grows upon the soul as the morning light, from its first dawn to the perfect day. Prov. 4 : 18. Every grace of the Spirit grows, if not sensibly, yet really ; for it is in discerning the growth of sanctification as in the growth of plants, which we perceive rather to have grown than to grow. And as it thrives in the soul by a deeper rooting of the habits, and more promptitude and spiritual-ity in acting ; so Christ and the soul proportionably, are united more and more inwardly and efficaciously, till at last it is wholly swallowed up in Christ's full and perfect enjoyment.

7. Although the several privileges and benefits mentioned are all truly and really bestowed with Christ upon believers, yet they *are not communicated to them in one and the same manner, but diversely, as their respective natures require.*

The four illustrious benefits mentioned in this text, are conveyed from Christ to us in three different ways and methods: his righteousness is made ours by *imputation;* his wisdom and sanctification by *renovation;* his redemption by our *glorification.*

I know the communication of Christ's righteousness to us by imputation, is not only denied, but scoffed at by papists; who own no righteousness but what is, at least, confounded with that which is inherent in us. The doctrine they regard as most absurd, everywhere endeavoring to load it with such absurdities as these: That if God imputes Christ's righteousness to the believer, and accepts what Christ has performed for him, as if he had performed it himself, then we may be accounted as righteous as Christ—we may be the redeemers of the world. False and groundless consequences! As if a man should say, my debt is paid by my surety, therefore I am as rich as he. "We think not," says Bradshaw, "that the righteousness of Christ is made ours according to its universal value, but according to our particular necessity; not to make others righteous, but to make us so; not that we have the formal intrinsic righteousness of Christ in us as it is in him, but a relative righteousness, which makes us righteous, even as he is righteous—not as to the quantity, but as to the truth of it: nor is it imputed to us as though Christ designed to make us the *causes* of salvation to others, but the *subjects* of salvation ourselves." Thus the Redeemer became sin for us, and thus we are made the righteousness of God in him. 2 Cor. 5 : 21. In this way Abraham, the father of believers, was justified, and in this way all believers, the children of Abraham, must be justified. Rom. 4 : 22–24. Thus is Christ's righteousness made ours.

But in conveying and communicating his *wisdom* and *sanctification*, he takes another method; for this is not *imputed*, but really *imparted* to us by the illuminating and regenerating work of the Spirit: these are graces really inherent in us: our righteousness comes from Christ as a *surety*, but our holiness comes from him as a quickening *head*, sending vital influences into all his members.

Now these gracious habits being formed in the souls of poor imperfect creatures, whose corruptions abide and work in the very same faculties where grace has its residence, it cannot be that our sanctification should be perfect and complete as is our justification which inheres only in Christ.   Gal. 5 : 17.

But *redemption*, that is, absolute and plenary deliverance from all the sad remains and consequences of sin, both upon soul and body, is made ours, or Christ is made redemption to us, when we are *glorified*: then, and not before, are these miserable effects removed; we put off these together with the body.   So that as *justification* cures the *guilt* of sin, and *sanctification* the *dominion* of sin, so *glorification* removes, together with its *existence* and being, all those *miseries* which it let in as a flood upon our whole man.   Eph. 5 : 26, 27.

INFERENCE 1.   *Learn from hence, what a naked, destitute, and empty thing a poor sinner is, in his natural unregenerate state.*   He is one that naturally and inherently has neither wisdom nor righteousness, sanctification nor redemption: all these must come from without himself, even from Christ, who is made all this to a sinner, or else he must eternally perish.   As we are born more weak and helpless than any other creature, so all our spiritual excellencies are borrowed excellencies, and we have nothing of which to boast.   "What hast thou that thou didst not receive? Now, if thou didst receive it, why dost thou glory, as if thou hadst not received it?"   1 Cor. 4 : 7.   What intolerable insolence and vanity would it be for a man that wears the rich and costly robe of Christ's righteousness, in which there is not one thread of his own spinning, to pride himself as if he had made it, and were beholden to none for it. O man, thine excellencies, whatever they are, are borrowed from Christ; they oblige thee to him, but he can be no more obliged to thee who wearest them, than the sun is obliged to him that borrows its light, or the fountain to him that draws its water for his use and benefit.

It has ever been the care of holy men, when they have viewed their own gracious *principles*, or best *performances*, still to disclaim themselves, and own free-grace as the sole author of all. Thus holy Paul, viewing the principles of the divine life in himself, the richest gift bestowed upon man in this world by Jesus Christ, how doth he renounce himself, and deny the least part of the praise and glory as belonging to him : "Now I live, yet not I, but Christ liveth in me," Gal. 2 : 20 ; and so for the best duties that ever he performed for God—and what mere man ever did more for God?—yet when, in a just and necessary defence, he was constrained to mention them, how carefully is *yet not I* presently added. "I labored more abundantly than they all; yet not I, but the grace of God which was with me." 1 Cor. 15 : 10. Let then the sense of your own emptiness by nature humble and the more increase your sense of obligation to Christ, from whom you receive all you have.

2. Hence we see that *none can claim benefit by imputed righteousness, but those that live in the power of inherent holiness.* To whomsoever Christ is made *righteousness*, to him he also is made *sanctification*. The gospel has not the least favor for licentiousness. It is every way as careful to press men to their duties as to instruct them in their privileges : "This is a faithful saying, and these things I will that thou affirm constantly, that they which have believed in God might be careful to maintain good works." Tit. 3 : 8. It is a loose principle, divulged by *libertines*, to the re-

proach of Christ and his gospel, that sanctification is not the evidence of our justification. And Christ is as much wronged by them who separate holiness from righteousness—as if a sensual vile life were consistent with a justified state—as he is in the contrary extreme, by those who confound Christ's righteousness with man's holiness in the point of justification; or who own no other righteousness but what is inherent in themselves. The former opinion makes him a *cloak* for sin, the latter a *needless sacrifice* for sin.

It is true, our sanctification cannot justify us before God; but what then, can it not evidence our justification before men? Is there no necessity or use for a holy life because it avails not in our justification? Is the preparation of the soul for heaven, by altering its frame and temper, nothing? Is the glorifying of our Redeemer, by a life of faith in the world, nothing? Does the work of Christ render the work of the Spirit needless? God forbid: he came not by blood only, but by water also. 1 John 5 : 6. When the apostle says, "Unto him that worketh not, but believeth on him that justifieth the ungodly, his faith is counted for righteousness," Rom. 4 : 5 ; the scope of it is not to characterize and describe the justified person as one that is slothful and has no mind to work; nor as rebellious and refractory, refusing obedience to the commands of God; but to represent him as a humbled sinner, who is convinced of his inability to work out his own righteousness by the law, and sees all his endeavors to obey the law fall short of righteousness, and therefore is said, in a law-sense, *not to work*, because he does not so work as to answer the purpose and end of the law, which accepts of nothing beneath perfect obedience. And when the ungodly are said to be justified, that character describes not the temper and frame of their hearts and lives after their justification, but what it was before ; not as it leaves, but as it found them.

3. How unreasonable and worse than brutish is the sin of *infidelity*, by which the sinner rejects Christ, and with him all those mercies and benefits which alone can relieve and cure his misery! He is by nature blind and ignorant, and yet he refuses Christ, who comes to him with heavenly light and wisdom; he is condemned by the terrible sentence of the law to eternal wrath, and yet rejects Christ, who tenders to him complete and perfect righteousness; he is wholly polluted and plunged into the pollutions of nature and practice, yet will have none of Christ, who would become sanctification to him. He is oppressed in soul and body, with the deplorable effects and miseries sin hath brought upon him, and yet is so in love with his bondage that he will neither accept Christ nor the redemption he brings to sinners.

O, what monsters, what beasts has sin turned its subjects into! "Ye will not come to me, that ye might have life." John 5 : 40. Sin has stabbed the sinner to the heart, the wounds are all mortal, eternal death is before him; Christ has prepared the only remedy that can heal his wounds, but he will not suffer him to apply it. He acts like one in love with death, and that judges it sweet to perish. So Christ tells us, "All they that hate me love death," Prov. 8 : 36; not in itself, but in its causes, with which it is inseparably connected. They are loath to burn, yet willing to sin; though sin kindles the everlasting flames. So that in two things the unbeliever shows himself worse than brutish: he cannot think of damnation, the effect of sin, without horror, and yet cannot think of sin, the cause of damnation, without pleasure; he is loath to perish to all eternity without remedy, and yet refuses and declines Christ as if he were an enemy, who only can and would deliver him from that eternal perdition.

How do men thus act as if they were in love with their own ruin! Many poor wretches now in the way to hell, how hard do they struggle to cast themselves away!

Christ meets them in the ordinances, where they studiously shun him; or checks them in their way by convictions, which they strive to overcome and conquer. Oh, how willing are they to accept a cure, a benefit, a remedy for any thing but their souls! You see, then, that sinners cannot, should they study all their days to do themselves a mischief, take a readier course to ruin themselves than by rejecting Christ in his gracious offers. Surely the sin of Sodom and Gomorrah is less than this sin. Mercy itself is exasperated by it, and the damnation of such as reject Christ, so seriously and frequently offered to them, is just, inevitable, and will be more intolerable than to any in the world besides. Neither heathens nor devils ever aggravated their sins by the wilful refusing of such an appropriate, offered, and only remedy.

4. *What a tremendous symptom of wrath and sad character of death* appears upon that man's soul, to which no effectual application of Christ can be made by the gospel. Christ with his benefits is frequently tendered to men in the gospel; they have been besought to accept him; these entreaties and persuasions have been urged by the greatest arguments, the command of God, the love of Christ, the inconceivable happiness or misery which unavoidably follow the accepting or rejecting of these offers, and yet nothing will affect them. All their pleas for unbelief have been confuted; their reason and conscience have stood convinced; they have been speechless, as well as Christless: not one sound argument is found with them to defend their infidelity, and they confess in general that such a course as theirs leads to destruction. They will allow that those who are in Christ are happy; and yet, when it comes to the point, their own closing with him, all arguments, all entreaties, are unsuccessful.

Lord, what is the reason of this obstinacy? In other things it is not so. If they be sick, they are so far from rejecting a physician, that they will send, and pray, and

pay him too. If they be arrested for debt, and any one
will be a surety, words can hardly express the sense they
have of such a kindness ; but though Christ would be both
a physician and surety, and whatever else their needs require, they will rather perish to eternity than accept him.
What may we fear to be the reason of this, but that they
are not of Christ's sheep. John 10 : 26 The Lord open
the eyes of poor sinners to apprehend not only how great
a sin, but how dreadful a sign this is.

5. If Christ, with all his benefits, be made ours by
God's special application, *what a day of mercy is the day of
conversion; what multitudes of choice blessings visit the converted
soul in that day!* "This day," said Christ to Zaccheus,
"is salvation come to this house." Luke 19 : 9. In this
day, Christ comes into the soul, and he comes not empty,
but brings with him all his treasures of "wisdom and
righteousness, sanctification and redemption." Troops of
mercies, yea, of the best of mercies, come with him. It
is a day of gladness and joy to the heart of Christ, when
he is espoused to and received by the believing soul : it
is a coronation day to a king. So you read, Song 3 : 11 ;
where is shadowed out the joy of Christ's heart, when
poor souls, by their high estimation of him and consent to
his government, do, as it were, crown him with glory and
honor, and make his heart glad.

Now, if the day of our espousals to Christ be the day
of the gladness of his heart, and he reckons himself thus
honored and glorified by us, what a day of joy and gladness should it be to our hearts, and how should we be
transported with joy, to see a King from heaven, with all
his treasures of grace and glory, bestowing himself freely
and everlastingly upon us, as our portion ! No wonder
that Zaccheus came down joyfully, Luke 19 : 6 ; that the
eunuch went home rejoicing, Acts 8 : 39 ; that the jailer
rejoiced, believing in God with all his household, Acts
16 : 34 ; that they that were converted did eat their meat

with gladness, praising God, Acts 2 : 41, 46 ; that there was great joy among them of Samaria, when Christ came among them in the preaching of the gospel. Acts 8 : 5, 8. I say, it is no wonder we read of such joy accompanying Christ into the soul, when we consider that in one day so many blessings meet together in it, the least of which is not to be exchanged for all the kingdoms of this world and the glory of them. Eternity itself will but suffice to bless God for the mercies of this one day

6. If Christ be made all this to every soul to whom he is effectually applied, what cause have those that are under the preparatory work of the Spirit, and are come nigh to Christ and all his benefits, to *stretch out their hands with vehement desire to Christ, and invite him into their souls!* The whole world is distinguishable into three classes of persons : such as are *far from Christ;* such as are *not far from Christ;* and such as are *in Christ.* They that are in Christ have heartily received him. Such as are far from Christ will not open to him ; their hearts are fast barred by ignorance, prejudice, and unbelief against him. But those that are under the preparatory workings of the Spirit are come nigh to Christ, who see their own indispensable necessity of him, and his suitableness to their necessities, in whom also encouraging hopes begin to dawn, and their souls would close sincerely and universally with him, Oh, what vehement desires, what strong pleas, what moving arguments should such persons urge and plead to win Christ and get possession of him ! They are in sight of their only remedy ; Christ and salvation are come to their very doors ; there wants but a few things to make them blessed for ever. This is the day in which their souls are exercised between hopes and fears : now they are much alone and deep in thoughtfulness, they weep and make supplication for a heart to believe, and that against the great discouragements which they encounter.

Reader, if this be the case of thy soul, it will not be

the least service I can render thee, to suggest such pleas as are proper now to be urged for the attainment of thy desires, and the closing of thy heart with Christ.

Plead *the absolute necessity* which now drives thee to Christ, tell him thy hope in all other refuges is utterly perished; thou art come like a starving beggar to the last door of hope. Tell him thou now beginnest to see the absolute necessity of Christ: thy body hath not so much need of bread, water, or air, as thy soul hath of Christ, and the wisdom and righteousness, sanctification and redemption that are in him.

Plead *the Father's gracious design* in furnishing and sending him into the world, and *his own design* in accepting the Father's call. "Lord Jesus, wast thou not 'anointed to preach good tidings to the meek, to bind up the broken-hearted, and to proclaim liberty to the captives, and the opening of the prison to them that are bound?' Isa. 61 : 1 Behold an object suitable to thine office: while I was ignorant of my condition, I had a proud rebellious heart, but conviction and self-acquaintance show me my sin: my heart was harder than the nether millstone, it was as easy to dissolve the obdurate rocks as to thaw and melt my heart for sin; but now God hath opened mine eyes, I sensibly feel the misery of my condition. I once thought myself at perfect liberty, but now I see that what I thought perfect liberty is perfect bondage; and never did a poor prisoner sigh for deliverance more than I. Since then thou hast given me a soul thus prepared, though still unworthy, for the exercise of thine office and the execution of thy commission. Lord Jesus, be, according to thy name, a Jesus, a Saviour unto me."

Plead *the unlimited and general invitation* made to such souls as you are to come to Christ freely. "Lord, thou hast made open proclamation, 'Ho, every one that thirsteth, come ye to the waters,' Isa. 55 : 1; and, 'Let him that is athirst come.' Rev. 22 : 17. In obedience to thy call, lo, I come; had I not been invited, my coming to thee, blessed Lord Jesus, had been an act of presumption, but this makes it an act of duty and obedience."

Plead *the unprofitableness of thy blood to God*. "Lord, there is no profit in my blood, it will turn to no more advantage to thee to destroy, than it will to save me: if thou send me to hell, as the merit of my sin calls upon thy justice to do, I shall be there dishonoring thee to all eternity, and the debt I owe thee will never be paid. But if Christ be applied to me for righteousness, the satisfaction will be complete. If the honor of thy justice lay as a bar to my pardon, it would stop my mouth; but when thy justice as well as thy mercy shall both rejoice together, and be glorified and pleased in the same act, what hinders but that Christ be applied to my soul?"

Plead *thy compliance* with the terms of the gospel: tell him, "Lord, my will complies fully and heartily to all thy gracious terms. I can now subscribe a blank: let God offer his Christ on what terms he will, my heart is ready to comply; I have no exception against any article of the gospel. And now, Lord, I wholly refer myself to thy pleasure; do with me what seemeth good in thine eyes, only give me an interest in Jesus Christ; as to all other concerns, I lie at thy feet, in full resignation of all to thy pleasure. Never yet did any perish in that posture and frame; and I hope I shall not be made the first instance and example."

7. If Christ, with all his benefits, be made ours by a special application, *how thankful and happy should believers be, in every condition into which God casts them in this world!* After such a mercy as this, let them never open their mouths any more to repine at the outward inconveniences of their condition. What are the things you want compared with the things you enjoy? What is a little money, health, or liberty, to "wisdom, righteousness, sanctification, and redemption?" All the crowns and

sceptres in the world are no price for the least of these mercies.

But your duty lies much higher than contentment. Be *thankful*, as well as content, in every state. "Blessed be 'the God and Father of our Lord Jesus Christ, who hath blessed us with all spiritual blessings in heavenly places in Christ." Eph. 1 : 3. O think what are men to angels, that Christ should pass by them to become a Saviour to men! And what art thou among men, that thou shouldst be taken and others left? And among all the mercies of God, what mercies are comparable to these conferred upon thee? O bless God in the lowest ebb of outward comforts, for such privileges as these.

And yet you will not come up to your duty in all this, except you be *joyful* in the Lord, and rejoice evermore, after the receipt of such mercies as these. "Rejoice in the Lord alway ; and again I say, Rejoice." Phil. 4 : 4. Has not the poor captive reason to rejoice when he has recovered his liberty ; the debtor to rejoice when all scores are cleared, and he owes nothing ; the weary traveller to rejoice, though he be not owner of a shilling, when he is come almost home, where all his wants shall be supplied? This is your case when Christ once becomes yours : you are the Lord's freeman, your debts to justice are all satisfied by Christ ; and you are within a little of complete redemption from all the troubles and inconveniences of your present state.

Thanks be to God for Jesus Christ.

CHAPTER II

THE BELIEVER'S UNION WITH CHRIST

"I in them, and Thou in me, that they may be made perfect in one." JOHN
17 : 23

THE design and end of the application of Christ to sinners is the communication of his benefits to them ; but all
communication of benefits necessarily implies communion,
and all communion as necessarily presupposes union with
his person : I shall therefore now treat of *the union between
Christ and believers;* this union being the principal act
wherein the Spirit's application of Christ consists.

In this verse we find a threefold union : one between
the Father and Christ, a second between Christ and believers, a third between believers themselves.

1. *Thou in me.* This is a glorious ineffable union, and
is fundamental to the other two. The Father is not only
in Christ in affection, as one dear friend is in another, who
is as his own soul ; nor only essentially in the identity and
sameness of nature and attributes, in which respect Christ
is " the express image of his person," Heb. 1 : 3 ; but he
is in Christ also as Mediator, by communicating the fulness
of the Godhead which dwells in him as God-man, in a transcendent and singular manner, so as it never dwelt nor
can dwell in any other. Col. 2 : 9.

2. *I in them.* Here is the union between Christ and
the saints. As if he had said, Thou and I are one essentially, they and I are one mystically : thou and I are one
by communication of the Godhead and the fulness of the
Spirit to me as Mediator ; they and I are one by my communication of the Spirit to them in measure.

3. Hence results a third union between believers them-

selves, *that they may be made perfect in one:* the same Spirit dwelling in them all, and equally uniting them all to me, as living members to their Head, there must be a dear and intimate union between themselves, as fellow-members of the same body.

Our subject at present is the second branch, the union between Christ and believers, from which we gather this proposition :

That there is a strict and dear union between Christ and all true believers.

The Scriptures have borrowed from the book of nature four elegant and lively metaphors to help us to understand the nature of this union with Christ ; but no one of them singly, nor all of them jointly, can give us a full and complete idea of this mystery.

" He that is *joined* to the Lord"—in the original, glued— "is one spirit." 1 Cor. 6 : 17. Yet this is but a faint and imperfect shadow of our union with Christ; for though this union by glue be intimate, it is not vital, as is that of the soul with Christ.

So of the *graff* and stock mentioned Rom. 6 : 5 ; for though it be there said that believers are implanted, or in-grafted, and this union between it and the stock be vital, for it partakes of the vital sap and juice, yet here also the metaphor is incomplete, for a graff is of a more excellent nature than the stock, and the tree receives its denomination from it, as from the more noble and excellent part ; but Christ, into whom believers are ingrafted, is infinitely more excellent than they, and they are denominated from him.

Another metaphor is that of the *conjugal union*, Eph. 5 : 31, 32 ; but though this be exceedingly dear and inti-mate, so that a man leaves father and mother and cleaves to his wife, and they two become one flesh, yet this union is not indissolvable, but may and must be broken by death; and then the survivor lives alone without any communion with or relation to the person that was once so dear. But the union between Christ and the soul cannot be dissolved by death, it abides to eternity.

The fourth metaphor is that of *the head and members* united by one vital spirit, so making one physical body. Ephes. 4 : 15, 16. But though one soul actuates every member, it does not knit every member alike near to the head ; but here every member is alike nearly united with Christ the head ; the weak are as near to him as the strong.

I. Let us then consider the *reality* and the *nature* of this union. That THERE IS SUCH A UNION between Christ and believers, appears,

1. From *the communion* between Christ and believers. In this the apostle is express: "Truly our fellowship is with the Father, and with his Son Jesus Christ." 1 John 1 : 3. It signifies such fellowship or copartnership as persons have by a joint interest in one and the same enjoyment, which is in common betwixt them. So we are *partakers of Christ.* Heb. 3 : 14. And the saints are called the companions, consorts, or fellows of Christ, Psalm 45 : 7 ; "and that not only in respect to his assumption of our mortality, and investing us with immortality, but it has a special reference and respect to the unction of the Holy Ghost, or graces of the Spirit, of which believers are partakers with him, and through him." Rivet. Now this communion of the saints with Christ is entirely and necessarily dependent upon their union with him, even as much as the branch's participation of the sap and juice depends upon its union and coalition with the stock : take away union, and there can be no communion or communication ; which is clear from 1 Cor. 3 : 22, 23 : "All are yours, and ye are Christ's, and Christ is God's ;" implying that all our participation of Christ's benefits is built upon our union with Christ's person.

2. The reality of the believer's union with Christ is

evident from the imputation of *Christ's righteousness to him*
for his justification.   That a believer is justified before
God by a righteousness without himself, is undeniable
from Rom. 3 : 24, "Being justified freely by his grace,
through the redemption that is in Christ Jesus." And
that Christ's righteousness becomes ours, is as clear from
Rom. 4 : 23, 24 ; but it can never be imputed to us, except we be united to him, and become one with him :
which is also plainly asserted in 1 Cor. 1 : 30, "But of
him are ye *in Christ Jesus*, who of God is made unto us
wisdom and righteousness, sanctification and redemption."
He communicates his merits to none but those that are
in him.

Hence all those vain cavils of papists, disputing against
our justification by the righteousness of Christ, and assert-
ing it to be by inherent righteousness, are solidly answered. When they demand, "How can we be justified by the
righteousness of another ?   Can I be rich with another
man's money, or preferred by another man's honors ?"
Our answer is, Yes, if that other be my surety or husband.   Indeed, Peter cannot be justified by the righteousness of Paul, but both may be by Christ's righteousness
imputed to them ; they being members, jointly knit to one
common head.   Principal and surety are one in obligation
and construction of law.   Head and members are one
body ; branch and stock are one tree ; and it is no strange
thing to see a graff live by the sap of another stock, when
once it is ingrafted into it.

3. The *sympathy* between Christ and believers proves
a union between them : Christ and the saints smile and
sigh together.   Paul tells us that he "filled up that which
was behind," the remainders, " of the afflictions of Christ
in his flesh," Col. 1 : 24 ; not as if Christ's sufferings were
imperfect, "for by one offering he hath perfected for ever
them that are sanctified," Heb. 10 : 14, but in these two
scriptures Christ is considered in a twofold capacity : he

suffered once in his own person, as Mediator ; these sufferings are complete and full, and in that sense he suffers
no more : he suffers also in his church and members, thus
he still suffers in the sufferings of every saint for his sake;
and though these sufferings in his mystical body are not
equal to the other in their weight and value, nor yet designed for the same use and purpose, to satisfy, by their
proper merit, offended justice ; nevertheless they are truly
reckoned the sufferings of Christ, because the head suffers
when the members do. How else can Acts 9 : 4, be
understood, where Christ the Head in heaven cries out,
" Saul, Saul, why persecutest thou me ?" when the foot
was trod upon on earth ? How doth Christ sensibly feel
our sufferings, or we his, if there be not a mystical union
between him and us ?

4. *The manner in which the saints shall be raised* at the
last day, proves this mystical union between Christ and
them ; for they are not to be raised as others, by the
naked power of God without them, but by the virtue of
Christ's resurrection as their Head, sending forth vital,
quickening influences into their dead bodies, which are
united to him as well as their souls. "But if the Spirit
of him that raised up Jesus from the dead dwell in you,
he that raised up Christ from the dead shall also quicken
your mortal bodies by his Spirit that dwelleth in you."
Rom. 8 : 11. The saints could not be raised in the last
resurrection by the Spirit of Christ dwelling in them, if
that Spirit did not knit and unite them to him, as members
to their head.

II. I shall endeavor to show the NATURE of this union,
according to the weak apprehensions we have of so sublime a mystery.

It is, to speak generally, an intimate conjunction of believers to Christ, by the imparting of his Spirit to them,
whereby they are enabled to believe and live in him. All
divine and spiritual life is originally in the Father, and com-

eth not to us but through the Son. John 5 : 26. To him hath the Father given to have an αυτοζωη, a quickening, enlivening power in himself ; and the Son communicates this life which is in him to none, but by the Spirit : "The Spirit of life in Christ Jesus hath made me free from the law of sin and death." Rom. 8 : 2

The Spirit must therefore first act in us, before we can live in Christ ; and when he does so, we are enabled to exert that vital act of faith whereby we receive Christ. All this we are taught by Christ himself : "As the living Father hath sent me, and I live by the Father, so he that eateth me," that is, by faith applies me, " even he shall live by me." John 6 : 57. So that these two, namely, the Spirit on Christ's part, and faith his work on our part, are the two ligaments by which we are knit to Christ.

But that we may the better understand the nature of this union, we shall consider it more particularly ; first remarking what it *is not*, that we may prevent misapprehension.

The saints' union with Christ is not one merely of *conceit* or notion, but really exists. I know the atheistical world censures all these things as fancies and idle imaginations, but believers know the reality of them : "At that day ye shall know that I am in my Father, and ye in me, and I in you." John 14 : 20.

The saints' union with Christ is not a *physical* union, as between the members of a natural body and the head : our nature indeed is assumed into union with the person of Christ, but the blessed and holy flesh of Christ alone has the honor to be so united as to make one person with him.

Nor is it an essential union, or union with *the divine nature*, so that our beings are thereby swallowed up and lost in the divine Being. Some there be indeed that talk at that wild rate, of being godded into God, and christed into Christ ; but O, there is an infinite distance between us and Christ, in respect to nature and excellency, notwithstanding this union.

The union I here speak of is not a *federal union*, or a union by covenant only; such a union indeed there is between Christ and believers, but that is consequential to and wholly dependent upon this.

Nor is it a mere *moral union* by love and affection, as when we say a friend is another self; the lover is in the person beloved. Such a union of hearts and affection there is between Christ and the saints, but this is of another nature: that we call a moral, this is a mystical union; that only knits our affections, but this our persons to Christ. But,

1. Though this union neither makes us one person nor essence with Christ, yet it *knits our persons most intimately to the person of Christ.* The church is Christ's body, Col. 1 : 24 ; not his natural, but his mystical body; that is to say, his body in a mystery, because it is to him as his natural body. The saints stand to Christ in the same relation that the natural members of the body stand to the head, and he stands in the same relation to them as the head to the natural members ; and consequently they stand related to one another, as the members of a natural body do to each other. Christ and the saints are not one, as the oak and the ivy that clasps it are one, but as the graff and stock are one : it is not an union by adhesion, but incorporation. Husband and wife are not so near, soul and body are not so near, as Christ and the believing soul are near to each other.

2. The mystical union is wholly supernatural, *wrought by the power of God only.* So it is said, " But of him are ye in Christ Jesus." 1 Cor. 1 : 30. We can no more unite ourselves to Christ, than a branch can incorporate itself into another stock ; it is of God, his proper and sole work.

There are only two ligaments or bands of union between Christ and the soul, namely, the Spirit on his part, and faith on ours. But when we say faith is the band of union on our part, the meaning is not, that-it is so our own act, as that it springs naturally from us, or is educed from the mere power of our own wills ; no, for the apostle expressly contradicts it : "Not of yourselves, it is the gift of God." Eph. 2 : 8. But we are the subjects of it ; and though the act on that account be ours, yet the power enabling us to believe is God's. Eph. 1 · 19, 20.

3. The mystical union is *an immediate union :* immediate, not as excluding means and instruments, for many are employed in effecting it ; but immediate, as excluding degrees of nearness among the members of Christ's mystical body In the natural body one member stands not as near to the head as another, but all the mystical members of Christ's body, the smallest as well as the greatest, have an immediate coalition with Christ : "To the church of God which is at Corinth, to them that are sanctified in Christ Jesus, called to be saints, with all that in every place call upon the name of Jesus Christ our Lord, *both theirs and ours.*" 1 Cor. 1 : 2.

4. The saints' mystical union with Christ is a *fundamental* union ; it is fundamental by way of sustentation ; all our fruits of obedience depend upon it : "As the branch cannot bear fruit of itself, except it abide in the vine, no more can ye, except ye abide in me." John 15 : 4. It is fundamental to all our privileges and comfortable claims : "All are yours, and ye are Christ's." 1 Cor. 3 : 23. And it is fundamental to all our expectations of glory : "Christ in you the hope of glory." Col. 1 : 27. So then, destroy this union, and with it you destroy all our fruits, privileges, and eternal hopes, at a stroke.

5. The mystical union is a most *efficacious* union, for through this union divine power is communicated to our souls, both to quicken us with the life of Christ, and to preserve and secure that life in us. Without the union of the soul to Christ, which is efficiently the Spirit's act,

there can be no communications of life from Christ to us.
Eph. 4 : 16. And the ενεργεια, or effectual working of the
Spirit of life in every part, of which the apostle speaks—
as though he had said, the first appearance of a new life,
a spiritual vitality diffused through the soul which was
dead in sin—our union with Christ is as necessary to maintain, as it was originally to produce. Why is not this life
again extinguished in us by so many deadly wounds as
are given it by temptations and corruptions, but that
Christ himself has said, "Because I live, ye shall live
also," John 14 : 19 ; while there is vital sap in me the root,
you that are branches in me cannot wither and die.

6. The mystical union is an *indissoluble* union : there is
an everlasting tie between Christ and the believer. In
this respect it excels all other unions. Death dissolves
the dear union between the husband and wife, friend and
friend, yea, between soul and body, but not between
Christ and the soul : the bands of this union perish not
in the grave. Who shall separate us from "the love of
Christ?" asks the apostle, Rom. 8 : 35. He bids defiance
to all his enemies, and triumphs in the firmness of this
union over all hazards that seem to threaten it. It is
with Christ and us, in this *mystical union*, as it is with
Christ himself in the *hypostatical union* of his two natures.
This union was not dissolved by his death, when the
natural union between his soul and body was ; nor can the
mystical union of our souls and bodies with Christ be dissolved, when the union between us and our dearest relations, yea, between the soul and body, is dissolved by
death. God calls himself the God of Abraham long after
his body was turned into dust.

7. It is an *honorable* union ; yea, the highest honor that
can be done to men, the greatest honor that was ever
done to our common nature, was by its assumption into
union with the second Person *hypostatically*, and the highest honor that was ever done to our single persons, was

their union with Christ *mystically*. To be a servant of Christ is a dignity transcendent to the highest advancement among men; but to be a member of Christ, how matchless is the glory! And yet, such honor have all the saints: "We are members of his body, of his flesh, and of his bones." Eph. 5 : 30.

8. It is a most *comfortable* union; yea, the ground of all solid comfort, both in life and death. Whatever troubles, wants, or distresses befall such, in this is abundant relief and support: Christ is mine, and I am his: what may not the redeemed soul make out of that? If I am Christ's, he will care for me, and indeed, in so doing, he does but care for his own. He is my head, and to him it belongs to care for the safety and welfare of his own members. Eph. 1 : 22, 23. He is not only a head to his own by way of *influence*, but to all things else by way of *dominion*, for their good. How comfortably may we, under this cheering consideration, repose ourselves upon him at all times and in all difficulties.

9. It is a *fruitful* union; the immediate end of it is fruit. We are married to Christ, "that we should bring forth fruit to God." Rom. 7 : 4. All the fruit we bear before our ingrafting into Christ is worse than none: till the person be in Christ, the work cannot be evangelically good and acceptable to God: we are "made accepted in the Beloved." Eph. 1 : 6. Christ is a fruitful root, and makes all the branches that live in him so too. John 15 : 5.

10. It is an *enriching* union; for by our union with his person we are immediately interested in all his riches. 1 Cor. 1 : 30. How rich and great a person do the little arms of faith clasp and embrace! "All are yours," 1 Cor. 3 : 22; all that Christ hath becomes ours, either by communication to us, or improvement for us: his Father, John 20 : 17; his promises, 2 Cor. 1 : 20; his providences, Rom. 8 : 28; his glory, John 17 : 24; all are ours by virtue of our union with him.

INFERENCE 1. If there be such a union between Christ and believers, *what transcendent dignity hath God put upon believers!*

Well might Constantine prefer the honor of being a member of the church to that of being head of the empire; for it is not only above all earthly dignities and honors, but, in some respects, above the honor which God hath put upon the angels of glory.

Great is the dignity of the angelic nature : the angels are the highest species of creatures ; they have the honor continually to behold the face of God in heaven : and yet in this one respect the saints are preferred to them ; they have a mystical union with Christ as their head, by whom they are quickened with spiritual life, which the angels have not.

It is true, here is an ανακεφαλαιωσις, or gathering together of all in heaven and earth under Christ as a common head. Eph. 1 : 10. He is the head of *angels* as well as saints, but in different respects. To angels he is a head of *dominion* and government, but to saints he is both a head of dominion and of vital *influence*—they are his chief and most honorable subjects, but not his mystical members ; they are as the barons and nobles in his kingdom, but the saints as the dear spouse and wife of his bosom. This dignifies the believer above the greatest angel. And as the nobles of the kingdom think it a preferment and honor to serve the queen, so the glorious angels think it no degradation or dishonor to them to serve the saints ; for to this honorable office they are appointed, to be ministering spirits for the good of them that shall be heirs of salvation. Heb. 1 : 14. The chiefest servant disdains not to honor and serve the heir.

Some imperious grandees would frown should some of these persons but presume to approach their presence ; but God sets them before his face with delight, and angels delight to serve them.

2. If there be such a strict and inseparable union between Christ and believers, then *the grace of believers can never totally fail.* Immortality is the privilege of grace, because sanctified persons are inseparably united to Christ, the fountain of *life:* "Your life is hid with Christ in God." Col. 3 : 3. While the sap of life is in the root, the branches live by it. Thus it is between Christ and believers, "Because I live, ye shall live also." John 14 : 19. See how Christ binds up their life in one bundle with his own, plainly intimating that it is as impossible for them to die as it is for himself : he cannot live without them.

True it is, the spiritual life of believers is encountered by many strong and fierce oppositions. It is also brought to a low ebb in some ; but we are always to remember that there are some things which pertain to the essence of that life in which the very being of it lies, and some things that pertain only to its well-being. All those things which belong to the well-being of the new creature, as manifestations, joys, and spiritual comforts, may for a time fail, yea, and grace itself may suffer great losses and remissions in its degrees, notwithstanding our union with Christ ; but still the essence of it is immortal, which is no small relief to gracious souls. When the means of grace fail, as it is threatened, Amos 8 : 11 ; when temporary formal professors drop away from Christ like withered leaves from the trees in a windy day, 2 Tim. 2 : 18 ; and when the natural union of their souls and bodies is suffering a dissolution from each other by death, when that *silver cord* is loosed, this *golden chain* holds firm. 1 Cor. 3 : 23.

3. Is the union so intimate between Christ and believers ? *How great and powerful a motive is this to make us open-handed and liberal in relieving the necessities and wants of every gracious person; for in relieving them, we relieve Christ himself.*

Christ *personally* is not the object of our pity and charity; he is at the fountain-head of all the riches in glory, Eph. 4 : 10; but Christ, in his members, is exposed to necessities and wants: he feels hunger and thirst, cold and pain, in his body the church; and he is refreshed, relieved, and comforted in their refreshments and comforts. Christ, the Lord of heaven and earth, in this view, is sometimes in need of a penny; he tells us his wants and poverty, and how he is relieved, Matt. 25 : 35, 40, a text believed and understood by very few. "I was a hungered, and ye gave me meat: I was thirsty, and ye gave me drink: I was a stranger, and ye took me in. Then shall the righteous answer, Lord, when saw we thee a hungered? etc. And the King shall answer, and say unto them, Verily, I say unto you, inasmuch as ye have done it unto one of the least of these my brethren, ye have done it unto me."

It was the saying of a great divine, that he thought scarcely any man on earth fully understood and believed this truth, and he thinks this is implied in the text, where the righteous themselves reply, "Lord, when saw we thee sick?" etc., intimating in the question, that they did not thoroughly understand the nearness, yea, *oneness* of those persons with Christ, for whom they did these things. And indeed it is incredible that a Christian can be hard-hearted and close-handed to that necessitous Christian, in refreshing and relieving of whom he verily believes that he ministers refreshment to Christ himself. O think again and again upon this scripture; consider what forcible and mighty arguments are here laid together to engage relief to the wants of Christians.

Here you see their near relation to Christ; they are one person; what you did to them, you did to him. Here you see also how kindly Christ takes it at our hands, acknowledging all those kindnesses that were bestowed upon him, even to a piece of bread: he receives it as a courtesy, who might demand it by authority, and bereave you of all immediately upon your refusal.

Yea, here you see one single branch or act of obedience, our charity to the saints, is singled out from among all the duties of obedience, and made the test and evidence of our sincerity in that great day, and men are blessed or cursed according to the love they have manifested in this way to the saints.

O then, let none that understand the relation the saints have to Christ as the members to the head, or the relation they have to each other thereby, as fellow-members of the same body, from henceforth suffer Christ to hunger, if they have bread to relieve him, or to be thirsty, if they have wherewith to refresh him : this union between Christ and the saints affords an argument beyond all other arguments to prevail with us. Methinks a little *rhetoric* might persuade a Christian to part with any thing he has for Christ, who parted with the glory of heaven, yea, and his own blood, for his sake.

4. Do Christ and believers make but one mystical person? *How unnatural and absurd then are all those acts of unkindness whereby believers wound and grieve Jesus Christ! This is as if the hand should wound its own head, from which it receives life, sense, motion, and strength.*

When Satan smites Christ by a wicked man, he wounds him with the hand of an enemy ; but when his temptations prevail upon the saints to sin, he wounds him as it were with his own hand : as the eagle and the tree in the fable complained, the one that he was wounded by an arrow winged with his own feathers, the other that it was cleaved asunder by a wedge hewn out of its own limbs.

Now the evil and disingenuousness of such sins are to be measured not only by the near relation Christ sustains to believers as their head, but more particularly from the several benefits they receive from him as such ; for in wounding Christ by their sins,

They wound their *Head of influence*, through whom

they live, and without whom they had still remained in the state of sin and death. Eph. 4 : 16. Shall Christ send life to us, and we return that which is death to him! O how absurd, how disingenuous is this!

They wound their *Head of government.* Christ is a *guiding* as well as a *quickening* head. Col. 1 : 18. He is your wisdom, he guides you by his counsel to glory : and must he be thus requited for all his faithful conduct! What do you, when you sin, but rebel against his government, refusing to follow his counsels, and obeying, in the mean time, a deceiver rather than him.

They wound their *consulting Head*, who cares, provides, and projects for the welfare and safety of the body. Christians, you know your affairs below have not been directed by your own wisdom, but that orders have been given from heaven for your security and supply from day to day. "O Lord, I know that the way of man is not in himself; it is not in man that walketh to direct his steps." Jer. 10 : 23. It is true, Christ is out of your sight, and you see him not; but he sees you, and orders every thing that concerns you. And is this a due requital of all the care he has taken for you? Do you thus requite the Lord for all his benefits? What, recompense evil for good? O, let shame cover you!

They wound their *Head of honor.* Christ your head is the fountain of honor to you : this is your glory, that you are related to him as your head ; you are, on this account, exalted above angels. Consider how vile a thing it is to reflect the least dishonor upon him from whom you derive all your glory. O consider, and bewail it.

5. Is there so strict and intimate a relation and union between Christ and the saints? *Then they can never want what is for their good.*

Every one naturally cares and provides for his own, especially for his own body ; yet we can more easily violate the law of nature, and be cruel to our own flesh, than

Christ can be so to his mystical body. I know it is hard to rest upon and rejoice in a promise, when necessities pinch and we see not from whence relief should arise; but O, what sweet satisfaction and comfort might a necessitous believer find in these considerations, would he but keep them upon his heart in such a day of straits.

Whatever my distresses are in number or degree, they are all *known*, even to the least circumstance, by Christ my head: he looks down from heaven upon all my afflictions, and understands them more fully than I that feel them. "Lord, all my desire is before thee; and my groaning is not hid from thee." Psalm 38 : 9.

He not only knows them, but *feels* them: "We have not a high-priest that cannot be touched with the feeling of our infirmities." Heb. 4 : 15. In all your afflictions he is afflicted; tender sympathy cannot but flow from such intimate union; therefore, in Matt. 25 : 35, he saith, *I* was a hungered, *I* was athirst, *I* was naked. For indeed his sympathy and tender compassion gave him as quick a resentment and as tender a sense of their wants as if they had been his own. Yea,

He not only knows and feels my wants, but hath enough in his hand, and much more than enough to *supply them all;* for all things are delivered to him by the Father. Luke 10 : 22. All the storehouses of heaven and earth are his. Phil. 4 : 19.

He bestows earthly good things, even upon his enemies; they have more than heart can wish. Psalm 73 : 7. He is bountiful to strangers, and can it be supposed he will in the mean time starve his own, and neglect those whom he loves as his own flesh? It cannot be.

Hitherto he hath not suffered me to perish in any *former* straits; when and where was it that he forsook me? This is not the first plunge of trouble I have been in; have I not found him a God at hand? How oft have I seen him in the mount of difficulties!

I have *his promise and engagement* that he will never leave me nor forsake me. Heb. 13 : 5, and John 14 : 18. If then the Lord Jesus knows and feels all my wants, and has enough, and more than enough to supply them ; if he gives even to redundance to his enemies, if he has not hitherto forsaken me, and has promised he never will, why then is my soul thus disquieted in me ? Surely there is no cause that it should be so.

6. If the saints are so nearly united to Christ, as the members to the head, *O then, how great a sin and full of danger is it, for any to wrong and persecute the saints ; for in so doing they persecute Christ himself.*

"Saul, Saul," saith Christ, "why persecutest thou *me*?" Acts 9 : 4. The righteous God holds himself obliged to vindicate oppressed innocency, though it be in the persons of wicked men ; how much more when it is in a member of Christ? "He that toucheth you toucheth the apple of his eye." Zech. 2 : 8. "He ordaineth his arrows against the persecutors." Psalm 7 : 13.

Oh, it were better thy hand should wither, and thine arm fall from thy shoulder, than ever it should be lifted up against Christ in the poorest of his members. Believe it, not only your violent actions but your hard speeches are all set down upon your doomsday-book ; and you shall be brought to an account for them in the great day. Jude 15. Beware what arrows you shoot, and be sure of your mark before you shoot them.

7. If there be such a union between Christ and the saints, *how peacefully may believers part with their bodies at death.*

Christ your head is risen, therefore you cannot be lost; nay, he is not only risen from the dead himself, but is also "become the first fruits of them that slept." 1 Cor. 15 : 20. Believers are his members, his fulness, he cannot therefore be complete without you : a part of Christ cannot perish in the grave, much less can it be left to burn in hell. Remember, when you feel the natural union dissolving, that this mystical union can never be dissolved ; the pangs of death cannot break this tie. And as there is a peculiar excellency in the believer's life, so there is a singular support and peculiar comfort in his death : "To me to live is Christ, and to die is gain." Phil. 1 : 21.

8. If there be such a union between Christ and believers, *how does it concern every man to try and examine his state whether he is really united with Christ or not, by the natural and proper effects which always flow from this union?*

Is there a *real communication* of Christ's holiness to the soul? We cannot be united with this root, and not partake of the vital sap of sanctification from him ; all that are planted into him, are planted into the likeness of his death and of his resurrection, Rom. 6 : 5, 6, that is, by mortification and vivification.

They that are so nearly united to him as members to the head, cannot but *love* him and value him above their own lives ; as we see in nature, the hand and arm will interpose to save the head. The nearer the union the stronger always is the affection.

The members are *subject* to the head. Dominion in the head implies subjection in the members. Eph. 4 : 24. In vain do we claim union with Christ as our head, while we are governed by our own wills, and our lusts give us law.

All that are united to Christ *bear fruit* to God. Rom. 7 : 4. Fruitfulness is the end of our union ; there are no barren branches growing upon this fruitful root.

9. *How much are believers engaged to walk as the members of Christ, in the visible exercise of all those graces and duties which the consideration of their near relation to him exacts from them.*

How *contented* and well pleased should we be with our outward lot, however Providence has cast it for us in this world. O do not repine, God hath dealt bountifully with you : upon others he hath bestowed the good things of this world ; upon you, himself in Christ.

How *humble* and lowly in spirit should you be under your great advancement. It is true, God hath magnified you greatly by this union ; but yet do not boast. You bear not the root, but the root you. Rom. 11 : 18. You shine, but with a borrowed light.

How *zealous* should you be to honor Christ, who hath put so much honor upon you. Be willing to give glory to Christ, though his glory should rise out of your shame. Never reckon that glory which goes to Christ to be lost to you : when you lie at his feet, in the most particular heart-breaking confessions of sin, let this please you, that therein you have given him glory.

How *circumspect* should you be in all your ways, remembering whose you are, and whom you represent. Shall it be said that a member of Christ was convicted of unrighteous and unholy actions ? God forbid. "If we say that we have fellowship with him, and walk in darkness, we lie." 1 John 1 : 8. "He that saith he abideth in him, ought himself also to walk even as he walked." 1 John 2 : 6.

How studious should you be of *peace among yourselves,* who are so nearly united to such a head, and thereby are made fellow-members of the same body. The heathen world was never acquainted with such an argument as the apostle urges for unity, in Eph. 4 : 3, 4.

How *joyful* and comfortable should you be, to whom Christ, with all his treasures and benefits, is effectually applied in this blessed union of your souls with him. This brings him into your possession : O how great, how glorious a person do these little weak arms of your faith embrace !

Thanks be to God for Jesus Christ.

CHAPTER III

THE GOSPEL MINISTRY AS AN EXTERNAL MEANS OF APPLYING CHRIST

" Now then we are ambassadors for Christ, as though God did beseech you by us : we pray you in Christ's stead, be ye reconciled to God." 2 Cor. 5 : 20.

THE effectual application of Christ principally consists in our union with him ; but ordinarily there can be no union without a gospel tender and an overture of him to our souls ; for, " how shall they believe in him of whom they have not heard ? and how shall they hear without a preacher ? and how shall they preach except they be sent ?" Rom. 10 : 14, 15.

If God would espouse poor sinners to his Son, there must be a treaty in order to it : that treaty requires inter- locution between the parties concerned in it ; but such is our frailty, that should God speak immediately to us him- self, it would confound and overwhelm us : God therefore graciously condescends and accommodates himself to our infirmity, in treating with us, in order to our union with Christ, by his *ambassadors*, and these not *angels*, whose converse we cannot bear, but *men* like ourselves, who are commissioned for the effecting of this great business be- tween Christ and us. " Now then we are ambassadors for Christ," etc. In which words you have,

1. Christ's ambassadors *commissioned*. " Now then we are ambassadors for Christ." The Lord Jesus thought it not sufficient to print the law of grace and the blessed terms of our union with him in the Scriptures, where men may read his willingness to receive them, and see the just and gracious terms and conditions upon which he offers to become theirs ; but has also set up and established a

standing office in the church, to expound the law, inculcate the precepts, and urge the promises he has given ; to woo and espouse souls to Christ, "I have espoused you to one Husband, that I may present you as a chaste virgin to Christ," 2 Cor 11 : 2 ; and this not simply from their own affection and compassion to miserable sinners, but also by virtue of their office and commission, whereby they are authorized and appointed to that work.

2. We have *the nature and design* of their commission.

The work to which they are appointed is to *reconcile the world to God ;* to bring these sinful, vain, rebellious hearts, which have naturally a strong aversion from God, to close with him according to the articles of peace contained in the gospel, that thereby they may be capable to receive the mercies and benefits purchased by the death of Christ, which they cannot receive in the state of enmity and alienation.

In this work they act *in Christ's stead*, as his *vicegerents.* He is no more in this world to treat personally with sinners, as he once did in the days of his flesh ; but he still continues the treaty with this lower world by his officers, requiring men to look upon them and obey them as they would himself, if he were corporeally present : "He that heareth you heareth me ; and he that despiseth you despiseth me." Luke 10 : 16.

The manner of their acting in this capacity is also prescribed ; and that is by humble, sweet, and condescending entreaties and beseechings. This best suits the meek and lamb-like Saviour whom they represent : thus he dealt with poor sinners himself, when he conversed among them ; he would not break the bruised reed, nor quench the smoking flax. Isa. 42 : 3. This is the way to allure and win the souls of sinners to Christ. Hence,

The preaching of the gospel by Christ's ambassadors is the principal means appointed for reconciling and bringing home sinners to Christ.

This doctrine is clear, from Rom. 10 : 14 ; 1 Cor. 1 : 21 ; and many other scriptures. We proceed to inquire what is *implied* in Christ's treating with sinners by his ambassadors or ministers ; what is *the great concern* about which they are to treat with sinners ; and in what consists *the efficacy* of preaching to bring sinners to Christ.

I. What is IMPLIED in Christ's treaty with sinners by his ambassadors or ministers.

1. It necessarily implies *the defection and fall of man* from his estate of favor and friendship with God : if no war with heaven, what need of ambassadors of peace ? The very office of the ministry is a proof of the fall. Gospel ordinances and officers came in upon the fall, and expire with the Mediator's dispensatory kingdom ; then shall he deliver up the kingdom to God, even the Father, 1 Cor. 15 : 24 ; after that, no more ordinances, no more ministers. What use can there be for them, when the treaty is ended ? They have done all they were ever intended for, when they have reconciled to God all his people among the lost and miserable posterity of Adam, and have brought them home to Christ in a perfect state. Eph. 4 : 12.

2. It implies the singular grace and admirable *condescension of God* to sinful man. That God will admit any treaty with him at all, is wonderful mercy ; it is more than he would do for the angels that fell ; *they* are reserved in everlasting chains, under darkness, unto the judgment of the great day. Jude 6. Christ took not on him their nature, but suffered myriads of them to perish, and fills up their vacant places in glory with sinful men and women, to whom the law awarded the same punishment.

But that God will entreat and beseech sinful men to be reconciled, is yet more wonderful. Barely to propound the terms of peace had been an astonishing mercy ; but to woo and beseech stubborn enemies to be at peace and accept their pardon, Oh, how unparalleled was this condescension !

3. It implies the great dignity and *honor* of the gospel ministry. We are *ambassadors for Christ.* Ambassadors represent and personate the prince that sends them ; and the honor or contempt done to them, reflects upon and is reckoned to the person of their master : " He that heareth you heareth me ; and he that despiseth you despiseth me." Luke 10 : 16. Neither their persons nor talents are the proper ground and reason of our respect to them, but their office and commission from Jesus Christ. We are fallen into the dregs of time, wherein a vile contempt is poured not only upon the persons, but the very office of the ministry ; and I could heartily wish that scripture, Mal. 2 : 7, 8, 9, were thoroughly considered by us ; possibly it might inform us of the true cause and reason of this sore judgment : but surely Christ's faithful ministers deserve a better entertainment than they ordinarily find in the world ; and if we did but seriously bethink ourselves, in whose name they come, and in whose stead they stand, we should receive them as the Galatians did Paul, as angels of God, even as Christ Jesus. Gal. 4 : 14.

4. Christ's treating with sinners by his ministers, who are his ambassadors, implies the strict obligation they are under to be *faithful* in their ministerial employment. Christ counts upon their faithfulness whom he puts into the ministry. 1 Tim. 1 : 12. They are accountable to him for all acts of their office. Heb 13 : 17. If they be silent, they cannot be innocent ; necessity is laid upon them, and woe to them if they preach not the gospel. 1 Cor. 9 : 16.

Yea, necessity is not only laid upon them to preach, but to keep close to their commission in preaching the gospel : " Our exhortation was not of deceit, nor of uncleanness, nor in guile ; but as we were allowed of God to be put in trust with the gospel, even so we speak ; not as pleasing men, but God, who trieth our hearts." 1 Thess. 2 : 3, 4. The word is not to be corrupted to please men, 2 Cor. 2 : 17 ; their business is not to make them their dis-

ciples, but Christ's ; not to seek theirs, but them, 2 Cor.
12 : 14 ; to keep close to their instructions, in the matter,
manner, and end of their ministry. So did Christ himself,
the treasure of wisdom and knowledge ; yet, being sent by
God, he saith, "My doctrine is not mine, but his that sent
me." John 7 : 16. And so he expects and requires that
his ambassadors keep close to the commission he has given
them, and be according to their measure faithful to their
trust, as he was to his.   Paul is to deliver to the people
that which he also received from the Lord. 1 Cor. 11 : 23.
And Timothy must keep that which was committed to him.
2 Tim. 1 : 14.

5. It implies the *removal* of the gospel ministry to be *a
very great judgment* to a people. The remanding of ambassadors presages an ensuing war. If the reconciling of
souls to God be the greatest work, then the removal of the
means and instruments for this end must be the sorest
judgment. Some account even the falling of the salt upon
the table ominous ; but surely the falling of them whom
Christ calls *the salt of the earth* is so indeed. What now
are those once famous and renowned places, from whence
Christ, as he threatened, hath removed the candlestick, but
dens of robbers and mountains of prey ?

6. It implies both the wisdom and condescension of
God to sinful men, in carrying on *a treaty of peace* with
them by such ambassadors, negociating between him and
them. Without a treaty there would be no reconciliation,
and no method to carry on a treaty like this ; for had the
Lord treated with sinners personally and immediately,
they had been overwhelmed with his awful majesty. The
appearance of God confounds the creature : "Let me not
hear again the voice of the LORD my God, neither let me
see this great fire any more, that I die not ;" yea, "so terrible was that sight, that Moses said, I exceedingly fear
and quake." Deut. 18 : 16 ; Heb. 12 : 21. Or had he commissioned *angels* for this employment, though they stand

not at such an infinite distance from us, yet such is the excellence of their glory, being the highest order of creatures, that their appearance would be more apt to astonish than persuade us; besides, they being creatures of another rank and kind, and not partaking with us either in the misery of the fall or benefit of the recovery by Christ, it is not to be supposed they should speak to us so feelingly and experimentally as these his ministers do. Ministers can open to you the mysteries of sin, feeling the workings thereof daily in their own hearts; they can discover to you the conflicts of the flesh and Spirit, as being daily exercised in that warfare; and then, being men of the same mould and temper, they can say to you as Elihu did to Job, "Behold, I am according to thy wish in God's stead: I also am formed out of the clay. Behold, my terror shall not make thee afraid, neither shall my hand be heavy upon thee." Job 33 : 6, 7.

So that, in this appointment, much of the divine wisdom and condescension to sinners is manifested: "We have this treasure in earthen vessels, that the excellency of the power may be of God, and not of us." 2 Cor. 4 : 7. God's glory and man's advantage are both promoted by this dispensation.

II. Consider THE GREAT CONCERN about which these ambassadors of Christ are to treat with sinners, namely, as the text informs us, their RECONCILIATION TO GOD.

Reconciliation with God is the restoring of men to that former friendship they had with God, which was broken by the fall, and is still continued by our enmity and aversion while we continue in our natural and unregenerate state. This is the greatest and most blessed design that ever God had in the world; an astonishing and invaluable mercy to men, as will clearly appear from the following particulars.

1. That God should be reconciled after such *a dreadful breach* as the fall of man made, is wonderful; no sin, all

things considered, was ever like this sin. If all the posterity of Adam in their several generations should do nothing else but bewail and lament this sin of his while this world continues, yet would it not be enough lamented—that a man so newly created out of nothing, and admitted the first moment into the highest order, crowned a king over the works of God's hands, Psalm 8 : 5 ; a man perfect and upright, without the least inordinate motion or sinful inclination ; a man whose mind was most clear, bright, and apprehensive of the will of God ; whose will was free, and able to have easily put by the strongest temptation ; a man in a paradise of delights, where nothing was left to desire for advancing the happiness of soul or body ; a man on whom depended not only his own, but the happiness of the whole world, so soon, upon so slight a temptation, to violate the law of his God, and involve himself and all his posterity with him in such a gulf of guilt and misery ; all which he might so easily have prevented. O wonderful, amazing mercy, that ever God should think of being reconciled, or have any purpose of peace towards him !

2. That God should be reconciled to *men*, and not to *angels*, a more high and excellent order of creatures, is yet more astonishing. When the angels fell, they were lost irrecoverably ; no hand of mercy was stretched out to save one of those *myriads* of excellent beings ; but chains of darkness were immediately clapped on them to reserve them to the judgment of the great day. Jude 6. That the milder attribute should be exercised to the inferior, and the severer attribute to the more excellent creature, is just matter for eternal admiration. Who would cast away vessels of gold, and save earthen potsherds ? Some indeed undertake to show us the reasons why the wisdom of God made no provision for the recovery of angels by a Mediator of reconciliation : partly from the high degree of the malignity of their sin, who sinned in the light of heav-

en ; partly because it was proper that the first breach of the divine law should be punished, to secure obedience for the future ; and besides, the angelical nature was not entirely lost, myriads of angels still continuing in their innocence and glory ; whereas all mankind were lost in Adam. But we must remember still the law made no distinction, but awarded the same punishment, and therefore it was mercy alone that made the difference, and mercy for ever to be admired by men : how astonishing is the grace of God, that moves in a way of reconciliation to us, out of design to fill up the vacant places in heaven, from which angels fell, with such poor worms as we are ! Angels excluded, and men received ! O stupendous mercy !

3. That God should be *wholly* reconciled to man, so that no fury remains in him against us, according to Isaiah 27 : 4, is still matter of further wonder. The design on which he sends his ambassadors to you, is not the allaying and mitigating of his wrath—which yet would be matter of great joy to the damned—but thoroughly to quench all his wrath, so that no degree thereof shall ever be felt by you. O blessed embassy ! Beautiful upon the mountains are the feet of them that bring such tidings. God offers you a full reconciliation, a plenary remission.

4. That God should be *freely* reconciled to sinners and discharge them without any, the least satisfaction to his justice from them, is and for ever will be marvellous in their eyes. O what mercy would the damned account it, if, after a thousand years of torment in hell, God would at last be reconciled to them, and put an end to their misery ! But believers are discharged without bearing any part of the curse, not one farthing of that debt is levied upon them.

Does any one ask how can this be, when God requires full satisfaction to his justice before any soul be discharged and restored to favor ; freely reconciled, and yet fully satisfied, how can this be ? We answer, this mercy comes freely to your hands, how costly soever it proved to Christ; and that free remission and full satisfaction are not contradictory and inconsistent, is plain from Rom. 3 : 24 : "Being justified freely by his grace, through the redemption that is in Christ Jesus ;" freely, and yet in the way of redemption. For though Christ, your Surety, has made satisfaction in your name and stead, yet it was his life, his blood, and not yours, that went for it, and this surety was of God's own appointment and providing, without your thoughts or contrivance. O blessed reconciliation! happy are the people that hear the joyful sound of it.

5. That God should *be finally reconciled* to sinners, so that never any new breach shall happen between him and them, so as to dissolve the league of friendship, is a most ravishing and transporting message. Two things give confirmation and full security to reconciled ones : the terms of the covenant, and the intercession of the Mediator. The covenant of grace gives great security to believers against new breaches between God and them. It is said, "I will make an everlasting covenant with them, that I will not turn away from them, to do them good ; but I will put my fear in their hearts, that they shall not depart from me." Jer. 32 : 40. The fear of the Lord is a choice preservative against second revolts, and therefore taken into the covenant. It is no *hinderance*, but a special *guard* to assurance. There is no doubt of God's faithfulness ; that part of the promise is easily believed, that he will not turn away from us to do us good : all the doubt is of the inconstancy of our hearts with God, and against that danger this promise makes provision.

Moreover, the *intercession* of Christ in heaven secures the saints in their reconciled state. "If any man sin, we have an Advocate with the Father, Jesus Christ the righteous : and he is the propitiation." 1 John 2 : 1, 2. He continually appears in heaven before the Father, as a lamb that had been slain, Rev. 5 : 6, and as the bow in the cloud, Rev. 4 : 3. So that as long as Christ thus appears in the presence of God for us, it is not possible our state of justification and reconciliation can be again dissolved. Such is the blessed *embassy* on which gospel ministers are employed; he hath committed to them the word of this reconciliation.

III. We inquire what and whence is this EFFICACY of preaching to reconcile and bring home sinners to Christ.

That its efficacy is great in convincing, humbling, and changing the hearts of men, is past all question. "The weapons of our warfare are not carnal, but mighty through God to the pulling down of strong-holds; casting down imaginations, and every high thing that exalteth itself against the knowledge of God, and bringing into captivity every thought to the obedience of Christ." 2 Cor. 10 : 4, 5. No heart so hard, no conscience so stupid, but this sword can pierce and wound; in an instant it can cast down all those vain reasonings and fond imaginations which the carnal heart has been building all its life long, and open a fair passage for convictions of sin, and the fears and terrors of wrath to come, into that heart that never was afraid of these things before. "When they heard this, they were pricked in the heart, and said unto Peter and to the rest of the apostles, Men and brethren, what shall we do?" Acts 2 : 37.

What shall we do? is the doleful cry of men at their wit's end; the voice of one in deepest distress : and such outcries have been no rarities under the preaching of the word; its power has been felt by persons of all orders and conditions; the great and honorable of the earth, as well as the poor and despicable. The learned and the ignorant, the civil and profane, the young and the old, all have felt the heart-piercing efficacy of the gospel.

If you ask whence hath the word preached this mighty power? The answer must be, neither from itself nor him that preaches it, but from the Spirit of God whose instrument it is, by whose blessing and concurrence with it it produces its blessed effects upon the hearts of men.

1. This efficacy and wonderful power is not from *the word itself*. Separated from the Spirit, it can do nothing; it is called "the foolishness of preaching." 1 Cor. 1 : 21. Foolishness, not only because the world so accounts it, but because in itself it is a weak, and therefore a very improbable way to reconcile the world to God. That the stony heart of one man should be broken by the words of another man ; that one poor sinful creature should be used to breathe spiritual life into another ; this could never be, if this sword were not managed by an omnipotent hand.

And besides, we know what works naturally, works necessarily : if this efficacy were inherent in the word, so that we should suppose it to work as other natural objects do, then it must needs convert all to whom it is at any time preached, except its effects were miraculously hindered, as the fire when it could not burn the three children ; but alas, thousands hear it that never feel its saving power. Isaiah 53 : 1, and 2 Cor. 4 : 3, 4.

2. It derives not this efficacy from the *instrument* by which it is ministered : let the gifts and abilities of ministers be what they will, it is impossible that ever such effects should be produced from the strength of their natural or gracious abilities. "We have this treasure in earthen vessels, that the excellency of the power may be of God, and not of us," 2 Cor. 4 : 7—in *earthen vessels*, as Gideon and his men had their lamps in earthen pitchers. And why is this precious treasure lodged in such weak, worthless vessels, but to convince us that the excellency of the power is of God, and not of us ; as it follows in the next words. To the same purpose speaks the same apostle, "So then, neither is he that planteth any thing, neither he that watereth ; but God that giveth the increase." 1 Cor. 3 : 7.

Not *any thing!* What can be more diminutively spo-

ken of gospel-preachers? But we must not understand
these words in a simple and absolute, but in a comparative and relative sense ; not as if they were not necessary
and useful in their place, but that how necessary soever
they be, and what excellent gifts soever God hath furnished
them with ; yet it is neither in their power nor choice to
make the word they preach effectual to men : if it were,
then the damnation of all that hear us must lie at our
door ; then also many thousands would have been reconciled to God, which are yet in the state of enmity. But
the effect of the gospel is not in our power.

3. But whatever efficacy it hath to reconcile men to
God it derives *from the Spirit of God*, whose coöperation
and blessing gives it all the fruit. Ministers, says Mr.
Burgess, are like trumpets, which make no sound if breath
be not breathed into them. Or like Ezekiel's wheels,
which move not until the Spirit move them ; or Elisha's
servant, whose presence does no good except Elisha's
spirit be there also. For want of the Spirit of God, how
many thousands of souls find the ministry to be nothing
to them? If it be something to the purpose to any soul,
it is the Lord that makes it so. This Spirit is not limited
by men's gifts or parts ; he concurs not only with the labors of those who have excellent gifts, but often blesses
mean, despicable gifts with far greater success.

Suppose, says Austin, there be two conduits in a town,
one very plain and homely, the other built of polished
marble, and adorned with excellent images, as eagles,
lions, angels ; the water refreshes as it is water, and not
as it comes from such or such a conduit. It is the Spirit
that gives the word all the virtue it hath : he is the Lord
of all saving influences : he has dominion over the *word*,
over our *souls*, over the *times* and *seasons* of conversion ;
and if any poor creature attends the ministry without
benefit, if he goes away as he came, without fruit, surely
we may say in this case, as Martha said to Christ in refer-

ence to her brother Lazarus, Lord, if thou hadst been here, my brother had not died; so, Lord, if thou hadst been in this prayer, in this sermon, this poor soul had not gone dead and carnal from under it.

INFERENCE 1. Is the preaching of the gospel by Christ's ambassadors the way which God takes to reconcile sinners to himself? *Then how inexcusable are all those that continue in their state of enmity, though the ambassadors of peace have been with them all their lives long, wooing and beseeching them to be reconciled to God!*

O invincible, obstinate, incurable disease, which is aggravated by the only proper remedy! Hath God been wooing and beseeching you by his ambassadors so many years to be reconciled to him, and will you not yield to any entreaties? Must he be made to speak in vain to charm the deaf adder? Well, when the milder attribute hath done with you, the severer attribute will take you in hand. The Lord hath kept an account of every year and day of his patience towards you. "These three years I come seeking fruit on this fig-tree, and find none." Luke 13 : 7. "I have spoken unto you, rising early and speaking, but you have not hearkened." Jer. 25 : 3. Well, be you assured that God holds both the glass of your time and the vials of his wrath; and so much of his abused patience as runs out of one, so much of his incensed wrath runs into the other. There is a time when this treaty of peace will end, when the Master of the house will rise up, and the doors be shut. Luke 13 : 25. Then will you be left without hope and without apology.

We read, indeed, of some poor and ineffectual pleas that will be made at the last day : "Lord, Lord, have we not prophesied in thy name; and in thy name have cast out devils; and in thy name done many wonderful works?" Matt. 7 : 22. These pleas will not avail; but as for you, what will you plead? Possibly many poor weak-headed persons may perish; many who had little opportunity to acquaint themselves with the way of salvation; many millions of heathen that never heard the name of Christ, nor came within the sound of salvation, may perish, and that justly. But whatsoever apologies any of these will make for themselves in the last day, to be sure you can make none. God hath given you a capacity and competent understanding; many of you are wise and subtle in all your other concerns, and only show your folly in the great concerns of your salvation. You cannot plead want of time, some of you are grown grey-headed under the gospel; you cannot plead want of means and opportunities, the ordinances and ministers of Christ have been with you all your life long to this day; surely if you be christless now, you must be speechless then.

2. Hence it also follows, *that the world owes better entertainment than it gives to the ministers of Christ : Christ's ambassadors deserve a better welcome than they find among men.*

The respect you owe them is founded upon their office and employment for you. Heb. 13 : 17, and 1 Thess. 5 : 12. They watch for your souls, dare any of you watch for their ruin? They bring glad tidings, shall they return with sad tidings to him that sent them? They publish peace, shall they be rewarded with trouble? O ungrateful world! We read in Eph. 6 : 20, of *an ambassador in bonds,* and he no ordinary one neither. We read also of a strange challenge made by another at his own death : " Which of the prophets have not your fathers persecuted? And they have slain them which showed before the coming of the Just One." Acts 7 : 52. Some that break the bread of life to you might want bread to eat, for any regard you have to them. The office of the ministry speaks the abundant love of God to you; your contempt and abuse of it speaks the abundant stupidity and malignity of your hearts towards God. What a sad protestation doth Jeremiah make against his ungrateful people : "Shall evil be recompensed for good? for they have digged a pit for my soul.   Remember that I stood before thee to speak good for them, and to turn away thy wrath from them." Jer. 18 : 20.

God's mercy is eminently discovered in the institution of, and Satan's malice is eminently discovered in the opposition to, the ministerial office.   Satan is a great and jealous prince, and it is no wonder he should raise all the forces he can to oppose the ambassadors of Christ : when, saith Gurnal, the gospel comes into his dominions, it doth, as it were, by sound of trumpet and beat of drum, proclaim liberty to all his slaves and vassals, if they will quit the tyrant that hath so long held their souls in bondage, and come under the sweet and easy government of Christ. And can the devil endure this, think you?   If Christ sends forth ambassadors, no wonder if Satan sends forth opposers : he certainly owes them a spite who undermine his government in the world.

3. Hence it follows, *that it nearly concerns all Christ's ambassadors to see that they themselves are in a state of reconciliation with God.*

Shall we stand in Christ's stead by *office*, and yet not be in Christ by union?   Shall we entreat men to be reconciled to God, and yet be at enmity with him ourselves ?   O let us take heed, lest after we have preached to others we ourselves should be castaways.   1 Cor. 9 : 27.   Of all men living we are the most miserable, if we be christless and graceless : our consciences will make more terrible applications of our doctrine to us in hell, than ever we made to the vilest of sinners on earth.   O, it is far easier to study and press a thousand truths upon others, than to feel the power of one truth upon our own hearts ; to teach others duties to be done, than duties by doing them.

They are sad *dilemmas* with which Baxter poses such graceless ministers : If sin be evil, why do you live in it ? If it be not, why do you dissuade men from it ?   If it be dangerous, how dare you venture on it? If it be not, why do you tell men so? If God's threatenings be true, why do you not fear them? If they be false, why do you trouble men needlessly with them, and put them into such frights without a cause? Take heed to yourselves, lest you should cry down sin and not overcome it; lest, while you seek to bring it down in others, you bow to it and become its slaves yourselves: it is easier to chide sin than to overcome it. That is a smart question, "Thou therefore which teachest another, teachest thou not thyself?" Rom. 2:21. A profane minister was once converted by reading that text, but how many have read it as well as he, who never trembled at the consideration of it as he did!

4. Is this the method God uses to reconcile men to himself, O then *examine yourselves, whether the preaching of the gospel has reconciled you to God.*

It is too manifest that many among us are in a state of enmity unto this day. We may ask, with the prophet, "Who hath believed our report? and to whom is the arm of the Lord revealed?" Isaiah 53:1. We offer you peace upon gospel terms, but our peace returns to us again; enemies you were to God, and enemies you still continue.

Many of you *have never been convinced* to this day of your state of enmity against God; and without conviction of this, reconciliation is impossible; without repentance there can be no reconciliation, and without conviction there can be no repentance. When we repent we lay down our weapons. Isaiah 27:4, 5. But how few have been brought to this. Alas, if a few poor, cold, heartless, ineffectual confessions of sin may pass for a due conviction and serious repentance, then have we been convinced, then have we repented; but you will find, if ever the Lord intend to reconcile you to himself, your convictions and humiliations for sin will be more than this, and will cost you more than a few cheap words against sin. "Ye sorrowed after a godly sort; what carefulness it wrought in you, yea, what clearing of yourselves, yea, what indignation, yea, what fear, yea, what vehement desire, yea, what zeal, yea, what revenge!" 2 Cor. 7 : 11.

Many of us *never treated seriously* with the Lord about peace, and how then are we reconciled to him? What, a peace without a treaty? Reconciliation without any consideration about it? It can never be. When was the time and where was the place that you were found in secret upon your knees, mourning over the sin of your nature and the evil of your ways? Certainly you must be brought to this; you must with a broken heart bewail your sin and misery. Friend, that stony heart of thine must feel remorse and anguish for sin; it will cost thee some sad days and sorrowful nights or ever thou canst have peace with God; it will cost thee many a groan, many a tear, many a hearty cry to heaven. If ever peace be made between God and thee, thou must "take with thee words, and turn to the Lord, saying, Take away all iniquity, and receive me graciously." O for one smile, one token of love, one hint of favor! The child of peace is not born without pangs and agonies of soul.

Many of us are not reconciled to *the duties* of religion and ways of holiness; how then is it possible we should be reconciled to God? What, reconciled to God, and unreconciled to the ways of God? By reconciliation we are *made nigh;* in duties of communion we *draw nigh;* and can we be made nigh to God, and have no heart to draw nigh to God? It can never be. Examine your hearts and say, Is not the way of strictness a bondage to you? Had you not rather be at liberty to fulfil the desires of the flesh and of the mind? Could you not wish that the Scriptures had made some things else your sins, and other things your duties? Do you delight in the law of God after the inner man, and *esteem his judgments concerning all things to be right?* Do you love secret prayer and delight in duties of communion with God; or rather, are they not an ungrateful burden and irksome imposition? Give conscience leave to speak plain.

Many of us are *not enemies to sin,* and how then are we reconciled to God? What, friends with God and our lusts too? It cannot be. "Ye that love the Lord, hate evil." Psa. 97 : 10. The same hour our reconciliation is made with God there is an everlasting breach made with sin: this is one of the articles or conditions of our peace with God, "Let the wicked forsake his way, and the unrighteous man his thoughts; and let him return unto the Lord, and he will have mercy upon him; and to our God, for he will abundantly pardon." Isaiah 55 : 7. But it is manifest in many of us, that we are no enemies to sin; we secretly indulge it, what bad names soever we call it. We will commit ten sins to cover one: we cannot endure the most serious, faithful, seasonable, private, tender, and necessary reproof for sin, but our hearts swell and rise at it; sure we are not reconciled to God while we embrace sin, his enemy, in our bosoms.

We *love not the children of God,* nor are we reconciled to them that bear his image, and how then can we be reconciled to God? "Every one that loveth him that begat, loveth him also that is begotten of him." 1 John 5 : 1. What, at peace with the Father and at war with the children? It cannot be. Do not some that hope they have made their peace with God, hate, revile, and persecute the children of God? Surely, when we are reconciled to the Lord, we are reconciled to his people: we shall then love a Christian as a Christian, and by this we may know that we have passed from death to life.

How can any man think himself to be reconciled to God who *never closed heartily with Jesus Christ* by faith. He is the only daysman and peacemaker; the only Mediator of reconciliation between God and man.

This is a sure truth, that all whom God accepts into favor are "made accepted in the Beloved." Eph. 1 : 6. If any man will make peace with God, he must take hold of his strength, accept and close with Christ, who is the power of God, or he can never make peace. Isa. 27 : 5. He must be "made nigh by the blood of Christ." Eph. 2 : 13. But, alas, both Christ and faith are strangers to many souls, who yet persuade themselves they are at peace with God. O fatal mistake !

5. We see *the high honor and responsibility of the ambassadors of reconciliation.* God hath put great honor upon you in this high and noble employment ; great is the dignity of your office ; to some you are the savor of death unto death, and to others a savor of life unto life; and who is sufficient for these things ? 2 Cor. 2 : 16. But yet the responsibility is no less than the dignity. O what manner of men should we be for judgment, seriousness, affection, patience, and exemplary holiness, to whom the management of so great a concern between God and man is committed.

How necessary are *judgment* and *prudence* in so weighty and difficult a work ! He had need be a man of wisdom that is to inform the ignorant of the nature and necessity of this great work, and win over their hearts to consent to the articles of peace propounded in the gospel—that has so many subtle temptations to answer, and so many intricate cases of conscience to resolve. There are many strongholds of Satan to be battered, and many stout and obstinate resistances made by the hearts of sinners which must be overcome ; and he had need be no novice in religion to whom so difficult a province is committed.

Let us be *serious* in our work, as well as judicious. Remember, O ye ambassadors of Christ, you bring a message from the God of heaven, of everlasting consequence to the souls of men. The eternal decrees are executed upon them in your ministry : to some you are "the savor of life

unto life," and to some "the savor of death unto death."
2 Cor. 2 : 16. Heaven and hell are matters of most awful
and solemn consideration. O, what an account have we
also shortly to give unto Him that sent us! These are
subjects of such deep concern as should swallow up our
very spirits ; the least they can do is to compose our hearts
unto seriousness in the management of them.

Be filled with *tender affections* towards the souls of men,
with whom you treat for reconciliation : you see a multitude
of poor souls upon the brink of eternal misery, and they
know it not, but promise themselves peace, and fill themselves with vain hopes of heaven ; and is there a more
moving, melting spectacle in the world than this ? O think
with what bowels of commiseration Moses and Paul were
filled, when the one desired rather to be blotted out of
God's book, and the other to be accursed from Christ, than
that Israel should not be saved. Exod. 32 : 32 ; Rom.
9 : 3. Think how the bowels of Christ yearned over Jerusalem, Matt. 23 : 37 ; and over the multitude, Matt. 9 : 36.
"Let this mind be in you, which was also in Christ Jesus."
Phil. 2 : 5.

Be *patient and long-suffering* towards sinners : such is
the value of one soul, that it is worth waiting all our days
to save it at last. "The servant of the Lord must not
strive ; but be gentle unto all men, apt to teach, patient,
in meekness instructing those that oppose themselves ; if
God peradventure will give them repentance." 2 Tim.
2 : 24, 25. The Lord waits with patience upon sinners,
and well may you. Consider yourselves, how long was
God treating with you ere you were won to him ? Be not
discouraged if your success at present answer not your
expectation.

Be sure to enforce your exhortations with a *godly example*, else you may preach out your last breath before
you gain one soul to God. The devil and the carnal hearts
of your hearers will put hinderances enough in the way of

your labors ; do not you put the greatest of all yourselves.
O study not only to preach exactly, but to live exactly ;
let the misplacing of one action in your lives trouble you
more than the misplacing of words in your discourses ; this
is the way to succeed in your embassy, and give up your
account with joy.

6. The exhortation *speaks to all those that are yet in a state
of enmity, and unreconciled to God.*

O that my words might prevail, and that you would
now be entreated to be reconciled to God ! The *ambassadors* of peace are yet with you, the *treaty* is not yet ended,
the Master of the house is not yet risen up, nor the door
of mercy and hope finally shut. Hitherto God hath waited
to be gracious ; O that the long-suffering of God might be
your salvation : a day is hasting when God will treat with
you no more, when a *gulf shall be fixed* between him and
you for ever. Luke 16 : 26. O what will you do when
the season of mercy and all hopes of mercy shall end together ; when God shall become inaccessible and irrecon-
cilable to you for evermore ?

O, what wilt thou do when thou shalt find thyself shut
up under eternal wrath ; when thou shalt feel the misery
thou art warned of ? Is this the place where I must be ?
Are these the torments I must endure ? What, for ever,
yea, for ever ? Will not God be satisfied with the sufferings of a thousand years ; no, nor millions of years ? Ah,
sinners, did you but clearly see the present and future
misery of unreconciled ones, and what that wrath of the
great and terrible God is, which is coming as fast as the
wings of time can bring it upon you, it would certainly
drive you to Christ or drive you out of your senses. O
it is a dreadful thing to have God for your eternal enemy ;
to have the great and terrible God causing his infinite
power to avenge the abuse of his grace and mercy.

Believe it, friends, it is a fearful thing to fall into the
hands of the living God : knowing the terrors of the Lord,

we persuade men ; an eternal weight hangs upon an inch of time.   O, that you did but know the time of your visitation ; that you would not dare to adventure and run the hazard of one day more in an unreconciled state !

7. This subject speaks to those *who have believed our report*, who have taken hold of God's strength and made peace with him ; who had not obtained mercy, but now have obtained mercy ; who once were afar off, but now are made nigh by the blood of Christ.

Admire and stand amazed at this mercy.   "O Lord, I will praise thee," saith the church : "though thou wast angry with me, thine anger is turned away, and thou comfortedst me." Isa. 12 : 1.   O how overwhelming a mercy is here before you !   God is at peace, at peace with you that were enemies in your minds by wicked works, Col. 1 : 21 ; at peace with you, and at enmity with millions as good by nature as you ; at peace with you that sought it not ; at peace for ever ; no dissolving this friendship for evermore.   O let this consideration melt your hearts before the Lord, and make you cry, "What am I, Lord, that mercy should take in me, and shut out fallen angels and millions of men !   O the riches, O the depths of the mercy and goodness of God !"

Beware of new breaches with God.   "He will speak peace unto his people, and to his saints ; but let them not turn again to folly." Psalm 85 : 8.   What though this state of friendship can never be dissolved, yet it is a dreadful thing to have it clouded : you may lose the sense of peace, and with it all the joy of your hearts and the comfort of your lives in this world.

Labor to reconcile others to God, especially those that are endeared to you by the bonds of nature.   When Paul was reconciled to God himself, his heart was full of heaviness for others that were not reconciled—for his brethren and kinsmen according to the flesh. Rom. 9 : 2, 3.   When Abraham was become God's friend himself, then he prayed, "O that Ishmael might live before thee !" Gen. 17 : 18.

Let your reconciliation with God relieve you under *all burdens of affliction* you shall meet with in your way to heaven. Let them that are at enmity with God droop under crosses and afflictions, but do not you do so. You "have peace with God through our Lord Jesus Christ." Rom. 5 : 1. Let the peace of God keep your hearts and minds. As nothing can comfort a man that must go to hell at last, so nothing should deject a man that shall, through many troubles, at last reach heaven.

CHAPTER IV

THE WORK OF THE SPIRIT THE INTERNAL AND MOST EFFECTUAL MEANS OF THE APPLICATION OF CHRIST

"No man can come to me, except the Father which hath sent me draw him." JOHN 6 : 44.

OUR last chapter informed you of the usefulness and influence of the preaching of the gospel, in order to the *application* of Christ to the souls of men. There must be, in God's ordinary way, the external ministerial offer of Christ before men can have union with him.

But yet all the preaching in the world can never effect this union with Christ in itself, and in its own virtue, except a supernatural and mighty power go forth with it. Let Boanerges and Barnabas try their strength, let the *angels* of heaven be the preachers, till God draw, the soul comes not to Christ.

No saving benefit is to be had by Christ without union with his person; there is no union with his person without faith; no faith is ordinarily wrought without the preaching of the gospel by Christ's ambassadors; and their preaching has no saving efficacy without God's drawing, as will evidently appear by considering these words and the occasion of them.

The occasion of these words is found, as the learned Cameron well observes, in the 42d verse, "And they said, Is not this Jesus, the son of Joseph, whose father and mother we know?" Christ had been pressing upon them in his ministry the great and necessary duty of faith; but notwithstanding the authority of the preacher, the holiness of his life, the miracles by which he confirmed his doctrine, they still objected against him, "Is not this the carpenter's son?" From whence Christ takes occasion for these words,

"No man can come to me, except the Father which hath sent me draw him." As if he had said, In vain is the authority of my person urged; in vain are all the miracles wrought in your sight to confirm the doctrine preached to you; till that secret, almighty power of the Spirit be put forth upon your hearts, you will not, you cannot come unto me.

The words are a negative proposition, in which the author and powerful manner of the divine operation in working faith are contained: there must be drawing before believing, and that drawing must be on the part of God. Every word has its weight: we will consider them in the order in which they lie in the text.

No man—not one, let his natural qualifications be what they will, let his external advantages in respect to means and helps be never so great—it is not in the power of any man—all persons, in all ages, need the same power of God, one as well as another—all men are by nature alike dead, impotent, and averse to faith. No man—not one among all the sons of men,

Can—or is able: he speaks of impotency to special and saving actions, such as believing in Christ; no act that is saving can be done without the concurrence of special grace. Other acts that have a remote tendency to it are performed by a more general concourse and common assistance; so men may come to the word and attend to what is spoken, remember and consider what the word tells them, but as to believing or coming to Christ, that no man can do of himself, or by a general and common assistance. No man can

Come unto me—believe in me unto salvation. Coming to Christ, and believing in him, are terms of the same import, and are both used to express the nature of saving faith, as is plain, verse 35, "He that cometh to me shall never hunger, and he that believeth on me shall never thirst;" it notes the terms from which and to which the

soul moves, and the voluntariness of the motion, notwithstanding that divine power by which the will is drawn to
Christ.

Except the Father—not excluding the other two persons; for every work of God relating to men is common
to all the three persons; nor only to imply that the Father
is the first in order of working; but the reason is hinted
in the next words.

Who hath sent me—God hath entered into covenant
with the Son, and sent him, and thus bound himself to
bring the promised seed to him, and this he does by drawing them to Christ by faith. So the next words tell us
that the Father doth

Draw him—that is, powerfully and effectually incline
his will to come to Christ; not by violence, but by a
benevolent bending of the will, which was averse. And
as it is not in the way of force and compulsion, so neither
is it by a simple *moral suasion*, by the bare proposal of
an object to the will, and so leaving the sinner to his own
election; but it is such a persuasion as has a mighty con-
trolling efficacy accompanying it: of which more anon.
Hence,

*It is utterly impossible for any man to come to Jesus Christ,
unless he be drawn unto him by the special and mighty power of
God.*

No man is compelled to come to Christ against his
will; he that cometh, comes willingly; but even that will
and desire to come is the effect of grace. "It is God
which worketh in you, both to will and to do of his good
pleasure." Phil. 2 : 13.

"If we desire the help and assistance of grace," says
Fulgentius, "even the desire is of grace; grace must first
be shed forth upon us, before we can begin to desire it."
"By grace are ye saved through faith, and that not of
yourselves, it is the gift of God." Eph. 2 : 8. Suppose
the utmost degree of natural ability; let a man be as

much disposed and prepared as nature can dispose or prepare him, and to all this add the proposal of the greatest arguments and motives to induce him to come—let all these have the advantage of the fittest season to work upon his heart ; yet no man will come till God draw him ; we move as we are moved : as Christ's coming to us, so our coming to him, are the pure effects of grace.

Three things here require explication : What the drawing of the Father imports ; in what manner he draws men to Christ ; and how it appears that none can come till they be so drawn.

I. WHAT THE DRAWING OF THE FATHER IMPORTS.

To open this, let it be considered that drawing is usually distinguished as *physical* or *moral*. The former is by force and compulsion, this by a sweet congruous efficacy upon the will. As to violence and compulsion, it is not God's way and method, it being both against the nature of the will of man, which cannot be forced, and against the will of Jesus Christ, who loves to reign over a free and willing people, "Thy people shall be willing in the day of thy power," Psa. 110 : 3, or, as that word may be rendered, they shall be *voluntarinesses*, as willing as willingness itself. It is not then by a forcible compulsion, but in a *moral* way of persuasion, that God the Father draws men to Jesus Christ : he draws *with the cords of a man*, as they are called, Hos. 11 : 4, by the rational conviction of the mind and conscience, and the effectual persuasion of the will.

But yet by *moral persuasion* we must not understand a simple and bare proposal or tender of Christ and grace, leaving it merely to the sinner's natural choice whether he will comply with it or not. For though God does not force the will contrary to its nature, yet there is a real internal efficacy implied in this *drawing*, or an immediate operation of the Spirit upon the heart and will, which, in a way congruous and suitable to its nature, takes away its rebellion and reluctance, and makes him who was unwilling, willing to come to Christ. And in this respect we own a *physical* as well as a *moral* influence of the Spirit in this work; and so Scripture expresses it: that ye may know "what is the exceeding greatness of his power towards us who believe, according to the working of his mighty power, which he wrought in Christ when he raised him from the dead." Eph. 1: 19, 20. Here is much more than a naked proposal made to the will; there is a *power* as well as a *tender;* greatness of power; and yet more, the exceeding greatness of his power; and this power hath an actual efficacy ascribed to it, he works upon our hearts and wills *according to the working of his mighty power, which he wrought in Christ when he raised him from the dead.* Thus he fulfils in us all the good pleasure of his will, and the work of faith with power. 2 Thess. 1: 11.

And this is that which the schools call effectual grace; and others an overcoming, conquering delight: thus the work is carried on with a most efficacious sweetness. So that the liberty of the will is not infringed, while the obstinacy of the will is effectually subdued and overruled. For want of this, there are so many *almost Christians* in the world; hence are all those vanishing and imperfect works which come to nothing, called in Scripture a morning cloud, an early dew. Had this mighty power gone forth with the word, they had never vanished or perished like embryos as they do. So then, God draws not only in a moral way, by proposing a suitable object to the will, but also in a physical way, or by immediate powerful influence upon the will; not infringing the liberty of it, but yet infallibly and effectually persuading it to come to Christ.

II. Let us consider the marvellous WAY AND MANNER in which the Lord draws the souls of poor sinners to Jesus Christ, and you will find he does it gradually, congruously, powerfully, effectually, and finally.

1. This blessed work is carried on by the Spirit *grad-

ually; bringing the soul step by step in the due method and order of the gospel to Christ. Illumination, conviction, compunction prepare the way to Christ; and then faith unites the soul to him : without humiliation there can be no faith. "Ye, when ye had seen it, repented not afterward, that ye might believe." Matt. 21 : 32. It is the burdensome sense of sin that brings the soul to Christ for rest. "Come unto me, all ye that labor and are heavy laden." Matt. 11 : 28. But without conviction there can be no compunction, no humiliation ; he that is not convinced of his sin and misery, never bewails it, nor mourns for it. Never was there one tear of true repentance seen to drop from the eye of an unconvinced sinner.

And without illumination there can be no conviction ; for what is conviction but the application of the light which is in the understanding, or mind of a man, to his heart and conscience? Acts 2 : 37. In this order, therefore, the Spirit ordinarily draws souls to Christ : he shines into their minds by illumination ; applies that light to their consciences by effectual conviction ; breaks and wounds their hearts for sin in compunction ; and then moves the will to embrace and close with Christ in the way of faith for life and salvation.

These several steps are more distinctly discerned in some Christians than in others ; they are more clearly to be seen in the *adult convert,* than in those that were drawn to Christ in their youth ; in such as were drawn to him out of a state of profaneness, than in those that had the advantage of a pious education ; but in this order the work is carried on ordinarily in all, however it differ in point of clearness in the one and in the other.

2. He draws sinners to Christ *congruously, or agreeably to the nature of man;* so he speaks, Hos. 11 : 4, "I drew them with cords of a man, with bands of love." Not as beasts are drawn and compelled, but as men are inclined and wrought to compliance by the rational conviction of

their judgments and the powerful persuasion of their wills. The minds of sinners are naturally blinded by ignorance, 2 Cor. 4 : 3, 4, and their affections ensnared by their lusts, Gal. 3 : 4 ; and while it is thus, no arguments or entreaties can possibly prevail to bring them off from the ways of sin to Christ. The way therefore which the Lord takes to win and draw them to Christ, is by rectifying their false apprehensions, and showing them infinitely more good in Christ than in all simple pleasures ; yea, by satisfying their understandings that there is goodness enough in Jesus Christ, to whom he is drawing them.

He shows them that there is *more good in Christ, than in all temporal good things which we are to deny or forsake* upon his account. This being once clearly and convincingly discovered to the understanding, the will is thereby prepared to quit all that entangles and withholds it from coming to Christ. No man loves money so much, but he will part with it for what is worth more to him. "The kingdom of heaven is like unto a merchant-man seeking goodly pearls ; who, when he had found one pearl of great price, went and sold all that he had, and bought it." Matt. 13 : 46. Such an invaluable *pearl* is Jesus Christ ; worth infinitely more than all a poor sinner has to part with for him, and a more real good than all sinful pleasures. These are but vain shadows. Prov. 23 : 5. Christ is a solid, substantial good ; yea, he is, and by conviction appears to be so. The world cannot justify and save, but Christ can. Christ is a more necessary good than the world, which is only for our temporal convenience, while he is of eternal necessity. He is a more durable good than any creature comfort is or can be : "The fashion of this world passeth away," 1 Cor. 7 : 31, but durable riches and righteousness are in him. Prov. 8 : 18. Thus Christ appears, in the day of conviction, infinitely more excellent than the world ; he outbids all the offers that the world can make, and this greatly forwards the work of drawing a soul to Jesus Christ.

And then to remove every thing out of the way to Christ, *God discovers to the soul enough in him to preponderate*, and much more than will recompense all the evils and sufferings it can endure for his sake. True, they that close with Christ close with his cross also ; they must expect to save no more than their souls by him. He tells us what we must expect : "If any man come to me, and hate not his father and mother, and wife and children, and brethren and sisters, yea, and his own life also, he cannot be my disciple. And whosoever doth not bear his cross and come after me, cannot be my disciple." Luke 14 : 26, 27.

To read such a text as this, with such a comment upon it as Satan and our flesh can make, is enough to frighten a man from Christ for ever. Nor is it possible by all the arguments in the world to draw any soul to Christ upon such terms as these, till the Lord convince it that there is enough, and much more than enough in Jesus Christ to recompense all the sufferings and losses we endure for him.

But when the soul is satisfied that these sufferings are but *external* upon the vile *body*, while the benefit which comes by Christ is *internal*, in a man's own *soul;* that these afflictions are but *temporal*, Rom. 8 : 18, while Christ and his benefits are *eternal*—this must needs prevail with the will to come over to Christ, notwithstanding the suffering to be endured, when the reality of this is shown to us by the Lord, and the power of God goes along with these discoveries. Thus the Lord draws us in our own way by rational convictions of the understanding and allurements of the will.

And this may be the reason why some poor souls misjudge the working of the Spirit of God upon themselves, thinking they never had the wonderful and mighty power of God in conversion acting upon their hearts, because they find all that is done upon their hearts is done in the ordinary course and method of nature. They consider, compare, are convinced, and then resolve to choose Christ and his ways; whereas they expected to feel some strange operation that should have the visible character of the immediate power of God upon them. Such a power indeed they might discern, if they would consider it as working in this way and method; but they cannot distinguish God's acts from their own, and that puzzles them.

3. The drawings of the Father are very *powerful.* The arm of the Lord is revealed in this work. Isaiah 53 : 1. It was a powerful word indeed that made the light at first shine out of darkness, and no less power is required to make it shine into our hearts. 2 Cor. 4 : 6. That day in which the soul is made willing to come to Christ, is called "the day of his power." Psalm 110 : 3.

The Scripture expresses the work of conversion by a threefold *metaphor,* namely, that of a *resurrection* from the dead, Rom. 6 : 4 ; that of *creation,* Eph. 2 : 10 ; and that of *victory* or *conquest,* 2 Cor. 10 : 4, 5. All these set forth the infinite power of God in this work, for no less than almighty power is required in each of them ; and if you strictly examine the distinct ideas, you will find the power of God more and more illustriously displayed in each of them. To raise the dead is the effect of almighty power; but then the resurrection supposes preëxistent matter. In the work of *creation,* there is no preëxistent matter ; but then there is no opposition : that which is not, rebels not against the power which gives it being. But *victory* and *conquest* suppose *opposition ;* all the power of corrupt nature arming itself and fighting against God, but yet not able to frustrate his design.

Let the soul whom the Father draws struggle ever so much, it shall come, yea, and come willingly too, when the drawing power of God is upon it. O the self-conflicts, the contrary resolves with which the soul finds itself distracted and rent asunder ! the hopes and fears ; the encouragements and discouragements ; they will, and they will not :

but victorious grace conquers all opposition at last. We find an excellent example of this in Augustin, who speaks of this very work, the drawing of his soul to Christ, and how he felt in that day two wills in himself, one old, the other new ; one carnal, the other spiritual ; and how in these their contrary motions and conflicts, he was torn asunder in his own thoughts and resolutions, suffering that unwillingly which he did willingly. And certainly, if we consider how deep the soul is rooted by natural inclination and long continued custom in sin, how extremely averse it is to the ways of strict godliness and death to sin ; how Satan, that invidious enemy, that strong man armed, fortifies the soul to defend his possession against Christ, and intrenches himself in the understanding, will, and affections, by deep-rooted prejudices against Christ and holiness, it is a wonder of wonders to see a soul quitting all its beloved lusts, and fleshly interests and endearments, and coming willingly under Christ's yoke.

4. The drawings of God are very *effectual.* There is indeed a common and *ineffectual* work upon hypocrites and apostates, called in Scripture a morning cloud and early dew. Hos. 6 : 4. These may believe for a time, and fall away at last. Luke 8 : 13. Their wills may be half won ; they may be drawn half way to Christ, and return again. So it was with Agrippa, Acts 26 : 28, Within a very little thou persuadest me to be a Christian. But in God's own children it is effectual. Their wills are not only *almost,* but *altogether* persuaded to embrace Christ and quit the ways of sin, how pleasant, gainful, and dear soever they have been. The Lord not only draws, but draws home those souls to Christ. "All that the Father giveth me shall come to me." John 6 : 37.

It is confessed that in drawing home the very elect to Christ there may be, and frequently are, many pauses, stands, and demurs ; they have convictions, affections, and resolutions stirring in them, which, like early blossoms, seem to be nipt and die away again. There is frequently, and especially in the young, a hopeful appearance of grace ; they make conscience of avoiding sins and performing duties ; they have sometimes great awakenings under the word ; they are observed to retire for meditation and prayer, and delight to be in the company of Christians ; and after all this, youthful lusts and vanities are found to stifle and choke these hopeful beginnings, and the work seems to stand, it may be some years, at a pause ; however, at last the Lord makes it victorious over all opposition, and sets it home with power upon their hearts.

5. Those whom the Father draws to Christ, he draws finally and for ever. "The gifts and calling of God are without repentance." Rom. 11 : 29. They are so as to God the giver, he never repents that he has called his people into the fellowship of his Son Christ Jesus ; and they are so on the believer's part, he is never sorry, whatever he afterwards meets with, that he came to Christ. There is a time when Christians are drawn to Christ, but there shall never be a time in which they shall be drawn away from Christ. John 10 : 29. There is no plucking them out of the Father's hand. It was common to a proverb in the primitive times, when they would express an impossibility, to say, "You may as soon draw a Christian from Christ as do it" When Christ asked that question of the disciples, "Will ye also go away ? Lord," said Peter, in the name of them all, "to whom shall we go ? Thou hast the words of eternal life." John 6 : 67. They who are thus drawn, do with full purpose of heart cleave unto the Lord.

III. I am to evince the impossibility of coming to Christ WITHOUT THE FATHER'S DRAWING, which will evidently appear on considering that the difficulty of this work is above all the power of nature to overcome ; and that the little power and ability which nature has, it will never employ to such a purpose as this, till the drawing power of God be upon the will of a sinner.

If all the power of nature were employed in this design, yet such are the difficulties of this work that it surmounts all the abilities of nature. This the Scripture very plainly affirms: "By grace are ye saved through faith; and that not of yourselves, it is the gift of God." Eph. 2 : 8. To think of Christ is easy, but to come to Christ is to nature impossible. Send forth cold and ineffectual wishes to Christ we may, but to bring Christ and the soul together requires the almighty power of God. Eph. 1 : 19. The grace of faith by which we come to Christ, is as much the free gift of God as Christ himself, who is the object of faith. To you it is freely given to believe. Phil. 1 : 29.

1. Consider *the subject* in which faith is wrought, or what it is that is drawn to Christ. It is *the heart of a sinner*, which is naturally no more disposed for this work than was the wood which Elijah laid in order upon the altar to take fire when he had poured so much water upon it as not only wet the wood, but filled up the trench round about it. 1 Kings 18 : 33. It is naturally a dark, blind, and ignorant heart, Job 11 : 12 ; and such a heart can never believe till He that commanded the light to shine out of darkness do shine into it. 2 Cor. 4 : 6. Nor will it avail any thing to say, though man be born in darkness and ignorance, yet afterwards he may acquire knowledge in the use of means, as we see many natural men do to a very high degree ; for this is not the light that brings the soul to Christ ; yea, this natural unsanctified light blinds the soul, and prejudices it more against Christ than ever it was before. 1 Cor. 1 : 21, 26.

As it is a blind, ignorant heart, so it is a *selfish* heart by nature : all its designs and aims terminate in self ; this is the centre and weight of the soul ; no righteousness but its own is sought after : that or none. Rom. 10 : 3. Now for a soul to renounce and deny self, in all its forms, modes, and interests, as every one doth that cometh to Christ ; to disclaim and deny natural, moral, and religious self, and

come to Christ as a poor, miserable, wretched, empty creature, to live upon his righteousness for ever, is as supernatural and wonderful as to see the hills and mountains
start from their bases and centres, and fly like wandering
atoms in the air.

Nay, this heart which is to come to Christ is not only
dark and selfish, but full of *pride*. Oh, it is a desperate
proud heart by nature ; it cannot submit to come to Christ
as Benhadad's servants came to the king of Israel, with
sackcloth on their loins and ropes upon their heads. To
take guilt, shame, and confusion of face to ourselves, and
acknowledge the righteousness of God in our eternal
damnation ; to come to Christ naked and empty, as one
that justifies the ungodly—I say, nature left to itself
would as soon be damned as do this : the proud heart will
never come to this till the Lord hath humbled and broken
it by his power.

2. Let us also take into consideration *the act of faith*, as
it is here described by the soul's coming to Jesus Christ,
and you will find a necessity of the Father's drawing ; for
this evidently implies that which is against the stream and
current of corrupt nature, and that which is above the sphere
and capacity of the most refined and accomplished nature.

It is *against the stream and current* of our corrupt nature
to come to Christ. Consider from what the soul departs
when it comes to Christ. In that day it leaves all its
lusts and ways of sin, how pleasant, sweet, and profitable
soever they have been : "Let the wicked forsake his way,
and the unrighteous man his thoughts : and let him return
unto the Lord." Isa. 55 : 7. *His way and thoughts*, that
is, both the practice of and delight he had in sin must
be forsaken, and the outward and inward man must be
cleansed from it. Now there are in the bosoms of unregenerate men such darling lusts, which have given them
so much pleasure, brought them so much profit, and been
born and bred up with them, and which, on all these

accounts, are so endeared to their souls, that it is easier
for them to die than to forsake them ; yea, nothing is more
common among such men, than to venture eternal damnation rather than suffer a separation from their sins.

And what is yet more difficult in coming to Christ, the
soul forsakes not only its sinful self, but its *righteous* self ;
not only its worst sins, but its best performances, accomplishments, and excellences.   This is one of the greatest
straits that nature can be put to.   Righteousness by works
was the first liquor that ever was put into the vessel, and
it still retains the relish and savor of it, and will to the end
of the world.   "For they being ignorant of God's righteousness, and going about to establish their own righteousness, have not submitted themselves unto the righteousness of God."   Rom. 10 : 3.   To come naked and empty
to Christ, and receive all from him as a free gift, is, to proud
corrupt nature, the greatest abasement and submission in
the world.

Let the gospel furnish its table with the richest dainties that ever the blood of Christ purchased, such is the
pride of nature that it disdains to taste them except it may
also pay for the same.   If the old hive be removed from
the place where it was wont to stand, the bees will come
home to the old place, yea, and many of them you shall
find will die there rather than go to the hive, though it
stand in a far better place than it did before.   Just so
stands the case with men.   The *hive* is removed, that is,
we are not to expect righteousness as Adam did, by obeying and working, but by believing and coming to Christ,
but nature would as soon be damned as do this : it still
goes about to establish its own righteousness.

Virtues and moral excellences are accounted the ornaments of nature : here is nature set off in its sumptuous
attire and rich embellishments, and now to renounce it,
disclaim and contemn it as dross and dung in comparison
of Christ, as believers do, Phil. 3 : 8 ; this, I say, is against

the grain of nature. We reckon it a strange instance of self-denial in Mahomet the Great, who being so enamoured with his beautiful Irene, would be persuaded, upon reasons of state, with his own hand to strike off her head, and that even when she appeared in all her rich ornaments before him, rather like such a goddess as the poets in their ecstasies use to feign, than a mortal creature. But there is a greater self-denial to our corrupt nature exercised in coming to Christ.

Again, we find the soul as much acting above the sphere and ability of improved nature as against the stream and current of corrupted nature ; for how wonderful and supernatural an adventure is that which the soul makes in the day that it comes to Jesus Christ. Surely, for any soul to venture itself for ever upon Jesus Christ whom it never saw, nay, upon Christ whose very existence its own unbelief calls in question ; and that when it is even weighed down to the dust with the sense of its own vileness and total unworthiness, feeling nothing in itself but sin and misery, the workings of death and fears of wrath—to go to Christ, of whose pardoning grace and mercy it never had the least experience, and without finding any ground of hope in itself that it shall be accepted ; this is as much above the power of nature as it is for a stone to rise from the earth and fix itself among the stars. Well might the apostle ascribe it to that almighty power which raised up Christ from the dead. Eph. 1 : 19, 20. If the Lord draw not the soul, and that omnipotently, it will never come from itself to Christ. But,

3. The natural impossibility of coming to Christ will more clearly appear, if we consider *the enemies* to faith, or what blocks are rolled by Satan and his instruments into the way to Christ : to mention, in this place, none but our own carnal reason, as it is armed and managed by the subtlety of Satan, what a wonder is it that any soul should come to Christ ! These are the strong-holds men-

tioned 2 Cor. 10 : 4, out of which those *objections*, fears, and discouragements sally, by which the soul is fiercely assaulted in the way to Christ:

"Wilt thou forsake all thy pleasures, merry company, and sensible comforts, to live a sad, retired, pensive life? Wilt thou beggar and undo thyself, let go all thy comforts in hand, for a hope of that which thine eyes never saw, and of which thou hast no certainty that it is any thing more than a fancy? Wilt thou that hast lived in reputation and credit all thy life, now become the scorn and contempt of the world? Thinkest thou thyself able to live such a strict, mortified, and self-denying life as the word of God requires? And what if persecution should arise, as thou mayest expect it will, canst thou forsake father and mother, wife and children, yea, and give up thine own life too, to a cruel and bloody death? Be advised before thou resolve in so important a matter. What thinkest thou of thy forefathers, that lived and died in the way thou art now living? Art thou wiser than they? Do not the generality of men walk in the same paths thou hast hitherto walked in? If this way lead to hell, as thou fearest it may, think then how many millions of men must perish as well as thyself; and is such a supposition consistent with the gracious and merciful nature of God? Besides, think what sort of people those are unto whom thou art about to join thyself in this new way. Are there not to be found among them many things to discourage thee and cool thy zeal? They are generally of the lower sort of men, poor and despicable. Seest thou not, though their profession be holy, how earthly, factious, and hypocritical many of them are found to be? And doubtless the rest are like them, though their hypocrisy be not yet discovered."

Oh, what demurs, what hesitations and doubts, is the soul clogged with in its way to Christ. But none of these can withhold and detain the soul when the Father draws: greater is he that is in us, than he that is in the world.

INFERENCE 1. *How thoroughly is the nature of man corrupted, and what an enemy is every man to his own happiness, that he must be drawn to it.* "Ye will not come to me, that ye might have life." John 5 : 40.

Life is desirable in every man's eyes, and eternal life is the most excellent; yet in this the world is agreed rather to perish for ever than come to Christ for life. Had Christ told us of fields and vineyards, sheep and oxen, gold and silver, honors and sensual pleasures, who would not have come to him for these? But to tell of mortification, self-denial, and sufferings for his sake, and all this for a happiness to be enjoyed in the world to come, nature will never like such a proposition as this.

You see where it sticks, not in a simple inability to believe, but in an inability joined with enmity; they neither can come nor will come to Christ. It is true, all that do come to Christ, come willingly; but thanks be to the grace of God, that has freed and persuaded the will, else they never had been willing to come. Who ever found his own heart first stir and move towards Christ? How long may we wait and expect before we shall feel our hearts naturally burn with desires after and love to Jesus Christ.

This aversion of the will and affections from God is one of the main roots of original sin. No argument can prevail to bring the soul to Christ till this be mastered and overpowered by the Father's drawing. In our motions to sin we need restraining, but in all our motions to Christ we as much need drawing. He that comes to heaven may say, Lord, if I had had mine own way, I had never come here : if thou hadst not drawn me, I should never have come to thee. O the riches of the grace of God! O unparalleled mercy and goodness, not only to prepare such a glory as this for an unworthy soul, but to put forth the exceeding greatness of thy power afterwards to draw an unwilling soul to the enjoyment of it!

2. *What enemies are they to God and the souls of men who do all they can to discourage and hinder the conversion of men to Christ.* God draws forward, and these do all that in them lies to draw backward, to prejudice and discourage men from coming to Jesus Christ in the way of faith : this is a direct opposition to God, and a plain confederacy with the devil.

O how many have been thus discouraged in their way to Christ by their worldly relations, I cannot say friends. Their greatest enemies have been the men of their own house. These have pleaded, as if the devil had hired and paid them, against the everlasting welfare of their own flesh. O cruel parents, brethren and sisters, that jeer, frown, and threaten, where they should encourage, assist, and rejoice. Such parents are the devil's children. Satan chooses such instruments as you are, above all others, for this work : he knows what influence and authority you have upon them and over them ; how they fear and love you, and are dependent upon you : so that none in all the world are likely to manage the design of their damnation so effectually as you.

Will you neither come to Christ yourselves, nor suffer your dear relations that would? Had you rather find them in the ale-house than in the closet? Did you instrumentally give them their being, and will you be the instruments of ruining for ever those lives they had from you? Did you so earnestly desire children, so tenderly nurse and provide for them, take such delight in them ; and, after all this, do you do what in you lies to damn and destroy them? If these lines shall fall into the hands of any such, O that God would set home the conviction and sense of this horrid evil upon their hearts.

And no less guilty of this sin are scandalous and loose professors, who furnish the devil with the greatest arguments he has to dissuade men from coming to Christ ; it is your looseness and hypocrisy by which he hopes to keep others from Christ. Take heed what you do, lest you go down to hell under the guilt of damning more souls than your own.

3. *Learn hence the true ground and reason of those amazing and supernatural effects that you behold and so admire in the world, as often as you see sinners forsaking their pleasant, profitable corruptions and companions, and embracing the ways of Christ and godliness.*

It is said, "They think it strange that you run not with them to the same excess of riot." 1 Pet. 4 : 4. It is the world's wonder to see their companions in sin forsake them; to see those that were once as profane and vain as themselves forsake their society, retire into their closets, mourn for sin, spend their time in meditation and prayer, embrace the severest duties, and content to run the greatest hazards for Christ; but they see not the almighty Power that draws them, which is too strong for all the sinful ties and engagements in the world to withhold and detain them.

A man would have wondered to see Elisha leave the oxen and run after Elijah, saying, "Let me go, I pray thee, and kiss my father and mother, and then I will follow thee;" when Elijah had said nothing to persuade him to follow him, only that, as he passed by, he cast his mantle on him. 1 Kings 19 : 19, 20. Surely the soul whom God draws will leave all and follow Christ, for the power of God resteth on it. All carnal ties and engagements to sin break and give way when the Father draws the soul to Christ in the day of his power.

4. *Is this the first spring of spiritual motion after Christ? Learn then how it comes to pass that so many excellent sermons and powerful persuasions are ineffectual, and cannot draw and win one soul to Christ.* Surely it is because ministers draw alone; and the special saving power of God goes not forth at all times alike with their endeavors.

Paul was a chosen vessel, filled with a greater measure of gifts and graces by the Spirit than any that went before him or followed after him ; and as his talents, so his diligence in improving them was beyond any example we read of among men : "He rather flew like a seraphim," says Chrysostom, "than travelled upon his Master's errand about the world."   Apollos was an eloquent preacher, and mighty in the Scriptures, yet Paul is nothing, and Apollos nothing ; but God that gives the increase.   1 Cor. 3 : 7. We are too apt to admire men, yea, and the best are but too apt to go forth in the strength of their own powers and preparations ; but God secures his own glory and magnifies his own power frequently in giving success to weaker endeavors and men of lower abilities, when he withholds it from men of more raised, refined, and excellent gifts.

It is our great honor, who are the ministers of the gospel, that we are workers together with God.   1 Cor. 3 : 9. In his strength we can prevail ; the weapons of our warfare are mighty through God.   2 Cor. 10 :4.   But if his presence, blessing, and assistance be not with us, we are nothing, we can do nothing.   If we prepare diligently, pray heartily, preach zealously, and our hearers go as they came, without any spiritual effects and fruits of our labors, what shall we say but as Martha said to Christ, "Lord, if thou hadst been here, my brother had not died ;" had the Spirit of God gone forth with his especial efficacy and blessing, with this prayer or that sermon, these souls had not departed dead and senseless from under it.

5. *Does all success and efficacy depend upon the Father's drawing ?   Let none then despair of their unregenerate relations, over whose obstinacy they mourn.*

What if they have been as many years under the preaching of the gospel as the poor man lay at the pool of Bethesda, and hitherto to no purpose ?   A time may come at last, as it did for him, when the Spirit of God may move upon the waters ; I mean, put a quickening and converting power into the means, and then the desire of your souls for them shall be fulfilled.

It may be you have poured out many prayers and tears to the Lord for them; you have cried for them as Abraham for his son, O that Ishmael might live before thee! O that this poor husband, wife, child, brother, or sister might live in thy sight; and still you see them continue carnal, dead, and senseless. Give not up your hopes, nor cease your pious endeavors; the time may come when the Father may draw as well as you, and then you shall see them quit all and come to Christ; and nothing shall hinder them. They are now drawn away of their own lusts; they are easily drawn away by their sinful companions; but when God draws, none of these shall withdraw them from the Lord Jesus. What is their ignorance, obstinacy, and hardness of heart before the mighty power that subdues all things to itself? Go therefore to the Lord by prayer for them, and say, Lord, I have labored for my poor relations in vain, I have spent my exhortations to little purpose; the work is too difficult for me, I can carry it no farther, but thou canst: O let thy power go forth; they shall be willing in the day of thy power.

6. If none can come to Christ except the Father draw them, then surely *none can be drawn from Christ except the Father leave them. That power which at first drew them to Christ can secure and establish them in Christ to the end.* "My Father, which gave them me, is greater than all; and no man is able to pluck them out of my Father's hand." John 10 : 29. When the power of God at first draws us out of our natural state to Christ, it finds us not only *impotent* but *obstinate*, not only unable but unwilling to come; and yet this power of God prevails against all opposition; how much more is it able to preserve and secure us when his fear is put into our inward parts, so that we dare not depart, we have no will to depart from him. Well then if the world say, I will ensnare thee; if the devil say, I will destroy thee; if the flesh say, I will betray thee; yet thou art secure and safe, as long as

God has said, "I will never leave thee, nor forsake thee." Heb. 13 : 5.

7. *Let this engage you to a constant attendance upon the ordinances of God, in which this drawing power of God is usually put forth upon the hearts of men.*

Beloved, there are certain seasons in which the Lord comes nigh to men in the ordinances and duties of his worship; and we know not at what time the Lord cometh forth by his Spirit upon this design: he many times comes in an hour when we think not of him: "I am found of them that sought me not." Isa. 65 : 1. It is good therefore to be found in the way of the Spirit. Had the poor man that lay so long at the pool of Bethesda reasoned thus with himself, "So long have I lain here in vain expecting a cure, it is to no purpose to wait longer;" and so had he been absent at that very time when the angel came down, he had, in all likelihood, carried his disease to the grave. How dost thou know but this very *Sabbath*, this sermon, this prayer, which thou hast no heart to attend, and art tempted to neglect, may be the season and instrument through which the Lord may do that for thy soul which was never done before?

8. *How are all the saints obligated to put forth all the power and ability they have for God, who hath put forth his infinite almighty power to draw them to Christ.*

God has done great things for your souls; he has drawn you out of the miserable state of sin and wrath; and that when he let others go, by nature as good as you: he has drawn you into union with Christ and communion with his glorious privileges. O that you would henceforth employ all the power you have for God in the duties of obedience, and in drawing others to Christ as much as in you lies, and say continually with the church, "Draw me, we will run after thee." Song 1 : 4.

Thanks be to God for Jesus Christ.

CHAPTER V

THE WORK OF THE SPIRIT MORE PARTICULARLY, BY WHICH THE SOUL IS ENABLED TO APPLY CHRIST

"And you hath he quickened, who were dead in trespasses and sins." Eph. 2:1

WE have seen our union with Christ in the general nature of it, and the means by which it is effected, both *external* by the preaching of the gospel, and *internal* by the drawing of the Father. We are now to bring our thoughts yet closer to this great mystery, and consider the bands by which Christ and believers are knit together in a blessed union.

If we heedfully observe the scripture expressions, and ponder the nature of this union, we shall find there are two bands which knit Christ and the soul together : 1. The *Spirit*, on Christ's part, *quickening* us with spiritual life, whereby Christ first takes hold of us ; and, 2. *Faith* on our part, when thus quickened, whereby we take hold of Christ; accordingly, this union with the Lord Jesus is expressed in Scripture sometimes by the one and sometimes by the other of these means or bands by which it is effected. Christ is sometimes said to be in us; so, Col. 1 : 27, "Christ is in you the hope of glory ;" and Rom. 8 : 10, " And if Christ be in you, the body is dead because of sin." At other times it is expressed by the other band on our part, as 1 John 5 : 20, "We are in him that is true, even in his Son Jesus Christ ;" and 2 Cor. 5 : 17, "If any man be in Christ, he is a new creature."

The difference between these is thus aptly expressed by Mr. Case : Christ is in believers by his *Spirit*. 1 John 4 : 13. The believer is in Christ by *faith*. John 1 : 12.

Christ is in the believer by *inhabitation.* Rom. 8 : 10. The believer is in Christ by *implantation.* Rom. 6 : 5. Christ is in the believer as the head is in the body, Col. 1 : 18 ; as the root in the branches, John 15 : 5. Believers are in Christ as the members are in the head, Eph. 1 : 23, or as the branches are in the root, John 15 : 1, 7. Christ in the believer implieth life and influence from Christ. Col. 3 : 4. The believer in Christ implieth *communion* and *fellowship* with Christ. 1 Cor. 1 : 30. When Christ is said to be in the believer, we are to understand it in reference to *sanctification.* When the believer is said to be in Christ, t is in order to justification."

Thus we apprehend being ourselves first apprehended by Jesus Christ. Phil. 3 : 12. We do not take hold of Christ till first he take hold of us ; no vital act of faith can be exercised till a vital principle be first inspired ; of both these bands of union we must speak distinctly, and first of *Christ quickening us by his Spirit,* in order to our union with him, of which we have an account in the scripture before us, "You hath he quickened, who were dead in trespasses and sins ;" in which words we find these two things :

1. The imparting of a vital principle of grace. *You hath he quickened.* The words *hath he quickened* are necessary to make clear the sense of the apostle, which else would have been more obscure, by reason of the long parenthesis between the first and fifth verses. They import the first vital act of the Spirit of God, or his first enlivening work upon the soul, in order to its union with Jesus Christ ; for as the blood of Christ is the fountain of all merit, so the Spirit of Christ is the fountain of all spiritual life ; and until he quicken us, impart the principle of divine life into our souls, we can put forth no vital act of faith to lay hold upon Jesus Christ.

This his quickening work is therefore first in the order of nature to our union with Christ, and fundamental to all other acts of grace done by us, from our first closing with Christ throughout the whole course of our obedience ; and this quickening act is said, verse 5, to be "together with Christ :" either denoting, as some expound it, that it is the effect of the same power by which Christ was raised from the dead, according to Eph. 1 : 20 ; or rather, to be *quickened together with Christ*, denotes that new spiritual life which is imparted to our dead souls in the time of our union with Christ : for it is Christ to whom we are conjoined and united in our regeneration, out of whom, as a fountain, all spiritual benefits flow to us, among which this vivification or quickening is one, and a most sweet and precious one.

Zanchy Bodius, and many others, will have this *quickening* to comprise both our justification and regeneration, and to stand opposed both to *eternal* and *spiritual* death, and it may well be allowed ; but it most properly imports our regeneration, wherein the Spirit, in an ineffable and mysterious way, makes the soul to live to God, yea, to live the life of God, which soul was before *dead in trespasses and sins*.

2. The words "hath he quickened" imply also the total indisposedness of the subjects by nature : they are dead in respect to *condemnation*, being under the damning sentence of the law, and dead in respect to the privation of spiritual life ; dead in opposition to justification, and dead in opposition to regeneration and sanctification.   And the fatal instrument by which their souls died is here showed them : you were dead in, or by *trespasses* and *sins;* this was the sword that killed your souls, and cut them off from God, Some curiously distinguish between trespasses and sins, as if one pointed at *original*, the other at *actual* sins ; but I suppose they are promiscuously used here, and serve to express the cause of their ruin, or means of their spiritual death and destruction : this was their case when Christ came to quicken them, *dead in sin;* and being so, they would never move themselves towards union with Christ.

but as they were moved by the quickening Spirit of God. Hence,

Those souls which have union with Christ are quickened with a supernatural principle of life by the Spirit of God.

The Spirit of God is not only a living Spirit, but he is the Spirit of life, or the life-giving Spirit. And without his breathing life into our souls, our union with Christ is impossible. We close with Christ by faith, but that faith being a vital act, presupposes a principle of life communicated to us by the Spirit; therefore it is said, "Whosoever liveth and believeth in me shall never die," John 11 : 26 : the vital act and operation of faith springs from this quickening Spirit. So, Rom. 8 : 1, 2, the apostle, having shown the blessed state of them that are in Christ, shows us in the second verse how we come to be in him: "The Spirit of life in Christ Jesus hath made me free from the law of sin and death."

There is indeed a quickening work of the Spirit which is *subsequent* to regeneration, consisting in his exciting, recovering, and actuating of his own graces in us; and from hence is the *growth* of a Christian; but I am here to speak of a quickening act of the Spirit *in our regeneration*, from which proceeds the spiritual life of a Christian, and will show what this spiritual life is in its nature and properties; in what manner it is wrought or inspired into the soul; for what end this life is so inspired; that this work is wholly supernatural; and why this quickening must be antecedent to our actual closing with Christ by faith.

I. THE NATURE AND PROPERTIES of this life consists in that *wonderful change which the Spirit of God makes upon the frame and temper of the soul, by implanting in it the principles of grace.*

A change it makes upon the soul, and that a marvellous one, no less than from death to life; for though a man be *physically* a living man, his soul hath union with his body, yet his soul having no union with Christ, he is *spir-*

itually dead. Luke 15 : 24, and Col. 2 : 13. Alas, it deserves not the name of life to have a soul serving only to preserve the body a little while from corruption ; to carry it up and down the world, and enable it to eat and drink, and talk and laugh, and then die. We begin to live when we begin to have union with Christ the Fountain of life by his Spirit communicated to us : from this time we are to reckon our life as some have done. There be many changes made upon men besides this : many are changed from profaneness to civility, and from mere civility to formality and a shadow of religion, who still remain in the state and power of spiritual death ; but when the Spirit of the Lord is poured out upon us, to quicken us with the new spiritual life, this is a wonderful change indeed : it gives us a new supernatural being, called a *new creature, the new man, the hidden man of the heart.* The natural essence and faculties of the soul still remain, but it is divested of the old qualities and endowed with new ones : "Old things are passed away ; behold, all things are become new." 2 Cor. 5 : 17.

And this change is not made by altering and rectifying the disorders of the life only, leaving the temper and frame of the heart still carnal ; but by implanting a supernatural, permanent principle in the soul. It shall be in him a well of water. John 4 : 14. Principles are to a course of action, as fountains or springs to the streams and rivers that flow from them, and are maintained by them ; and hence the constancy of renewed souls in the course of godliness.

Nor is this principle or habit *acquired* by accustoming ourselves to holy actions, as natural habits are acquired by frequent acts, which beget a *disposition*, and thence grow up to a *habit* or second nature ; but it is implanted in the soul by the Spirit of God. So we read, "A new heart also will I give you, and a new spirit will I put within you," Ezek. 36 : 25 ; it grows not up out of our natures, but is wrought in us. As it is said of the two witnesses, Rev. 11 : 11, who lay dead in a *civil sense* three days and a half, that "the Spirit of life from God entered into them ;" so it is here in a spiritual sense, the Spirit of life from God enters into the dead, carnal heart. But we shall more fully discern the nature of this spiritual life by considering the properties of it ; among which these are very remarkable.

1. The soul that is joined to Christ is quickened with a *divine life;* so we read 2 Pet. 1 : 4, where believers are said to be "partakers of the divine nature ;" a very high expression, and that must be understood in a way proper to believers ; we partake of it by the inhabitation of the Spirit of God in us : "Know ye not that ye are the temple of God, and that the Spirit of God dwelleth in you ?" 1 Cor. 3 : 16. The Spirit who is God by nature dwells in and actuates the soul whom he regenerates, and by sanctifying it causes it to live a *divine life;* from this life of God the unsanctified are said to be alienated, Eph. 4 : 18, but believers are partakers of it.

2. And being divine, it must be the most *excellent* and transcendent life that any creature can live in this world : it surmounts the natural, rational, and moral life of the unsanctified, as much as the angelical life excels the life of flies and worms of the earth. Some think it a rare life to live in sensual pleasures, while Scripture will not allow so much as the name of life to them, but tells us they are dead while they live. 1 Tim. 5 : 6. Certainly it is a wonderful elevation of the nature of man to be quickened with this divine and spiritual life. There are two ways wherein the blessed God hath honored poor man above the very angels of heaven. One was by the union of our nature, in Christ, with the divine nature ; the other is by uniting us to Christ, and thereby communicating spiritual life to us : this latter is a most glorious privilege, and in one respect a more singular mercy than the former ; for the

honor which was done to our nature by Christ assuming it, is common to all, good and bad, even they that perish have yet that honor; but to be implanted in Christ by regeneration, and live upon him as the branch does upon the vine, this is a peculiar privilege, a mercy kept from the world that is to perish, and only communicated to God's people, who are to live eternally with him in heaven.

3. This life imparted by the regenerating Spirit, is a most *pleasant life.* All delights, all pleasures, all joys, which are not fantastic and delusive, have their spring and origin here : "To be spiritually-minded is life and peace," Rom. 8 : 6, a most serene, placid life ; such a soul becomes, so far as it is influenced and sanctified by the Spirit, the very region of life and peace : it hath its pleasures in it, such as a stranger intermeddles not with. Prov. 14 : 10. Regeneration is the point from which all true pleasure commences ; you never live a cheerful day till you begin to live to God : therefore it is said when the *prodigal son* was returned to his father and reconciled, then "*they began to be merry.*" Luke 15 : 24. None can by words make another understand what that pleasure is which the renewed soul feels in its communion with the Lord, and in the sealings and witnessings of his Spirit. That is a very apt and well-known similitude which Peter Martyr used, and the Lord blessed to the conversion of the noble marquis Galeacus : If, said he, a man should see a company of people dancing upon the top of a remote hill, he would be apt to conclude they were a company of wild, distracted people ; but if he draw nearer, and behold the excellent order and hear the ravishing sweet music that are among them, he will quickly alter his opinion of them, and be for dancing with them himself. All the delights in the sensual life are but as the putrid waters of a corrupt pond where toads lie croaking and spawning, compared to the crystal streams of the most pure and pleasant fountain.

4. This life of God, with which the regenerate are

quickened in their union with Christ, as it is a pleasant,
so it is also *a growing, increasing life:* "The water that I
shall give him shall be in him a well of water springing
up into everlasting life." John 4 : 14. It is not in our
sanctification as it is in our justification : our justification
is complete and perfect, no defect is found there ; but the
new creature labors under many defects : all believers are
equally justified, but not equally sanctified.   Therefore
you read that " the inward man is renewed day by day,"
2 Cor. 4 : 16 ; and Christians are exhorted "to grow in
grace, and in the knowledge of our Lord and Saviour."
1 Pet. 3 : 18.   If this work were perfect, and finished at
once, as justification is, there could be no renewing day
by day, nor growth in grace.   The apostle indeed prays
for the Thessalonians, that God would sanctify them
wholly, perfectly.   1 Thess. 5 : 23.   And this is matter of
prayer and hope ; for at last it will grow up to perfection ;
but this perfect holiness is reserved for the perfect state
in the world to come, and none but deluded, proud spirits
boast of it here ; but when " that which is perfect is come,
then that which is in part shall be done away."   1 Cor.
13 : 10.   And upon the imperfection of the new creature
in every faculty, that warfare and daily conflict spoken of,
Gal. 5 : 17, and experienced by every Christian, is ground-
ed ; grace rises gradually in the soul, as the sun doth in
the heavens, "that shineth more and more unto the perfect day."   Prov. 4 : 18.

5. This life with which the regenerate are quickened,
is also an *everlasting life.*   "This is the **record**, that God
hath given to us eternal life, and this life is in his Son."
1 John 5 : 11.   This principle of life is the seed of God ;
and that remains in the soul for ever.   1 John 3 : 9.   It
is no transient, vanishing thing, but a fixed, permanent
principle, which abides in the soul for ever.   A man may
lose his *gifts,* but grace abides ; the soul may and must be
separated from the body, but grace cannot be separated

from the soul: when all forsake us, this will not leave us. This principle implanted by the Spirit is therefore vastly different, both from the extraordinary gifts of prophecy wherein the Spirit was sometimes said to come upon men under the Old Testament, 1 Sam. 10 : 6, 10, and from the common vanishing effects he sometimes produces in the unregenerate, of which we have frequent accounts in the New Testament. Heb. 6 : 4, and John 5 : 35. It is one thing for the Spirit to visit a man in the way of present influence and assistance, and another thing to dwell in a man as in his temple.

II. Having seen the nature and properties of the spiritual life, we are concerned, in the next place, to inquire HOW IT IS WROUGHT by the Spirit.

1. And here we must say, first of all, that the work is wrought in the soul very *mysteriously;* so Christ tells Nicodemus, " The wind bloweth where it listeth, and thou hearest the sound thereof, but canst not tell whence it cometh, or whither it goeth ; so is every one that is born of the Spirit." John 3 : 8. There are many opinions among philosophers about the origin of wind, but we have no certain knowledge of it ; we describe it by its effects and properties, but know little of its origin : and if the works of God in nature are so abstruse and unsearchable, how much more are these sublime and supernatural works of the Spirit ? We are not able to solve the phenomena of nature, we can give no account of our own formation in the womb. Eccl. 11 : 5. Who can exactly describe how the parts of the body are formed and the soul infused ? It is curiously wrought in the lower parts of the earth, as the Psalmist speaks, Psalm 139 : 15 ; but how, we know not. Basil saith divers questions may be moved about a *fly,* which may puzzle the greatest *philosopher :* we know little of the forms and essences of natural things, much less of the profound and abstruse spiritual things.

2. But though we cannot pry into these secrets by the

eye of reason, God hath revealed to us in his word, that
it is wrought by *his own almighty power.* Eph. 1 : 19.
The apostle ascribes this work to *the exceeding greatness* of
the power of God; and this must needs be, if we consider
how the Spirit of God expresses it in Scripture by a new
creation—a giving being to something out of nothing.
Eph. 2 : 10. In this it differs from all the effects of human
power, for man always works upon some preëxistent matter, but here is no such matter. Nothing is found in man
to contribute towards this work; this supernatural life is
not, nor can it be educed out of natural principles; this
wholly transcends the sphere of all natural power: but of
this more anon.

3. This also we may affirm, that *the whole soul and spirit*
is the recipient of this divine life, and thus it is called a
new creature, a new man, having an integral perfection and
fulness of all its parts and members: it becomes light in
the mind, John 17 : 3; obedience in the will, 1 Peter 1 : 2;
in the affections a heavenly temper and tenderness, Col.
3 : 1, 2. And here, we must observe, lies one main difference between a regenerate soul and a hypocrite: the one
is all of a piece, as I may say, the principle of spiritual life
runs into all and every faculty and affection, and sanctifies
or renews the whole man; whereas the change upon the
hypocrite is but partial and particular: he may have new
light, but no new love; a new tongue, but not a new
heart; this or that vice may be reformed, but the whole
course of his life is not altered.

4. This imparting of spiritual life is done *instantaneous-
ly,* as all *creation work* is; hence it is resembled to that
plastic power which, in a moment, made the light to shine
out of darkness. So God shines into our hearts. 2 Cor.
4 : 6. It is true, a soul may be a long time under the preparatory work of the Spirit, under convictions and humiliations, purposes and resolutions; he may be attending
means and ordinances, but when the Spirit comes to

quicken the soul it is done in a moment; and O what a blessed moment is this, upon which the whole weight of our eternal happiness depends; for it is Christ in us, Christ formed in us the hope of glory. Col. 1 : 27. And our Lord expressly tells us, that except we be regenerate and born again, we cannot see the kingdom of God.

III. Consider *the* DESIGN AND END of God in this his quickening work. If we consult the Scriptures, we shall find this principle of life is given us in order to our glorifying God in this world by a *life of obedience*, and our *enjoying God in the world to come*.

1. Spiritual life is imparted in order to a course of *obedience in this world*, whereby God is glorified. So we read in Eph. 2 : 10, "Created in Christ Jesus unto good works, which God hath before ordained that we should walk in them :" habits are to actions as the root is to the fruit, it is for the fruit that we plant the root and ingraff the branches. So in Ezek. 36 : 27, "I will put my Spirit within you, and cause you to walk in my statutes, and ye shall keep my judgments and do them." This is the immediate design not only of the first principle of life imparted to the soul, but of all the exciting, actuating, and assisting works of the Spirit afterwards.

This principle makes a *sincere and true* obedience when it flows from an inward vital principle of grace. The hypocrite is moved by something from without, as the applause of men, the accommodation of fleshy interests, the force of education ; or if there be any thing from within that moves him, it is but self-interest, to quiet a disturbing conscience and support his vain hopes of heaven ; but he never acts from a new principle, a new nature, inclining him to holy actions. Sincerity mainly lies in the harmony and correspondence of actions to their principles : from this influence of the Spirit it is that men hunger and thirst for God, and go to their duties as hungry men do to their meals.

O reader, pause a little upon this ere thou pass on, ask

thy heart whether it be so with thee : are holy duties natural to thee ? Does thy soul move and work after God by a kind of supernatural instinct? This then will be to thee a good evidence of thy integrity.

From this principle of life also results the *excellence* of our obedience ; for by virtue thereof it becomes free and voluntary, not forced and constrained ; it drops like honey, of its own accord, out of the comb, Song 4 : 11 ; or as waters from the fountain, without forcing. John 4 : 14. An unprincipled professor must be pressed hard by some weight of affliction, ere he will yield one tear or pour out a prayer. "When he slew them, then they sought him." Psalm 78 : 34. The *freedom* of obedience is the excellence of it, God's eye is much upon that, 1 Cor. 9 : 17 ; yea, and the *uniformity* of our obedience, which is also a special part of the beauty of it, results from hence : this is it which makes us holy *in all manner of conversation*, or in every point and turning of our conversations, as the original imports. 1 Pet. 1 : 15. Whereas he that is moved by this or that external accidental motive must needs be very uneven, like "the legs of a lame man," as the expression is. Prov. 26 : 7, which "are not equal :" now a word of God, and then the discourse runs muddy and profane or carnal again. All the evenness and uniformity in the several parts of a Christian's life are the effect of this principle of spiritual life.

2. Another aim and design of God in imparting this principle of life is, thereby to prepare and qualify the soul for the enjoyment of himself *in heaven :* "Except a man be born again, he cannot see the kingdom of God." John 3 : 3. All that shall possess that inheritance must be begotten again to it, as the apostle speaks, 1 Pet. 1 : 3, 4. This principle of grace is the very seed of that glory ; it is eternal life in the root and principle. John 17 : 3. By this the soul is attempered and qualified for that state and employment. What is the life of glory but the vision of

God, and the soul's assimilation to God by that vision? From both which results that unspeakable joy and delight which passeth understanding. But what vision of God, assimilation to God, or delight in God can that soul have which was never quickened with the supernatural principle of grace? The temper of such souls is expressed in that sad character, "My soul loathed them, and their soul also abhorred me." Zech. 11 : 8. For want of this vital principle it is that the very same duties and ordinances which are the delight and highest pleasure of the saints, are no better than a mere drudgery and bondage to others. Mal. 1 : 13. Heaven would be no heaven to a dead soul ; this principle of life, in its daily growth and improvement, is our meetness as well as our evidence for heaven.

IV. THIS QUICKENING WORK IS WHOLLY SUPERNATURAL ; it is the sole and proper work of the Spirit of God. So Christ himself expressly asserts it : "That which is born of the flesh is flesh ; and that which is born of the Spirit is spirit : the wind bloweth where it listeth, and thou hearest the sound thereof, but canst not tell whence it cometh, nor whither it goeth ; so is every one that is born of the Spirit." John 3 : 6-8. Believers are the birth or offspring of the Spirit, who produceth the new creature in them in a manner unintelligible even to themselves. So far is it above their own ability to produce, that it is above their capacity to understand the way of its production : as if you should ask, Do you know from whence the wind comes? No. Do you know whither it goes ? No. But you hear and feel it when it blows? Yes. So is every one that is born of the Spirit ; he feels the efficacy and discerns the effects of the Spirit on his own soul, but cannot understand or describe the manner of their production. This is not only above the carnal, but above the renewed mind to comprehend. We really contribute nothing to the production of this principle of life. We may indeed be said to concur with the Spirit in it ;

there is found in us a capacity, aptness, or receptiveness of it; our nature is endowed with such faculties and powers as are meet subjects to receive and instruments to act it; but God only quickens the rational nature with spiritual life. "Who maketh thee to differ from another? And what hast thou that thou didst not receive?" 1 Cor. 4 : 7. The Scriptures not only assert that without him we can do nothing, and that our sufficiency is of God, John 15 : 5; Matt. 12 : 34; 2 Cor. 3 : 5; but they declare that the carnal mind "is enmity against God," and that we were "enemies in our minds by wicked works." Rom. 8 : 7; Col. 1 : 21. That which is born of the flesh is flesh, a perishing thing; but this principle of spiritual life is not subject to dissolution, it is the water that springs up into everlasting life, John 4 : 14; the seed of God, which remaineth in the regenerate soul. 1 John 3 : 9. And all this, because it is born not of corruptible, but of incorruptible seed. 1 Pet. 1 : 23. Our new birth is represented to us in the Scriptures as a resurrection from the dead, a new creation, Eph. 5 : 14; 4 : 24; and thus all is ascribed to grace.

If nature could produce in any degree this spiritual life, then the best natures would be soonest quickened with it; and the worst natures not at all, or last, and least of all: but we find apparently the worst natures often regenerated, and the best left in the state of spiritual death. With how many sweet virtues was the young man adorned, Mark 10 : 21, yet graceless: and what a sink of sin was Mary Magdalene, Luke 7 : 37, yet sanctified. And there is scarce any thing that affects and melts the hearts of Christians more than this comparative consideration, when they consider vessels of gold cast away, and leaden ones chosen for such noble uses. So that it is plain enough to all wise and humble souls, that this new life is wholly of supernatural production.

V. I shall briefly represent THE NECESSARY ANTECEDENCY of this quickening work of the Spirit to our first closing with Christ by faith ; and this will appear if you consider the nature of the vital act of faith, which is the soul's receiving of Christ and resting upon him for pardon and salvation ; in which two things are necessarily included:

1. The *renouncing of all other* hopes and dependences whatsoever. Self in all its acceptations, natural, sinful, and moral, is now to be denied and renounced for ever, else Christ can never be received, Rom. 10 : 3, not only self in its vilest pollutions, but self in its richest ornaments and endowments ; but this is as impossible to the unrenewed and natural man, as it is for rocks or mountains to start from their centre and fly like wandering atoms in the air : nature will rather choose to run the hazard of everlasting damnation, than escape it by a total renunciation of its beloved lusts or self-righteousness ; this supernatural work necessarily requires a supernatural principle. Rom. 8 : 2.

2. The *opening the heart fully to Christ*, without which Christ can never be received, Rev. 3 : 20, is also the effect of the quickening Spirit, the Spirit of life which is in Christ Jesus. Sooner may we expect to see the flowers and blossoms open without the influence of the sun, than the heart and will of a sinner open to receive Christ without a principle of spiritual life first derived from him ; and this will be past doubt to all that consider not only the impotence, but the ignorance, prejudice, and aversion of nature, by which the door of the heart is barred and chained against Christ. John 5 : 40. So that if any have the heart opened to receive him, it is the Lord that opens it by his almighty power.

INFERENCE 1. If such be the nature and necessity of this principle of divine life, it follows *that unregenerate men are no better than dead men.* So the text represents them, "You hath he quickened who were dead in trespasses and sins :" spiritually dead though naturally alive, yea, and lively too as any other persons in the world.

To all those things that are *natural*, they are alive: they can understand, reason, discourse, project, and con trive, as well as others; they can eat, drink, and build, plant, and receive the natural comfort of these things, as much as any others. So their life is described, Job 21 : 12: they "take the timbrel and harp, and rejoice at the sound of the organ; they spend their days in wealth." And James 5 : 5, "Ye have lived in pleasure on the earth," as the fish lives in the water, its natural element, and yet this natural, sensual life is not allowed the name of life, 1 Tim. 5 : 6; such persons are *dead while they live;* it is a base and ignoble life to have a soul only to preserve the body, or to enable a man for a few years to eat and drink, and talk and laugh, and then die. But spiritually considered, they are dead; without life, sense, or motion towards God and the things that are above: their understandings are dead, 1 Cor. 2 : 14, and receive not the things that are of God; their wills are dead, and move not towards Jesus Christ. John 6 : 65. Their affections are dead, even to the most excellent and spiritual objects; and all their duties are dead duties, without life or spirit. This is the sad case of the unregenerate world.

2. *This speaks encouragement to ministers and parents to expect success at last, even with those that yet give little hope of conversion.*

The work you see is the Lord's; when the Spirit of life comes upon their dead souls they shall believe, and be made willing; till then we do but plough upon the rocks; yet let not our hand slack in duty; pray for them and plead with them; you know not in which prayer or exhortation the Spirit of life may breathe upon them. "Can these dry bones live?" Yes, if the Spirit of life from God breathe upon them they can, and shall live: what though their dispositions be averse to all things that are spiritual and serious, yet even such have been regenerated when more sweet and promising natures have been passed by and left under spiritual death. Mr. Ward said of his brother, a man of great gifts, yet of a very bad temper, though my brother Rogers has grace enough for two men, he has not half enough for himself. It may be you have prayed and striven long with your relations and to little purpose, yet be not discouraged. How often was Mr. John Rogers, that famous and successful divine, a grief of heart to his relations in his younger years, proving a wild young man, to the great discouragement of his pious friends; yet, at last, the Lord graciously changed him, so that Mr. Richard Rogers would say, when he would exercise the utmost degree of charity or hope for any that at present were vile and worthless, *I will never despair of any man for* John Rogers' *sake.*

3. *How honorable are Christians by their new birth!* They are "born, not of blood, nor of the will of the flesh, nor of the will of man, but of God," John 1 : 13, not in a mere natural way, but in a spiritual and supernatural : they are the offspring of God, the children of the Most High, as well by regeneration as by adoption; which is the greatest advancement of the human nature, next to its union with the divine nature of Christ. Oh, what honor is this for a poor sinful creature, to have the very life of God breathed into his soul! All other dignities of nature are trifles compared with this; this makes a Christian a sacred hallowed thing, the living temple of God, 1 Cor. 6 : 19, the special object of his delight.

4. *How deplorable is the condition of the unregenerate world.* They are but as *dead men.* As there is no *beauty* in the dead, all their loveliness goes away at death, so there is no spiritual beauty or loveliness in any that are unregenerate. It is true, many of them have excellences which adorn their conversation in the eyes of men; but what are all these but so many sweet flowers strewed over a body where no life is. The dead have no *pleasure* or delight; even so the unregenerate are incapable of the

delights of the Christian life ; "to be spiritually-minded is life and peace," Rom. 8 : 6 ; that is, this is the only serene, placid, and pleasant life. The dead have no *heat*, they are cold as clay ; so are all the unregenerate towards God and things above ; their affections to him are cold and frozen : that which makes a gracious heart melt will not make an unregenerate heart move. The dead must be *buried*, so must the unregenerate be buried out of God's sight ; buried in the lowest hell, in the place of darkness for ever. John 3 : 3. Woe to the unregenerate ; good had it been for them had they never been born !

5. *How greatly are all men concerned to examine their condition with respect to spiritual life and death!* It is very common for men to presume upon their union with and interest in Christ. This privilege is by common mistake extended generally to all that profess the Christian religion and practise the external duties of it, when, in truth, no more are united to Christ than are quickened by the Spirit of life which is in Christ Jesus. Rom. 8 : 1, 2. O try your interest in Christ by this rule. If I am quickened by Christ, I have union with Christ. If there be *spiritual sense* in your souls, there is spiritual life in them. There are senses belonging to the spiritual as well as to the animal life, Heb. 5 : 14 ; they can feel and sensibly groan under soul pressures and burdens of sin. Rom. 7 : 24. The dead feel not, moan not under the burdens of sin as the living do : they may be sensible indeed of the evil of sin with respect to themselves, but not as against God ; damnation may scare them, but pollution doth not ; hell may frighten them, but not the offending of God.

If there be spiritual *hunger and thirst*, it is a sweet sign of spiritual life ; this sign agrees to Christians of a day old. Even new-born babes desire the sincere milk of the word. 1 Pet. 2 : 2. If spiritual life be in you, you know how to expound that scripture, " As the hart panteth after the water-brooks, so panteth my soul after thee, O God," Psa.

42 : 1, without any other interpreter than your own experience; you will feel somewhat like the gnawing of an empty stomach making you restless during the interruption of your daily communion with the Lord.

If there be *spiritual conflicts* with sin, there is spiritual life in your souls. Gal. 5 : 17. Not only a combat between *light* in the higher, and *sense* in the lower faculties; not only opposition to more gross external corruptions, that carry more infamy and horror with them than other sins do; but the heart will be the seat of war; and the more inward and secret any lust is, by so much the more will it be opposed and mourned over.

In a word, the weakest Christian may, upon impartial observation, find such signs of spiritual life in himself—if he will allow himself time to reflect upon the bent and frame of his own heart—as desires after God; conscience of duties; fears, cares, and sorrows about sin; delight in the society of heavenly and spiritual men; and a loathing and burden in the company of vain and carnal persons.

OBJECTION. O, but I have a very dead heart to spiritual things.

ANSWER. It is a sign of life, that you feel and are sensible of that deadness; and besides, there is a great difference between *spiritual deadness* and *death:* the one is the state of the unregenerate, the other is the *disease* of regenerate men.

OBJECTION. Some signs of spiritual life are clear to me, but I cannot close with others.

ANSWER. If you can really close with any, it may satisfy you, though you be dark in others; for if a child cannot walk, yet if it can take its food—if it cannot take its food, yet if it can cry—yea, if it cannot cry, yet if it breathe, it is alive.

CHAPTER VI

THE ACT BY WHICH WE EFFECTUALLY APPLY CHRIST TO OUR OWN SOULS; OR, SAVING FAITH

"But as many as received him, to them gave he power to become the sons of God, even to them that believe on his name." JOHN 1 : 12

No sooner is the soul quickened by the Spirit of God, but it answers, in some measure, the end of God in that work, by its *active reception of Jesus Christ in the way of believing.* What this vital act of faith is upon which depends our interest in Christ and everlasting blessedness, this scripture will show; in which observe three things:

1. *The privilege conferred* is a very high and glorious one, than which no created being is capable of greater: "power to become the sons of God." The word rendered power is one of large extent and signification, and is by some rendered this right, by others this dignity, by others this prerogative, this privilege, or honor. It implies a title or right to *adoption*, not only with respect to the present benefits of it in this life, but also to that blessed inheritance which is laid up in heaven for the sons of God. Oh, what an honor, dignity, and privilege is this!

2. *The subjects* of this privilege are described: "As many as received him." This text describes them by that very grace, *faith*, which gives them their title and right to Christ and his benefits; and by that very act of faith, which primarily confers their right to his person, and secondarily to his benefits, namely, *receiving him.* There are many graces besides faith, but faith only is the grace that gives us right to Christ; and there are many acts of faith besides receiving, but this receiving or embracing Christ

is the justifying and saving act: "As many as received him," *as many*, be they of any nation, sex, age, or condition. For "there is neither Greek nor Jew, circumcision nor uncircumcision, Barbarian, Scythian, bond, nor free: but Christ is all, and in all." Col. 3:11. Nothing but unbelief bars men from Christ and his benefits. As many as *received* him: the word signifies "to accept, take," or, as we fitly render it, to receive, assume, or take to us; a word most aptly expressing the nature and office of faith, yea, the very justifying and saving act; and we are also heedfully to note its special object, not *his* but *Him*, his person as he is clothed with his offices, and not only his benefits and privileges; these are secondary and consequential to our *receiving him*. So that it is a receiving, assuming, or accepting the Lord Jesus Christ which must have respect to the tenders and proposals of the gospel, "for therein is the righteousness of God revealed from faith to faith," Rom. 1:17, therein is Jesus Christ revealed, proposed, and offered unto sinners as the only way of justification and salvation; which gospel offer, as before was shown, is therefore ordinarily necessary to believing. Romans 10:11, etc.

3. This description is yet farther explained by the additional exegetical clause, *even to them that believe on his name*. Here the terms are varied, though the things expressed in both are the same; what he there called *receiving*, is here called *believing on his name*, to show us that the very essence of saving faith consists in our receiving Christ. By *his name* we are to understand Christ himself; it is usual to take these two, believing in him and believing in his name, as terms convertible and of the same import. Hence we draw this proposition:

The receiving of the Lord Jesus Christ is that saving and vital act of faith which gives the soul right both to his person and benefits.

We cannot act spiritually till we begin to live spiritually : the Spirit of life must first join himself to us in his quickening work, as shown in the last chapter. This being done, we begin to act spiritually, by taking hold upon or receiving Jesus Christ, which is the point now to be considered.

The soul is the life of the body, faith is the life of the soul, and Christ is the life of faith. There are several kinds of faith besides saving faith, and in saving faith there are several acts besides the justifying or saving act ; but *this receiving act*, which is our present subject, is that upon which both our righteousness and eternal happiness depend ; by this it is that we are justified and saved : "To as many as received him, to them gave he power to become the sons of God." Yet it doth not justify and save us by reason of any proper dignity that is found in this act, but by reason of the object it receives or apprehends. The same thing is often expressed in Scripture by other terms, as "*coming* to Christ," John 6 : 35 ; *trusting* or *staying* upon Christ, Isa. 50 : 10 ; but whatever is found in those expressions is all comprehended in this.

I proceed, then, to explain the nature of this receiving of Christ, and show what it includes ; to prove that this is the justifying and saving act of faith ; to show the excellency of this act of faith ; to remove some mistakes, and give a true account of the dignity and excellency of this act ; and then to bring home all in a proper application.

I. I will endeavor to explain THE NATURE of this receiving of Christ, and show what is implied in it ; indeed, it involves many deep mysteries and things of greatest weight. People are generally very ignorant and unacquainted with the importance of this expression. They have slight thoughts of faith who never passed under the illuminating, convincing, and humbling work of the Spirit : but we shall find that saving faith is quite another thing,

and differs in its whole kind and nature from that traditional faith and common assent which is so fatally mistaken for it in the world.

1. It is evident that no man can receive Jesus Christ
in *the darkness of natural ignorance:* we must understand
and discern who and what he is whom we receive to be
"the Lord our righteousness." If we know not his person and his offices, we do not take, but mistake Christ.
It is a good rule in the civil law, *Non consentit qui non
sentit.* A mistake of the person invalidates the match.
They that take Christ for a mere man, or deny the satisfaction of his blood, or divest him of his human nature, or
deny any of his most glorious and necessary offices, let
them cry up as high as they will his spirituality, glory,
and exemplary life and death, they can never receive
Jesus Christ aright. This is such a flaw in the very
foundation of faith as undoes and destroys all. All saving faith is founded in light and knowledge, and therefore
it is called *knowledge,* Isa. 53 : 11 ; and *seeing* is inseparably connected with *believing,* John 6 : 40. Men must hear
and learn of the Father before they can come to Christ.
John 6 : 45. The receiving act of faith is directed and
guided by knowledge. I will not presume to state the
degree of knowledge which is absolutely necessary to the
reception of Christ ; I know the first actings of faith are,
in most Christians, accompanied with much darkness and
confusion of understanding : but yet we must say in the
general, that wherever faith is, there is so much light as
is sufficient to discover to the soul its own sins, dangers,
and wants, and the all-sufficiency, suitableness, and necessity of Christ for the supply and remedy of all ; and without this Christ cannot be received. "Come unto me, all
ye that labor and are heavy laden, and I will give you
rest." Matt. 11 : 28.

2. The receiving of Christ necessarily implies *the assent
of the understanding* to the truths of Christ revealed in the

gospel; his person, natures, offices, his incarnation, death, and satisfaction; which assent, though it be not in itself saving faith, yet is the foundation and groundwork of it; it being impossible the soul should receive and embrace what the mind does not assent to as true and infallibly certain. True faith *rests upon the testimony of God* as unquestionable. This assent of faith is called our receiving the witness of God, 1 John 5 : 9; our setting to our seal that God is true, John 3 : 33. The divine verity is the very object of faith : into this we resolve our faith "Thus saith the Lord," is that firm foundation upon which our assent is built. And thus we see good reason to believe those profound mysteries of the incarnation of Christ; the union of the two natures in his wonderful person; the union of Christ and believers; though we cannot understand these things by reason of the darkness of our minds. It satisfies the soul to find these mysteries in the written word; upon that foundation it firmly builds its assent; and without such an assent of faith there can be no embracing of Christ. All acts of faith and religion, without assent, are but as so many arrows shot at random into the open air, they signify nothing for want of a fixed, determinate object.

It is therefore the policy of Satan, by injecting atheistical thoughts—with which young converts often find themselves greatly tried—to undermine and destroy the whole work of faith. But God makes his people victorious over them; yea, and they do assent to the truths of the word even at the time when they think they do not, as appears by their tenderness and fear of sin, their diligence and care in duty. If I discern these things in a Christian's life, he must excuse me if I believe him not when he says he does not assent to the truths of the gospel.

3 Our receiving Christ necessarily implies our hearty *approbation*, liking, and estimation; yea, the acquiescence

of our very souls in Jesus Christ as the most excellent, suitable, and complete remedy for all our wants, sins, and dangers that ever could be prepared by the wisdom and love of God for us. We must receive him with such a frame of heart as rests upon and trusts in him, if ever we receive him aright. To them that believe he is precious. 1 Pet. 2 : 7. This is the only sovereign remedy in all the world that is full and efficacious enough to cure our wounds ; and as Christ is most highly esteemed and heartily approved as the only remedy for our souls, so the sovereign grace and wisdom of God are admired, and the way and method he has taken to save poor souls by Jesus Christ most heartily approved, as the most apt and excellent method both for his glory and our good, for it is plain that none will espouse themselves with conjugal affection to the person whom they esteem not as the best for them that can be chosen. None will forsake and quit all for His sake, except they account him as the spouse did, " The chiefest among ten thousand."

There are two things in Christ which must gain the greatest approbation in the soul of a poor convinced sinner and bring it to rest upon him. It can find nothing in Christ that is distasteful or *unsuitable* to it, as it finds in the best creatures. In him is no *weakness*, but a fulness of all saving power, " able to save to the uttermost ;" no *pride*, causing him to scorn and contemn the most wretched soul that comes to him ; no inconstancy or *levity*, to cause him to cast off the soul whom he hath once received ; no *passion*, but a Lamb for meekness and patience. There is no spot to be found in him, He is " altogether lovely." Song 5 : 16.

And again, as the believer can find nothing in Christ that is distasteful, so he finds *nothing wanting* in Christ that is necessary or desirable. Such is the fulness of wisdom, righteousness, sanctification, and redemption in Christ, that nothing is left to be desired but the full enjoyment of him. O, saith the soul, how completely happy shall I be if I can but win Christ! I would not envy the nobles of the earth were I but in Christ. I am hungry and athirst, and Christ is meat indeed and drink indeed. This is the best thing in all the world for me, because so necessary and so suitable to the needs of a soul ready to perish. I am a law-condemned and a self-condemned sinner, trembling for fear of the execution of the curse upon me every moment; in Christ is complete righteousness to justify my soul; O there is nothing better for me than Christ. I see myself plunged, both in nature and practice, into the odious pollutions of sin, and in Christ is a fountain opened for sin and for uncleanness; his blood is a fountain of *merit*, his Spirit is a fountain of holiness and purity; none but Christ, none but Christ. O the manifold wisdom and unsearchable love of God, to prepare and furnish a Saviour so fully answering all the needs, all the distresses, all the fears and burdens of a poor sinner! Thus the believing soul approves of Christ as best for it; and thus in believing it gives glory to God. Rom. 4 : 21.

4. Receiving Christ consists in the *consent and choice of the will;* and this is the opening of the heart and stretching forth of the soul to receive him. "Thy people shall be willing in the day of thy power." Psalm 110 : 3.

It is the great design and main scope of the gospel to bring over the wills of poor sinners to this. It was the great complaint of Christ against the incredulous Jews, "Ye will not come unto me, that ye might have life." John 5 : 40. The saving, justifying act of faith lies principally in the consent of the will, which consent is the effect of the almighty power of God. Eph. 1 : 19 He allures and draws the will to Christ, and he *draws with the cords of a man*—that is, he prevails with it by rational arguments The soul being prepared by conviction of its lost and miserable state by sin, and that there is but one door of hope open to it for an escape from the wrath to come, which is Christ; being also satisfied of the fulness and completeness of his saving ability, and of his willingness to apply it for our salvation upon such just and equal terms; this cannot but prevail with the will of a poor distressed sinner to consent and choose him.

5. The last and principal thing included in our receiving Christ is, the respect that this act of acceptance has *to the terms upon which Christ is tendered to us* in the gospel. "So we preach, and so ye believed." 1 Cor. 15 : 11. Faith answers to the gospel offer as the impress upon the *wax* does to the engraving in the *seal;* and this is of principal consideration, for there is no receiving Christ upon any other terms but his own proposed in the gospel to us. He will never come lower, nor make them easier than they are; we must either receive him upon these, or part with him for ever, as thousands do, who could agree to some articles of the gospel terms, but rather choose to be damned for ever than submit to all. This is the great controversy between Christ and sinners; upon this many thousands break off the treaty and part with Christ, because he will not come to their terms; but every true believer receives him upon his own; their acceptance of him by faith is in all things consentaneous to the overtures made by him in the written word. So he tenders himself, and so they receive him, as will be evident in the following particulars :

(1.) The gospel offers Christ to us *sincerely and really,* and so the true believer receives and accepts him, even with a "faith unfeigned." 1 Tim. 1 : 5. If ever the soul be serious and in earnest in any thing, it is so in this. Can we suppose him that flies for his life to the *refuge city,* to be serious and in earnest to escape the *avenger of blood* who pursues him? Then is the heart of a convinced sinner serious in this matter; for under this figure is the work of faith presented to us. Heb. 6 : 18.

(2.) Christ is offered to us in the gospel *entirely* and *undividedly*, as clothed with all his offices, priestly, prophetical, and regal, as Christ Jesus the Lord, Acts 16 : 31 ; and so the true believer receives him. The hypocrite, like the harlot, is for dividing, but the sincere believer finds his need of every office of Christ, and knows not how to want any thing that is in him. His ignorance makes him necessary and desirable as a *prophet;* his guilt makes him necessary as a *priest;* his strong and powerful lusts and corruptions make him necessary as a *king;* and in truth he sees not any thing in Christ that he can spare ; he needs all that is in Christ, and admires infinite wisdom in nothing more than the investing Christ with all these offices, which are so suited to the poor sinner's wants and miseries. As the three offices are undivided in Christ, so they are in the believer's acceptance ; and before this trial no hypocrite can stand, for all hypocrites reject and quarrel with something in Christ ; they like his pardon better than his government. They call him indeed Lord and Master, but it is an empty title they bestow upon him ; for, let them ask their own hearts if Christ be Lord over their *thoughts* as well as *words*, over their *secret* as well as *open* actions, over their *darling* lusts as well as others ; let them ask, who will appear to be Lord and Master over them when Christ and the world come in competition— when the pleasures of sin shall stand upon one side, and sufferings to death and deepest points of self-denial upon the other side ? Surely it is the greatest affront that can be offered to the divine wisdom and goodness to separate in our acceptance what is so united in Christ for our salvation and happiness. As without any one of these offices the work of our salvation could not be completed, so without acceptance of Christ in them all, our union with him by faith cannot be completed. The gospel offer of Christ includes all his offices, and gospel faith just so receives him ; to submit to him, as well as to be redeemed by him; to imitate him in the holiness of his life, as well as to reap the fruits of his death. It must be an entire receiving of the Lord Jesus Christ.

(3.) Christ is offered to us in the gospel *exclusively* as the only Saviour of sinners, with whose blood and intercession nothing is to be mixed; but the soul of a sinner is singly to rely and depend on him, and no other. Acts 4 : 12; 1 Cor. 3 : 11. And so faith receives him. "I will make mention of thy righteousness, even of thine only." Psalm 71 : 16. "And be found in him, not having mine own righteousness, which is of the law, but that which is through the faith of Christ." Phil. 3 : 9. To depend partly upon Christ's righteousness, and partly upon our own, is to set one foot upon a rock and the other in a quicksand. Either Christ will be to us all in all, or nothing, in point of righteousness and salvation; he affects not social honor; as he did the whole *work,* so he expects the sole *praise.* If he be not able to save to the uttermost, why do we depend upon him at all? and if he be, why do we lean upon any beside him?

(4.) The gospel offers Christ *freely* to sinners as the *gift* of God, John 4 : 10; Isa. 55 : 1; Rev. 22 : 17; and so faith receives him. The believer comes to Christ with an empty hand, not only as an undeserving, but as a hell-deserving sinner; he comes to Christ as to one that justifies the ungodly. "To him that worketh not, but believeth on him that justifieth the ungodly, his faith is counted for righteousness." Rom. 4 : 5. By him that worketh not the apostle means a convinced, humbled sinner, who finds himself utterly unable to do the task the law sets him, that is, perfectly to obey it; and therefore in a law sense he is said not to work, for it is all one as to the intent and purpose of the law, not to work, and not to work perfectly. This he is convinced of, and therefore comes to Christ as one that is in himself ungodly, acknowledging that the righteousness by which alone he can stand before God is in Christ, and not in himself in whole or in part. And, by the way, let this encourage poor souls that are daunted for want of due qualifications for closing with and embracing Christ. Nothing qualifies a man for Christ more than a sense of his unworthiness of him, and the want of all excellences or ornaments that may commend him to divine acceptance.

(5.) The gospel offers Christ *orderly* to sinners, first his *person,* then his *privileges.* God first gives his Son, and then with him, or as a consequence of that gift, he gives us all things. Rom. 8 : 32. In the same order must our faith receive him. The believer doth not marry the *portion* first and then the *person,* but to be found in him is the first and great care of a believer.

I deny not but it is lawful for any to have an eye to the benefits of Christ. Salvation from wrath is and lawfully may be intended and aimed at : "Look unto me and be saved, all the ends of the earth." Isa. 45 : 22. Nor do I deny but there are many poor souls who, being in deep distress and fear, may and often do look mostly to their own safety at first ; and that there is much confusion, as well in the actings of their faith as in their condition ; but sure I am that it is the proper order in believing, first to accept the person of the Lord Jesus. Heaven is no doubt very desirable, but Christ is more : "Whom have I in heaven but thee?" Psalm 73 : 25. Union with Christ is, in the order of nature, antecedent to the communication of his privileges, and so it ought to be in the order and method of believing.

(6.) Christ is *advisedly* offered in the gospel to sinners, as the result of God's eternal counsel, a project of grace upon which his heart and thoughts have been much set. Zech. 6 : 13. The counsel of peace was between the Father and the Son. And so the believer receives him, most deliberately weighing the matter in his most deep and serious thoughts ; for this is a time of much solicitude and thoughtfulness. The soul's espousals are acts of judgment on our part as well as on God's. Hos. 2 : 19. We are therefore bid to sit down and count the cost. Luke 14 : 28. Faith, or the actual receiving of Christ, is the result of many previous debates in the soul. The matter has been pondered over and over. The objections and discouragements, both from the self-denying terms of the gospel and our own vileness and deep guilt, have been ruminated and lain upon our hearts day and night ; and after all things have been balanced in the most deep consideration, the soul is determined to this conclusion, " I must have Christ : be the terms never so hard, be my sins never so great and many, I will yet go to him and venture my soul upon him ; if I perish, I perish. I have thought out all my thoughts, and this is the result, union with Christ here, or separation from God for ever must be my lot."

Thus doth the Lord open the hearts of his people, and win the consent of their wills to receive Jesus Christ upon the deepest consideration and debate of the matter in their own most solemn thoughts. They understand and know that they must deeply deny themselves, take up his cross and follow him, Matt. 16 : 24, renounce not only *sinful*, but *religious* self. These things are hard and difficult, but yet the necessity and excellency of Christ make them appear eligible and rational.

By all this you see faith is another thing than what the sound of that word, as it is generally understood, signifies to the understandings of most men.

II. Our next work will be to evince this receiving of Christ to be THE SPECIAL SAVING FAITH OF GOD'S ELECT. This is that faith of which such great and glorious things are spoken in the gospel, which whosoever hath shall be saved, and he that hath it not shall be damned. This I shall prove by the following arguments :

ARG. 1. That faith which gives the soul right and title

to spiritual *adoption*, with all the privileges and benefits thereof, is true and saving faith. Our right and title to spiritual adoption arise from our union with Jesus Christ; we being united to the Son of God, are by virtue of that union reckoned or accounted sons: "Ye are all the children of God by faith in Christ Jesus." Gal. 3 : 26. The effect of saving faith is union with Christ's person; the consequence of that union is adoption, or right to the inheritance. "To as many as received him, to them gave he power," or right, "to become the sons of God." A false faith has no such privilege annexed to it; no unbeliever is thus dignified, no stranger entitled to this inheritance.

Arg. 2. That only is saving and justifying faith which is *in all true believers*, in none but true believers, and in all true believers at all times. There is no other act of faith but this *fiducial receiving of Christ* as he is offered, that agrees to all true believers, to none but true believers, and to all true believers at all times.

There are three acts of faith, *assent*, *acceptance*, and *assurance*. The Papists generally give the essence of saving faith to the first, mere *assent*. There are some who give it to the last, *assurance*. But neither can be correct. *Assent* is not solely applicable to true believers or justified persons. *Assurance* applies to justified persons and them only, but not to all justified persons and at all times. *Assent* is too low to contain the essence of saving faith: it is found in the unregenerate as well as the regenerate, yea, in devils as well as men. James 2 : 19. It is supposed and included in justifying faith, but it is not the justifying or saving act. *Assurance* is as much too high, being found only in some eminent believers; and in them too but at times. There are many true believers to whom the joy and comfort of assurance is denied; they may say of their union with Christ, as Paul said of his vision, "whether in the body or out of the body, I cannot tell"— "whether in Christ or out of Christ, I cannot tell."

A true believer may "walk in darkness, and see no light." Isa. 50 : 10. Nay, a man must be a believer before he know himself to be so; the *direct act of faith* is before the *reflex act:* so that the justifying act of faith lies neither in *assent* nor in *assurance.* *Assent* says, I believe that Christ is, and that he is the Saviour of his people. *Assurance* says, I believe and am sure that Christ died for me, and that I shall be saved through him. So that *assent widens* the nature of faith too much, and *assurance* on the other hand *straitens* it too much; but *acceptance*, which says, "I take Christ in all his offices to be mine," fits it exactly, and belongs to all true believers, and to none but true believers, and to all true believers at all times. This therefore must be the justifying and saving act of faith.

ARG. 3. That and no other is the justifying and saving act of faith to which *the properties and effects* of saving faith belong, or in which only they are found. By saving faith Christ is said to *dwell in our hearts,* Eph. 3 : 17; but it is neither by assent nor assurance, but by acceptance, and receiving him, that he dwells in our hearts : not by assent, for then he would dwell in the unregenerate; nor by assurance, for he must dwell in our hearts before we can be assured of it : therefore it is by acceptance.

By faith we are *justified.* Rom. 5 : 1. But neither assent nor assurance, for the reasons above, do justify; therefore it must be by the receiving act, and no other.

The Scripture ascribes great *difficulties* to that faith by which we are saved, as being most opposed to the corrupt nature of man; but of all the acts of faith, none is clogged with such difficulties, or conflicts with such opposition as the receiving act does; this act is attended with the greatest difficulties, fears, and deepest self-denial. In assent, a man's reason is convinced, and naturally yields to the evidence of truth. In assurance there is nothing against a man's will or comfort, but much for it; every one desires it : but it is not so in the acceptance of Christ

upon the self-denying terms of the gospel, as will hereafter be evinced. We conclude, therefore, that in this
consists the nature and essence of saving faith.

III. Having seen what the receiving of Jesus Christ
is, and that it is the faith by which we are justified and
saved, I next come to open the DIGNITY AND EXCELLENCY of
this faith, whose praises are in all the Scriptures. There
you find it renowned by the title of precious faith, 2 Pet.
1 : 1 ; enriching faith, Jas. 2 : 5 ; the work of God, John
6 : 29 ; the great mystery of godliness, 1 Tim. 3 : 16 ;
with many more rich epithets throughout the Scriptures
bestowed upon it.

Simply as a saving grace, faith has but the same excellence with all other precious saving graces. As it is
the fruit of the Spirit, it is more precious than gold, Prov.
8 : 11, 19 ; and so are all other graces : in this sense they
all shine with equal glory, and that a glory transcending
all the glory of this world; but then consider faith *rela
tively*, as the instrument by which the righteousness of
Christ is apprehended and made ours, and in this view it
excels all other graces. This is the grace that is singled
out from among all other graces to *receive Christ*, by which
office it is dignified above its fellows. As Moses was
honored above the many thousands of Israel, when God
took him up into the mount and admitted him nearer to
himself than any other of all the tribes might come, so
faith is honored above its fellow-graces in being singled
out and solemnly anointed to this high office in our justification. It is that precious eye that looks unto Christ as
the stung Israelites did to the brazen serpent, and derives healing virtue from it to the soul. It is the grace
which instrumentally saves us. Eph. 2 : 8. As it is
Christ's glory to be the door of salvation, so it is faith's
glory to be the golden key that opens that door.

What shall I say of faith ? It is the bond of union ;
the instrument of justification ; the spring of spiritual

peace and joy; the means of spiritual life and subsistence; and therefore the great scope and drift of the gospel, which aims at and presses nothing more than to bring men to believe.

1. Faith is the *bond of our union* with Christ; that union is begun in our vivification, and completed in our actual receiving of Christ; the first is the bond of union on the Spirit's part, the second a bond of union on our part. Christ "dwells in our hearts by faith." Eph. 3 : 17 Thus it is a door opened to let in many rich blessings to the soul; for, by uniting us to Christ, it brings us into special favor and acceptance with God, Eph. 1 : 6 ; makes us the special objects of Christ's conjugal love and delight, Eph. 5 : 29 ; and draws from his heart sympathy and a tender sense of all our miseries and burdens. Hebrews 4 : 15.

2. It is *the instrument* of our justification. Rom. 5 : 1. Till Christ be thus received by us we are in our sins— under guilt and condemnation; but when faith comes, then comes freedom : "By him all that believe are justified from all things." Acts 13 : 39 ; Rom. 8 : 1. It apprehends or receives the pure and perfect righteousness of the Lord Jesus, wherein the soul, how guilty and sinful soever it be in itself, stands faultless and spotless before the presence of God; all bonds to punishment are, upon believing, immediately dissolved; a full and final pardon sealed. O precious faith! Who can sufficiently value it?

What respect, reader, wouldst thou have to the hand that should bring thee a pardon when on the ladder or block! A pardon, which thou canst not read without tears of joy, is brought thee by the hand of faith. O inestimable grace! This clothes the pure righteousness of Jesus upon our defiled souls, and so causes us to become "the righteousness of God in him," or as it is, 1 John 3 : 7, "righteous as he is righteous;" not with a formal inherent righteousness of our own, but with a relative imputed righteousness from another.

I know this most excellent and most comfortable doctrine of imputed righteousness is not only *denied* but *derided* by Papists. Stapleton calls it the monstrous birth of Luther's brain ! But, blessed be God, this comfortable truth is well secured against all attempts of its adversaries. Let their blasphemous mouths call it in derision, as they do, *putative righteousness*, that is, a mere fancied or conceited righteousness ; yet we know assuredly Christ's righteousness is imputed to us, and that in the way of faith. Rom. 5 : 17 ; and 2 Cor. 5 : 21. This was the way in which Abraham, the father of them that believe, was justified ; and the way in which all believers, the children of Abraham, must in like manner be justified. Romans 4 : 22–24. Who can express the worth of faith in this one respect, were this all it did for our souls ?

3. It is the *spring* of our spiritual peace and joy ; and that as it is the instrument of our *justification.* If it be an instrument of our justification, it cannot but be the spring of our consolation, "Being justified by faith, we have peace with God." Rom. 5 : 1. In uniting us with Christ, and apprehending and applying his righteousness to us, it becomes the seed or root of all the peace and joy of a Christian's life. Joy, the child of faith, therefore bears its name, "The joy of faith." Phil. 1 : 25. So 1 Peter 1 : 8, "Believing, ye rejoice with joy unspeakable." We cannot forbear rejoicing when by faith we are brought to the sight and knowledge of such a privileged state. When faith has first given and then cleared our title to Christ we cannot but rejoice, and that with joy unspeakable.

4 It is the *means* of our spiritual livelihood and subsistence ; all other graces, like birds in the nest, depend upon what faith brings in to them ; take away faith, and all the graces languish and die : joy, peace, hope, patience,

and all the rest depend upon faith, as the members of the natural body do upon the vessels by which blood and spirits are conveyed to them. "The life which I now live in the flesh I live by the faith of the Son of God." Gal. 2 : 20. It provides our ordinary food and extraordinary cordials : "I had fainted unless I had believed." Psalm 27 : 13.

5. As faith is all this to our souls, it is no wonder that it is *the main scope* and drift of the gospel to press and bring souls to believing : it is the gospel's grand design to bring up the hearts of men to faith. The urgent *commands* of the gospel aim at this. 1 John 3 : 23 ; Mark 1 : 14, 15 ; John 12 : 36. Hither also look the great *promises* and encouragements of the gospel. John 5 : 35, 37 ; Mark 16 : 16. And the opposite sin of *unbelief* is everywhere fearfully aggravated and threatened. John 16 : 8, 9 ; and 3 : 18, 36.

IV. But lest we commit a mistake here, to the prejudice of Christ's honor and glory, which must not be given to another, no, not to faith itself, I am to show UPON WHAT ACCOUNT faith is thus dignified and honored ; that so we may give unto *faith* the things that are *faith's*, and to Christ the things that are Christ's.

I find four opinions about the interest of faith in our justification : some will have it to justify us *formally*, not relatively, that is, by its own intrinsical value and worth ; and this is the *popish* sense of justification by faith. Again, some affirm, that though faith be not our perfect legal righteousness, considered as a work of ours, yet the *act* of believing is imputed to us for righteousness, that is, God graciously accepts it instead of perfect legal righteousness, and so in his esteem it is our evangelical righteousness. Others contend that faith justifies and saves us, as it is *the condition* of the new covenant ; while others will have it to justify us as an *instrument* apprehending or receiving the righteousness of Christ : which last opinion

I must adopt, when I consider that my text calls it a *receiving of Christ.* Most certain it is,

1. That it doth not justify in the *popish sense,* on account of its own proper worth and dignity ; for then justification would be of debt, not of grace ; contrary to Rom. 3 : 23, 24. This would also frustrate the very scope and end of the death of Christ ; for if righteousness come by the law, by the way of works and desert, then is Christ dead in vain. Gal. 2 : 21. This way of our justification by faith would be so far from excluding, that it would establish boasting, expressly contrary to the apostle, Rom. 3 : 26, 27. In this view of faith there should be no defects or imperfections in it, for a defective or imperfect thing can never be the ground of our justification before God ; if it justify by its own worth and proper dignity. it must have no flaw or imperfection in it, which is contrary to the consciousness of all believers. Nay, in this view, it is the same thing to be justified by faith, and to be justified by works, which the apostle so carefully distinguishes and opposes. Phil. 3 : 9, and Rom. 4 : 6. So that we conclude it does not justify, in the popish sense, for any worth or proper excellence in itself.

2. It is equally evident that faith does not justify us by *the act of believing being imputed or accepted* by God as our evangelical righteousness, instead of perfect legal righteousness. In the former opinion you have the dregs of popery, and here you have refined popery. Let all know we have as high an esteem for faith as any men in the world, but yet we will not rob Christ to clothe faith.

We cannot embrace this opinion, because we must then dethrone Christ to exalt faith : we are willing to give to faith all that is due to it, but we dare not despoil Christ of his glory for faith's sake : *he is* "the Lord our righteousness." Jer. 23 : 6. We dare not set the servant above the master. We acknowledge no righteousness but what the obedience and satisfaction of Christ yields us. His blood, not our faith; his satisfaction, not our believing it, is the ground of our justification before God.

Again, we dare not yield this point, lest we undermine all the comfort of Christians, by resting their pardon and peace upon *a weak, imperfect work of their own.* O, how tottering and unstable must their foundation be that stand upon such ground as this! What alterations are there in our faith, what mixtures of unbelief at all times, and prevalency of unbelief at some times; and is this a foundation to build our justification and hope upon? If we lay the stress here, we build upon very loose ground, and must be at continual loss both as to safety and comfort.

Nor dare we so wrong the justice and truth of God as to affirm that he esteems and imputes our poor weak faith for perfect legal righteousness.* We know that the judgment of God is always according to truth; if the justice of God require full satisfaction, surely it will not say it is satisfied by any acts of ours, when all that we can do amounts not to one mite of the vast sum we owe to God.

3. And for the third opinion, that it justifies as the *condition of the new covenant;* though some of great name and worth among our Protestant divines seem to go that way, yet I cannot see, according to this opinion, any reason why repentance may not as properly be said to justify us as faith, for it is a condition of the new covenant as much as faith; and if faith justify as a condition, then every other grace that is a condition must justify as well as faith. I acknowledge faith to be a condition of the covenant, but cannot allow that it *justifies as a condition.*

I therefore must profess myself best satisfied in the

* Because faith receives Christ our righteousness, and ascribes all to the grace of God in him; therefore we are said to be justified by it only on account of Christ, and not as it is our work. Confes. Helv.

last opinion, which speaks it an instrument in our justification : it is *the hand which receives* the righteousness of Christ that justifies us, and that gives it its value above all other graces ; as when we say a diamond ring is worth one hundred pounds, we mean not the gold that receives, but the stone that is set in it is worth so much. Faith, considered as a habit, is no more precious than other gracious habits are, but considered as an instrument to receive Christ and his righteousness, it excels them all ; and this instrumentality of faith is noted in the phrases, *by faith,* and *through faith.* Rom. 3 : 22, 25. Thus much of the nature and excellency of saving faith.

CHAPTER VII

SAVING FAITH—CONTINUED

"But as many as received him, to them gave he power to become the sons of God, even to them that believe on his name." JOHN 1 : 12

HAVING considered the nature and excellency of saving faith, with its relation to justification, as an instrument in receiving Christ and his righteousness, I now come to make APPLICATION of this weighty and fruitful doctrine. And

This point yields us MANY GREAT AND USEFUL TRUTHS for our information.

INFERENCE I. Is the receiving of Christ the vital and saving act of faith, which gives the soul right to the person and privileges of Christ? then it follows *that the rejecting of Christ by unbelief must be the damning and soul-destroying sin* which cuts a man off from Christ and all the benefits purchased by his blood. If there be life in receiving, there must be death in rejecting Christ.

There is no grace more excellent than faith ; no sin more execrable and abominable than unbelief. Faith is the saving grace, and unbelief the damning sin : "He that believeth not shall be damned." Mark 16 : 16. See John 3 : 18, 36, and 8 : 24.

In the justification of a sinner, as there must be free grace as an impulsive cause, and the blood of Christ as the meritorious cause, so, of necessity, there must be faith as the instrumental cause, to receive and apply what the free grace of God designed, and the blood of Christ purchased for us. For where several causes concur to produce one effect, the effect is not produced till the last cause be in action.

"To him gave all the prophets witness, that through

his name, whosoever believeth in him shall receive remission of sins." Acts 10 : 43. Faith in its place is as necessary as the blood of Christ in its place ; it is "Christ *in you* the hope of glory." Col. 1 : 27. Not Christ in the womb, not Christ in the grave, nor Christ in heaven, except he be also *Christ in you.*

Though Christ be come in the flesh ; though he died and rose again for the dead ; yet if you believe not, you must for all that "*die in your sins.*" John 8 : 24. And what a dreadful thing is this ! better die any death whatever than die in your sins. If you die in your sins, you will also rise in your sins, and stand at the bar of Christ in your sins ; you can never receive remission till first you have received Christ. O cursed unbelief, which damns the soul ; dishonors God, 1 John 5 : 10 ; slights Jesus Christ, the wisdom of God, as if the glorious design of redemption by his blood, the triumph and masterpiece of divine wisdom, were mere foolishness, 1 Cor. 1 : 23, 24 : it frustrates the great design of the gospel, Gal. 4 : 11 ; and consequently it must be the sin of sins, the worst and most dangerous of all sins ; leaving a man under the guilt of all his other sins.

2. If such a receiving of Christ as has been described be saving and justifying faith, *then faith is a work of greater difficulty than most men understand it to be, and there are but few sound believers in the world.*

Before Christ can be received, the heart must be emptied and opened ; but most men's hearts are full of self-righteousness and vain confidence : this was the case of the Jews, "Being ignorant of God's righteousness, and going about to establish their own righteousness, have not submitted themselves to the righteousness of God." Rom. 10 : 3.

Man's righteousness was once in himself, and whatever liquor is first put into the vessel it ever afterwards savors of it. It is with Adam's posterity as with *bees* which have been accustomed to go to their own hive and carry all thither; if the *hive* be removed to another place, they will still fly to the old place, hover up and down about it, and rather die there than go to a new place. So it is with most men. God hath removed their righteousness from *doing* to *believing;* from *themselves* to *Christ;* but who shall prevail with them to forsake self? Nature will venture to be damned rather than do it: there is much submission in believing, and great self-denial: a proud self-conceited heart will never stoop to live upon the stock of another's righteousness.

Besides, it is no easy thing to persuade men to receive Christ as their Lord in all things, and submit their necks to his strict and holy precepts, though it be a great truth that "Christ's yoke doth not gall, but grace and adorn the neck that bears it ;" that the truest and sweetest liberty is in our freedom from our lusts, not in our fulfilling them; yet who can persuade the carnal heart to believe this? And much less will men ever be prevailed with to forsake father, mother, wife, children, inheritance, and life itself, to follow Christ; and all this on account of spiritual and invisible things. Yet this must be done by all that receive the Lord Jesus Christ upon gospel terms ; yea, and before the soul has any encouraging experience of its own, to balance the manifold discouragements of sense and carnal reason, improved by the utmost craft of Satan to dismay it; for experience is the fruit and consequence of believing. So that it may well be placed among the great mysteries of godliness, that Christ is believed on in the world. 1 Tim. 3 : 16.

3. Hence it will follow *that there may be more true be-lievers in the world than know or dare conclude themselves to be such.*

As many ruin their own souls by placing the essence of saving faith in naked assent, so some rob themselves of their own comfort by placing it in full assurance.

Faith, and the sense of faith, are two distinct and separable mercies : you may have truly received Christ, and not receive the knowledge or assurance of it. Isaiah 50 : 10. Some there be that say, thou art our God, of whom God never said, ye are my people ; these have no authority to be called the sons of God : others there are, of whom God says, these are my people, who yet dare not call God their God ; these have authority to be called the sons of God, but know it not. They have received Christ, that is their safety ; but they have not yet received the knowledge and assurance of it, that is their trouble : the father owns his child in the cradle, who yet knows him not to be his father.

There are two reasons why many believers, who might argue themselves into peace, live without the comforts of their faith : this may arise,

(1.) From *the want of evidence* that they have truly received Christ. Many great *objections* lie against it, which they cannot clearly answer.

One objection is this : Light and knowledge are necessarily required to the right receiving of Christ, but *I am dark and ignorant ;* many carnal, unregenerate persons seem to know more than I do, and to be more able to discourse of the mysteries of religion than I am.

ANSWER. But you ought to distinguish between the *kinds* and *degrees* of knowledge, and you would then see that your bewailed ignorance is no bar to your interest in Christ. There are two kinds of knowledge. There is a *natural knowledge* even of spiritual objects, a spark of nature blown up by an advantageous education ; and though the objects of this knowledge be spiritual things, yet the light in which they are discerned is but a mere natural light. And there is *a spiritual knowledge* of spiritual things, the *teaching of the anointing*, as it is called, 1 John 2 : 27 ; that is, the effect and fruit of the Spirit's sanctifying work upon our souls, when the experience of a man's own heart informs and teaches his understanding, when by the working of grace in our own souls we come to understand its nature; this is spiritual knowledge.

Now a little of this spiritual knowledge is a better evidence of a man's interest in Christ than the most raised and excellent degree of natural knowledge. As the philosopher says, One dram of knowledge of the most excellent things, is better than much knowledge of common things; so here a little spiritual knowledge of Jesus Christ that has life and savor in it, is more than all the natural sapless knowledge of the unregenerate, which leaves the heart dead, carnal, and barren : it is not the *quantity*, but the *kind;* not the *measure*, but the *savor.* If you know so much of the evil of sin as renders it the most bitter and burdensome thing in the world to you, and so much of the necessity and excellency of Christ as renders him the most sweet and desirable thing in the world to you, though you may be defective in many degrees of knowledge, yet this is enough to prove yours to be the fruit of the Spirit: you may have a sanctified heart though you have an irregular or weak head : many that knew more than you, are in *hell;* and some that once knew as little as you, are now in *heaven:* God has not prepared heaven only for clear and subtle heads. A little sanctified and effectual knowledge of Christ's person, offices, suitableness, and necessity, may bring thee thither, when others, with all their curious speculations, may perish for ever.

But you object again, *"Assent* to the truths of the gospel is necessarily included in saving faith, and though it be not the justifying and saving act, yet it is presupposed and required to it. Now I have many staggerings and doubtings about the certainty and reality of these things ; many horrid atheistical thoughts, which shake the assenting act of faith in the very foundation, and hence I fear I do not believe."

ANSWER. There may be, and often is, a true and sin-

cere *assent* in the soul that is assaulted with violent atheistical suggestions from Satan, and thereupon questions
the truth of it.   And this is a very clear evidence of the
reality of our assent, that whatever doubts or contrary
suggestions there be, yet we dare not in our practice contradict or slight those truths or duties which we are
tempted to disbelieve.   We are assaulted with atheistical
thoughts, and tempted to slight and cast off all fear of sin
and practice of religious duties ; yet when it comes to the
point of practice we dare not commit a known sin, the awe
of God is upon us ; we dare not omit a known duty, the
tie of conscience is found strong enough to hold us close
to it ; in this case it is plain we do really assent when we
think we do not.

A man thinks he does not love his child, yet carefully
provides for him in health, and is full of griefs and fears
about him in sickness : now, so long as I see all fatherly
duties performed, and affection to his child's welfare manifested, let him say what he will as to the want of love to
him, while I see this he must excuse me if I do not believe
him when he says he has no love to him.   Just so is it in
this case : a man says I do not assent to the being, necessity, or excellency of Jesus Christ ; yet in the mean time
his soul is filled with cares and fears about securing an
interest in him ; he is found panting and thirsting for him
with vehement desires ; nothing in all the world would
give him such joy as to be well assured of an interest in
him.   While it is thus with any man, let him say or think
what he will of his assent, it is manifest by this that he
does truly and heartily assent, and there can be no better
proof of it than these real effects produced by it.   But,

(2.) If these and other objections were never so fully
answered, yet believers are afraid to draw *the conclusion*
that they truly receive Christ.   For,

The conclusion is *of infinite importance* to them : it is the
everlasting happiness of their souls, than which nothing is

or can be of greater weight upon their spirits : the blessing seems so great and so good, that they still suspect the truth and certainty of it, as never being sure enough. Thus when the women that were the first messengers and witnesses of Christ's resurrection, came and told the disciples those wonderful and joyful tidings, it is said that "their words seemed to them as idle tales, and they believed them not," Luke 24 : 10, 11 ; they thought it was too good to be true, too great to be hastily received ; and so it is in this case.

Again, the sense they have of *the deceitfulness of their own hearts,* and the daily working of hypocrisy there, makes them afraid to conclude in so great a point as this. They know that very many daily delude themselves in this matter ; they know also that their own hearts are full of falseness and deceit ; they find them so in their daily observation ; and what if they should prove so in this case? Why then they are lost for ever. They also know there is not such danger in their fears and jealousies as there would be in vain confidence and presumption : by the one, they are only deprived of their present comforts, but by the other they would be ruined for ever ; and they therefore choose rather to dwell with their own fears, though they be uncomfortable companions, than run the danger of so great a mistake, which would be infinitely more fatal. And this being the common case of most Christians, it follows that there must be many true believers in the world who dare not conclude themselves to be such.

(4.) If the right receiving of Jesus Christ be true saving and justifying faith, *then those that have the least and lowest degree and measure of saving faith, have cause for ever to admire the bounty and riches of the grace of God towards them.*

If you have received never so little of his bounty by the hand of Providence in the good things of this life, yet if he have given you any measure of true saving faith, he has dealt bountifully indeed with you : this mercy alone is enough to balance all other wants and inconveniences. If you are poor in the world, but rich in faith, James 2 : 5, O let your hearts receive the full sense of this bounty of God to you ; say with the apostle, "Blessed be the God and Father of our Lord Jesus Christ, who hath blessed us with all spiritual blessings in heavenly places in Christ," Eph. 1 : 3, and you will in this one mercy find matter enough for praise and thanksgiving, wonder and admiration to your dying day, yea, to all eternity : for consider,

The smallest measure of saving faith which is found in any of the people of God *receives Jesus Christ ;* and in receiving him, what mercy is there which the believing soul does not receive in him, and with him? Rom. 8 : 32. O believer, though the arms of thy faith be small and weak, yet they embrace a great Christ, and receive the richest gift that ever God bestowed upon the world. No sooner art thou become a believer, but Christ is in thee the hope of glory ; and thou hast authority to become a son of God; thou hast the broad seal of heaven to confirm thy title and claim to the privileges of adoption, for "to as many as received him, to them gave he power to become the sons of God." *To as many,* be they strong or weak, if they really receive Christ by faith, there is authority or power given ; so that it is no act of presumption in them to say, God is our Father, heaven is our inheritance. O precious faith ! the treasures of ten thousand worlds cannot purchase such privileges as these ; all the crowns and sceptres of the earth, sold at full value, are no price for such mercies.

Again, the least degree of saving faith brings the soul into a state of *perfect and full justification.* For if it receives Jesus Christ, it must in him, and with him, receive a free, full, and final pardon of sin : the least measure of faith receives remission for the greatest sins. "By him all that believe are justified from all things." Acts 13 : 39. It unites thy soul with Christ, and then, as the necessary consequent of that union, there is no condemnation, Rom. 8 : 1; or as in the original, not one condemnation, how many soever our sins have been.

The least measure or degree of saving faith is also a *greater mercy* than God has bestowed or ever will bestow upon many that are far above you in outward respects. *All men have not faith;* nay, but a remnant of men believe. Few of the nobles and potentates of the world have such a gift as this: they have houses and lands, yea, crowns and sceptres, but no faith, no Christ, no pardon; they have authority to rule over men, but no authority to become the sons of God. 1 Cor. 1 : 26. Say therefore in thy most debased, straitened, afflicted condition, "Return to thy rest, O my soul, for the Lord hath dealt bountifully with thee."

The least degree of saving faith is *more than all the power of nature* can produce. There must be a special revelation of the arm of the Lord in that work. Isa. 53 : 1. Believers are not born of the flesh, nor of blood, nor of the will of man, but of God. John 1 : 13. All believing motions towards Christ are the effects of the Father's drawing. John 6 : 44. A glorious power goes forth from God to produce it, whence it is called "the faith of the operation of God." Col. 2 : 12. So then let not believers despise the day of small things, or overlook the great and infinite mercy which is included in the least degree of saving faith.

5. *Learn hence the impossibility of their salvation who neither know the nature nor enjoy the means of saving faith.* My soul pities and mourns over the infidel world. Ah, what will become of the millions of poor unbelievers? there is but one door of salvation, Christ; and but one key of faith to open the door.

As that key was never given to the heathen world, so it is laid aside or taken away from the people by their cruel guides all over the *popish* world; were you among them you should hear nothing else pressed as necessary to your salvation but a blind, implicit faith, to believe as the church believes ; that is, to believe, they know not what. To believe as the *pope* believes is no more than to believe as an infidel believes, for such that false church herself confesses he may be,* and though such a thing as an explicit faith is sometimes spoken of among them, yet it is but *sparingly* discoursed of : they love not to accustom the people's ears to such a doctrine ; one of themselves confesses that there is so deep a silence respecting explicit, particular faith in the Romish church, that you may find many everywhere that believe no more of these things than heathen philosophers.† And when it is preached or written of, it is *falsely described;* for they place the whole nature and essence of justifying and saving faith in a naked assent, which the devils have as well as men. James 2 : 19. No more than this is pressed upon the people at any time, as necessary to their salvation.

And even this particular explicit faith, when it is spoken or written of, is *exceedingly slighted.* I think, if the *devil* himself were in the *pulpit,* he could hardly tell how to bring men to a more low and slight esteem of faith ; to represent it more as a very trifle, or a quite needless thing, than these his agents have done. Some‡ say if a man believe with a particular explicit faith, if he actually assent to the Scripture truths once in a year, it is enough. Yea, and others§ think it too much to oblige people to believe once in twelve months, and for their ease tell them if they believe once in twelve years it is sufficient ; and, lest this should be too great a task, others‖ affirm that if it be

* For the pope's internal faith is not necessary to the church. Canus in loc.   Theol. p. 344.

† Navarr. cap. 11, p. 142.

‡ Petr. a S. Joseph. sum. Art. 1, p. 6.

§ Bonacina. Tom. 2, in 1 precept.

‖ Jo. San. Disp. 41, n. 32.

done but once in their whole life, and that at the point of death, it is enough, especially for the rude and common people. What a doctrine is here! It was a saying long ago of Gregory: A wicked minister is the devil's *goosehawk*, that goes a birding for hell; and Oh, what game have these hawks of hell among such numerous flocks of people! O, bless God while you live for your deliverance from popery, and see that you prize the gospel and the means of grace you enjoy at a higher rate, lest God bring you once more under that yoke which neither you nor your fathers could bear.

6. Does saving faith consist in a due and right receiving of the Lord Jesus Christ? Then let me persuade you to EXAMINE YOURSELVES in this great point of faith. Reflect solemnly upon the transactions that have been between Christ and your souls; think closely on this subject of meditation. If all you were worth in the world lay in one precious stone, and that stone were to be tried by the skilful lapidary whether it were true or false, whether it would fly or endure under the smart stroke of his hammer, surely your thoughts could not be unconcerned about the issue; but all that you are worth in both worlds depends upon the truth of your faith which is now to be tried. O then read not these lines with a careless eye, but seriously ponder the matter before you. You would be loath to put to sea, though it were but to cross the channel, in a rotten leaky vessel; and dare you venture into the ocean of eternity in a false, rotten faith? God forbid. You know the Lord is coming to try every man's faith as by fire, and that we must stand or fall for ever with the sincerity or hypocrisy of our faith. Surely you can never be too exact and careful about that on which your whole estate depends, and that for ever.

Now there are three things upon which we should have a very tender and watchful eye for the discovery of the sincerity of our faith:

(1.) If you would discern the sincerity of your faith, examine whether those *antecedent and preparative works* of the Spirit which usually introduce and usher it into the souls of God's elect were ever found in you. Such are illumination, conviction, self-despair, and earnest cries to God.

Illumination is a necessary antecedent to faith. You cannot believe till God has opened your eyes to see your sin, your misery by sin, and your remedy in Jesus Christ alone. You find this act of the Spirit to be the first in the order both of nature and time, and introductory to all the rest, "To turn them from darkness to light, and from the power of Satan to God." Acts 26 : 18. As faith without works, which must be a consequent to it, is dead, so faith without light, which must be an antecedent to it, is blind : faith is the hand by which Christ is received, but knowledge is the eye by which that hand is directed. Has God opened your eyes to see sin and misery in another manner than ever you saw them before? For certainly if God has opened your eyes by saving illumination, you will find as great a difference between your former and present apprehensions of sin and danger, as between a painted lion upon the wall or a sign-post, and the real living lion that meets you roaring in the way.

Conviction is an antecedent to believing. Where this goes not before, no faith follows. The Spirit first convinces of sin, then of righteousness. John 16 : 8. So Mark 1 : 15, "Repent ye, and believe the gospel :" believe it, O man, that breast of thine must be wounded, that vain and frothy heart of thine must be pierced and stung with conviction and sorrow for sin ; thou must have some sick days and restless nights for sin, if ever thou rightly close with Christ by faith. It is true, there is much difference found in the strength, depth, and continuance of conviction and spiritual troubles in converts ; but sure it is, the child of faith is not ordinarily born without some pangs. Conviction is the application of that light which God makes to shine in our minds, to our particular case and condition by the conscience; and surely when men come to see their miserable and sad state by a true light, it cannot but wound them, and that to the very heart.

Self-despair, or a total and absolute loss in ourselves about deliverance and the way of escape, either by ourselves or any other mere creature, must likewise go before faith. So it was with the early believers: "Men and brethren, what shall we do?" Acts 2:27. These are the words of men at a total loss; it is the voice of poor distressed souls, that saw themselves in misery, but knew not, nor could devise any way of escape from it, by any thing they could do for themselves, or any other creature could do for them. Gal. 3:23. And hence the apostle uses that emphatical word, "*Shut up* unto the faith," as men besieged and distressed in a garrison in a time of storm, when the enemy pours in upon them through the breaches and overpowers them. There is but one *sally-port* or gate at which they can escape, and to that they all throng, as despairing of life if they take any other course. Just so do men's convictions besiege them, distress them, beat them off from all their holds and intrenchments, and bring them to a pinching distress in themselves, shutting them up to Christ as the only way of escape.

"Duties cannot save me, reformation cannot save me; nor angels nor men can save me; I must have Christ, or condemnation for ever. I thought once, that a little repentance, reformation, restitution, and a stricter life might be a way to escape the wrath to come; but I find the bed is too short and the covering too narrow: all is but loss, dung, dross, in comparison with Jesus Christ. If I trust to those Egyptian reeds, they will not only fail me, but pierce and wound me too: I see no hope within the whole horizon of sense."

Hence come *vehement and earnest cries to God* for faith,

for Christ, for help from heaven, to transport the soul out of this dangerous condition to that strong rock of salvation; to bring it out of this furious, stormy sea of trouble, where it is ready to be wrecked every moment, into that safe and quiet harbor, Christ. O when a man sees his misery and danger, and no way to escape but Christ, and that this work of faith is the operation of God; how will the soul return again and again upon God, with such cries as in Mark 9 : 24, "Lord, help my unbelief!" "Lord, enable me to come to Christ; give me Christ, or I perish for ever! What profit is there in my blood? Why should I die in the sight and presence of a Saviour? O Lord, it is thine own work, a most glorious work : reveal thine arm in this work upon my soul, I pray thee; give me Christ, if thou deny me bread; give me faith, if thou deny me breath. It is more necessary that I believe, than that I live."

O reader, reflect upon the days and nights that are past, the places where thou hast been conversant : where are the bedsides or the secret corners where thou hast besieged heaven with such cries? If God has thus enlightened, convinced, distressed thy soul, and thus set thee a mourning after Christ, it will be one good sign of faith in thy soul; for here are certainly the *harbingers* and forerunners of it, that ordinarily make way for faith in the souls of men.

(2.) If you would be satisfied of the sincerity and truth of your faith, examine what states of mind have *accompanied* the exercise of it; what frame and temper your soul was in at the time when you think you received Christ. For certainly in those that receive Christ, excepting those into whose hearts God has wrought faith in a more still and insensible way by his blessing upon pious education, such accompanying frames of spirit may be remarked as these following.

The heart is deeply *serious*, and as much in earnest in

this matter as ever it was, or can be, about any thing in the world. This you see in the example of the jailer; he came in trembling and astonished. Acts 16:29. It is the most solemn and important matter that ever the soul had before it in this world, or ever shall or can have. How much are the hearts of men affected in their outward straits and distresses about the concerns of the body: "What shall I eat? what shall I drink? wherewithal shall I and mine be fed and clothed?" But certainly the straits that souls are in about salvation must be allowed to be greater than these; and such questions as that of the jailer's, "Sirs, what must I do to be saved?" make deeper impressions upon the heart, than what shall I eat or drink? Some indeed have their thoughts sinking deeper into these things than others; but all are most solemnly concerned about their condition: frothiness and frolics are gone, and the heart settles itself in the deepest earnest about its eternal state.

The heart that receives Jesus Christ is in a frame of *deep humiliation and self-abasement.* O, when a man begins to apprehend the first approaches of grace, pardon, and mercy by Jesus Christ to his soul; when he is convinced of his utter unworthiness and desert of hell, and can scarcely expect any thing from the just and holy God but damnation, how do the first dawnings of mercy melt and humble him! "O Lord, what am I, that thou shouldst feed me and preserve me; that thou shouldst but for a few years spare me! But that ever Jesus Christ should love me, and give himself for me; that such a wretched sinner as I should obtain union with his person, pardon, peace, and salvation by his blood! Lord, whence is this to such a worm as I? And will Christ indeed bestow himself upon me? shall so great a blessing as Christ ever come to such a soul as mine? will God in very deed be reconciled to me in his Son? what, to me—to such an enemy as I have been? Shall my sins, which are so many, so horrid, so much aggravated beyond the sins of most men, be forgiven? O, what am I, vile dust, base wretch, that ever God should do this for me!" And how is that scripture fulfilled and made good, "That thou mayest remember, and be confounded, and never open thy mouth any more because of thy shame, when I am pacified toward thee for all that thou hast done, saith the Lord God." Ezek. 16 : 63. Thus that poor broken-hearted believer stood behind Christ weeping and washing his feet with tears, as one quite melted down and overcome with the sense of mercy to such a vile sinner. Luke 7 : 38.

The soul that receives Jesus Christ is in a *weary condition*, restless and full of disquietness, neither able to bear the burden of sin, nor knowing how to be discharged from it, except Christ will give it ease. Come unto me, that is, believe in me, ye that are weary and heavy laden. Matt. 11 : 28. If they do not look into their own souls, they know there is no *safety*, and if they do, there is no *comfort*. O, the burden of sin overweighs them; they are ready to fall, to sink under it.

The soul that rightly receives Christ is not only in a weary, but in a *longing* condition : never did the heart pant for the water-brooks, never did the hireling desire the shadow, never did a condemned person long for a pardon, more than the soul longs after Jesus Christ. "O," said David, "that one would give me of the water of the well of Bethlehem to drink." O, saith the poor humbled sinner, that one would give me of the opened fountain of the blood of Christ to drink! O for one drop of that precious blood! O for one encouraging smile from Christ! O now, were ten thousand worlds at my command, and Christ to be bought, how freely would I lay them all down to purchase him! but he is the *gift* of God. O that God would give me Christ, even if I must go in rags, and hunger and thirst all my days in this world!

The soul, in the time of its closing with or receiving Christ, is in a *state of conflict*. It hangs between hope and fear, encouragements and discouragements, which occasions many a sad pause in the way of Christ. Sometimes the number and nature of its sins discourage it; then the riches and freeness of the grace of Christ erect hope again. There is little hope, saith unbelief; nay, it is utterly impossible, saith Satan, that ever such a wretch as thou shouldst find mercy: now the hands hang down. O, but then there is a necessity, an absolute necessity; I have not the choice of two, but am shut up to one way of deliverance; others have found mercy, and the invitation is to all that are weary, and athirst; he saith, him that cometh to him he will in no wise cast out: now new hopes inspire the soul, and the hands that hung down are strengthened.

(3.) Examine the *consequents and effects* of faith, if you would be satisfied of the truth and sincerity of it: such as,

An evangelical and ingenuous melting of the heart under the apprehensions of grace and mercy: "They shall look upon me whom they have pierced, and they shall mourn." Zech. 12 : 10.

Love to Christ, his ways, and people. Faith worketh by love, Gal. 5 : 6, that is, it represents the love of God, and then makes use of the sweetness of it by way of argument, to constrain the soul to all acts of obedience where it may testify the reality of its love to God and Christ.

Heart-purity. "Purifying their hearts by faith." Acts 15 : 9. It doth not only cleanse the hands, but the heart. No principle in man but faith can do this. Morality may hide corruption, but faith only *purifies* the heart from it.

Obedience to the commands of Christ. "The obedience of faith." Rom. 16 : 26. The very name of faith is called upon obedience; for it accepts Christ as Lord, and urges upon the soul the most powerful arguments in the world to draw it to obedience.

In a word, let the poor doubting believer, that questions his faith, reflect upon those things that are unquestionable in his own experience, which being well considered will greatly tend to his satisfaction in this point.

It is very doubtful to you whether you believe; but yet in the mean time it may be past doubt, being a matter of clear experience, that you have been deeply convinced of sin, driven from all carnal refuges, made willing to accept Jesus Christ upon what terms soever you might enjoy him. You doubt whether Christ be yours; but it is past doubt that you have a most high and precious esteem of Christ, that you heartily long for him, that you prize and love all that bear his image; that nothing would please your heart like a transformation into his likeness; that you would rather your soul should be filled with his Spirit than your house with gold and silver. It is doubtful whether Christ be yours; but it is past doubt that one smile from Christ, one token of his love, would do you more good than all the honors and smiles of the world; and nothing so grieves you as that you grieve him by sin. You dare not say that you have received him; nor can you deny but that you have had many sick days and nights for him; that you have gone into many secret places with yearning after him. Whether he be yours or not, you cannot tell; but that you are resolved to be his, this you can tell. Whether he will save you is but a doubt; but that you resolve to lie at his feet, and wait only on him, and never look to another for salvation, there is no doubt.

Well, well, poor pensive soul, if it be so, arise, lift up thy dejected head, take thine own Christ into thine arms. These are undoubted signs of a real closure with Christ; thou makest thyself poor, and yet hast great riches : such things as these are not found in them that despise and reject Christ by unbelief.

7. This doctrine may be improved by way of *appeal to unbelievers*, who from hence must be pressed, as ever they expect to see the face of God in peace, to receive Jesus

Christ as he is now offered to them in the gospel. This is the very scope of the gospel. I shall therefore press it by three great considerations : what is in Christ whom you are to receive ; what in the offer of Christ by the gospel ; and what in the rejecting of that offer.

MOTIVE 1. Consider well *what is in Christ,* whom I persuade you this day to receive. Did you know what is in Christ, you would never neglect or reject him as you do.

God is in Christ. 2 Cor. 5 : 19. The Deity hath chosen to dwell in his flesh ; he is "God manifest in the flesh." 1 Tim. 3 : 16. A Godhead dwelling in flesh is the world's wonder ; so that in receiving Christ, you receive God himself. The authority of God is in Christ. "My name is in him." Exod. 23 : 21. "Him hath God the Father sealed," John 6 : 27 ; he hath the commission, the great seal of heaven to redeem and save you. All power in heaven and earth is given to him, Matt. 28 : 18 ; he comes in his Father's name to you, as well as in his own name. The wisdom of God is in Christ, 1 Cor. 1 : 24 ; yea, in him are hid all the treasures of "wisdom and knowledge." Col. 2 : 3. Never did the wisdom of God display itself before the eyes of angels and men as it has done in Christ. The angels desire to look into it, 1 Pet. 1 : 12, yet they are not so much concerned in the project and design of this wisdom in redemption as you are.

The *fulness of the Spirit* is in Christ ; yea, it fills him so as it never did, nor will fill any creature, "God giveth not the Spirit by measure unto him." John 3 : 34. All others have their limits and measures, but the Spirit is in Christ without measure. O how lovely and desirable are those men that have a large measure of the Spirit in them ; but he is anointed with the Spirit of holiness *above his fellows.* Psalm 45 : 7. Whatever grace is found in all the saints which makes them desirable and lovely, wisdom in one, faith in another, patience in a third, they all centre in Christ as the rivers do in the sea.

The righteousness of God is in Christ, by which only a poor guilty sinner can be justified before God. We are "made the righteousness of God in him." 2 Cor. 5 : 21. He is "the Lord our righteousness," Jer. 23 : 6, the author of our righteousness, or the Lord who justifies us; by that name he will be known and called by his people, than which none can be sweeter.

The *love* of God is in Christ; yea, the very yearning of divine love is in him. What is Christ, but the love of God wrapt up in flesh and blood? "In this was manifested the love of God towards us," 1 John 4 : 9, 10, and herein is love, that God sent his Son: this is the highest flight that ever divine love made; and higher than this it cannot mount. O love unparalleled and admirable!

The *mercies and compassions* of God are all in Christ. Jude 21. Mercy is the thing that poor sinners want, it is what they cry for at the last gasp; it is the only thing that can do them good. O what would they give to find mercy in that great day? Why, if you receive Christ you shall with him receive mercy; but out of him there is no mercy to be expected from the hands of God; for God will never exercise mercy to the prejudice of his justice; and it is in Christ that justice and mercy meet and embrace each other.

The *salvation* of God is in Christ, "Neither is there salvation in any other." Acts 4 : 12. Christ is the *door* of salvation, and faith is the *key* that opens that door to men. If you therefore believe not, if you do not receive Jesus Christ as God has offered him, you exclude yourselves from all hope of salvation. The devils have as much ground to expect salvation as you. You see what is in Christ to induce you to receive him.

MOTIVE 2. I beseech you, consider what there is *in the offer* of Christ to sinners to induce you to receive him. Consider well *to whom* and *how* Christ is offered in the gospel.

To *whom* is he offered? Not to the fallen angels, but to you; they lie in chains of darkness. Jude 6. As he took not their nature, so he designs not their recovery, and therefore will have no treaty at all with them; but he is offered to you, creatures of an inferior rank and order by nature. Nor is he offered to the *damned*, the treaty of peace is ended with them. Christ will never make them another tender of salvation. Nor is he offered to millions as good as you now living in the world. The sound of Christ and salvation is not come to their ears, but he is offered to you by the special favor and bounty of heaven; and will you not receive him? Oh, then, how will the devils, the damned, and the heathen upbraid your folly, and say, "Had we had one such tender of mercy, of which you have had thousands, we had not been now in this place of torment."

Again, consider *how* Christ is offered to you: *freely as the gift of God* to your souls; you are not to *purchase* him, but only to *receive* him. "Ho, every one that thirsteth, come ye to the waters, and he that hath no money; come," etc. Isa. 55 : 1. He is offered *importunately*, by repeated entreaties. "As though God did beseech you by us, we pray you in Christ's stead, be ye reconciled to God." 2 Cor. 5 : 20. O what amazing condescension is here in the God of mercy! God now beseeches you; wilt thou not yield to the entreaties of thy God? O then, what wilt thou say for thyself when thou shalt entreat and cry for mercy, and God will not hear thee?

MOTIVE 3. Consider *the sin and danger there is in refusing* or neglecting the present offers of Christ in the gospel, and surely there is much sin in it : the very malignity of sin and the sum of all misery lies here; for in refusing Christ,

You put the greatest contempt and slight upon *all the attributes of God*. He has made his justice, his mercy, his wisdom, and all his attributes to shine in their brightest glory in Christ. Never was there such a display of the glory of God made to the world in any other way. O then, what is it to reject and despise Jesus Christ, but to offer the greatest affront to the glory of God that is possible?

You hereby *frustrate the very design* of the gospel to yourselves; you receive the grace of God in vain. 2 Cor. 6 : 1. As good, yea, better had it been for you that Christ had never come into the world; or if he had, that your lot had fallen in the dark places of the earth, where you had never heard his name; yea, "good had it been for that man if he had never been born."

Hereby a man *murders his own soul:* "I said therefore unto you, that ye shall die in your sins; for if ye believe not that I am he, ye shall die in your sins." John 8 : 24. Unbelief is self-murder; you are guilty of the blood of your own soul; life and salvation were offered you, and you rejected them. Yea,

The refusing of Christ by unbelief will *aggravate your damnation* above all others that perish in ignorance of Christ. O, it will be more tolerable for heathens than for you; the greatest measures of wrath are reserved to punish the worst of sinners, and among sinners none will be found worse than unbelievers.

8. This doctrine may also be very useful to *believers in persuading them to various excellent duties,* among which I shall single out two principal ones.

The first is to *bring up their faith of acceptance to the faith of assurance.* You that have received Jesus Christ truly, give yourselves no rest till you are fully satisfied that you have done so; acceptance brings you to heaven hereafter, but assurance will bring heaven into your souls now. O, what a life of delight and pleasure doth the assured believer live! What pleasure is it to him to look back and consider where he once was, and where he now is; to look forward, and consider where he now is, and where shortly he shall be! "I was in my sins, I am now in Christ; I am in Christ now, I shall be with Christ, and that for ever, after a few days. I was upon the brink of hell, I am now upon the very borders of heaven; I shall be in a very little while among the innumerable company of angels and glorified saints, bearing part with them in the song of Moses and of the Lamb for evermore."

And why may not you that have received Christ receive the comfort of your union with him? All the grounds and helps of assurance are furnished to your hand; there is a real union between Christ and your souls which is the very groundwork of assurance. You have the Scriptures before you, which contain the signs of faith and the very things within you that answer those signs in the word. So you read, and so, just so you might feel it in your own hearts, would you attend to your own experience. The Spirit of God is ready to seal you; it is his office and his delight so to do. O give diligence to this work; attend to the study of the Scriptures and of your own hearts more, and grieve not the Holy Spirit of God, and you may arrive to the very desire of your hearts.

The other duty is to *bring-up your life* to the excellent principles and rules of faith: "As ye have received Christ Jesus the Lord, so walk ye in him." Col. 2 : 6. Live as you believe; you received Christ sincerely in your first close with him, O maintain no less seriousness and sincerity in all your ways to the end of your lives : you received him entirely and *undividedly* at first, let there be no exceptions against any of his commands afterwards. You received him *exclusively* of all others, see that you watch against all self-righteousness and self-conceitedness now, and mingle nothing of your own with his blood, whatever gifts or enlargements in duty God shall give you afterwards.

You received him *advisedly* at first, weighing and considering the self-denying terms upon which he was offered to you : O show that it was real, and that you see no cause to repent of the consecration made, whatever you shall meet with in the ways of Christ and duty ; convince the world of your constancy and cheerfulness in all your sufferings for Christ, that Christ with his cross, Christ with a prison, Christ with the greatest afflictions, is worthy of all acceptation. "As ye have received him, so walk ye in him." Let him be as sweet, as lovely, as precious to you now as he was in the first moment you received him ; yea, let your love to him, delight in him, and self-denial for him increase with your acquaintance with him day by day.

9. I close with a few words of *direction to all that are made willing to receive the Lord Jesus Christ;* and surely it is well that help be given to poor Christians in this matter : it is a time of trouble, fear, and great temptation ; mistakes are easily made of dangerous consequence ; attend heedfully, therefore, to a few directions :

In your receiving Christ, beware you *do not mistake the means for the end.* Many do so, but see you do not. Prayer, sermons, reformations are means to bring you to Christ, but they are not Christ ; to close with those duties is one thing, and to close with Christ is another thing. If I go into a *boat,* my design is not to dwell there, but to be carried to the place where I desire to be landed : so it must be in this case ; all your duties must land you upon Christ—they are means to bring you to Christ.

See that you receive Christ, *not for a present help merely, but for your everlasting portion.* Many inquire after Christ, pray for Christ, cast themselves, in their way, upon Christ and the satisfaction of his blood, when the efficacy and terror of conscience is upon them, and they feel the sting of guilt within ; but as soon as the storm is over, and the rod that conscience shook over them is laid by, there is no more talk of Christ : alas, it was not Christ, but quietness that they sought. Beware of mistaking peace for Christ.

In receiving Christ, *come empty-handed to him,* believing

on him who justifies the ungodly, Rom. 4 : 5, and know that the deepest sense of your own vileness, emptiness, and unworthiness is the best frame of heart that can accompany you to Christ. Many persons stand off from Christ for want of fit qualifications ; they think they are not prepared for Christ as they should be : they would not come naked and empty, but would have something to commend them to the Lord Jesus for acceptance. O, this is the pride of men's hearts and the snare of the devil ! Let "him that hath no money" come. You are not to come to Christ because you are qualified, but that you may be qualified with whatever you want; and the best qualification you can bring, is a deep sense that you have no worth nor excellency at all in you.

In receiving Christ, *beware of dangerous delays.* O follow on that work till it be finished. You read of some that are almost persuaded, and of others not far from the kingdom of God; O take heed of what the prophet says, Hosea 13 : 13. Delays here are full of danger; life is uncertain, so are means of grace. The manslayer needed no motives to quicken his flight to the city of refuge.

See that you receive Christ *with all your heart.* To receive Christ, is to receive his person clothed with all his offices ; and to receive him with all your heart, is to receive him into your understanding, will, and affections. Acts 8 : 37. As there is nothing in Christ that may be refused, so there is nothing in you from which he must be excluded.

Finally, understand that the opening of your hearts to receive the Lord Jesus Christ, is not a work done by any power of your own, but *the arm of the Lord* is revealed therein. Isa. 53 : 1. It is therefore your duty and interest to be daily at the feet of God, pouring out your soul to him in secret, that he may work in you the genuine faith of his own people.

Thanks be to God for Jesus Christ.

CHAPTER VIII

THE BELIEVER'S FELLOWSHIP WITH CHRIST

"Therefore God, thy God, hath anointed thee with the oil of gladness above thy fellows." PSALM 45:7

THE method of grace in uniting souls with Jesus Christ has been shown : thus does the Spirit, whose office it is, make application of Christ to God's people ; the result and next fruit of which is *communion* with Christ in his graces and benefits. Our *union* with Christ is the very ground-work and foundation of our sweet, soul-enriching *communion* and participation of spiritual privileges : we are first en-grafted into Christ, and then suck the sap and fatness of the root ; first married to the person of Christ, then en-dowed and instated in the privileges and benefits of Christ. To this communion with Christ the portion of Scripture selected now calls our attention.

The words are a part of that excellent psalm, or *song of love*, wherein the spiritual espousals of Christ and the church are figuratively and very elegantly celebrated and shadowed. The subject of this psalm is the same as of the whole book of the Canticles, in which the spiritual espousals of Christ and the church are set forth and repre-sented to us. Among many rapturous and elegant ex-pressions in praise of this glorious bridegroom Christ, this is one : "God, thy God, hath anointed thee with the oil of gladness above thy fellows ;" that is, enriched and filled thee in a singular and peculiar manner with the fulness of the Spirit, whereby thou art consecrated to thy office ; and by reason whereof thou outshinest and excellest all the saints, who are thy *fellows* or copartners in these graces. So that in these words you have two parts ; the saints' *dignity*, and Christ's *preëminence*.

1. The saints' *dignity*, which consists in this, that they are Christ's *fellows*. The Hebrew word is very full and copious, and is translated consorts, companions, copartners, partakers; that is, such as are partakers with him in the anointing of the Spirit; who do in their measure receive the same Spirit, being anointed with the same grace, and dignified with the same titles. 1 John 2 : 27 ; Rev. 1 : 6. Does the Spirit of holiness dwell in him? so it does in them too. Is Christ *King* and *Priest*? so are they by the grace of union with him. He "hath made us kings and priests unto God and his Father." This is the saints' dignity, to be Christ's fellows, consorts, or copartners ; so that whatever spiritual grace or excellence is in Christ, it is not appropriated to himself, but they share it with him ; for indeed he was filled with the fulness of the Spirit for their sakes. As the sun is filled with light not to shine to itself, but to others, so is Christ with grace. But,

2. Whatever *dignity* is here ascribed to the saints, there is and still must be a *preëminence* acknowledged and ascribed to Christ : if they are anointed with the Spirit of grace, much more abundantly is Christ: "God, thy God, hath anointed thee with the oil of gladness above thy fellows."

By the *oil of gladness* understand the Spirit of holiness, compared here to oil, of which there was under the law a *civil* and a *sacred* use. It had a sacred and a solemn use in the inauguration and consecration of the Jewish kings and high-priests ; it had also a civil and common use for anointing their bodies, to make their limbs more agile and nimble ; to make the face shine, for it gave a lustre, freshness, and liveliness to the countenance. By the Spirit of grace poured forth upon Christ, he was prepared for and consecrated to his offices ; he was anointed "with the Holy Ghost and with power." Acts 10 : 38. And as this precious oil runs down from Christ the head, to the borders of his garments ; I mean, as it is shed upon believers, so it exceedingly beautifies their faces and makes them shine with glory—it renders them apt and ready to every good work. It kindles and maintains the flame of divine love in their souls, and like a lamp, enlightens their minds in the knowledge of spiritual things.

And this oil is here called the oil of *gladness*, because it is the cause of all joy and gladness to them that are anointed with it. The anointing or instalment of sovereign princes is the day of the gladness of their hearts; and among the common people oil was liberally used at all their *festivals*, but never on their days of mourning. Whence it becomes excellently expressive of the nature and use of the Spirit of grace, who is the cause and author of all joy in believers. John 17 : 13.

With this oil of gladness is Christ said to be anointed *above his fellows*, to have a far greater share of the Spirit of grace than they; for to every one of the saints "is given grace according to the measure of the gift of Christ." Eph. 4 : 7. But to him the Spirit is not given by measure. John 3 : 34. "It pleased the Father, that in him should all fulness dwell," Col. 1 : 19, and "of his fulness we all receive grace for grace." John 1 : 16. The saints partake with him and through him in the same Spirit of grace, for which reason they are his fellows; but all the grace poured out upon believers comes exceeding short of that which God hath poured out upon Jesus Christ. The words thus explained teach us that,

All true believers have a real communion or fellowship with the Lord Jesus Christ.

From the saints' union with Christ results naturally and immediately a most sweet and blessed communion and fellowship with him in graces and spiritual privileges: "Blessed be the God and Father of our Lord Jesus Christ, who hath blessed us with all spiritual blessings in heavenly places." In giving us his Son, he freely gives us all things. Rom. 8 : 32. So 1 Cor. 1 : 30, "Of him are ye in Christ Jesus, who of God is made unto us wisdom, righteousness, sanctification, and redemption." And once more, "All are yours, and ye are Christ's." 1 Corinthians 3 : 22, 23.

That the scope of this discourse be not mistaken, let the reader observe that I am not here treating of the saint's communion or fellowship with God in his duties, as in prayer, hearing, the ordinances, etc., but of the interest which believers have in the good things of Christ, by virtue of *the mystical union between them through faith.*

There is a fellowship or communion the saints have with Christ in holy duties, wherein Christians let forth their hearts to God by desires, and God lets forth his comforts and refreshments again into their hearts ; they open their mouths wide, and he fills them : this communion with God is the joy and comfort of a believer's life, but I am not to speak of that here. It is not any *act* of communion, but *the state* of communion, from which all acts of communion flow, of which I am now to treat. Between Christ and his people there is a fellowship, or joint interest, on which ground they are called *coheirs with Christ.* Rom. 8 : 17. In the explication of this point, I shall show in what Christ and believers have fellowship ; by what means they come to have this fellowship ; and the dignity to which it raises them.

I. IN WHAT do Christ and believers have fellowship. And here I remark negatively, that the saints have *no fellowship* with Christ in those things that belong to him as God ; such as his consubstantiality, coequality, and coeternity with the Father. Neither men nor angels partake in these things ; they are the proper and incommunicable glory of the Lord Jesus. Nor have the saints any communion or fellowship in the honor and glory of his *mediatorial* work, his sanctification to God, or redemption of his people. It is true, we have the benefit and fruit of his mediation and satisfaction : his righteousness is imputed to us for our personal justification; but we share not in the least with Christ in the glory of this work; nor have we an inherent righteousness in us, as Christ has; nor can we justify and save others, as Christ does: we have nothing to do with his peculiar honor and praise in these things. Though we have the benefit of being saved, we may not pretend to the honor of being saviors as Christ is to ourselves or others. "Christ's righteousness," says Bradshaw, "is not made ours as to its universal value, but as to our particular necessity; nor is it imputed to us as causes of salvation to others, but as subjects to be saved by it ourselves." But there are many glorious and excellent things which are in common between Christ and believers, though in them all he hath the preëminence; he shines in the fulness of them as the sun, and we with a borrowed and lesser light.

1. Believers have communion with Christ in his *names and titles;* they are called Christians from Christ, from him the whole family in heaven and earth is named. Eph. 3 : 15. This is that worthy name the apostle speaks of, James 2 : 7. He is the Son of God, and they also, by their union with him, have power or authority to become the sons of God. John 1 : 12. He is the heir of all things, and they are joint-heirs with him. Rom. 8 : 17. He is both King and Priest, and he hath made them kings and priests. Rev. 1 : 6.

2. They have communion with him in his *righteousness*, the righteousness of Christ is made theirs, 2 Cor. 5 : 21; he is "the Lord our righteousness." Jer. 23 : 6. True, the righteousness of Christ is not inherent in us as it is in him; but our union with him is the ground of the imputation of his righteousness to us. 2 Cor. 5 : 21. We are made the righteousness of God in him. Phil. 3 : 9.

This is a most inestimable privilege, the very ground of all our other blessings and mercies. O what a benefit is this to a poor sinner that owes to God infinitely more than he is ever able to pay by doing or suffering, to have such a rich treasure of merit as lies in Christ to discharge, in one entire payment, all his debts to the last farthing. "Surely shall one say, In the Lord have I righteousness," Isa. 45 : 24, even as a poor woman that owes more than she is worth, in one moment is discharged of all her obligations by her marriage to a wealthy man.

3. Believers have communion with Christ in his *holiness or sanctification,* for of God he is made unto them not only righteousness, but sanctification also ; and as in the former privilege they have merit in the blood of Christ to justify them ; so here they have the Spirit of Christ to sanctify them, 1 Cor. 1 : 30 ; and therefore we are said of his fulness to receive "grace for grace," John 1 : 16 ; that is, say some, grace upon grace, manifold graces, or abundance of grace ; or grace answerable to grace, as in the seal and wax there is line for line and cut for cut exactly answerable to each other ; or grace for grace, that is, say others, the free grace of God in Christ for the sanctification or filling of our souls with grace : be it in which sense it may, it shows the communion believers have with Jesus Christ in grace and holiness. Now, holiness is the most precious thing in the world, it is the image of God and chief excellency of man : it is our evidence for glory, yea, and the first fruits of glory. In Christ dwells the fulness of grace, and from him our head it is derived and communicated to us ; thus "he that sanctifieth, and they who are sanctified, are all of one." Heb. 2 : 11. More particularly,

4. Believers have communion with Christ *in his death;* they die with him : "I am crucified with Christ," Gal. 2 : 20 ; that is, the death of Christ has a real killing and mortifying influence upon the lusts and corruptions of my heart and nature. True it is, he died for sin one way, and we die to sin another way : he died to *expiate* it, we die to it when we *mortify* it. The death of Christ is the death of

sin in believers; and this is a very glorious privilege; for the death of sin is the life of your souls; if sin do not die in you by mortification, you must die for sin by eternal damnation. If Christ had not died, the Spirit of God, by which you now mortify the deeds of the body, could not have been given unto you: then you must have lived vassals to your sins, and died at last in your sins: but the fruit, efficacy, and benefit of Christ's death is yours for killing those sins in you which else had been your ruin.

5. Believers have communion with Christ in *his life and resurrection* from the dead; as he rose from the dead, so do they, and that by the power and influence of his *vivification* and resurrection. It is the Spirit of life which is in Christ Jesus that makes us free from the law of sin and death. Rom. 8 : 2. Our spiritual life is from Christ: "You hath he quickened, who were dead in trespasses and sins," Eph. 2 : 1; and hence Christ is said to live in the believer: "I live; yet not I, but Christ liveth in me," Gal. 2 : 20; and it is no small privilege to partake of the very life of Christ, which is the most excellent life that any creature can live; yet such is the happiness of all the saints, the life of Christ is manifest in them, and such a life as shall never see death.

6. Believers have fellowship with Jesus Christ *in his glory*, which they shall enjoy in heaven with him: they "shall be ever with the Lord," 1 Thess. 4 : 17; and that is not all—though, as one saith, it were a kind of heaven but to look through the keyhole and have but a glimpse of Christ's blessed face—but they shall partake of the glory which the Father hath given him; for so he speaks, John 17 : 22, 24; and more particularly, they shall sit with him in his throne, Rev. 3 : 21; and when he comes to judge the world, he will come to be glorified in the saints. 2 Thess. 1 : 10.

Thus you see what glorious and inestimable things are and will be in common between Christ and the saints—

his titles, his righteousness, his holiness, his death, his life, his glory.   I do not say that Christ will make any saint equal with him in glory ; that is impossible ; he will be known from all the saints in heaven, as the sun is distinguished from the stars ; but they shall partake of his glory, and be filled with his joy.

II. I would show THE WAY AND MEANS by which we come to have fellowship with Jesus Christ in these excellent privileges ; and this I shall do briefly in the following positions.

1. No man has fellowship with Christ in any special saving privilege by nature, howsoever it be cultivated or improved, but only *by faith uniting him to the Lord Jesus Christ ;* it is not the privilege of our first, but second birth. This is plain from John 1 : 12, 13 : "But to as many as received him, to them gave he power to become the sons of God, even to them that believe on his name ; who are born not of blood, nor of the will of the flesh, nor of the will of man, but of God." We are by nature children of wrath, Eph. 2 : 3, we have fellowship with Satan in sin and misery : the wild branch has no communication of the sweetness and fatness of a more noble and excellent root until it be ingrafted upon it, and have immediate union with it. John 15 : 1, 2.

2. Believers themselves have not an equal share one with another in all the benefits and privileges of their union with Christ, but in some there is an equality and in others an inequality ; *to every one according to the measure and gift of Christ.* In justification they are all equal : the weak and the strong believer are alike justified, because it is one and the same perfect righteousness of Christ which is applied to the one and to the other ; so that there are no different degrees of justification, but all that believe are justified from all things, Acts 13 : 39 ; and "there is no condemnation to them that are in Christ Jesus," Rom. 8 : 1, be they never so weak in faith or defective in de-

grees of grace. But there is difference in the measures of
their sanctification; some are men, and others babes in
Christ. 1 Cor. 3 : 1. The faith of some flourishes and
grows exceedingly, 2 Thess. 1 : 3; the things that are in
others are ready to die. Rev. 3 : 2. It is a plain case,
that there is great variety in the degrees of grace and
comfort among them that are jointly interested in Christ,
and equally justified by him.

3. The saints have not fellowship and communion with
Christ in the forementioned benefits and privileges by
one and the same medium, but *by various mediums and
ways, according to the nature of the benefits in which they participate.* For instance, they have partnership and communion with Christ, as has been said, in his righteousness,
holiness, and glory, but they receive these distinct blessings by divers mediums of communion : we have communion with Christ in his righteousness by the way of
imputation; we partake of his holiness by his imparting
it to us, and of his glory in heaven by the beatifical vision. Our justification is a relative change, our sanctification a real change, our glorification a perfect change by
redemption from all the remains both of sin and misery.
Thus hath the Lord appointed several blessings for believers in Christ, and several channels of conveying them
from him to us : by imputed righteousness we are freed
from the guilt of sin; by imparted holiness we are freed
from the dominion of sin; and by our glorification with
Christ we are freed from all the remains both of sin and
misery brought in by sin upon our natures.

4. *Christ imparts to all believers all the spiritual blessings
that he is filled with, and withholds none from any that have
union with him, be these blessings never so great, or they that
receive them never so weak and contemptible in outward respects.*
Ye are the children of God by faith in Jesus Christ. Gal.
3 : 26. The salvation that comes by Jesus Christ is styled
the *common salvation*, Jude 3, and heaven the inheritance

of the saints in light, Col. 1 : 12. "There is neither Greek nor Jew, circumcision nor uncircumcision, Barbarian, Scythian, bond nor free; but Christ is all, and in all." Col. 3 : 11. As if the apostle had said, there is no privilege in the one to commend them to God, and no want of any thing in the other to debar them from God; let men have or want outward excellences, as beauty, honor, riches, nobility, gifts of the mind, sweetness of nature, and all such ornaments, what is that to God? He looks not at these things, but respects them, and communicates his favor to them as they are in Christ: *He is all, and in all.* The gifts and blessings of the Spirit are given to men as they are in Christ, and without respect to any external differences made in this world among men : hence we find excellent treasures of grace in mean and contemptible persons in the world ; poor in the world and rich in faith, and heirs of the kingdom ; and as all believers, without difference, receive from Christ, so they are not debarred from any blessing that is in Christ: "All is yours, for ye are Christ's." 1 Cor. 3 : 22, 23. With Christ, God "freely gives us all things." Rom. 8 : 32.

5. *The communion believers have with Christ in spiritual benefits is a very great mystery, far above the understandings of natural men.* There are no footsteps of this thing in all the works of creation ; therefore the apostle calls it "the unsearchable riches of Christ." Eph. 3 : 8. The word signifies that which has no footsteps to trace it by ; yea, it is so deep a mystery that the angels themselves stoop to look into it. 1 Pet. 1 : 12. "Eye hath not seen, nor ear heard, neither have entered into the heart of man, the things which God hath prepared for them that love him ; but God hath revealed them unto us by his Spirit." 1 Cor. 2 : 9, 10.

III. I am to show THE DIGNITY AND EXCELLENCE of this fruit of our union with Christ, and that a greater glory and honor cannot be put upon man than to be thus in fellowship with him. "The glory which thou gavest me I have given them, that they may be one, even as we are one." John 17 : 22. Let it be considered,

1. *With whom* we are associated, even the Son of God; with him that is "over all, God blessed for ever." Our association with angels is a high advancement, for angels and saints are fellow-servants in the same family, Rev. 19 : 10, and through Christ we are come to an innumerable company of angels, Heb. 12 : 22. But what is all this to our fellowship with Jesus Christ himself, and that in another manner than angels have? For though Christ be to them a head of dominion, yet not a head of vital influence, as he is to his mystical body the church; this therefore is to them a mystery, which they greatly desire to study and pry into.

2. *What we are* that are dignified with this title, the *fellows* or *copartners* with Jesus Christ: not only dust by nature, but such wretched sinners by nature and the sentence of the law, as ought to be associated with devils and partakers with them of the wrath of Almighty God to all eternity.

3. *The benefits* we are partakers of, in and with the Lord Jesus Christ; and indeed they are wonderful and astonishing so far as they do already appear, and yet we see but little of them compared with what we shall see. "Now are we the sons of God, and it doth not yet appear what we shall be; but we know that when he shall appear we shall be like him, for we shall see him as he is." 1 John 3 : 2. Oh, what will that be, to see him as he is, and to be transformed into his likeness!

4. *The manner* in which we are brought into this fellowship with Christ; which is yet more admirable. The apostle gives us a surprising account of it in 2 Cor. 8 : 9 : "For ye know the grace of our Lord Jesus Christ, that, though he was rich, yet for your sakes he became poor, that ye through his poverty might be rich:" he empties

himself of his glory, that we might be filled ; he is made a curse, that we might enjoy the blessing ; he submits to be crowned with thorns, that we might be crowned with glory and honor ; he puts himself into the number of worms, Psa. 22 : 6, that we might be made equal to the angels. Oh, the inconceivable grace of Christ !

5. The *reciprocal* nature of the communion which is between Christ and believers. We do not only partake of what is his, but he partakes of what is ours : he has fellowship with us in all our wants, sorrows, miseries and afflictions ; and we have communion with him in his righteousness, grace, sonship, and glory : he takes part of our misery, and we take part of his blessedness ; our sufferings are his sufferings. Col. 1 : 24. Oh, what an honor is it to thee, poor man, to whom a great many would not turn aside to ask how thou doest ; to have a King, yea, the Prince of all the kings of the earth, pity, relieve, sympathize, groan, and bleed with thee, sit by thee in all thy troubles, and give thee his cordials ; say thy troubles are my troubles, and thy afflictions are my afflictions ; whatever toucheth thee, toucheth me also. O what name shall we give unto such grace as this?

6. Consider the *perpetuity* of this privilege. Your fellowship with Christ is interminable, and abides for ever. Christ and the saints shall be glorified together, Rom. 8 : 17 ; while he hath any glory they shall partake with him. It is said indeed, that there shall be a time when Christ will deliver up the kingdom to the Father, 1 Cor. 15 : 24 ; but the meaning is not, that he will ever cease to be the Head of his saints, or they cease to be his members : no, the relation never ceases ; justification, sanctification, and adoption are everlasting ; no enemy can despoil us of them.

INFERENCE 1. Are the saints Christ's fellows? *What honorable persons then are they ; and how should they be esteemed and valued in the world.* If a king, who is the fountain of honor, do but raise a man by his favor, and dignify him by bestowing some honorable title upon him, what respect and deference is presently paid him by all persons. But what are all the vain and empty titles of honor to the glorious and substantial privileges with which believers are dignified and raised above all other men by Jesus Christ? He is the Son of God, and they are the sons of God also; he is the Heir of all things, and they are joint-heirs with Christ; he reigns in glory, and they shall reign with him; he sits upon the throne, and they shall sit with him in his throne. O that this vile world did but know the dignity of believers; they would never slight, hate, abuse, and persecute them as they do. And Oh that believers did but understand their own happiness and privileges by Christ; they would never droop and sink under every small trouble as they now do.

2. *How abundantly has God provided for all the necessities and wants of believers!* Christ is a storehouse filled with blessings and mercies, and it is all for them; from him they "receive abundance of grace, and of the gift of righteousness." Rom. 5 : 17. "Of his fulness they all receive grace for grace." John 1 : 16. All the fulness of Christ is made over to them for the supply of their wants: "My God shall supply all your need according to his riches in glory by Christ Jesus." Phil. 4 : 19. If all the riches of God can supply your needs, then they shall be supplied. Say not, Christ is in the possession of consummate glory, and I am a poor creature struggling with many difficulties, and toiling in the midst of many cares and fears in the world; for care is taken for all thy wants, and orders given from heaven for their supply: "My God shall supply all your need." O say with a melting heart, I have a full Christ, and he is filled for me: I have his pure and perfect righteousness to justify me, his holiness to sanctify me, his wisdom to guide me, his comforts to refresh me, his power to protect me, and his all-sufficiency

to supply me. O be cheerful, be thankful; you have all your hearts can wish: and yet be humble; it is all from free-grace to empty and unworthy creatures.

3. *How absurd, disingenuous, and unworthy of a Christian is it, to deny or withhold from Christ any thing by which he may be served or honored.* Doth Christ communicate all he hath to you, and can you withhold any thing from Christ? On Christ's part it is not *mine* and *thine*, but *ours*, or *mine* and *yours:* "I ascend unto my Father, and your Father; and to my God, and your God." John 20 : 17. But Oh this cursed idol *self*, which appropriates all to its own designs and uses. How liberal is Christ, and how penurious are we to him! Some will not part with their credit for Christ, when yet Christ abased himself unspeakably for them. Some will not part with a drop of blood for Christ, when Christ spent the whole treasure of his blood freely for us; yea, how loath are we to part with a shilling for Christ to relieve him in his distressed members, though "we know the grace of our Lord Jesus Christ, that though he was rich, yet for our sakes he became poor, that we through his poverty might be rich!" O ungrateful return! O base and disingenuous spirits! The things Christ gives us are great, and the things we deny to him are small: he parts with the greatest, and yet is denied the least. The things he communicates to us are none of ours, we have no right nor title by nature, or any desert of ours, to them; the things we deny or grudge to Christ are by all titles his own, and he has the fullest and most unquestionable title to them all: what he gives to us, he gives to them that never deserved it; what we withhold from him, we withhold from one who has deserved that and infinitely more from us than we have or are.

He interested you freely in all his riches when you were enemies; you stand upon trifles with him, and yet call him your best and dearest friend: he gave himself and all he has to you, when you could claim nothing from him; you refuse to part with these things for Christ, who may not only claim them upon the highest title, his own sovereignty and absolute property, but by your own act who profess to have given all in covenant to him. On what he gives, you return no profit to him; but what you give or part with for him is to your greatest advantage. O that the consideration of these things might shame and humble your souls.

4. *Certainly no man is or can be supposed to be a loser by conversion, seeing from that day whatever Christ is or has becomes his.* O what an inheritance are men possessed of by their new birth! Some men cry out, Religion will undo you; but with what eyes do these men see? Surely you could never so reckon, except your souls were so worldly as to reckon pardon, peace, adoption, holiness, and heaven for nothing; that invisibles are nonentities, and temporals the only realities. It is true, the converted soul may lose his estate, his liberty, yea, his life for Christ; but what then? Are they losers that exchange brass for gold; or part with their present comforts for a hundred-fold advantage? Mark 10 : 29, 30. So that none need be frightened at religion for the losses that attend it, while Christ and heaven are gained by it : they that count religion their loss, have their portion only in this life.

5. *How securely is the saints' inheritance settled upon them, seeing they are in common with Jesus Christ.* Christ and his saints are joint-heirs, and the inheritance cannot be alienated but by his consent : he must lose his interest, if you lose yours. Indeed, Adam's inheritance was by a single title, and moreover it was in his own hand, and so he might, as indeed he soon did, divest himself and his posterity of it; but it is not so between Christ and believers : we are secured in our inheritance by Christ our coheir, who will never alienate it, and therefore it was truly observed that Job was happier upon the dunghill than Adam

was in paradise. The covenant of grace is certainly the best tenure : as it has the best mercies, so it gives the fullest security to enjoy them.

6. *How rich and full is Jesus Christ, who communicates abundantly to all the saints, and yet has still infinitely more in himself than has ever been received by them all!* Take all the faith of Abraham, all the meekness of Moses, all the patience of Job, all the wisdom of Solomon, all the zeal of David, all the industry of Paul, and all the tender-heartedness of Josiah; add to this all the grace that is poured, though in lesser measure, into all the elect vessels in the world, yet still it is far short of that which remains in Christ: "He is anointed with the oil of gladness above his fellows ;" and in all things he hath and must ever have the preëminence. There are many thousand stars glittering above our heads, and one star differs from another star in glory, yet there is more light and glory in one sun than in many thousand stars. Grace beautifies the children of men exceedingly, but still it is true of Christ, "Thou art fairer than the children of men ; grace is poured into thy lips." Psalm 45 : 2. For all grace is secondarily and derivatively in the saints, but it is primitively and originally in Christ. John 1 : 16. Grace is imperfect and defective in them, but in him it is in its most absolute perfection and fulness. Col. 1 : 19. In the saints it is mixed with abundance of corruption, but in Christ it is altogether unmixed and exclusive of its opposite. Heb. 7 : 26. So that as the heathen said of moral virtue, I may much more say of Christ, that were he to be seen with mortal eyes, he would compel love and admiration from all men, for "he is altogether lovely." Song 5 : 16.

7. *What delight and singular advantage must there be in the communion of the saints, who have communion with Jesus Christ in all his graces and benefits.* "That which we have seen and heard declare we unto you, that ye also may have fellowship with us ; and truly our fellowship is with the

Father, and with his Son Jesus Christ." 1 John 1 : 3.   O
it is sweet to have fellowship with those that have fellowship with God in Jesus Christ.   Christ has communicated
graces to the saints in different measures and degrees ;
and as they all receive from Christ the fountain, so it is
sweet and most delightful to be improving themselves by
spiritual communion one with another.   Yea, one is furnished with one grace more eminently than another for
this end, that the weak may be assisted by the strong, as
Mr. Torshell well observes.   Athanasius was prudent and
active, Basil of a heavenly sweet temper, Chrysostom laborious without affectation, Ambrose resolved and grave,
Luther courageous, and Calvin acute and judicious.   Thus
every one has his proper gift from Christ, the fountain of
gifts and graces. 1 Cor. 7 : 7.   One has quickness of parts,
another solidity of judgment ; one is zealous, another well-
principled ; one is wary and prudent, another open and
plain ; one is trembling and melting, another cheerful and
joyous ; one must impart his light, another his heat.   The
eye, the knowing man, cannot say to the *hand*, the active
man, I have no need of thee.   And Oh, how sweet would
it be if gifts, graces, and experiences were frequently and
humbly imparted.   But idle notions, earthly-mindedness,
self-interest, and want of more communion with Christ,
have almost destroyed the comfort of Christian fellowship
in the world.

   8. *In a word, those only have ground to claim interest in*
Christ who do really participate of his graces, and in whom are
found the effects and fruits of their union and communion with
him.   If you have interest in Christ, you have communion
in his graces and benefits ; and if you have such communion, it will appear in your maintaining daily *actual com-*
munion with God in duties, by which will be produced the
increase of your sanctification by fresh participations from
the fountain.   As *cloth* which is often dipped into the *vat*
receives the deeper dye and livelier tincture, so will your

souls by assiduous communion with God. It will also be discerned in your deeper humiliation and spiritual sense of your own vileness : the more any man partakes of God, and is acquainted with him, and assimilated to him, the more base and vile in his own sight he still grows. Job 42 : 5, 6 ; Isa. 6 : 5. It will appear in your more vehement longings after the full enjoyment of God in heaven. 1 Pet. 1 : 8, and Rom. 8 : 23. You that have the first-fruits will groan within yourselves after the full harvest and satisfying fruition ; you will not be so taken with things below as to be content with the best lot on earth for your everlasting portion. Oh, if these communicated drops be so sweet, what is there in Christ the fountain!

Thus I have shown *the method of grace in bringing home Christ and his benefits to God's people by union in order to communion with him.*

Thanks be to God for Jesus Christ.

THE WHOLE SUBJECT APPLIED IN A SOLEMN INVITATION TO COME TO CHRIST, WITH MOTIVES FROM HIS TITLES AND BENEFITS.

CHAPTER IX

ALL MEN INVITED TO APPLY JESUS CHRIST

"Come unto me, all ye that labor and are heavy-laden, and I will give you rest." MATT. 11 : 28

THE *providing or procuring* of our redemption by Jesus Christ having been discussed in the former treatise—the Fountain of Life—and the way and means by which Christ is *applied* to sinners in the foregoing part of this treatise, I now come to the general practical improvement of the whole ; which in the first place shall be by way of *exhortation*, to invite and persuade all men to come to Christ. In all the foregoing discourses, Christ has been represented in his *garments of salvation*, red in his apparel, prepared and offered to sinners as their all-sufficient and only remedy ; in those which follow, he will be represented in his *perfumed garments*, coming out of his *ivory palaces*, Psalm 45 : 8, to allure and draw all men unto him.

For a general head to this practical application, which will be large, I have chosen this scripture, "Come unto me, all ye that labor and are heavy-laden, and I will give you rest." These words are the voice of our Lord Jesus Christ himself, in which there is a vital, ravishing sound. It is your mercy to have such a joyful sound in your ears this day.

It is manifest that these words have an immediate

relation to the foregoing verse, wherein Christ opens his commission, and declares the fulness of his authority and saving power, and the impossibility of coming to God any other way. "All things are delivered unto me of my Father: and no man knoweth the Son, but the Father; neither knoweth any man the Father, save the Son, and he to whomsoever the Son will reveal him." Verse 27. The text is brought in proleptically to obviate the discouragements of any poor convinced and humbled soul who might thus object: "Lord, I am satisfied of the fulness of thy saving power, but greatly doubt whether ever I shall have the benefit thereof; for I see so much sin and guilt in myself, so great vileness and utter unworthiness, that I am overweighed and even sink under the burden of it; my soul is discouraged because of sin." This objection is here met: "Come unto me, all ye that labor and are heavy-laden;" let not the sense of your sin and misery drive you from your only remedy; be your sins never so many, and the sense and burden of them never so heavy, yet for all that, *come unto me:* you are the persons whom I invite and call. I came not to call the righteous, but sinners to repentance. In these words three things are especially remarkable.

1. The soul's spiritual distress and burden expressed in two very emphatical words, "Ye that *labor* and are *heavy-laden.*" The word which we translate *labor* signifies a laboring even to faintness and tiring, to the consumption and waste of the spirits; and the other word signifies a pressure by a burden that is too heavy to be borne, so that we even sink down under it.

Chrysostom and some others after him expound this burden of the legal *rites* and *ceremonies*, which were as a heavy burden indeed, such as neither they nor their fathers could bear. Under the task and burden of these legal observances, they did sweat and toil to obtain a righteousness to justify them before God, and all in vain. But others more properly expound it of the burden of sin in general, the corruption of nature and evils of practice which souls are convinced have brought them under the curse, and will bring them to hell, and they therefore labor and strive all that in them lies, by repentance and reformation, to clear themselves from it; but all in vain while they strive in their own strength. Such are they that are here called to come to Christ.

2. The invitation of burdened souls to Christ. " *Come unto me*, all ye that labor and are heavy-laden ;" believe in me, lean and rest your burdened souls upon me. I am able to ease all your burdens ; in me are that righteousness and peace which you seek in vain in all legal rites and ceremonies, or in your repentance, reformations, and duties ; they will give you no ease, will be no benefit to you, except you come unto me   Faith is often expressed under this idea, see John 6 : 37, and 7 : 37 ; and it is to be further noted, that *all* burdened souls are invited to come : "*All ye that labor*." Whatever your sin or guilt have been, whatever your fears or discouragements are. yet come, that is, believe in me

3. Here is the encouragement Christ gives to this duty, *I will give you rest;* I will refresh you, I will give you rest from your labor ; your consciences shall be pacified, your hearts at rest and quiet in the pardon, peace, and favor of God which I will procure for you by my death. But here it must be heedfully noted, that this promise of rest in Christ is not made to men simply as they are sinners, nor yet as they are burdened and heavy-laden sinners, but as they *come to Christ*, as they are believers. For let a man break his heart for sin, let him mourn as a dove and shed as many tears for sin, if it were possible, as ever there fell drops of rain upon the ground, yet if he come not to Christ by faith, his repentance shall not save him, nor all his sorrows bring him true rest.   Hence we draw these three propositions :

1. *Some souls are heavy-laden with the burdensome sense of sin.*

2. *All burdened souls are solemnly invited to come to Christ.*

3. *There is rest in Christ for all that come to him under the heavy burden of sin.*

Prop. 1. Some souls are heavy-laden with the burdensome sense of sin.

I do not say all are so, for "fools make a mock at sin." Prov. 14 : 9. It is so far from being burdensome to some, that it is a *sport* to them. Prov. 10 : 23. But when a man's eyes are opened to see the evil of sin, and the eternal misery that follows it—sin and hell being linked together with such strong chains as nothing but the blood of Christ can loose—then no burden is like that of sin : " A wounded spirit who can bear ?" Prov. 18 : 14.

I. Consider the efficacy of the law of God upon the consciences of men, when it comes in its spirituality and power to convince and humble the soul of a sinner of what inward trouble for sin is.

1. *The memory of sin long since committed is refreshed and revived as if it had been but yesterday.* There are fresh recognitions of sin long since forgotten. What was done in our youth is brought back again, and by a new impression of fear and horror set home upon the trembling conscience. "Thou writest bitter things against me, and makest me to possess the iniquities of my youth." Job 13 : 26. Conscience can call back the days that are past, and draw up a new charge upon the score of old sins. Gen. 42 : 21. All that ever we did is recorded and entered into the book of conscience, and now is the time to open that book when the Lord will convince and awaken sinners. We read in Job 14 : 17, of sealing up iniquities in a bag, which is an allusion to the *clerk of the assizes*, that takes all the indictments made against persons at the assizes, and seals them up in a bag in order to a trial. This is the first office and work of conscience ; upon which depend,

2. Its *accusations*. These accusations of conscience are terrible, who can stand before them? They are full, they are clear, and all of them referring to the approaching judgment of the great and terrible God. Conscience dives into all sin, secret as well as open, and into all the circumstances and aggravations of sin, as being committed against light, against mercy, against the strivings, warnings, and regrets of conscience; so that we may say of the efficacy of conscience as it is said, Psa. 19 : 6, of the influence of the *sun*, nothing is hid from the heat and power thereof. "Come," saith the woman of Samaria, "see a man which told me all things that ever I did." John 4 : 29. Christ convinced her but of one sin by his discourse, but conscience by that one brought in and charged all the rest upon her. And as the accusations of conscience are full, so they are clear and undeniable. A man becomes self-convinced, and there remains no shift, excuse, or plea to defend himself. A thousand witnesses cannot prove any point more clearly than one testimony of conscience. The man "was speechless," Matt. 22 : 12, a mute, muzzled, as the word signifies, by the clear testimony of his own conscience. These accusations are the second work of conscience, and they make way for,

3. The *sentence* and *condemnation* of conscience. And truly this is an insupportable burden. The condemnation of conscience is nothing else but its application of the condemning sentence of the law to a man's person. The law curseth every one that transgresseth it. Gal. 3 : 10. Conscience applies this curse to the guilty sinner. It sentences the sinner in God's name and authority, from which there is no appeal. The voice of conscience is the voice of God, and what it pronounces in God's name and authority he will confirm and ratify. "If our heart," our conscience, "condemn us, God is greater than our heart, and knoweth all things." 1 John, 3 : 20. This is that torment which no man can endure. See the effects of it in Cain, in

Judas, and in Spira; it is a real foretaste of hell-torments. This is that *worm that never dies.* Mark 9 : 44. As a worm in the body is bred of the corruption there, so the accusations and condemnations of conscience are bred in the soul by the corruption and guilt that are there. As the worm in the body preys and bites upon the tender, sensible, inward parts, so does conscience touch the very quick. This third effect or work to sentence and condemn makes way for conscience,

4. *To upbraid and reproach the sinner under his misery;* and this makes a man a very *terror to himself.* To be pitied in misery is some relief, but to be upbraided and reproached doubles our affliction. You know it was one of the aggravations of Christ's sufferings to be reproached by the tongues of his enemies while he hung in torments upon the cursed tree; but all the scoffs and reproaches, the bitter jeers and sarcasms in the world are nothing to those of a man's own conscience, which will cut to the very bone : Oh, when a man's conscience shall say to him in the day of trouble, as Reuben to his afflicted brethren, "Spake I not unto you, saying, Do not sin against the child; and ye would not hear? therefore, behold, also his blood is required." Gen. 42 : 22. So conscience, "Did I not warn you, threaten you, persuade you in time against these evils? but you would not hearken to me; therefore, behold, now you must suffer to all eternity for it. The wrath of God is kindled against thy soul for it; this is the fruit of thy own wilful madness and obstinacy. Now thou shalt know the price of sinning against God, against light and conscience." O this is terrible! Every bite of conscience makes a poor soul startle and cry in terror, O the worm; O the bitter foretaste of hell! A wounded spirit who can bear?

This is a fourth wound of conscience, and it makes way for a fifth; for here it is as in the pouring out of the vials, and the sounding of those woe-trumpets in the Revelation—one woe is past, and another cometh. After all these deadly blows of conscience upon the very heart of a sinner, comes another as dreadful as any that is yet named:

5. The fearful *expectation of wrath to come* which it begets in the soul of a guilty sinner. Of this you read, Heb. 10 : 27 : "A fearful looking for of judgment, and fiery indignation." And this makes the stoutest sinner faint and sink under the burden of sin ; for the tongue of man cannot declare what it is to lie down and rise with those fearful expectations. The case of such sinners is somewhat like that described in Deut. 28 : 65–67 : "The Lord shall give thee a trembling heart, and failing of eyes, and sorrow of mind : and thy life shall hang in doubt before thee ; and thou shalt fear day and night, and shalt have none assurance of thy life. In the morning thou shalt say, Would God it were even ! and at even thou shalt say, Would God it were morning ! for the fear of thy heart wherewith thou shalt fear, and for the sight of thine eyes which thou shalt see." Only in this it differs : in this scripture you have the terror of those described whose temporal life hangs in doubtful suspense, but in the persons I am speaking of it is a trembling under the apprehensions and expectations of the vengeance of eternal fire.

Believe it, friends, words cannot express what those poor creatures feel that lie down and rise up under these fears and alarms of conscience. Lord, what will become of me ? I am free among the dead, yea, among the damned. I hang by the frail thread of a momentary life, which will and must break shortly, and may break the next moment, over the everlasting burnings : no pleasant bread is to be eaten in these days, but what is like the bread of condemned men.

Thus you see what the burden of sin is when God makes it bear upon the consciences of men ; no burden of affliction is like it; losses of dearest relations, sorrows for an only son, are not so pungent and penetrating as these.

No creature enjoyments are pleasant under these inward troubles. In other troubles they may bring relief, but here they are nothing; the wound is too deep to be healed by any thing but the blood of Jesus Christ; conscience requires as much to satisfy it, as God requires to satisfy him. "When God is at peace with thee," saith conscience, "then will I be at peace with thee; but till then expect no rest nor peace from me. Pleasures and diversions shall never stop my mouth; go where thou wilt, I will follow thee like thy shadow; be thy portion in the world sweet as it may, I will drop gall and wormwood into thy cup, that thou shalt taste no sweetness in any thing till thou hast got thy pardon." These inward troubles for sin alienate the mind from all former pleasures and delights; there is no more taste or savor in them than in the white of an egg. Music is out of tune; all instruments jar and groan. Ornaments have no beauty: what heart hath a poor creature to deck that body in which dwells such a miserable soul; to feed and pamper the body that has been the soul's inducement to and instrument in sin, and must be its companion in everlasting misery?

These inward troubles for sin *awaken a dread of death* beyond what the soul ever saw in it before. Now it looks like the *king of terrors* indeed. You read of some that through fear of death are all their lifetime subject to bondage. Heb. 2 : 15. O what a lively comment is a soul in this case able to make upon such a text. They would not fear the pale horse, nor him that sits on him, though his name be *Death*, if it were not for what follows him, Rev. 6 : 8; but when they consider that hell follows, they tremble at the very name or thoughts of death.

Such is the nature of these inward troubles of spirit, that *they swallow up the sense of all outward troubles.* Alas, these are all lost in the deeps of soul-sorrows, as the little rivulets are in the vast sea. A small matter formerly would discompose a man; now ten thousand outward troubles are light, for saith he, "Why doth a living man complain?" Am I yet on this side of eternal burnings? O let me not complain then, whatever my condition be. Have I losses in the world, or pains in my body? alas, these are not to be named with the loss of God, and the feeling of his wrath and indignation for evermore." Thus you see what inward troubles for sin are.

II. But HOW ARE SOULS SUPPORTED UNDER SUCH TROUBLES? How is it that all who feel them do not sink under them? The answer is,

1. Though this be a very sad time with the soul—much like that of Adam between the breach of the first covenant and the first promise of Christ made to him—yet the souls that are thus heavy-laden do not sink, because *God has a most tender care over them* and regard to them; underneath them are the everlasting arms, and hence they sink not : were they left to grapple with these troubles in their own strength, they could never stand. But God takes care of these mourners, that their spirits do not fail before him, and the souls that he has made ; I mean those whom he is in this way preparing for and bringing to Christ.

2. The Lord is pleased to nourish still some *hope* in the soul, under the greatest fears and troubles of spirit. Though it have no comfort or joy, yet it hath some hope, and that keeps up the heart. The afflicted soul "putteth his mouth in the dust ; if so be there may be hope." Lam. 3 : 29. He saith, "It is good for a man to hope, and quietly to wait for the salvation of God." There are usually some glimmerings or dawnings of mercy through Christ in the midnight darkness of inward troubles. In hell there is no hope to enlighten the darkness, but it is not so upon earth.

3. The *experience of others* who have been in the same deeps of trouble, is of use to keep up the soul above water. The experience of another is of great use to prop up a desponding mind while as yet it has none of its own; and indeed, for the support of souls in such cases they were recorded. "For this cause I obtained mercy, that in me first Jesus Christ might show forth all long-suffering, for a pattern to them which should hereafter believe on him to life everlasting," 1 Tim. 1 : 16 ; for an encouraging *pattern*, an eminent precedent to all poor sinners that were to come after him, that none might absolutely despair of finding mercy through Christ. You know if a man be sick, and none can tell what the disease is, or say that they ever heard of such a disease before, it is most alarming; but if one and another come to the sick man's bedside and tell him, Sir, be not afraid, I have been in the very same case that you now are, and so have many more, and all did well at last ; this is half a cure to the sick man. So it is here a great support to hear the experience of other saints.

4. As the experiences of others support the soul under these burdens, so the riches of free grace through Jesus Christ *uphold* it. It is rich and abundant, plenteous redemption ; and it is free, and to the worst of sinners. Psalm 130 : 7, 8 ; Isaiah 1 : 18. Under these troubles it finds itself in the way and proper method of mercy, for so our text, a text that hath upheld many thousand drooping hearts, states it. All this gives hope and encouragement under trouble.

5. Though the state of the soul be sad and sinking, yet Jesus Christ usually makes haste in the extremity of trouble to relieve it by sweet and seasonable discoveries of his grace. It is with Christ as it was with Joseph, whose bowels yearned towards his brethren, and he was in pain till he had told them, "I am Joseph your brother." This is sweetly exhibited to us in that excellent parable of the

prodigal, Luke 15: when his father saw him, being yet a great way off, he ran, and fell upon his neck, and kissed him. Mercy runs nimbly to help when souls are ready to fall under the pressure of sin.

III. But *why does God make* THE BURDEN OF SIN LIE SO HEAVY UPON THE SOULS OF SINNERS? I answer,

1. He does it to *divorce their hearts* from sin, by giving them an experimental taste of the bitterness and evil there is in sin. Men's hearts are naturally glued with delight to their sinful courses; all the persuasions and arguments in the world are too weak to separate them from their beloved lusts. The morsels of sin they roll with delight under their tongues, and when such bitter potions as these are administered, what "sorrow, yea, what indignation" does it work in them. See 2 Cor. 7:11. This is the way, the best and most effectual way to separate the soul of a sinner from his lusts; for in these troubles conscience says, "Thy way and thy doings have procured these things unto thee; this is thy wickedness, because it is bitter, because it reacheth unto thy heart." Jer. 4:18.

2. The Lord does this to make *Christ most welcome* and desirable to the soul. Christ is not *sweet* till sin be made *bitter* to us. "They that be whole need not a physician, but they that are sick." Matt. 9:12. If once God wounds the heart of a sinner with the stinging sense of sin, then nothing is so precious, so necessary, so vehemently desired and panted for as Jesus Christ. O that I had Christ if I went in rags, if I fed upon no other food all my days but the bread and water of affliction! This is the language of a soul filled with the sense of the evil of sin.

3. The Lord does this to advance *the riches of his free grace* in the eyes of sinners. Grace never appears grace till sin appears to be sin. The deeper our sense of the evil of sin, the deeper will be our apprehensions of the

free grace of God in Christ. The louder our groans have been under the burden of sin, the louder will our acclamations and praises be for our salvation from it by Jesus Christ. To me, saith Paul, the chiefest of sinners, was this grace given. 1 Tim. 1 : 15, 16. Never does the grace of a prince so melt the heart of a traitor as when trial, sentence, and all preparations for his execution have passed before his unexpected pardon comes.

4. The Lord does this to *prevent relapses* into sin : " In that ye sorrowed after a godly sort, what carefulness it wrought !" 2 Cor. 7 : 11. The bird that is delivered out of the talons of the hawk trembles at the sight of him. After such a deliverance as this, should we again break his commandments ? Ezra 9 : 13, 14. Ask a penitent soul that has been in the deeps of sorrow for sin, Will you return to your former course of sin again? and it sounds in his ears as if you should ask him, Will you run into the fire? Will you go to the rack again ? O no, it has cost him dear already.

5. This the Lord does to make them both skilful and compassionate in *relieving others* that are under like inward troubles. None can speak so judiciously, so pertinently, so feelingly to another's case as he that has been in the same case himself ; this furnishes him with the tongue of the learned to speak a word in season to the weary soul ; by this means they are able to comfort others with the same comforts wherewith they themselves have been comforted of God. 2 Cor. 1 : 4.

Thus you have had a brief account what the burden of sin is, how souls are supported under that burden, and why the Lord causes sin to lie so heavy upon the souls of some sinners.

INFERENCE 1. Is there such a load and burden in sin? *What then was the burden that our Lord Jesus Christ felt and bore for us, upon whom lay the whole weight of our sins!* Isaiah 53 : 6. He has made the iniquities of us all to

meet on him. Our burden is heavy, but nothing to
Christ's. O there is a vast difference between that which
Christ bore and that which we bear. We feel but the
single weight of our own sins; Christ felt the whole
weight of all our sins. You do not feel the whole weight
there is in any one sin: alas, it would sink you if God
should let it bear in all its aggravations and effects upon
you. "If thou, Lord, shouldest mark iniquities, O Lord,
who shall stand?" Psalm 130 : 3. You would sink presently; you can no more stand under it than under the
weight of a mighty mountain. But Christ bore all the
burden upon himself. His understanding was deep and
large; he knew the extent of its evil, which we do not.
We have many reliefs and helps under our burden, he
had done. We have friends to counsel, comfort, and pity
us; all his friends forsook him and fled in the day of his
trouble. We have comforts from heaven; he had frowns
from heaven: "My God, my God," saith he in that doleful day, "why hast thou forsaken me?" There is no comparison between our load and Christ's.

2. If there be such a burden in sin, *then certainly sinners will pay dear for all the pleasure they find in sin in the
days of their vanity.* What one says of crafty counsels
we may say of all sins: "Though they seem pleasant in
their first appearance, they will be found sad in the
event;" they are honey in the mouth, but the gall of asps
in the belly; they tickle the fancy, but rend the conscience.
O sinner, thy mirth will be turned into mourning, as sure
as thou livest: that vain and frothy breast of thine shall
be wounded: thou shalt feel the sting and pain as well
as relish the sweet and pleasure of sin. O that thou
wouldst but give thyself the leisure seriously to ponder
these scriptures: Prov. 20 : 17 ; and 23 : 31, 32 ; Job
20 : 12, 13, 14 ; James 1 : 15 ; Rom. 6 : 21 ; methinks they
should have the same effect as the handwriting upon the
wall had upon the jovial king in the height of a frolic.

Dan. 5 : 5. Reason thus with thine own heart, and thou
wilt find the conclusion unavoidable : Either I shall repent
for sin, or I shall not ; if I do not, then must I howl under
the wrath of God for sin, in the lowest hell for evermore ;
if I do, then by what I have now read of the throbs and
wounds of conscience, I see what this heart of mine, this
vain heart of mine, must feel in this world. O how much
wiser was the choice that Moses made, the worst of sufferings rather than the best of sin, the pleasures of sin
which are but for a season ! Heb. 11 : 25.

3. Is there such a burden in sin, *then the most tender
compassion is due to souls afflicted and heavy-laden with sin.*
Their condition cries for pity, whatever their tongues do ;
they seem to call upon you, as Job upon his friends,
"Have pity upon me, have pity upon me, O ye my friends;
for the hand of God hath touched me." Job 19 : 21.
And Oh, let all that have felt the wounds and anguish of
an afflicted conscience themselves, learn from their own
experience tenderly to pity and help others. "Ye which
are spiritual, restore such a one in the spirit of meekness,
considering thyself." Gal. 6 : 1. Israel were commanded
to be kind to strangers, for says God, you know the
heart of a stranger. And surely, if any case in the world
require help, pity, and all compassionate tenderness, this
does ; and yet how do some slight the spiritual troubles of
others ! Parents slight them in their own children, masters in their servants ; the more brutish and wicked they.
O had you but felt yourselves what they feel, you would
never treat them as you do. But let this comfort such
poor creatures, Christ knows their sorrows, and will pity
and help them ; yea, he felt them himself, that he might
have compassion upon you. If men will not pity you,
God will ; if men are so cruel as to persecute him whom
God hath smitten, God will pour balm into the wounds
that sin has made : if they will not be concerned about
your troubles, except it be to aggravate them, God will

not serve you so. But certainly you that have passed through the same difficulties cannot be without compassion to them that are now grappling with them. .

4. *How inexpressibly dreadful is the state of the damned, who must bear the burden of all their sins upon themselves, without relief or hope of deliverance!* "Where their worm dieth not, and the fire is not quenched." Mark 9 : 44. O, if sin upon the soul that is coming to Christ for deliverance be so burdensome, what is it upon the soul that is shut out from Christ and all hope of deliverance for ever? For ponder these differences between these two burdens :

No soul is so *capacious* now to take in the fulness of the evil and misery of sin, as they are who are gone down to the place of torments. Even as the joys of God's face above are unknown to them that have the foretastes and first-fruits of them here by faith, so the misery of the damned is unknown even to them that have in their conscience now the bitterest taste of sin ; as we have the visions of heaven, so we have the visions of hell also, but through a glass darkly.

No burden of sin presses *continually* upon the soul here as it does there. Afflicted souls on earth have intermissions, but in hell there are no lucid intervals, the wrath of God there is still flowing. Isa. 30 : 33.

No burden of sin lies here *so long* as on the damned, who must bear it : our troubles about sin are but short, though they should run parallel with the line of life ; but the troubles of the damned are parallel with the endless line of eternity.

Under these troubles the soul hath hope, but there all hope is cut off. The gospel is full of hope, it breathes nothing but hope to sinners that are moving Christ-ward under their troubles ; but in hell the pangs of desperation rend their consciences for ever. So that, upon all accounts, the state of the damned is inexpressibly dreadful.

5. *If the burden of sin be so heavy, how sweet must the*

pardon of sin be to a sin-burdened soul: Is it a refreshment to a prisoner to have his chains knocked off; a comfort to a debtor to have his debts paid, and his obligations cancelled? What joy must it be to a sin-burdened soul to hear the voice of pardon and peace in his trembling conscience. Is the light of the morning pleasant to a man after a weary, tiresome night; the spring of the year pleasant after a tedious winter? They are nothing so sweet as the favor, peace, and pardon of God to a soul that has been long restless and anxious under the terrors and fears of conscience. For though after pardon and peace a man remembers sin still, yet it is as one that remembers the dangerous pits and deep waters from which he has been wonderfully delivered. O the inconceivable sweetness of a pardon! Who can read it without tears of joy? Are we glad when the grinding pain of the stone, or racking fits of the colic, are over? And shall we not be transported when the accusations and condemnations of conscience are over? Tongue cannot express what these things are; the joy is something that no words can convey to the understanding of another that never felt the anguish of sin.

6. *In how sad a case are those that never felt any burden in sin, that never were kept waking and restless one night for sin.* There is a *burdened* conscience, and there is a *benumbed* conscience. The first is more painful, but the last more dangerous. O it is a fearful blow of God upon a man's soul, to strike it senseless and stupid, so that though mountains of guilt lie upon it, it feels no pain or pressure; and this is so much more sad, because it incapacitates the soul for Christ, and is a presage and forerunner of hell. It would grieve the heart of a man to see a delirious person, in the rage and height of a fever, laugh at those that are weeping for him, call them fools, and tell them he is as well as any of them: much so is the case of many thousand souls; the God of mercy pity them.

I shall further improve the subject by giving some COUNSEL to souls that are weary and heavy-laden with the burden of sin, in order to their obtaining true rest and peace. And,

(1.) *Satisfy not yourself in fruitless complaints to men.* Many do so, but they are never the nearer to Christ. I grant it is lawful in spiritual distresses to complain to men, yea, and it is a great mercy if we have any near us in times of trouble who are judicious, tender, and faithful, into whose bosoms we may pour our sorrows ; but to rest in this short of Christ, is no better than a snare of the devil to destroy us. Is there not a God to go to in trouble ? The best of men, in the neglect of Christ, are but physicians of no value. Be wise and cautious in your choice of Christian friends, to whom you open your complaints ; some are not clear themselves in the doctrine of Christ and faith, others are of a dark and troubled spirit as you are, and will but entangle you more. "As for me, is my complaint to man ? and if it were so, why should not my spirit be troubled ?" Job 21 : 4. One hour between Christ and thy soul in secret will do more for thy true relief, than all other counsellors and comforters can do.

(2.) *Beware of a false peace, which is more dangerous than your trouble for sin can be.* Many men are afraid of their troubles, but I think they have more cause to fear their peace. There is a twofold peace that ruins most men— peace in sin, and peace with sin. O how glad are some persons when their troubles are gone ; but I dare not rejoice with them. It is like him that rejoices that his ague is gone when it has left him in a deep consumption. You are rid of your troubles, but God knows how you have left them ; your wounds are skinned over, better they were kept open. Surely they have much to answer for that help on these delusions, healing the hurt of souls slightly by "crying, Peace, peace, when there is no peace."

The false peace you beget in them will be a real trouble to yourselves in the issue. Jer. 6 : 14.

(3.) *Let all that are under inward troubles for sin take heed of drawing desperate conclusions against themselves and the final state of their own souls.* Though your case be sad, it is not desperate ; though the night be troublesome and tedious, keep on the way to Christ, and light will spring up. To mourn for sin is your duty ; to conclude there is no hope for you in Christ, is your sin. You have wronged God enough already, do not add a further and greater abuse to all the rest by an absolute despair of mercy. It was your sin formerly to presume beyond any promise ; it is your sin now to despair against many commands. I would say as the apostle in another case, I would not have you mourn as men that have no hope : your condition is sad, but it is not as once it was. You were once full of sin and void of sense ; now you have the sense of sin, which is no small mercy. You were once quite out of the way and method of mercy ; now you are in that very path where mercy meets the elect of God. Keep hope, therefore, at the bottom of all your troubles.

(4.) *Observe whether your troubles for sin produce such fruits and effects in your soul as theirs do which end at last in Christ and everlasting peace.* One that is truly burdened with sin will not allow himself to live in the secret practice of sin ; either your trouble will put an end to your course of sinning, or your sinning will put an end to your troubles. Consult 2 Cor. 7 : 11. True sorrow for sin will give you very low and vile thoughts of yourself : as you were covered with *pride* before, so you will be covered with *shame* after God has convinced and humbled you. Rom. 6 : 21. A soul really burdened with sin will never stand in his own justification before God, nor extenuate it in his confessions to him. Psa. 51 : 3, 4. The burden of sin will make all other burdens of affliction seem light. Lam. 3 : 22 ; Micah 7 : 9. The more you feel sin, the less

you feel affliction. A soul truly burdened for sin will take
no hearty joy or comfort in any outward enjoyment of this
world, till Christ come and speak peace to the soul. Lam.
3 : 28. Just so the soul sits alone and keeps silence;
merry company is a burden, and music is but howling
to him.

(5.) *Beware of those things that make your troubles longer
than they ought to be.* There are errors and mistakes that
hold poor souls much longer in their fears and terrors than
else they might be. One of these is ignorance of the nature of saving faith, and the necessity of it. Till you come
to believe, you cannot have peace; and while you mistake
the nature, or apprehend not the necessity of faith, you
are not likely to find the path of peace. Another error is
laboring to heal the wounds that the law has made upon
your conscience by a more strict obedience to it for the
future in the neglect of Christ and his righteousness. But
the last and principal counsel is,

(6.) *Hasten to Christ by faith, and you shall find rest;*
and till then all the world cannot give you rest. The
sooner you transact with Christ in the way of faith, the
sooner you shall be at peace and enter into his rest; for
those that believe do now enter into rest. You may labor
and strive, look this way and that, but all in vain; Christ
and peace come together. No sooner do you come to
him, roll your burden on him, and receive him as he offers
himself, but the soul feels itself eased on a sudden:
"being justified by faith, we have peace with God."
Rom. 5 : 1.

PROP. 2. SIN-BURDENED SOULS ARE SOLEMNLY INVITED TO
COME TO CHRIST.

This point sounds sweetly in the ear of a distressed
sinner; it is the most joyful voice that ever the soul heard;
the voice of blessing from mount Gerizim, the ravishing
voice from mount Zion, "Ye are come to Jesus the Mediator." It will lead me to show what it is to come to

Christ; how Christ invites men to come to him; and why his invitation is directed to burdened souls.

I. We inquire WHAT IT IS to come to Christ. In general, to come to Christ is a phrase of the same import with believing in Christ. "He that cometh to me shall never hunger; and he that believeth on me shall never thirst." John 6 : 35. Coming to Christ is believing in Christ; and believing in Christ is coming to Christ. The expressions are synonymous, importing the self-same thing, only that in *coming* to Christ there are many rich and excellent things hinted to us which no other word can so aptly convey to our minds.

1. It hints to us that the souls of convinced and burdened sinners not only discern the *reality* of Christ, or that he is, but also the necessity of *applying* Christ, and that their eternal life is in their union with him; for it is most certain that the object of faith must be determinate and fixed; the soul must believe that Christ is, or there can be no motions of the soul after him: all coming presupposes a fixed object to which we come. "He that cometh to God must believe that God is." Heb. 11 : 6. Take away this, and all motions after Christ presently stop. No wonder then that souls, in their first motions to Christ, find themselves clogged with so many atheistical temptations, shaking their assent to the truth of the gospel at the very root and foundation of it; but they that truly come to Christ, see that *he is*, and that their life and happiness lie in their union with him, else they would never come to him upon such terms as they do.

2. Coming to Christ implies *despair* of salvation any other way. The way of faith is a supernatural way, and souls will not attempt it until they have tried all natural ways to help and save themselves, and find it all in vain; therefore the text describes these comers to Christ as weary persons that have been laboring and striving all other ways for rest, but can find none; and so are con-

strained to relinquish all their fond expectations of salvation in any other way, and come to Christ as their last and only remedy.

3. Coming to Christ shows an *almighty power* acting upon the soul. "No man can come to me, except the Father, which hath sent me, draw him." John 6 : 44. None come to Christ by a pure unaided natural power of their own. It was not a stranger thing for Peter to come to Christ walking upon the waves of the sea, than for his or any man's soul to come to Christ in the way of faith.

4. Coming to Christ shows *the voluntariness* of the soul in its motion to Christ. True, there is no coming without the Father's drawing ; but that drawing has nothing of compulsion in it ; it does not destroy, but powerfully and with an overcoming sweetness persuades the will. It is not forced or driven, but it *comes;* being made willing in the day of God's power. Psalm 110 : 3. Ask a poor distressed sinner in that season, Are you willing to come to Christ? "O rather than live ! life is not so necessary as Christ is. O with all my heart : ten thousand worlds for Jesus Christ, if he could be purchased, were nothing to his value in mine eyes !" The soul's motion to Christ is free and voluntary, it is *coming.*

5. It implies that the soul is to rest in no duties or ordinances which are only means by which we come to Christ, but is to come by them or through them to Jesus Christ, and take up its rest *in him only.* No duties, no reformations, no ordinances of God, however excellent in themselves, and however necessary in their proper place, can give rest to the weary and heavy-laden soul ; it cannot centre in any of them, and you may see it cannot, because it still gravitates and inclines to another thing, even Christ, and cannot terminate its motion till it be come to him. Christ is the object to which a believer moves ; and therefore he cannot sit down by the way and be satisfied, as if he were at his journey's end. Ordi-

nances and duties are means to bring us to Christ, but are not to be to any man instead of Christ.

6. Coming to Christ implies a hope or *expectation from Christ* in the coming soul. If he has no hope, why does he move forward? As well sit still and resolve to perish where he is, as come to Christ, if there is no ground to expect salvation by him. Hope is the spring of action; if you cut off hope, you hinder faith; a sinner cannot move to Christ except he be satisfied at least of the possibility of mercy and salvation by him. Hence it is that when comers to Christ are struggling with doubts and fears of the issue, the Lord is pleased to enliven their faint hopes by setting home such scriptures as these: "Him that cometh to me I will in no wise cast out." John 6 : 37. "He is able to save to the uttermost them that come unto God by him." Heb. 7 : 25. This gives life to hope, and hope animates to exertion.

7. Coming to Christ for rest implies that believers have and lawfully may have an eye to *their own happiness* in closing with the Lord Jesus Christ. The poor soul comes for rest; it comes for salvation; its eye and aim are upon it; and this aim of the soul at its own good is sanctioned by the expression of Christ, "Ye will not come unto me, that ye might have life." John 5 : 40. If Christ blame them for not coming to him that they might have life, surely he would not have blamed them had they come to him for life.

8. But the principal thing implied in coming to Christ is the *all-sufficiency of Christ* to answer the needs and wants of distressed souls, and their betaking themselves accordingly to him only for relief, being content to come to Christ for whatever they need, and live upon the fulness that is in him. If there were not an all-sufficiency in Christ, no soul would come to him; for this is the very ground upon which men come. Heb. 7 : 25. "He is able to save them to the uttermost that come to God by him :"

9*

to the uttermost; in the greatest difficulties and dangers. He has a fulness of saving power, and this encourages souls to come to him. One beggar does not wait at the door of another, but all at the doors of those they conceive able to relieve them. And as this implies the fulness of Christ as our Saviour, so it must intimate the emptiness and humility of the soul as a comer to him. This is called submission. Rom. 10 : 3. Proud nature must be deeply distressed, humbled, and moulded into another temper, before it will be persuaded to live upon these terms, to come to Christ for every thing it wants, to live upon Christ's fulness in the way of grace and favor, and have no stock of its own to live upon. O this may seem hard, but it is the way of faith.

II. Let us see HOW Christ invites men to come to him. And you will find the means employed in this work are either *internal* and *principal*, namely, the Spirit of God, who is Christ's vicegerent, and comes to us in his name and room to persuade us to believe, John 15 : 26; or *external*, namely, the preaching of the gospel by commissioned ambassadors, who *in Christ's stead beseech men to be reconciled to God*, to come to Christ by faith in order to their reconciliation and peace with him. But all means and instruments employed in this work of bringing men to Christ entirely depend upon the blessing and concurrence of the Spirit of God, without whom they avail nothing. How long may ministers preach before one soul comes to Christ, except the Spirit coöperate in that work. Now as to the manner in which men are persuaded and their wills wrought upon by the Holy Spirit to come to Christ, I observe,

1. There is an *illustrating work* of the Spirit upon the minds of sinners, opening their eyes to see their danger and misery. Till these be discovered, no man stirs from his place. It is sense of danger that rouses the secure sinner, distresses him, and makes him look about for de-

liverance, crying, *What shall I do to be saved?* And it is
the discovery of Christ's ability to save which is the
ground and reason, as was observed above, of its motion to Christ. Hence, seeing the Son is joined with
believing or coming to him in John 6 : 40.

2. There is the *authoritative call* or commanding voice
of the Spirit in the word ; a voice that is full of majesty
and power. "This is his commandment, that we should
believe on the name of his Son Jesus Christ." 1 John
3 : 23. This call of the Spirit to come to Christ removes
one great obstacle, the fear of presumption, out of the
soul's way to Christ, and instead of presumption in coming, makes it rebellion and inexcusable obstinacy to refuse
to come. This answers all pleas against coming to Christ
arising from our unworthiness and deep guilt, and mightily
encourages the soul to come to Christ, whatever it has
been or done.

3. There are soul-encouraging *promises* to all that come
to Christ in obedience to the command. Such is that in
my text, "I will give you rest ;" and that in John 6 : 37,
"Him that cometh to me I will in no wise cast out." And
these breathe life and encouragement into poor souls that
fear and are daunted through their own unworthiness.

4. There are *dreadful threatenings* denounced by the
Spirit in the word against all that refuse or neglect to
come to Christ, which are of great use to engage and
quicken souls in their way to Christ. "He that believeth
not shall be damned ;" shall "die in his sins." Mark
16 : 16 ; John 8 : 24. "The wrath of God abideth on
him." John 3 : 36. Which is as if the Lord had said,
Sinners, be not undecided in coming to Christ ; do not
be always treating and never resolving ; for if there be
justice in heaven or fire in hell, every soul that comes not
to Christ must perish to all eternity. Upon your own
heads be the destruction of your own souls for ever if you
will not come to him.

5. There are *moving examples* set before souls in the word to prevail with them to come, alluring and encouraging examples of such as have come to Christ under the deepest guilt and discouragement, and yet found mercy. "This is a faithful saying, and worthy of all acceptation, that Jesus Christ came into the world to save sinners; of whom I am chief. Howbeit for this cause I obtained mercy, that in me first Jesus Christ might show forth all long-suffering, for a pattern to them which should hereafter believe on him to life everlasting." 1 Tim. 1 : 15, 16. Who would not come to Christ after such an example as this? And if this will not prevail, there are dreadful examples recorded setting before us the miserable condition of such as refuse the calls to come to Christ. "By which also he went and preached unto the spirits in prison; which sometime were disobedient, when once the long-suffering of God waited in the days of Noah." 1 Peter 3 : 19, 20. The meaning is, the sinners that lived before the flood but are now in hell had the offers of grace, but despised them, and now lie for their disobedience in prison under the wrath of God in the lowest hell.

6. There is an effectual *persuading*, overcoming, and victorious work of the Spirit upon the hearts and wills of sinners under which they come to Jesus Christ. Of this I have spoken at large before in the *fourth* chapter, and therefore shall not add any thing more here. Such is the way in which souls are prevailed upon to come to Jesus Christ.

III. If you inquire why Christ makes his invitations TO WEARY AND HEAVY-LADEN SOULS, and to no other, the answer is, briefly,

1. Because in so doing he follows the commission received from the Father: "The Spirit of the Lord God is upon me; because he hath anointed me to preach good tidings unto the meek; he hath sent me to bind up the broken-hearted, to proclaim liberty to the captives, and the opening of the prison to them that are bound." Isa. 61 : 1

You see here how Christ's commission directs him: his Father sent him to poor broken-hearted sinners. "He came not to call the righteous, but sinners to repentance." Matt. 9 : 13.

2. The order of the Spirit's work in bringing men to Christ, shows us to whom the invitation and offers of grace in Christ are to be made ; for none are convinced of righteousness, that is, of the complete and perfect righteousness in Christ for their justification, until first they are convinced of sin; and consequently no man comes to Christ by faith till convictions of sin have awakened and distressed him. John 16 : 8–10. This being the order of the Spirit's operation, the same order must be observed in gospel offers and invitations.

3. It behooves Christ to provide for his own glory as well as for our safety ; and not to expose one to secure the other, but to save us in the way which will bring him most honor and praise. And certainly such a way is this : first convincing and humbling the souls of men, and then bringing them to rest in himself.

Let those that never saw or felt the evil of sin be told of rest, peace, and pardon in Christ, and they will but despise it as of no value. "The whole need not a physician, but they that are sick." Luke 5 : 31. Tell a man that thinks himself sound and whole to go to a physician, and he will but laugh at the suggestion ; but if the same man feel an acute disease, and is made to groan under strong pain, if he come to know what sick days and restless nights are, and to apprehend his life to be in imminent danger, then messengers are sent one after another in post-haste to the physician ; he begs him with tears to do what in him lies for his relief ; he thankfully takes the bitterest medicine, and praises the care and skill of his physician with tears of joy. Thus the patient's safety and the physician's honor are both secured. So is it in this method of grace.

INFERENCE 1. If sin-burdened souls are solemnly invited to come to Christ, *then whatever guilt lies upon the conscience of a poor humbled sinner, it is no presumption, but his duty, to come to Christ, notwithstanding his vileness and great unworthiness.*

Let it be observed how happily that word *all* is inserted in Christ's invitation for the encouragement of sinners: "Come unto me, *all* ye that labor." Let no broken-hearted sinner exclude himself when he is not by me excluded from mercy: my grace is my own, I may bestow it where I will, and upon whom I will. It is not I, but Satan that shuts up my mercy from humbled souls that are made willing to come unto me; he calls that your presumption, which my invitation makes your duty.

OBJECTION 1. But I fear my case is excepted by Christ himself in Matt. 12 : 31, where blasphemy against the Holy Ghost is exempted from pardon: I have had many blasphemous thoughts injected into my soul.

ANSWER. Art thou a burdened and heavy-laden soul? If so, thy case is not in that or any other scripture exempted from mercy, for the unpardonable sin is always found in an obdurate heart; as that sin finds no pardon with God, so neither is it followed with contrition and sorrow in the soul that commits it.

OBJECTION 2. But if I am not guilty of that sin, I am certainly guilty of many great and heinous abominations too great for me to expect mercy, and therefore I dare not go to Christ.

ANSWER. The greater your sins have been, the more need you have to go to Jesus Christ. Let not a *motive* to go to Christ be made an *obstacle* in your way to him. Great sinners are expressly called, Isa. 1 : 18; great sinners have come to Christ and found mercy, 1 Cor. 6 : 11; and it is a high reproach and dishonor to the blood of Christ and the mercy of God, which flows so freely through him, to object the greatness of sin to either of them. Certainly you have not sinned beyond the *extent of mercy*, or beyond the *efficacy of the blood of Christ;* but pardon and peace may be had, if you will thus come to Christ for it.

OBJECTION 3. O, but it is now too late; I have had many thousand calls, and refused them; many purposes in my heart to go to Christ, and quenched them; my time therefore is past, and now it is to no purpose.

ANSWER. If the time of grace be past and God intends no mercy for thee, how is it that thy soul is now filled with trouble and distress for sin? Is this the frame of a man's heart that is past hope? Do such signs as these appear in men that are hopeless? Besides, the time of grace is a *secret* hid in the breast of God, but coming to Christ is a *duty* plainly revealed. And why will you object a thing that is secret and uncertain against a duty that is so plain and evident? Nor do you yourselves believe what you object; for at the same time that you say your season is over and it is too late, you are notwithstanding found repenting, mourning, praying, and striving to come to Christ. Certainly if you knew it were too late, you would not be found laboring in the use of means. Go on, therefore, and the Lord be with you. It is not presumption, but obedience to come when Christ calls, as he here doth: "Come unto me, all ye that labor and are heavy-laden."

2. Hence it follows *that none have cause to be troubled when God makes the souls of their friends sick with the sense of sin.* It was the saying of Hieron to Sabinian, Nothing makes my heart sadder than that nothing can make my heart sad. It is matter of joy to all that rightly understand the matter when God smites the heart of any man with the sense of sin: of such sickness it may be said, "This sickness is not unto death, but for the glory of God." Yet how do many carnal relations lament and bewail this as a misery, as an undoing to their friends and acquaintances; as if then they must be reckoned lost, and never till then

when Christ is finding and saving them. Oh, if your hearts were spiritual and wise, their groans for sin would be as music in your ears. When they go alone to bewail their sin, you would go alone also to bless God for the mercy that ever you should live to such a happy day: you would say, Now is my friend in the blessed pangs of the new birth; now is he in the very way of mercy— never in so hopeful a condition as now. I had rather he should groan now at the feet of Christ, than groan hereafter under the wrath of God for ever. Oh, parents, beware, as you love the souls of your children, that you do not damp and discourage them, tempt or threaten them, divert or hinder them in such cases as this, lest you bring the *blood* of their *souls* upon your own heads.

3. It also follows *that those to whom sin was never any burden, are not yet come to Christ, nor have any interest in him.* We may as well suppose a child to be born without pangs, as a soul to be born again and united to Christ without any sense or sorrow for sin. I know many have great *alarms of conscience* that never were made duly sensible of the evil of sin; many are afraid of *burning* that never were afraid of *sinning.* Slight and transient troubles some have had, but they vanished like the early cloud or morning dew. Few men are without checks of conscience at one time or other; but instead of going to the closet, they run to the *ale-house* or *tavern* for cure. If their sorrow for sin had been right, nothing but the sprinkling of the blood of Christ could have appeased their consciences. Heb. 10 : 22. How should the consideration of this rend the hearts of such persons. Methinks, reader, if this be thy case, it should send thee away with an aching heart; thou hast not yet tasted the bitterness of sin, and if thou do not, thou shalt never taste the sweetness of Christ, his pardon and peace.

4. *How great a mercy is it for sin-burdened souls to be within the sound and call of Christ in the gospel.* There are

many thousands in pagan and popish parts of the world that labor under distress of conscience, but have no knowledge of relief, no such means of peace and comfort as we have that live within the joyful sound of the gospel. If the conscience of a papist be burdened with guilt, all the relief he has is to afflict his body in order to quiet his soul; a penance or pilgrimage is all the relief they have. If a pagan be in trouble for sin, he has no knowledge of Christ or of a satisfaction made by him; he asks, Shall I give my *first-born* for my transgression, the *fruit of my body* for the sin of my soul? The damned endure the terrible blows and wounds of conscience for sin, they roar under that terrible lash, but no voice of peace or pardon is heard among them. It is not, "Come unto me, ye that labor and are heavy-laden," but, "Depart from me, ye cursed."

Blessed are your ears, for you hear the voice of peace; you are come to Jesus the Mediator, and to the blood of sprinkling. Oh, you can never set a due value upon this privilege.

5. *How sweet and unspeakably relieving is the closing of a burdened soul with Jesus Christ by faith. It is rest to the weary soul.*

Soul troubles are wasting troubles; the pains of a distressed conscience are the most acute pains. A poor soul would fain be at rest, but knows not where; he tries this duty and that, but finds none. At last, in a way of believing, he casts himself with his burden of guilt and fear upon Christ, and there is the rest his soul desired. Christ and rest come together; till faith bring you to the bosom of Jesus you can find no true rest; the soul is rolling and tossing, sick and weary, upon the billows of its own guilt and fears. Now the soul is come, like a ship tossed with storms and tempests, out of a raging ocean into the quiet harbor; or like a *lost sheep*, that hath been wandering in weariness, hunger, and danger, into the fold. Is a soft bed in a quiet chamber sweet to one that is spent and tired with travel? Is the sight of a shore sweet to the shipwrecked mariner who looked for nothing but death? Much more sweet is Christ to a soul that comes to him pressed in conscience and broken in spirit under the sinking weight of sin.

How did they of old rejoice, after a long and dangerous voyage, to see Italy again; crying, with loud and united voices, which made the very heavens ring again, Italy! Italy! But no shore is so sweet to the weather-beaten passenger as Christ is to a broken-hearted sinner: this brings the soul to a sweet repose. "We which have believed do enter into rest." Heb. 4 : 3. And this endears the way of faith to their souls ever after.

6. *Learn hence the usefulness of the law to bring souls to Jesus Christ.* It is utterly useless as a covenant to justify us, but exceedingly useful to convince and humble us; it cannot relieve nor ease us, but it can and does awaken and rouse us. It is a mirror to show us the face of sin, and till we have seen that, we cannot see the face of Jesus Christ.

The law, like the fiery serpent, stings and torments the conscience; this drives us to the Lord Jesus, lifted up in the gospel, like the brazen serpent in the wilderness, to heal us. The use of the law is to make us feel our sickness; this makes us look out for a physician: "I was alive without the law once; but when the commandment came, sin revived, and I died." Rom. 7 : 9. The hard, proud hearts of men require such a hammer to break them to pieces.

7. *It is the immediate duty of weary and heavy-laden sinners to come to Christ by faith, and not stand off from Christ, or delay to accept him upon any terms whatsoever.*

Christ invites and commands such to come unto him; it is therefore your sin to neglect, draw back, or defer, whatever seeming reasons and pretences there may be to the contrary. When the *jailer* was brought to distress, that made him cry, "Sirs, what must I do to be saved?" the counsel the apostles gave him was, "Believe on the Lord Jesus Christ, and thou shalt be saved." Acts 16 : 30, 31. And for your encouragement, know that he who calls you to come, knows your burden, what your sins have been and troubles are, yet he calls you : if your sin hinder not Christ from *calling*, neither should it hinder you from *coming*. He that calls you is able to ease you, "to save to the uttermost all that come to God by him." Heb. 7 : 25. Whatever fulness of sin be in you, there is a greater fulness of saving power in Christ. He that calls you to come, never yet rejected any poor burdened soul that came to him ; and hath said he never will. "Him that cometh to me I will in no wise cast out." John 6 : 37. Fear not, therefore ; he will not begin with thee, or make thee the first instance and example of the feared rejection.

Bethink thyself, what wilt thou do, and whither wilt thou go, if not to Jesus Christ? Nothing shall ease or relieve thee till thou dost come to him. Thou art under a happy necessity to go to him ; with him only is found rest for the weary soul.

PROP. 3. THERE IS REST IN CHRIST FOR ALL THAT COME UNTO HIM UNDER THE HEAVY BURDEN OF SIN.

Rest is a sweet word to a weary soul ; all seek it, but none but believers find it. "We which have believed," saith the apostle, "do enter into rest." Heb. 4 : 3. "He doth not say they *shall*, but they *do* enter into rest ; noting their spiritual rest to be already begun by faith on earth in the tranquillity of conscience, and to be consummated in heaven in the full enjoyment of God." There is a sweet calm upon the troubled soul after believing, an ease or rest of the mind, which is an unspeakable mercy to a poor weary soul. Christ is to it as the ark was to the dove when she wandered over the watery world and found no place to rest the sole of her foot. Faith centres the unquiet spirit of man in Christ; brings it to repose itself and its burden on him. It is the soul's dropping anchor in a storm, which stays and settles it.

The great debate which cost so many anxious thoughts is now issued in this resolution: I will venture my all upon Christ; let him do with me as seemeth him good. It was impossible for the soul to find rest while it knew not how to be secure from the wrath to come; but when all is embarked in Christ for eternity, and the soul fully resolved to lean upon him and to trust to him, it feels the beginning of eternal rest in itself: it finds a heavy burden unloaded from its shoulders; it is come, as it were, into a new world. The word *rest*, in this place, denotes—and is so rendered by some—a *recreation;* it is restored, renewed, and recreated, as it were, by the sweet repose it hath upon Christ. Believers, know that faith is the sweetest recreation you can take. Others seek to divert their troubles by sinful recreations, vain company, and the like; but they little know the recreation and sweet restoring rest that faith gives the soul. You find in Christ what they seek in vain in the world. Believing is the highest recreation known in this world.

But to prevent mistakes three *cautions* need to be premised, lest we stumble at the threshold, and so lose our way all along afterwards.

CAUTION 1. *You are not to think that all the soul's fears, troubles, and sorrows are at an end as soon as it is come to Christ by faith.* They will have many troubles in the world after that, it may be more than ever they had in their lives. They will be infested with many temptations; the assaults of Satan may be more violent upon their souls than ever. They will not at once be wholly freed from sin, nor from inward trouble and grief of soul about sin; that rest remains for the people of God.

CAUTION 2. *We must not think all believers do immediately enter into the full, actual sense of rest and comfort, but they presently enter into the* STATE *of rest.* "Being justified by faith, we have peace with God," Rom. 5 : 1 ; that is, we enter into the state of peace immediately. "Light is sown for the righteous, and gladness for the upright in heart." Psalm 97 : 11. He is a rich man that has a thousand acres of corn in the ground, as well as he that has so much in his barn, or its value in his purse. They have rest and peace in the seed of it, when they have it not in the fruit ; they have rest in the promise, when they have it not in possession. He is a rich man that hath good bonds and bills for a great sum of money, if he have not twelve pence in his pocket. All believers have rest and peace granted them under God's own hand, in many promises which faith brings them under ; and we know that the truth and faithfulness of God stand engaged to make good to them every line and word of the promise. So that though they have not a full and clear actual sense and feeling of rest, they are, nevertheless, by faith come into the state of rest.

CAUTION 3. *We must not think that faith itself is the soul's rest, it is only the means of it.* We cannot find rest in any work or duty of our own, but we may find it in Christ, whom faith apprehends for justification and salvation.

Having thus guarded the point against misapprehensions, I proceed to show how our coming to Christ by faith brings us to rest in him. And here let us consider what those things are that burden, grieve, and disquiet the soul before its coming to Christ ; and how it is relieved by coming to the Lord Jesus.

I. Some things that BURDEN THE SOUL before it comes to Christ.

1. One principal ground of trouble is *the guilt of sin upon the conscience*, of which I spoke in the former point. The curse of the law lies heavy upon the soul, so heavy that nothing is found in all the world able to relieve it.

As you see in a condemned man : spread a table in prison with the greatest dainties, and send for the rarest musicians, all will not charm his sorrow ; but if you can produce an authentic *pardon*, you ease him presently.   Just so it is here : faith plucks the thorn out of the conscience, unites the soul with Christ, and thus that ground of trouble is removed ; for "there is no condemnation to them that are in Christ Jesus."   Rom. 8 : 1.   The moment the soul comes to Christ, it has passed from death to life, and is no more under the law, but grace.   If a man's debt be paid by his surety, he need not fear to show his face boldly abroad ; he may freely meet the serjeant at the prison door.

2. The soul of a convinced sinner is exceedingly burdened with the *sins* which have defiled and polluted it. Conviction discovers the universal pollution of heart and life, so that a man loathes and abhors himself by reason thereof : if he do not look into his own corruptions, he cannot be safe ; and if he do, he cannot bear the sight of them.   Nothing can give rest but what gives relief against this evil ; and this is done only by faith uniting the soul with Jesus Christ.   For though the pollution of sin be not at once and perfectly taken away by coming to Christ, yet the burden thereof is exceedingly eased ; for, upon our believing, there is a heart-purifying principle planted in the soul, which by degrees cleanses that fountain of corruption, and will at last perfectly free the soul from sin.   "Purifying their hearts by faith."   Acts 15 : 9. The sinner being once in Christ, He is concerned for the soul as a member of his own mystical body, to purify and cleanse it, that at last he may present it perfect to the Father, without spot or wrinkle, or any such thing.   Eph. 5 : 27.   The reigning power of sin is gone immediately upon believing, and the very existence and being of it shall at last be destroyed.   O what rest must this give under those troubles for sin.

3. It was an intolerable burden to the soul to be under the continual *fears of death and damnation;* his life has been a life of bondage ever since the Lord opened his eyes to see his condition. Poor souls lie down with trembling for fear what a night may bring forth. It is a sad life indeed to live in continual bondage of such fears; but faith sweetly relieves the trembling conscience by removing the guilt which causes its fears. The sting of death is sin. When guilt is removed, fears vanish. "Smite, Lord, smite," said Luther, "for my sins are forgiven." Now if sickness come, it is another thing than it was wont to be. " The inhabitant shall not say, I am sick; the people that dwell therein shall be forgiven their iniquity." Isa. 33 : 24. A man scarcely feels sickness in comparison to what he did while he was without Christ and hope of pardon.

4. A convinced sinner, out of Christ, sees *every thing against him;* nothing yields him any comfort; every thing increases and aggravates his burden when he looks to things past, present, or to come. If he reflect upon things past, his soul is filled with anguish to remember the sins committed, the seasons neglected, the precious mercies abused; if he look upon things present the case is equally doleful, he is Christless and comfortless; and if he look forward to the future, that gives him a deeper cut to the heart than any thing else; for though it be sad and miserable for the present, yet he fears it will be much worse hereafter : all these are but the beginning of sorrows. And thus the poor awakened sinner is encompassed with misery on every side.

II. But on his coming to Christ all things are marvellously CHANGED; a quite contrary face of things appears, every thing gives hope and comfort. So speaks the apostle, "All things are yours; whether life or death, or things present, or things to come; all are yours, and ye are Christ's, and Christ is God's. 1 Cor. 3 : 21–23. They are ours, that is, for our advantage, benefit, and comfort. More particularly upon our coming to Christ,

1. Things *past* are ours; they conduce to our advantage and comfort. Now the soul can begin to read the gracious end and design of God in all its preservations and deliverances, whereby it has been reserved for such a day as this. O it melts his heart to consider that while his companions in sin and vanity are cut off he is spared, and that for a day of such mercy as the day of his espousals with Christ. Now all his past sorrows and deep troubles of spirit which God hath exercised him with, begin to appear the greatest mercies that ever he received, being all necessary and leading to this blessed union with Christ.

2. Things *present* are ours, though it be not yet with us as we would have it: our union with Christ is not sure enough, the heart is not pure enough; sin is too strong, and grace too weak; many things are still out of order; yet can the soul bless God with tears of joy and praise that he is where he is, though he be not yet where he would be. O it is a blessed life to live as a poor recumbent by acts of trust and affiance, though as yet he have but little evidence; to be resolved to trust all with Christ, though he be not yet certain of the issue. O this is a comfortable station, a sweet condition compared with what it was, either when the soul wallowed in sin in the days before conviction, or was swallowed up in fears and troubles for sin after conviction. Now it hath hope though it want assurance, and hope is sweet to a soul coming out of such deep distresses : now it sees the remedy and is applying it, whereas before the wound seemed desperate : now all hesitations and debates are at an end in the soul ; it is no longer unresolved what to do; all things have been deeply considered, and after consideration issued into this resolve, "I will go to Christ ; I will venture all upon his command and call ; here I will embark my eternal in-

terests ; here I fix, and here I resolve to live and die." O how much better is this than that floating life it lived before, rolling upon the billows of inward fears and troubles, not able to drop anchor anywhere, nor knowing where to find a harbor !

3. *Things to come* are ours ; and this is the best and sweetest of all : man looks onward to the future ; his eye is much upon things to come, and it will not satisfy him that it is well at present except he have a prospect that it shall be so hereafter.   But now the soul has committed itself and all its concerns to Christ for eternity, and this being done it is greatly relieved against evils to come.

I cannot, says the believer, think all my troubles over, and that I shall never meet any more afflictions ; but I leave all these things where I have left my soul : he that hath supported me under inward, will carry me through outward troubles also.   I cannot think all my *temptations* to sin past : Oh, I may yet meet with sore assaults from Satan ; yet it is infinitely better to be watching, praying, and striving against sin, than it was when I was obeying it in the lusts of it.   God, that hath delivered me from the love of sin, will, I trust, preserve me from ruin by sin. I know also death is to come ; I must feel its pangs and agonies ; but yet the aspect of death is much more pleasant than it was.   I come, Lord Jesus, to thee, who art the death of death, whose death hath disarmed death of its sting.   Thus you see briefly how by faith believers enter into rest ; how Christ gives rest, even at present, to them that come to him, and all this but as a beginning of their everlasting rest.

INFERENCE 1. Is there rest in Christ for weary souls that come unto him ?   *Then certainly it is a device of Satan against the peace and welfare of men's souls to discourage them from coming to Christ in the way of faith.*

He is a restless spirit himself, and would make us so too : he goeth about as a roaring lion seeking whom he may devour. It frets his proud and envious mind to see others find rest when he finds none; and he obtains his end fully if he can but keep souls from Christ. Look therefore upon all those objections and discouragements raised in your heart against coming to Christ as so many artifices and cunning devices of the devil to destroy and ruin your souls. It is true they have a very specious appearance; they are gilded over with pretences of the justice of God, the heinous nature of sin, the want of due and befitting qualifications to meet so holy and pure a God, the lapsing of the season of mercy, and a hundred others of like nature; but I beseech you lay down this as a sure conclusion and hold it fast, that whatever it be that discourages and hinders you from coming to Christ is directly against the interest of your souls, and the hand of the devil is certainly in it.

2. Hence also it follows *that unbelief is the true reason of all that disquietness and trouble with which the minds of poor sinners are so racked and tortured.*

If you will not believe, you cannot be established; till you come to Christ, peace cannot come to you: Christ and peace are undivided. Consider this: you have tried all other ways; you have tried duties, and no rest comes; you have tried reformation, restitution, and a stricter course of life, yet your wounds are still open and bleeding: these things, I grant, are in their place both good and necessary; but of themselves, without Christ, they are utterly insufficient to give what you expect from them: why will you not try the way of faith? why will you not carry your burden to Christ? O that you would be persuaded to it; how soon would you find what so long you have been seeking in vain! How long will you thus oppose your own good? how long will you keep yourselves upon the rack of conscience? Is it easy to go under the throbs and wounds of an accusing and condemning conscience? You know it is not: you look for peace, but no good comes; for a time of healing, and behold trouble. Alas, it must and will be so until you are in the way of faith, which is the true and only method to obtain rest.

3. *What cause have we all to admire the goodness of God in providing for us a Saviour in whom we may find rest to our souls.*

How has the Lord filled and furnished Jesus Christ with all that is suitable to a believer's wants. Does the guilt of sin terrify his conscience? Lo, in him is perfect righteousness to remove that guilt, so that it shall neither be imputed to him nor reflected by his conscience in the way of condemnation as it was before. In him also is a fountain opened for washing and for cleansing the pollution of sin from our souls; in him is the fulness both of merit and of the Spirit, two sweet springs of peace to the souls of men: well might the apostle call him, "Christ the wisdom of God," and well might the church say, "He is altogether lovely." Had not God provided Christ for us, we had never known rest to all eternity.

4. *How unreasonable and wholly inexcusable in believers is the sin of backsliding from Christ.* Have you found rest in him when you could not find it in any other? Did he receive and give peace to your soul when all other persons and things were physicians of no value? And will you after this backslide from him? O what madness! No man in his right mind would leave the pure, cold, refreshing stream of a crystal fountain to go to a filthy puddle or an empty cistern; such are the best enjoyments of this world in comparison with Jesus Christ.

That was a melting expostulation of Christ with the disciples when some had forsaken him, "Will ye also go away?" John 6 : 67. And it was a very suitable reply they made: Lord, whither away from thee should we go? From thee, Lord! No; where can we mend ourselves? Be sure of it, whenever you go from Christ, you go from rest to trouble. Had Judas rest? had Spira rest? and do you think you shall have rest? No, no: "The backslider in heart shall be filled with his own ways." Prov. 14 : 14. "Cursed be the man that departeth from him: he shall be as the heath in the desert, that seeth not when good cometh, and shall inhabit the parched places of the wilderness." Jer. 17 : 5, 6. If fear of sufferings and worldly temptations ever draw you off from Christ, you may come to those straits and terrors of conscience that will make you wish yourselves back again with Christ in a prison, with Christ at a stake.

5. *Let all that come to Christ learn to make him the rest and peace of their souls in all the troubles and outward distresses they meet.*

Rest may be found in Christ in any condition; he is able to give you peace in all your troubles. So he tells you, John 16 : 33, "These things have I spoken unto you, that in me ye might have peace. In the world ye shall have tribulation." By peace, he means not a deliverance from troubles by taking off affliction from them, or taking them away by death from all afflictions; but it is something they enjoy from Christ in the very midst of troubles, and amidst all their afflictions, that quiets and gives them rest, so that troubles cannot hurt them. Certainly, believers, you have peace in Christ when there is little in your own hearts; and your hearts might be filled with peace too, if you would exercise faith upon Christ for that end. It is your own fault if you are without rest in any condition in this world. Set yourselves to study the *fulness* of Christ and to clear your *interest* in him; believe what the Scriptures reveal of him, and live as you believe, and you will quickly find the peace of God filling your hearts and minds.

Blessed be God for Jesus Christ.

CHAPTER X

FIRST TITLE OF CHRIST—THE PHYSICIAN OF SOULS

"But when Jesus heard that, he said unto them, They that be whole need not a physician, but they that are sick." MATT. 9 : 12

HAVING in the former discourses considered the *nature* and *method* of the *application* of Christ to sinners, it remains now that I press it upon every soul, as it expects peace and pardon from God, to *apply* and *put on Jesus Christ*, that is, to get union with him by faith while he is yet held forth in the free and gracious tenders of the gospel. Pursuing the general application of the subject as entered upon in the last chapter, in the gracious invitation to come to Christ, divers arguments will be further urged, both from *the titles* of Christ, and *the privileges* conferred by him.

The TITLES of Christ are so many motives or arguments fitted to persuade men to come to him; among which, Christ as *the Physician of souls* comes under our first consideration in the text before us.

The occasion of these words of Christ was the call of Matthew the publican, who having first opened his heart, next opened his house to Christ, and entertained him there. This strange and unexpected change wrought upon Matthew quickly brings in all the neighborhood, and many publicans and sinners resorted thither; at which the pride of the Pharisees began to swell. From this occasion they took offence at Christ, and in this verse Christ addressed them in a manner fitted both for their conviction and his own vindication. "He said unto them, They that be whole need not a physician, but they that are sick."

He gives it, says one, as a reason why he conversed so much with publicans and sinners, and so little among the Pharisees, because there was more work for him: Christ came to be a physician to sick souls; Pharisees were so well in their own conceit that Christ saw that they would have little to do with him, and so he applied himself to those who were more sensible of their sickness. In these words,

1. The *secure sinner* is described, both with respect to his own apprehensions of himself as one that is whole, and also by his low value and esteem for Christ: he sees no need of him; "they that be whole need not a physician."

2. The *convinced and humbled* sinner is here also described, and that both by his state, he is *sick;* and by his valuation of Jesus Christ, he greatly needs him: they that are sick need the physician.

3. We have Christ's treatment of both: the former he rejects and passes by, as those with whom he hath no concern; the latter he converses with in order to their cure.

The words thus opened are fruitful in observations. I shall now insist upon only this one, which suits the scope of my discourse:

The Lord Jesus Christ is the only Physician for sick souls.

The world is a great *hospital,* full of sick and dying souls, all wounded by one and the same mortal weapon, sin. Some are without a sense of their misery, and value not a physician; others are sensible of danger, mourn under the apprehension of their condition, and sadly bewail it. The merciful God has, in his abundant compassion to the perishing world, sent a Physician from heaven, and given him his orders under the great seal of heaven for his office, Isaiah 61 : 1, 2, which he opened and read in the audience of the people : "The Spirit of the Lord is upon me, because he hath anointed me to preach the gospel to the poor ; he hath sent me to heal the broken-hearted, to preach deliverance to the captive, and recovering of sight to the blind, to set at liberty them that are bruised." Luke 4 : 18. He is the tree of life, whose leaves are for the healing of the nations : he is the Lord that healeth us ; and that even as he is "the Lord our righteousness." The brazen serpent that healed the Israelites in the wilderness was an excellent type of our great physician Christ, and is expressly applied to him, John 3 : 14. He rejects none that come, and heals all whom he undertakes with. But more particularly, I will point out those diseases which Christ heals in sick souls, and by what means he heals them ; and show the excellence of this Physician above all others : there is none like Christ, he is the only Physician for wounded souls.

I. We will inquire into THE DISEASES which Christ the Physician cures, and they are reducible to two—sin and sorrow.

1. The *disease of sin;* in which three things are found exceeding burdensome to sick souls : the guilt, the dominion, and the inherence of sin—all cured by this Physician.

(1.) The *guilt* of sin ; this is a mortal wound, a stab in the very heart of a poor sinner. It is a groundless distinction that papists make of sins *mortal* and *venial;* all sin in its own nature is mortal. " The wages of sin is death." Rom. 6 : 23. Yet though it be so in its own nature, Christ can and doth cure it by the sovereign balm of his own precious blood. " In whom we have redemption through his blood, the forgiveness of sins, according to the riches of his grace." Eph. 1 : 7. This is the deadliest wound the soul of man feels in this world. What is guilt, but the obligation of the soul to everlasting punishment and misery ? It puts the soul under the sentence of God to eternal wrath ; the condemning sentence of the great and terrible God ; than which nothing is found more dreadful and insupportable : put all pains, all poverty, all afflictions, all miseries in one scale, and God's condemnation in the other, and you weigh but so many feathers against a talent of lead.

This disease our great physician Christ cures by remission, which is the dissolving of the obligation to punishment; the loosing of the soul that was bound over to the wrath and condemnation of God. Col. 1 : 13, 14 ; Heb. 6 : 18 ; Micah 7 : 18, 19. This remission being made, the soul is immediately cleared from all its obligation to punishment. There is no condemnation. Rom. 8 : 1. All bonds are cancelled, the condemnation of all sins, original and actual, great and small, is removed. This cure is performed upon souls by the blood of Christ ; nothing is found in heaven or earth besides his blood, that is able to heal this disease. "Without shedding of blood there is no remission," Heb. 9 : 22 ; nor is it any blood that will do it, but that only which dropped from the wounds of Christ. "With his stripes we are healed." Isa. 53 : 5 His blood only is innocent and precious blood, 1 Peter 1 : 19 ; blood of infinite worth and value ; blood of God, Acts 20 : 28 ; blood prepared for this very purpose. Heb. 10 : 5. This is the blood that performs the cure ; and how great a cure is it ! for this cure the souls of believers shall be praising and magnifying their great Physician in heaven to all eternity. "Unto Him that loved us, and washed us from our sins in his own blood, to him be glory and dominion for ever and ever." Rev. 1 : 5, 6.

(2.) The next evil in sin cured by Christ is its *dominion* over the souls of sinners. Where sin is in dominion the soul is in a very sad condition ; for it darkens the understanding, depraves the conscience, stiffens the will, hardens the heart, misplaces and disorders all the affections ; and thus every faculty is wounded by the dominion of sin over the soul. How difficult is the cure of this disease ! It passes the skill of angels or men to heal it, but Christ undertakes it and makes a perfect cure of it at last, and this he does by his Spirit. As he cures the guilt of sin by pouring out his blood for us ; so he cures its dominion by pouring out his Spirit upon us. Justification is the cure of guilt, sanctification the cure of the dominion of sin.

As the dominion of sin darkens the *understanding*, 1 Cor. 2 : 14, so the Spirit of holiness which Christ sheds upon his people cures the blindness of that noble faculty and restores it again. Eph. 5 : 8. They that were darkness hereby become light in the Lord ; the anointing of the Spirit teacheth them all things. 1 John 2 : 27.

As the dominion of sin depraved and defiled the *conscience*, Tit. 1 : 15, disabling it for the performance of all its offices and functions, so that it would neither apply nor tremble at the word ; so when the Spirit of holiness is shed forth, O what a tender sense fills the renewed conscience ! For what small things will it smite and rebuke ! How strongly will it bind to duty and bar against sin.

As the dominion of sin stiffened the *will* and made it stubborn and rebellious, so Christ, by sanctifying it, brings it to be obedient to the will of God. "Lord, what wilt thou have me to do ?" Acts 9 : 6.

As the power of sin hardened the *heart* so that nothing could affect it, or make any impression upon it ; when sanctification comes upon the soul, it thaws and breaks it, as hard as it was, and makes it dissolve in the breast of a sinner in godly sorrow. "I will take away the stony heart out of your flesh, and I will give you a heart of flesh." Ezek. 36 : 26. It will now melt ingenuously under the threatenings of the word, 2 Kings 22 : 19, or the strokes of the rod, Jer. 31 : 18, or the manifestations of grace and mercy. Luke 7 : 38.

As the power of sin disordered all the *affections*, so sanctification sets them right. Psalm 4 : 6, 7. Thus you see how sanctification becomes the rectitude, health, and due temper of the soul, so far as it prevails, curing the diseases with which sin filled the soul. True it is, this cure is not perfected in this life ; there are still some remains of the old diseases in the holiest souls, notwithstanding sin is dethroned from its dominion over them ; but the cure is begun, and daily advances towards perfection, and at last will be complete.

(3.) The *inherence* of sin in the soul is a sore disease, the very root of all our other complaints. This made the holy apostle bemoan himself and wail so bitterly because of sin that dwelt in him. Rom. 7 : 17. And the same misery is bewailed by sanctified persons all the world over. It is a wonderful mercy to have the guilt and dominion of sin cured, but we shall never be perfectly sound and well till the existence or indwelling of sin in our natures be also cured : when that is done we shall feel no more pain nor sorrow for sin ; and this our great *Physician* will at last perform in us. But as the cure of guilt was by our *justification*, the cure of the dominion of sin by our *sanctification*, so the third and last, which perfects the whole cure, will be by our *glorification;* and till then it is not to be expected. For sin, like ivy in the old walls, will never be gotten out till the wall be pulled down, and it is then pulled up by the roots. This cure Christ will perform in a moment, upon our dissolution. For it is plain that none but perfect souls, freed from all sin, are admitted into heaven. Eph. 5 : 27 ; Heb. 12 : 23 ; Rev. 21 : 27. And it is as plain that no such perfection is found in any man on this side death, 1 John 1 : 8 ; 1 Kings 8 : 46 ; Phil. 3 : 12 ; a truth sealed by the sad experience of all the saints on earth. And if such perfection must be before the saints can be perfectly happy, and no such thing is done in this life, it remains that it must be done immediately upon their dissolution, and at the very time of their glorification. As sin came in at the time of the union of their souls and bodies, so it will go out at the time of their separation by death; then will Christ complete this glorious work, and perfect that cure which hath been so long under his hand in this world; and thenceforth sin shall have no power upon them. It shall never tempt them more, it shall never defile them more, it shall never grieve and sadden their hearts any more; henceforth it shall never cloud their evidences, darken their understandings, or give the least interruption to their communion with God. When sin is gone, all these its mischievous effects will be gone with it. While you are under Christ's cure upon earth, but not perfectly healed, your understandings mistake, your thoughts wander, your affections are dead, and your communion with God is daily interrupted; but it shall not be so in heaven, where the cure is perfect; you shall not there know, love, or delight in God in the manner you do this day, for you are not as yet come to the rest and to the inheritance which the Lord your God giveth you.

2. As sin is the disease of the saints, so also is *sorrow;* the best saints must pass through the valley of Bacha to heaven. How many tears fall from the eyes of the saints on account of outward as well as inward troubles, even after their reconciliation with God. Through much tribulation we must enter into the kingdom of God. Acts 14 : 22. Whatever distress or trouble any poor soul is in upon any account whatsoever, if that soul belongs to Jesus Christ he will take care of it for the present, and deliver it at last by a complete cure.

Christ cures troubles by *sanctifying* them to the souls of his people, and makes their very troubles medicinal and healing to them. Trouble is a scorpion, and has a deadly sting, but Christ is a wise physician, and extracts a sovereign oil out of this scorpion that heals the wound it makes. By afflictions our wise Physician prevents or cures greater troubles by lesser—inward sorrows by outward ones. "By this therefore shall the iniquity of Jacob be purged;

and this is all the fruit to take away his sin." Isaiah 27 : 9.

Christ also cures outward troubles by inward *consolations*, which are made to rise in the inner man as high as the waters of affliction do upon the outward man. 2 Cor. 1 : 5. One drop of spiritual comfort is sufficient to sweeten a whole ocean of outward trouble. It was a high expression of an afflicted father, whom God comforted, just upon the death of his dear and only son, with some clearer manifestations of his love than usual : " Oh, might I but have such consolations as these, I could be willing, were it possible, to lay an only son into the grave every day I have to live in the world." Thus all the troubles of the world are cured by Christ. " In the world ye shall have tribulation ; but in me ye shall have peace."

Christ cures all outward troubles in his people *by death*, which is their removal from the place of sorrows to peace and rest for evermore. Then God wipes all tears from their eyes, and the days of their mourning are at an end ; they then put off the garments and spirit of mourning, and enter into peace. Isa. 57 : 2. They come to that place and state where tears and sighs are unknown : one step beyond the state of this mortality brings us quite out of the sight and hearing of all troubles and lamentations.

II. I shall show that Jesus Christ is the ONLY PHYSICIAN of souls, and this will be evident in divers respects.

1. None so *wise* and judicious as Jesus Christ to understand and comprehend the nature, depth, and danger of soul diseases. O how ignorant and unacquainted are men with the state and case of afflicted souls ! But Christ hath "the tongue of the learned, that he should know how to speak a word in season to him that is weary." Isa. 50 : 4. He only understands the weight of sin, and the depth of inward troubles for sin.

2. None so *able* to cure and heal the wounds of afflicted souls as Christ is ; he only has the medicines that can

cure a sick soul. The blood of Christ, and nothing else in heaven or earth, is able to cure the wounds which guilt inflicts upon a trembling conscience; let men try all other receipts, and costly experience shall convince them of their insufficiency. Conscience may be benumbed, but pacified it can never be but by the blood of Christ. Heb. 10 : 2.

3. None so *tender-hearted* and *sympathizing* with sick souls as Jesus Christ; he can have compassion, because he has had experience. Heb. 5 : 2. If I must come into the surgeon's hands with broken bones, give me one whose own bones have been broken, who hath felt the anguish in himself. Christ knows by experience the anguish of inward troubles, the weight of God's wrath, and the terrors of a forsaking God, more than any or all the sons of men; this makes him tender over distressed souls. "A bruised reed shall he not break, and the smoking flax shall he not quench." Isa. 42 : 3.

4. None cures in so *wonderful a method* as Christ; he heals us by his stripes. Isa. 53 : 5. The physician dies, that the patient may live; his wounds must bleed, that ours may be healed; he feels the smart and pain, that we may have ease and comfort. No physician but Christ can cure others in this way.

5. None so *ready* to relieve a sick soul as Christ; he is within the call of a distressed soul at all times. Art thou sick for sin, weary of sin, and made truly willing to part with sin? lift up but thy sincere cry to the Lord Jesus for help, and he will quickly be with thee. When the prodigal, the emblem of a convinced, humbled sinner, said in himself, I will return to my father, the father ran to meet him. Luke 15 : 20.

6. None so *willing* to receive and undertake for all distressed and afflicted souls as Jesus Christ is; he refuses none that come to him. "Him that cometh to me I will in no wise cast out." John 6 : 37. Whatever their sins have been, or their sorrows are; however they have

wounded their own souls with the deepest gashes of guilt;
how desperate and helpless soever their case appears in
their own or others' eyes, he never puts them off or discourages them, if they are but willing to come. Isa.
1 : 18, 19.

7. None so *successful* as Christ: he never fails of performing a perfect cure upon those he undertakes; never
was it known that any soul failed of cure in his hands.
John 3 : 15, 16. Christ suffers none to perish that commit themselves to him.

8. None so free and *generous* as Christ: he doeth all
gratis; he sells not his medicines, though they are of infinite value, but freely gives them. "He that hath no
money, let him come." Isa. 55 : 1. If any are sent away,
it is the rich, Luke 1 : 53, not the poor and needy: those
only fail that will not accept the remedy as a free gift, but
seek to purchase it at a price.

9. None *rejoice in the recovery of souls* more than Christ.
Oh, it is unspeakably delightful to him to see the efficacy
of his blood upon our souls. He shall see the travail of
his soul, that is, the success of his death and sufferings,
and shall be satisfied. Isa. 53 : 11. When he foresaw
the success of the gospel in the world, it is said, "in that
hour Jesus rejoiced in spirit." Luke 10 : 21.

INFERENCE 1. *How inexpressible is the grace of God in
providing such a physician as Christ*, for the sick and dying
souls of sinners! Oh, blessed be God, that there is balm
in Gilead, and a Physician there! that our case is not
desperate, forlorn, and remediless, as that of the devils
and the damned is. There is but one case exempted from
cure, and that such as is not incident to any sensible,
afflicted soul, Matt. 12 : 31; and this only excepted, all
manner of sins and diseases are susceptible of a cure.
Though there be a disease which is incurable, yet take
this for thy comfort, that never any soul was sick or sensibly burdened with it, who was yet willing to come to

Jesus Christ for healing; for under that sin the will is so wounded that they have no desire to Christ. O inestimable mercy, that the worst sinner may have a perfect cure! There are thousands and ten thousands now in heaven and earth who said once, Never was any case like mine; so dangerous, so hopeless. The greatest of sinners have been perfectly recovered by Christ. 1 Tim. 1 : 15; 1 Cor. 6 : 11. O mercy never to be duly estimated!

2. *What a powerful restraint from sin is the method ordained by God for the cure of it!* "With his stripes we are healed." Isa. 53 : 5. The Physician must die that the patient may live; nothing but the blood, the precious blood of Christ is found in heaven or earth able to heal us. Heb. 9 : 22, 26. This blood of Christ must be freshly applied to every new wound sin makes upon our souls, 1 John, 2 : 1, 2; every new sin wounds him afresh. O think of this again and again, you that so easily yield to the solicitations of Satan. Is it so easy and so cheap to sin, as you seem to make it? Does the cure of souls cost nothing? True, it is free to us, but was it so to Christ? No, it was not; he knows the price of it, though you do not. Have you forgot also your own sick days and nights for sin, that you are so careless in resisting and preventing it? Surely it is not easy for saints to wound Christ and their own souls at one stroke. If you renew your sins, you must also renew your sorrows and repentance, like David, Psa. 51; 2 Sam. 12 : 13; you must feel again the anguish and pain of a troubled spirit with which the saints are not unacquainted; of which they may say, as the church, "Remembering mine affliction and my misery. the wormwood and the gall. My soul hath them still in remembrance." Lam. 3 : 19, 20.

3. If Christ be the only physician of sick souls, *what sin and folly is it for men to take Christ's work out of his hands and attempt to be their own physician.*

Thus do those that superstitiously endeavor to heal

their souls by afflicting their bodies—not Christ's blood, but their own must be the remedy ; and as blind papists, so many carnal and ignorant Protestants strive, by confession, restitution, reformation, and a stricter course of life, to heal the wounds that sin hath made upon their souls, without respect to the blood of Christ ; but this course shall not profit them at all.   It may for a time divert, but can never heal them : the wounds so skinned over will open and bleed again.   God grant it be not when our souls shall be out of the reach of the true and only remedy.

4. *How sad is the case of those souls to whom Christ has not yet been a physician.*   They are mortally wounded by sin, and are likely to die of their sickness ; no healing applications have hitherto been made unto their souls : and this is the case of the greatest part of mankind, yea, of them that live under the discoveries of Christ in the gospel.   This appears in that their eyes have not yet been opened to *see their sin and misery,* in which illumination the cure of souls begins.   Acts 26 : 18.   To this day he hath not given them eyes to see, Deut. 29 : 4, but that terrible stroke of God which blinds and hardens, mentioned Isa. 6 : 9, 10, is too visibly upon them—no hope of healing till the sinner's eyes be opened to see his sin and misery. Again, nothing will separate them from their lusts ; a sure sign they are not under Christ's cure, nor were ever made sick of sin.   Oh, if ever Christ be a physician to thy soul, he will make thee loathe what now thou lovest, and say to thy most pleasant and most profitable lusts, "Get ye hence."   Isa. 30 : 22.   Till then, there is no ground to think that Christ is a physician to you.   They have no sensible need of Christ, nor make any earnest inquiry after him, as most certainly they would do if they were in the way of healing and recovery.   These, and many other sad symptoms, too plainly show the disease of sin to be in its full strength upon their souls ; and

if it so continue, how dreadful will be the issue! Isa. 6 : 9, 10.

5. *What cause have they to be glad who are under the hand and care of Christ in order to a cure, and who find their souls in a hopeful way of recovery.* Can we rejoice when the strength of a natural disease is broken, and nature begins to recover ease and vigor again? And shall we not much more rejoice when our souls begin to mend and recover sensibly, and comfortable signs of health and life appear upon them; particularly when the understanding, which was ignorant and dark, has the light of life beginning to dawn into it, 1 John, 2 : 27; when the will, which was rebellious and inflexible to the will of God, is brought to comply with that holy will, saying, "Lord, what wilt thou have me to do?" Acts 9 : 6; when the heart, which was harder than adamant, is brought to contrition for sin, and can mourn as heartily over it as ever a father did for a beloved and only son; when its aversion from God is gone, and the thoughts are fixed upon God, and spiritual things begin to grow pleasant to the soul; when times of duty are longed for, and the soul never more pleased than in such seasons; when the hypocrisy of the heart is purged out, so that we begin to do all that we do heartily, as unto the Lord, and not unto men, Col. 3 : 23; 1 Thess. 2 : 4; when we begin to make conscience of secret sins, Psa. 119 : 113, and of secret duties, Mat. 6 : 5, 6; when we have an equal respect to all God's commandments, Psa. 119 : 8, and our hearts are under the holy and awful eye of God, which overawes our souls. Gen. 17 : 1. Oh, what sweet signs of a recovering soul are these. Surely such are in the skilful hand of the great Physician, who will perfect what yet remains to be done.

6. This point yields *advice and direction to souls that are under the disease of sin;* and they are of two classes, to each of which I will distinctly speak.

(1.) *To those that are in their first troubles for sin,* and know not what course to take for ease and safety, I would say,

Shut your ears against *the dangerous counsels* of carnal persons or relations; for as they themselves are unacquainted with these troubles, so also are they with all proper remedies; and it is very usual with the devil to convey his temptations to distressed souls by such hands, because by them he can do it with least suspicion. It was Augustine's complaint that his own father took little care for his soul; and many parents act, in this case, as if they were employed by Satan.

Be not *too eager to get out of trouble*, but be content to take God's way, and wait upon him. It is true, times of trouble are apt to seem tedious, but a false peace will endanger you more than a long trouble; a man may lengthen his own troubles to the loss of his own peace, and may shorten them to the hazard of his own soul.

Open your case to *wise and experienced Christians*, and especially the ministers of Christ, whose office it is to direct you in these difficulties; and let not your troubles lie, like a smothering fire, always in your own breasts. I know men are more ashamed to open their sins under conviction, than they were to commit them before conviction; but this is your interest, and the true way to your rest and peace. If there be with you, or near you, an interpreter, one of a thousand, to show you your righteousness and remedy, as it lies in Christ, neglect not your own souls in a sinful concealment of your case: it will be the joy of their hearts to be employed in such work as this.

Be much *with God in secret*, open your hearts to him, and pour your complaints into his bosom. The 102d Psalm bears a title very suitable to your case and duty; yea, you will find, if God intend a cure upon your souls, that nothing will be able to keep God and your souls asunder: whatever your incumbrances in the world be, some time will be daily redeemed, to be spent between God and you.

Plead hard with God in *prayer* for help and healing. "Heal my soul, for I have sinned against thee," Psa. 41 : 4. Tell him Christ has his commission sealed for such as you are : he was sent to "bind up the broken-hearted." Isa. 61 : 1. Tell him he came into the world "to seek and save that which was lost," and such are you now, in your own apprehension. Lord, what profit is there in my blood? And why is my heart wounded with the sense of sin, and mine eyes open to see my danger and misery? Are not these the first dawnings of mercy upon sinners? O let it appear that the time of mercy, even the set time, is now come.

Understand your peace to be *in Christ only*, and faith to be the only way to Christ and rest ; let the great inquiry of your soul be after Christ and faith ; study the nature and necessity of these, and cry to God day and night for strength to carry you to Christ in the way of faith.

(2.) *To those that have been longer under the hands of Christ*, and are still in trouble, whose wounds bleed still, and all they do will not bring rest, to such I only add a few words.

Consider whether you have rightly closed with Christ since your first awakening, and whether there be not some way of sin in which you still live : if so, no wonder your wounds are kept open and your souls are strangers to peace.

If you are conscious of no such defect in the foundation, consider how much of this trouble may arise from your natural constitution and temper, which, being melancholy, will be distrustful ; you may find it so in other cases of less moment, and be sure Satan will not be wanting to improve it.

Acquaint yourselves more with the nature of true justifying faith; a mistake in this has prolonged the troubles of many; if you look for it in no other act but assurance, you may easily overlook it as it lies in the mean time in your acceptance. A proper conception of saving faith would go far in the cure of many troubled souls.

Be more careful to shun sin than to get yourselves clear of trouble: it is sad to walk in darkness, but worse to lie under guilt. Say, Lord, I would rather be grieved myself than be a grief to thy Spirit. O keep me from sin, how long soever thou keep me under sorrow. Wait on God in the way of faith, and thy wounds shall be healed by thy great Physician.

Thanks be to God for Jesus Christ.

CHAPTER XI

SECOND TITLE OF CHRIST—"THE MERCY "

"To perform the mercy promised to our fathers, and to remember his holy covenant." LUKE 1:72

THIS scripture is part of Zachariah's prophecy at the rising of that bright star John, the harbinger and forerunner of Christ. These are some of the first words he spoke after God had loosed his tongue, which for a time was struck dumb for his unbelief. His tongue is now at liberty to proclaim to all the world the unspeakable riches of mercy through Jesus Christ in a song of praise : in which observe the mercy celebrated, redemption by Christ, verse 68 ; the description of Christ, verse 69 ; the faithfulness of God in our redemption, verse 70 ; the benefit of being so redeemed by Christ, verse 71 ; and the exact accomplishment of all the promises made to the fathers in sending Christ, the mercy promised, into the world : "to perform the mercy promised to our fathers." In these words,

1. You have *a mercy freely promised* by God the Father from the beginning of the world, and often repeated in succeeding ages to the fathers, in his covenant transactions. This mercy is Jesus Christ, of whom he speaks in this prophecy ; the same which he styles, "A horn of salvation in the house of David," verse 69.

The mercy of God in Scripture is put, first, for the free and undeserved favor of God to man, and this favor may respect him either as undeserving or as ill-deserving. It respected innocent man as undeserving, for Adam could put no obligation upon his benefactor. It respects fallen man as ill-deserving. Innocent man could not merit favor, and fallen man merited wrath : the favor or mercy of God to both is every way free. But second, the word *mercy* is also taken for *the effects* of God's favor, which are either principal and primary, or subordinate and secondary. Of secondary and subordinate mercies there are multitudes, both temporal respecting the body, and spiritual respecting the soul. But *the principal and primary mercy is but one, and that is Christ*, the first-born of mercy, from whom are all other mercies ; and who is therefore called by a singular emphasis in our text, *The Mercy;* that is, the mercy of all mercies, without whom no drop of saving mercy can flow to any of the sons of men, and in whom are all the tender bowels of divine mercy yearning over poor sinners. *The mercy, and the mercy promised.* The first promise of Christ was made to Adam, Gen. 3 : 15, and it was frequently renewed afterwards to Abraham, to David, and as the text speaks, "unto the fathers," in their respective generations.

2. We find here also the promised mercy faithfully *performed:* "To perform the mercy promised." What mercy soever the love of God engaged him to promise, the faithfulness of God stands engaged for its performance. Christ the promised mercy is not only performed *truly*, but he is also performed according to the promise in all its circumstances *exactly*. So he was promised to the fathers, and just so performed to us their children. We are thus taught that

Jesus Christ, the Mercy of mercies, was graciously promised and faithfully performed by God to his people.

Three things are here to be considered : why Christ is styled The Mercy ; what kind of mercy Christ is to his people ; and how this mercy was performed.

I. Christ is THE MERCY, emphatically so called : the peerless and matchless mercy.

1. Because he is the *first-fruit* of the mercy of God to sinners. The mercies of God are infinite : mercy gave to the world and us our being ; all our protection, provision, and comforts in this world are the fruits of mercy, the free

gifts of divine favor : but Christ is the first and chief ; all
other mercies, compared with him, are but fruits from that
root, and streams from that fountain of mercy ; the very
bowels of divine mercy are in Christ, as in verse 78,
"through the tender mercy," or as in the Greek, the
yearning bowels of the mercy of God.

2. Christ is the mercy, because all the mercy of God
to sinners is dispensed and conveyed through Christ to
them. John 1 : 16 ; Col. 2 : 3 ; Eph. 4 : 7. Christ is the
medium of all divine communications, the *channel* of grace :
through him are both the flow of mercy from God to us,
and the returns of praise from us to God. Vain therefore
are all expectations of mercy out of Christ. No drop of
saving mercy runs except in this channel.

3. Christ is the mercy, because all inferior mercies
derive their nature, value, sweetness, and duration from
Christ, the fountain-mercy of all other mercies.

They derive their *nature* from Christ ; for apart from
him those things which men call mercies, are rather traps
and snares than mercies to them. Prov. 1 : 32. The time
will come when the rich that are christless will wish, O
that we had been poor ! and nobles not ennobled by the
new birth, O that we had been among the lower rank of
men ! All these things that pass for valuable mercies,
like cyphers, signify much when such an important figure
as Christ stands before them, else they signify nothing to
any man's benefit.

They derive their *value* as well as nature from Christ.
For how little does it signify to any man to be rich, honorable, and successful in all his designs in this world, if after
all he must lie down in hell !

All other mercies derive their *sweetness* from Christ, and
are but insipid without him. There is a twofold sweetness
in things ; one natural, another spiritual : those that are
out of Christ can relish the first, believers only relish both.
They have the natural sweetness there is in mercy itself,

and a sweetness supernatural from Christ and the covenant, the way in which they receive them.   Hence it is that some men taste more spiritual sweetness in their daily bread, than others do in the Lord's supper; and the same mercy, by this means, becomes a feast to soul and body at once.

All mercies have their *duration* from Christ.   All christless persons hold their mercies upon the greatest contingencies and uncertainty; if they are continued during this life, that is all: there is not one drop of mercy after death. But the mercies of the saints are continued to eternity; the end of their mercies on earth is the beginning of their better mercies in heaven.   There is a twofold end of mercies, one perfective, another destructive: the death of the saints perfects and completes their mercies; the death of the wicked destroys and cuts off their mercies.   For these reasons Christ is called the mercy.

II. Let us inquire WHAT KIND OF MERCY CHRIST IS; and we shall find many transcendent properties to commend him to our souls.

1. He is *free* and undeserved mercy, called, upon that account, "The gift of God."   John 4 : 10.   And to show how free this gift was, God gave him to us when we were enemies.   Rom. 5 : 8.   That mercy must be free which is given not only to the undeserving, but to the ill-deserving; the benevolence of God was the sole cause of this gift. John 3 : 16.

2. Christ is a *full* mercy, replenished with all that answers to the wishes or wants of sinners, in him alone is found whatever the justice of God requires for satisfaction, or the necessities of souls require for their supply.   Christ is full of mercy; in him are all kinds of mercies; and in him are the highest and most perfect degrees of mercy; "for it pleased the Father that in him should all fulness dwell."   Col. 1 : 19.

3. Christ is the *seasonable* mercy, given by the Father

to us in due time, Rom. 5 : 6 ; in the fulness of time, Gal. 4 : 4 ; a seasonable mercy in his exhibition to the world in general, and in his application to the soul in particular ; the wisdom of God fixed upon the best time for his incarnation, and takes the best for its application. When a poor soul is distressed and ready to perish, then comes Christ. All God's works are done in season, but none more seasonable than this great work of salvation by Christ.

4. Christ is the *needful* mercy, there is an absolute necessity for Jesus Christ ; hence in Scripture he is called the "bread of life," John 6 : 35 ; he is bread to the hungry. He is the "water of life," Rev. 22 : 17, as cold water to the thirsty soul. He is a ransom for captives, Matt. 20 : 28 ; a garment to the naked, Rom. 13 : 14. Bread is not so necessary to the hungry, nor water to the thirsty, nor a ransom to the captive, nor a garment to the naked, as Christ is to the soul of a sinner. The life of our souls is in Jesus Christ.

5. Christ is a *fountain-mercy*, and all other mercies flow from him. A believer may say of Christ, "All my springs are in thee ;" from his merit and his Spirit flow our redemption, justification, sanctification, peace, joy in the Holy Ghost, and blessedness in the world to come : "In that day there shall be a fountain opened." Zech. 13 : 1.

6. Christ is a *satisfying* mercy : he that is full of Christ can feel the want of nothing. "I determined not to know any thing among you, save Jesus Christ and him crucified." 1 Cor. 2 : 2. Christ bounds and terminates the vast desires of the soul : he is the very sabbath of the soul. How hungry, empty, and straitened on every side is the soul of man in the abundance and fulness of all outward things till it come to Christ : the weary motions of a restless soul, like those of a river, cannot be at rest till they pour themselves into Christ the ocean of blessedness

7. Christ is a *peculiar* mercy applied to a remnant among men : some would extend redemption as large as the world, but the gospel limits it to those only that believe ; and believers are upon that account called " a peculiar people." 1 Pet. 2 : 9. The offers of Christ indeed are large and general, but the application of Christ is to few. Isa. 53 : 1. The greater cause have they to whom Christ comes, to lie with their mouths in the dust, astonished and overwhelmed with the sense of so peculiar and distinguished a mercy.

8. Jesus Christ is a *suitable* mercy, suited in every respect to all our needs and wants, 1 Cor. 1 : 30, in whom the admirable wisdom of God is illustriously displayed. " Ye are complete in him." Col. 2 : 10. Are we enemies ? He is reconciliation. Are we sold to sin and Satan ? He is redemption. Are we condemned by the law ? He is the Lord our righteousness. Hath sin polluted us ? He is a fountain opened for sin and for uncleanness. Are we lost by departing from God ? He is the way to the Father. Rest is not so suitable to the weary, nor bread to the hungry, as Christ is to the wants of the sinner.

9. Christ is a *wonderful* mercy ; his name is called *Wonderful*, Isa. 9 : 6 ; and as his name is, so is he—a wonderful Saviour. His person is a wonder. "Great is the mystery of godliness ; God was manifest in the flesh." 1 Tim. 3 : 16. His abasement is wonderful. Phil. 2 : 6, 7, 8. His love is a wonderful love ; his redemption full of wonders ; angels desire to look into it. He is and will be admired by angels and saints to all eternity.

10. Jesus Christ is an incomparable and *matchless* mercy. Draw the comparison how you will between Christ and all other enjoyments, you will find none in heaven or earth to equal him. He is more than all externals, as the light of the sun is more than that of a candle. Nay, even the worst of Christ is better than the best of the world ; his reproaches are better than the

world's pleasures. Heb. 11 : 25. He is more than all spirituals, as the fountain is more than the stream. He is more than justification, as the cause is more than the effect ; more than sanctification, as the person himself is more than the image or picture. He is more than all peace, all comfort, all joy, as the tree is more than the fruit. Nay, draw the comparison between Christ and things eternal, and you will find him better than they ; for what is heaven without Christ? "Whom have I in heaven but thee?" Psalm 73 : 25. If Christ should say to the saints, take heaven among you, but I will withdraw myself from you, the saints would weep, even in heaven itself, and say, Lord, heaven will be no more heaven to us except thou be there, who art thyself the joy of heaven.

11. Christ is an *unsearchable* mercy ; who can fully express his wonderful name ? Prov. 30 : 4. Who can count his unsearchable riches? Eph. 3 : 8. Hence it is that saints never tire in the study or love of Christ, because new wonders are eternally rising out of him. He is a deep which no line of any understanding, angelic or human, can fathom.

12. Christ is an *everlasting* mercy ; "the same yesterday, and to-day, and for ever." Heb. 13 : 8. All other enjoyments are perishable ; time, like a moth, will fret them out ; but the riches of Christ are durable riches. Prov. 8 : 18. The graces of Christ are durable graces. John 4 : 14. All creatures are flowers that appear and fade in their month ; but this Rose of Sharon, this Lily of the Valley never withers. Thus you see the mercy performed with its desirable properties.

III. The last thing to be opened is THE MANNER OF GOD'S PERFORMING HIS MERCY to his people. This he did,

1. *Really and truly.* As he had promised, so he made good the promise : " Let all the house of Israel know assuredly that God hath made that same Jesus whom ye have crucified, both Lord and Christ." Acts 2 : 36. The

manifestation of Christ in the flesh was no delusion, but a most evident and palpable truth: that "which we have heard, which we have seen with our eyes, which we have looked upon, and our hands have handled." 1 John 1 : 1. A truth so certain that the assertors of it appealed to the very enemies of Christ for certainty. Acts 2 : 22. Yea, not only the sacred, but profane writers witness to it; not only the evangelists and apostles, but even the heathen writers of those times, both Roman and Jewish, as Suetonius, Tacitus, Pliny the younger, and Josephus the Jewish antiquary, all acknowledge it.

2. As God really and truly performed Christ the promised mercy, so he performed this promised mercy *exactly* agreeable to the promises, types, and predictions made of him to the fathers, even in the most minute circumstances. This is a great truth for our faith to be established in: let us therefore cast our eyes both upon the promises and performances of God with respect to Christ, the mercy of mercies. See how he was represented to the fathers long before his manifestation in the flesh; and what he appeared to be when he was really exhibited in the flesh.

1. As to his *person and qualifications*, as it was *foretold*, so it was *fulfilled*. His original was said to be unsearchable and eternal, Micah 5 : 2, and so he affirmed himself to be: "I am Alpha and Omega, the first and the last." Rev. 1 : 11. "Before Abraham was, I am." John 8 : 58. His two natures united into one person were plainly foretold, Zech. 13 : 7, " *The man* that is *my Fellow*," and such a one God performed. Rom. 9 : 5. His immaculate purity and holiness were foretold· "To anoint the most Holy." Dan. 9 : 24. "Which of you convinceth me of sin?" John 8 : 46. His offices were foretold: the prophetical office predicted, Deut. 18 : 15, and fulfilled in him, John 1 : 18; his priestly office foretold, Psalm 110 : 4, fulfilled, Heb. 9 : 14; his kingly office foretold, Micah 5 : 2,

and in him fulfilled, his very enemies being judges. Matt. 27 : 37.

2. As to his *birth*, the time, place, and manner were foretold to the fathers, and exactly performed to a tittle.

The *time* predicted more generally in Jacob's prophecy, Gen. 49 : 10, when the sceptre should depart from Judah, as indeed it did in Herod the Idumean : more particularly in Daniel's seventy weeks, from the decree of Darius, Daniel 9 : 24, answering exactly to the time of his birth ; a prophecy so cogent and full of proof, that Porphyry, the great enemy of Christians, had no other evasion but that it was devised after the event ; which yet the Jews, though as bitter enemies to Christ as himself, will by no means allow to be true.   And lastly, the time of his birth was exactly pointed at in Haggai's prophecy, Hag. 2 : 7, 9, compared with Malachi 3 : 1.   He must come while the second temple stood ; at that time there was a general expectation of him, John 1 : 19, and at that very time he came.   Luke 2 : 38.

The *place of his birth* was foretold to be Bethlehem Ephratah, Micah 5 : 2, and so it was, Matt. 2 : 5, 6. He was to be brought up in Nazareth, Zech. 6 : 12 : "Behold the man whose name is the Branch."   The word is *Netzer*, whence is the word Nazarite.   And there indeed was our Lord brought up.   Matt. 2 : 23.

His parent was to be a *virgin*, Isa. 7 : 14 ; punctually fulfilled, Matt. 1 : 20–23.

His *tribe* was foretold to be Judah.   Gen. 49 : 10.   "It is evident," saith the apostle, "that our Lord sprang out of Judah."   Heb. 7 : 14.

His *harbinger* or forerunner was foretold, Mal. 4 : 5, 6; fulfilled in John the Baptist, Luke 1 : 16, 17.

The obscurity and *meanness of his birth* were predicted, Isa. 53 : 2 ; Zech. 9 : 9 ; to which the event answered, Luke 2 : 12.

3. His *doctrine and miracles* were foretold, Isa. 35 : 4,

5, 6, the accomplishment of which in Christ is evident in the history of all the evangelists.

4. His *death* for us was foretold by the prophets : " Messiah shall be cut off, but not for himself." Daniel 9 : 26. " He was wounded for our transgressions." Isaiah 53 : 5. And so he was. John 11 : 50. The very kind and manner of his death was prefigured in the brazen serpent his type, and answered in his death upon the cross. John 3 : 14.

5. His *burial* in the tomb of a rich man was foretold, Isaiah 53 : 9, and accomplished most exactly. Matthew 27 : 59, 60.

6. His *resurrection* from the dead was typified in Jonah, and fulfilled in Christ's abode three days and nights in the grave. Matt. 12 : 40.

7. The wonderful *spread* of the gospel in the world, even to the isles of the Gentiles, was prophesied, Isaiah 49 : 6, to the truth whereof we are not only witnesses, but happy instances and examples of it. Thus the promised mercy was performed.

INFERENCE 1. *If Christ be the mercy of mercies, the medium of conveying all other mercies from God to men,* then in vain do men hope for mercy out of Jesus Christ.

I know many poor sinners comfort themselves with this when they come upon a bed of sickness : " I am sinful, but God is merciful." It is very true, God is merciful ; plenteous in mercy ; his mercy is great above the heavens ; mercy pleaseth him ; and all this they that are in Christ shall find experimentally, to their comfort and salvation. But what is all this to thee, if thou art Christless ? There is not one drop of saving mercy that comes in any other channel than Christ to the soul of any man. You may enjoy the riches, honors, and pleasures of this world for a season ; but there are two bars between you and all spiritual mercies, namely, the guilt of sin and the pollution of sin ; and nothing but your own union with

Christ can remove these, and so open the passage for spiritual mercies to your soul.

"But I will repent of sin, strive to obey the commands of God, make restitution for the wrongs I have done, cry to God for mercy, bind my soul with vows and strong resolutions against sin for time to come: will not, all this lay a groundwork for hope of mercy to my soul?" No, this will not, this cannot do it.

All your *sorrows* and tears for sin cannot obtain mercy. Could you shed as many tears for any sin you have committed, as all the children of Adam have shed since the creation of the world, they would not purchase the pardon of that one sin; for the law requires full satisfaction, and will not discharge any soul without it. The repentance of a soul finds, through Christ, acceptance with God, but out of him it is nothing.

All your *strivings* to obey the commands of God and live more strictly for time to come will not obtain mercy. "Except your righteousness shall exceed the righteousness of the scribes and Pharisees, ye shall in no case enter into the kingdom of heaven." Matt. 5 : 20.

Your *restitution* and reparation of wrongs you have done cannot obtain mercy. Judas restored, and yet was damned. Man is satisfied, but God is not. Remission is the act of God. He must loose your conscience from the bond of guilt, or it can never be loosed.

All your *cries* to God for mercy will not avail if you are out of Christ. Matt. 7 : 21 ; Job 27 : 9. A righteous judge will not reverse the just sentence of the law, though the prisoner at the bar fall upon his knees and cry for mercy.

Your *vows* and engagements to God for time to come cannot obtain mercy. Being made in your own strength, it is impossible you should keep them ; and if you could, it is impossible they should obtain remission and mercy. Should you never sin more for time to come, yet how shall God be satisfied for past sins? Justice must have satisfaction, or you can never have remission, Rom. 3 : 25, 26 ; and no work wrought by man can satisfy divine justice ; nor is the satisfaction of Christ made over to any for their discharge, but to such only as are in him : therefore never expect mercy out of Christ.

2. Is Christ greater and more necessary than all other mercies ? *then let no inferior mercy satisfy you for your portion.*

God has mercies of all kinds to give, but Christ is the chief, the mercy of all mercies ; Oh, be not satisfied without that mercy ! When Luther had a rich present sent him he protested that God should not put him off so ; and David was of the same mind. Psalm 17 : 14, 15. If the Lord should give you the desires of your heart in the good things of this life, let not that satisfy you while you are Christless ; for what is there in these earthly enjoyments whereof the vilest men have not a greater fulness than you? Job 21 : 7–11 ; Psalm 17 : 10, and 73 : 3, 12. What comfort can all these things give to a soul already condemned as thou art? John 3 : 18. What sweetness can be in them while they are all unsanctified things to you? enjoyment and sanctification are two distinct things. Psalm 37 : 16 ; Prov. 10 : 22. Thousands of unsanctified enjoyments will not yield your soul one drop of solid spiritual comfort. And what pleasure can you take in these things of which death must shortly strip you naked? You must die, and whose then shall all those things be for which you have labored? Be not so foolish as to think of leaving a great name behind you : it is but a poor felicity, as Chrysostom well observes, to be tormented where thou art, and praised where thou art not. The sweeter your portion has been on earth, the more intolerable will your condition be in hell ; yea, these earthly delights not only increase the torments of the damned, but also, as they are instruments of sin, prepare the souls of men for damnation : "Surely the prosperity of fools shall destroy them." Prov. 1 : 32. Rest not till Christ, the mercy of mercies, be the root and fountain, yielding and sanctifying all other mercies to you.

3. Is Christ, the mercy of mercies, infinitely better than all other mercies? *then let all that are in Christ be content and well satisfied, whatever other mercies the wisdom of God sees fit to deny them.* You have a Benjamin's portion, a plentiful inheritance in Christ; will you yet complain? Others have splendid houses upon earth, but you have "a house not made with hands, eternal in the heavens." 2 Cor. 5 : 1. Others are clothed with rich and costly apparel; your souls are clothed with the white, pure robes of Christ's righteousness. "I will greatly rejoice in the Lord, my soul shall be joyful in my God; for he hath clothed me with the garment of salvation, he hath covered me with the robe of righteousness, as a bridegroom decketh himself with ornaments, and as a bride adorneth herself with her jewels." Isa. 61 : 10. Let those that have full tables, heavy purses, rich lands, but no Christ, be rather objects of your pity than envy. God has not a better mercy to give than Christ, thy portion; in him all necessary mercies are secured to thee, and thy wants and straits sanctified to thy good. Oh, therefore never open thy mouth to complain against the bountiful God!

4. Is Christ the mercy, in whom are all the tender mercies of God towards poor sinners? *then let none be discouraged in going to Christ by reason of their sin and unworthiness.* His very name is *mercy.* Poor drooping sinner, encourage thyself in the way of faith; the Saviour to whom thou art going is mercy itself to broken-hearted sinners moving towards him. Jesus Christ is so merciful to poor souls that come to him, that he has received and pardoned the chiefest of sinners—men that stood as remote from mercy as any in the world. 1 Tim. 1 : 15; 1 Cor. 6 : 11. Those that shed the blood of Christ have yet been washed in that blood from their sin. Acts 2 : 36, 37. Mercy

receives sinners without exception of great and heinous ones. "If any man thirst, let him come unto me and drink." John 7 : 37. Gospel invitations run in general terms to all sinners that are heavy-laden. Matt. 11 : 28. When Mr. Bilney the martyr heard a minister preaching in this manner : "O thou old sinner, who hast been serving the devil these fifty or sixty years, dost thou think that Christ will receive thee now?" "Oh," said he, "what a preaching of Christ is here ! Had Christ been thus preached to me in the day of my trouble for sin, what glad tidings had it been !" Blessed be God, there is a sufficiency both of merit and mercy in Jesus Christ for all sinners, for the vilest among sinners whose hearts shall be made willing to come unto him. So merciful is the Lord Jesus Christ that he moves first, Isa. 61 : 1, 2 ; so merciful that he upbraids none, Ezek. 18 : 22 ; so merciful that he will not despise the weakest desires of souls if sincere, Isa. 42 : 3 ; so merciful that nothing more grieves him than our unwillingness to come unto him for mercy, John 5 : 40 ; so merciful that he waiteth to the last upon sinners to show them mercy, Rom. 10 : 21 ; Matt. 23 : 37 ; in a word, so merciful that it is his greatest joy when sinners come unto him, that he may show them mercy. Luke 15 : 5, 22.

OBJECTION. But it cannot enter into my thoughts that I should obtain mercy.

ANSWER. You measure God by yourself : "If a man find his enemy, will he let him go well away?" 1 Sam. 24 : 19. Man will not, but the merciful God will, upon the submission of his enemies to him. Besides, you are discouraged because you have not tried. Go to Jesus Christ, poor distressed sinner ; try him, and then report what a Saviour thou hast found him to be.

OBJECTION. But I have neglected the time of mercy, and now it is too late.

ANSWER. How know you that? Have you seen the book of life, or turned over the records of eternity? Or are you unwarrantably intruding into the secrets of God which belong not to you? Besides, if the treaty were at an end, how is it that thy heart is now distressed for sin and solicitous after deliverance from it?

OBJECTION. But I have waited long, and yet see no mercy for me.

ANSWER. May not mercy be coming and you not see it? or have you not waited at the wrong door? If you wait for the mercy of God through Christ in the way of humiliation and faith, assuredly mercy shall come to you.

5. Has God performed the mercy promised to the fathers, the great mercy, the capital mercy, Jesus Christ? *then let no man distrust God for the performance of lesser mercies contained in any promise of Scripture.* The performance of this mercy secures the performance of all other mercies to us; for Christ is a greater mercy than any other which yet remains to be given. Rom. 8 : 32. This mercy virtually comprehends all other mercies, 1 Cor. 3 : 21–23; and the promises that contain all other mercies are ratified and confirmed to believers in Christ. 2 Cor. 1 : 20. It was much more improbable that God should bestow his own Son upon the world, than that he should bestow any other mercy upon it. Has he given thee Christ? He will give thee bread to eat, raiment to put on, support in troubles, and whatsoever else thy soul or body shall need. The great mercy, Christ, makes way for all other mercies to the souls of believers.

6. *How mad are they that part with Christ, the best of mercies, to secure and preserve any temporal mercies to themselves!* Thus Demas and Judas gave up Christ to gain a little of the world. O soul-undoing bargain! How dear do they pay for the world, that purchase it with the loss of Christ and their own peace for ever!

Blessed be God for Jesus Christ, the mercy of mercies.

CHAPTER XII

THIRD TITLE OF CHRIST—"ALTOGETHER LOVELY"

" Yea, he is altogether lovely." Song 5: 16

At the ninth verse of this chapter you have an inquiry proposed to the spouse by the daughters of Jerusalem, "What is thy beloved more than another beloved?" To this question she returns her answers in the following verses, wherein she asserts his excellency. In verse 10 she declares, "He is the chiefest among ten thousand;" and she confirms that general assertion by an enumeration of his particular excellencies to verse 16, where she closes up her character and encomium of her beloved in the words we have read: "Yea, he is altogether lovely."

The words are an affirmative proposition setting forth the transcendent loveliness of the Lord Jesus Christ, and naturally resolve themselves into three parts:

1. The *subject*, *He* the Lord Jesus Christ, after whom she had been seeking, concerning whom these daughters of Jerusalem had inquired, whom she had endeavored so graphically to describe in his particular excellencies. This is the great and excellent subject of whom she here speaks.

2. What she affirms of him, that he is a *lovely one*, as in the original. The term signifies earnestly to desire, covet, or long after that which is most pleasant, grateful, delectable, and admirable. It is both in the abstract and the plural number, which speaks Christ to be the very essence of all delights and pleasures, the very soul and substance of them. As all the rivers are gathered into the ocean, so Christ is the ocean in which all true delights and pleasures meet.

3. The *manner* of the affirmation: He is "altogether lovely," lovely in all and in every part; as if she had said, Look on him in what respect or particular you will; cast your eye upon this lovely object and view him any way; turn him in your serious thoughts which way you will: consider his person, his offices, his works, or any thing belonging to him, you will find him "altogether lovely;" there is nothing ungrateful in him, there is nothing lovely without him. Hence,

Jesus Christ is the loveliest person souls can set their eyes upon.
"Thou art fairer than the children of men." Psa. 45:2. That is said of Jesus Christ which cannot be said of any creature, that he is "altogether lovely." Let us then weigh the import of this phrase, "altogether lovely," and then show in what respect Christ is so.

I. LET US WEIGH THIS EXCELLENT EXPRESSION, and particularly consider what is contained in it.

1. *It excludes all unloveliness* from Jesus Christ. So says Vatablus, There is nothing in him which is not amiable. And in this respect Christ infinitely transcends the most excellent and lovely creatures; for whatsoever loveliness is found in them it is not without imperfection: the fairest pictures must have their shadows; the most transparent stones must have their foils to set off their beauty; the best creature is but a bitter-sweet at best: if there be somewhat pleasing, there is also somewhat displeasing. But it is not so in our altogether lovely Saviour; his excellencies are pure and unmixed: he is a sea of sweetness without one drop of gall.

2. "Altogether lovely." As there is nothing unlovely found in him, so *all that is in him is wholly lovely;* as every ray of gold is precious, so every thing that is in Christ is precious. Who can weigh Christ in a pair of balances and tell you what his worth is? His price is above rubies, and all that thou canst desire is not to be compared with him. Prov. 8 : 11.

3. "Altogether lovely." He is *comprehensive of all things that are lovely;* he seals up the sum of all loveliness. Things that shine as single stars with a particular glory all meet in Christ as a glorious constellation. "It pleased the Father that in him should all fulness dwell." Col. 1 : 19. Cast your eyes among all created beings, observe strength in one, beauty in a second, faithfulness in a third, wisdom in a fourth; but you shall find none excelling in them all as Christ doth. He is bread to the hungry, water to the thirsty, a garment to the naked, healing to the wounded, and whatever a soul can desire is found in him. 1 Cor. 1 : 30.

4. "Altogether lovely." *Nothing is lovely in opposition to him,* or in separation from him. If he be altogether lovely, whatever is opposite to or separate from him can have no loveliness in it; take away Christ, and where is the loveliness of any enjoyment? The best creature-comfort out of Christ is but a broken cistern, it cannot hold one drop of true comfort. Psalm 73 : 26. It is with the loveliest creature as with a beautiful image in the glass— turn away the face and where is the image? Riches, honors, and comfortable relations are sweet when the face of Christ smiles upon us through them; but without him what empty trifles are they all.

5. "Altogether lovely" *Transcending all created excellencies* in beauty and loveliness. If you compare Christ and other things, be they never so lovely, never so excellent and desirable, Christ carries away all loveliness from them. "He is before all things." Col. 1 : 17. Not only before all things in time, nature, and order, but in dignity, glory, and true excellence. In all things he must have the preëminence.

All other loveliness is *derivative* and secondary, but the loveliness of Christ original and primary. Angels and men, the world and all that is desirable in it, receive what excellence they have from him—they are streams from the fountain. But as the waters in the fountain itself are more abundant, so are they more pure and pleasant than in the streams.

The loveliness and excellence of all other things is but *relative*, consisting in its reference to Christ and subserviency to his glory; but Christ is lovely considered absolutely in himself: he is desirable for himself, other things are so for him.

The beauty and loveliness of all other things is *perishing*, but the loveliness of Christ is fresh to all eternity: the sweetness of the best creatures is a fading flower; if not before, yet certainly at death it must fade away. "Doth not their excellency which is in them go away?" Job 4 : 21. Yes, whether natural excellencies of the body, or acquired endowments of the mind, lovely features, amiable qualities, attracting excellencies, all these like pleasant flowers are withered, faded, and destroyed by death; but Christ is the same yesterday, to-day, and for ever. Heb. 13 : 8.

The beauty and excellence of creatures are *ensnaring* and dangerous: a man may make them an idol, and dote upon them beyond the bounds of moderation, but there is no danger of excess in the love of Christ.

The loveliness of every creature is of a *satiating* nature; our estimation of it abates and sinks by our nearer approach to it, or longer enjoyment of it: creatures, like pictures, are fairest at a due distance, but it is not so with Christ; the nearer the soul approaches him, and the longer it lives in the enjoyment of him, the more sweet and desirable he is.

All other loveliness is *unsatisfying* to the soul of man: there is not room enough in all created things for the soul of man to dilate and expatiate itself; it still feels itself confined and narrowed within those limits. This arises from the unsuitableness of the creature to the nobler and more excellent soul of man, which, like a ship in a narrow river, hath not room to turn, and besides, is ever and anon striking ground and foundering in those shallows. But Jesus Christ is every way adequate to the vast desires of the soul; in him it hath sea-room enough; there it may spread all its sails with no fear of touching the bottom.

II. I proceed to show IN WHAT RESPECTS Jesus Christ is altogether lovely. And,

1. He is altogether lovely *in his person:* a Deity dwelling in flesh. John 1 : 14. The wonderful union of the divine and human nature in Christ renders him an object of admiration and adoration to angels and men. 1 Tim. 3 : 16. God never presented to the world such a vision of glory before. And consider how the human nature of our Lord Jesus Christ is replenished with all the graces of the Spirit, so as never any of all the saints was filled. O how lovely doth this render him! "God giveth not the Spirit by measure unto him." John 3 : 34. This makes him fairer than the children of men, grace being poured into his lips. Psalm 45 : 2. If a small measure of grace in the saints makes them such desirable companions, what must the riches and fulness of the Spirit of grace, filling Jesus Christ without measure, make him in the eyes of believers?

2. He is altogether lovely *in his offices.* Let us but consider the suitableness, fulness, and comfort of them.

Consider the *suitableness* of the offices of Christ to the miseries and wants of men, and we cannot but adore the infinite wisdom of God in his investiture with them. We are by nature blind and ignorant, at best but groping in the dim light of nature after God. Acts 17 : 27. Jesus Christ is a light to lighten the Gentiles. Isa. 49 : 6. When this great Prophet came into the world, then did the day-spring from on high visit us. Luke 1 : 78. The state of nature is a state of alienation from and enmity against God; Christ comes into the world an atoning sacrifice, making peace by the blood of his cross. Col. 1 : 20. All the world by nature are in bondage and captivity to Satan ; Christ comes with kingly power to rescue sinners as a prey from the mouth of the terrible one.

Let the *fulness* of his offices as prophet, priest, and king be also considered, by reason whereof he is able to save to the uttermost all that come to God by him. Heb. 7 : 25. The three offices, comprising in them all that our souls need, become a universal relief to all our wants ; and therefore,

Unspeakably *comfortable* must the offices of Christ be to the souls of sinners. If light be pleasant to our eyes, how pleasant is that light of life springing from the Sun of righteousness ! Mal. 4 : 2. If a pardon be sweet to a condemned malefactor, how sweet must the sprinkling of the blood of Jesus be to the trembling conscience of a law-condemned sinner ! If a rescue from a cruel tyrant be sweet to a poor captive, how sweet must it be to the ears of enslaved sinners to hear the voice of liberty and deliverance proclaimed by Jesus Christ ! Out of the several offices of Christ, as out of so many fountains, all the promises of the new covenant flow, as so many soul-refreshing streams of peace and joy. All the promises of illumination, counsel, and direction flow out of the *prophetical office;* all the promises of reconciliation, peace, pardon, and acceptation flow out of the *priestly office,* with the sweet streams of joy and spiritual comfort depending thereupon ; all the promises of converting, increasing, defending, directing, and supplying grace flow out of the *kingly office* of Christ : indeed, all promises may be reduced to the three offices ; so that Jesus Christ must needs be altogether lovely in his offices.

3. Jesus Christ is altogether lovely *in his relations.*

(1.) He is a lovely *Redeemer.* He came to open the prison-doors to them that are bound. Isa. 61 : 1. This Redeemer must be a lovely one, if we consider the depth of

misery from which he redeemed us, even "from the wrath
to come." 1 Thess. 1 : 10. How lovely was Titus in the
eyes of the poor enthralled Greeks, whom he delivered
from their bondage ; this so endeared him to them, that
when their liberty was proclaimed they even trod one
another to death to see the herald that proclaimed it ; and
all the night following, with instruments of music, danced
about his tent, crying, with united voices, " A saviour, a
saviour !"

Or whether we consider the numbers redeemed, and
the means of their redemption. "They sung a new song,
saying, Thou art worthy to take the book, and to open
the seals thereof : for thou wast slain, and hast redeemed
us to God by thy blood out of every kindred, and tongue,
and people, and nation." Rev. 5 : 9. He redeemed us
not with silver and gold, but with his own precious blood,
by way of *price*, 1 Peter 1 : 18, 19 ; with his outstretched
and glorious arm, by way of *power*, Col. 1 : 13 ; he redeemed us *freely*, Eph. 1 : 7 ; *fully*, Rom. 8 : 1 ; *seasonably*,
Gal. 4 : 4 ; and out of special and peculiar *love*, John
17 : 9. In a word, he hath redeemed us *for ever*, never
more to come into bondage. 1 Peter 1 : 5 ; John 10 : 28.
O how lovely is Jesus Christ in the relation of a Redeemer
to God's elect.

(2.) He is a lovely *bridegroom* to all that he espouses to
himself. How does the church glory in him in the words
following my text : "This is my Beloved, and this is my
Friend, O ye daughters of Jerusalem." As much as to
say, heaven and earth cannot show such another ; which
needs no fuller proof than the following particulars :

He espouses to himself, in mercy and in loving-kind-
ness, such defiled and altogether unworthy souls as we
are, Deut. 7 : 7 ; he chooseth us not because we were,
but that he might make us lovely, Eph. 5 : 27 ; he passed
by us when we lay in ruin, and said unto us, Live ; and
that was the time of love. Ezek. 16 : 6. He expects

nothing from us, and yet bestows himself and all that he has upon us. Our poverty cannot enrich him, but he made himself poor to enrich us. 2 Cor. 8 : 9 ; 1 Cor. 3 : 22.

No husband loves the wife of his bosom as Christ loved his people. He loved the church, and gave himself for it. Eph. 5 : 25. No one bears with weakness and provocation as Christ does ; the church is called "the Lamb's wife." Rev. 21 : 9. No husband is immortal as Christ is ; death separates all other relations, but the soul's union with Christ is not dissolved in the grave ; yea, the day of a believer's death is his marriage day, the day of his fullest enjoyment of Christ. No husband can say to his wife what Christ says to the believer, "I will never leave thee, nor forsake thee." Heb. 13 : 5. No bridegroom advances his bride to such honors by marriage as Christ does ; he brings his people to God as their father, and from that day the glorious angels think it no dishonor to be their servants, Heb. 1 : 14 ; they admire the beauty and glory of the spouse of Christ. Rev. 21 : 9. No marriage was ever consummated with such triumphal solemnity as the marriage of Christ and believers shall be in heaven. "She shall be brought to the king in raiment of needlework ; the virgins her companions that follow her shall be brought unto thee. With gladness and rejoicing shall they be brought : they shall enter into the king's palace." Psalm 45 : 14, 15. Among the Jews the marriage house was called the house of praise ; there was joy in all hearts, but none like the joy that will be in heaven when believers, the spouse of Christ, shall be brought thither. God the Father will rejoice to behold the blessed accomplishment and consummation of the glorious designs of his love. Jesus Christ the Bridegroom will rejoice to see the travail of his soul, the blessed issue of all his bitter pangs and agonies. Isaiah 53 : 11. The Holy Spirit will rejoice to see the perfection of the sanctifying design which was committed to his hand, 2 Cor. 5 : 5 ; to see the souls whom he once found as rough stones, shine as the bright polished stones of the spiritual temple. Angels will rejoice : great was the joy when the foundation of this design was laid in the incarnation of Christ, Luke 2 : 13 ; great must their joy be when the top-stone is set up with shouting, crying, Grace, grace. The saints themselves shall rejoice unspeakably when they shall enter into the King's palace, and be for ever with the Lord. 1 Thess. 4 : 17.

(3.) Christ is altogether lovely as an *Advocate*. "If any man sin, we have an Advocate with the Father, Jesus Christ the righteous, and he is the propitiation," 1 John 2 : 1, 2 ; it is he who pleads the cause of believers in heaven, appears for them in the presence of God to prevent all new breaches, and continues the state of friendship and peace between God and us. He makes our cause his own, and acts for us in heaven as for himself. Heb. 4 : 15. He is touched with the tender sense of our troubles and dangers, and is not only one with us by way of representation, but also in sympathy and affection. He follows our suit in heaven as his great design and business ; therefore, in Heb. 7 : 25, he is said to "live for ever to make intercession for us," as if our concerns were so regarded by him there that he gives himself wholly to that work.

He pleads the cause of believers by *his blood*. We are said to be come to the blood of sprinkling that speaketh better things than that of Abel. Heb. 12 : 24. Every wound he received for us on earth is opened to plead with God on our behalf in heaven ; hence it is that, in Rev. 5 : 6, he is represented standing before God, *as a lamb that had been slain ;* as it were exhibiting in heaven those deadly wounds received on earth from the justice of God on our account. Other advocates spend their breath, Christ his blood. He pleads the cause of believers freely. In a word, he obtains for us all the mercies for which he pleads ; no cause which he undertakes can fail. Rom. 8 : 33, 34. O what a lovely Advocate is Christ for believers.

(4.) Christ is altogether lovely in the relation of a *Friend*, for in this relation he is pleased to own his people. Luke 12 : 4. There are certain things in which one friend manifests his affection and friendship to another, but none like Christ.

No friend is so *open-hearted* to his friend as Christ is to his people ; he reveals the very counsels and secrets of his heart to them. "Henceforth I call you not servants ; for the servant knoweth not what his Lord doeth ; but I have called you friends ; for all things that I have heard of my Father I have made known unto you." John 15 : 15.

No friend in the world is so *bountiful* to his friend as Jesus Christ is to believers. "Greater love hath no man than this, that a man lay down his life for his friends." John 15 : 13. He has exhausted the precious treasures of his invaluable blood to pay our debts. O what a lovely friend is Jesus Christ to believers.

No friend *sympathizes* so tenderly with his friend in affliction. In all our afflictions he is afflicted. Heb. 4 : 15. He feels all our sorrows, wants, and burdens as his own. Whence it is that the sufferings of believers are called the sufferings of Christ. Col. 1 : 24.

No friend in the world takes the *complacency* in his friend that Jesus Christ does in believers. How is the Lord Jesus pleased to glory in his people ; how is he delighted with those gracious ornaments which himself bestows upon them !

No friend in the world loves his friend with so fervent and strong *affection* as Jesus Christ loves believers. Jacob loved Rachel, and endured for her sake the parching heat of summer and cold of winter ; but Christ endured the storms of the wrath of God, the heat of his indignation, for our sakes. David manifested his love to Absalom in wishing, "O that I had died for thee!" Christ manifested his love to us in death itself, in our stead and for our sake.

No friend in the world is so constant and unchangeable in friendship as Christ. "Having loved his own which were in the world, he loved them unto the end." John 13 : 1. He bears with millions of provocations and injuries, and yet will not break friendship with his people. Peter denied him, yet he did not disown him.

I might farther show the loveliness of Christ in his ordinances and in his providences, in his communion with us and communications to us, but there is no end to the account of Christ's loveliness; I will rather choose to press believers to their duties towards this altogether lovely Saviour.

INFERENCE 1. Is Jesus Christ altogether lovely, then I beseech you *set your souls upon him.* Methinks such an object as here represented should compel love from the coldest and hardest heart. Away with this vain, deceitful world, which deserves not the thousandth part of the love you give it; let all stand aside and give way to Christ. O did you but know his worth and excellency, what he is in himself, what he has done for and deserved from you, you would need no arguments of mine to persuade you to love him.

2. *Esteem nothing lovely but as it is enjoyed in Christ, or improved for him.* Love nothing for itself, as separate from Jesus Christ. We all sin in the excess of our affections towards earthly objects, and in transferring to them the love which we owe to Christ alone.

3. *Let us all be humbled for the baseness of our hearts, that are so free in their affections to trifles, and so hard to be persuaded to the love of Christ.* O how many pour out streams of love and delight upon earthly objects, while no arguments can draw forth one drop of love from their obdurate

and unbelieving hearts to Jesus Christ. I have read of one Joannes Mollius, who was observed to go often alone and to weep bitterly; and being pressed by a friend as to the cause of his troubles, "Oh," said he, "it grieves me, that I cannot bring this heart of mine to love Jesus Christ more fervently."

4. *Represent Christ as he is to the world, by your conduct towards him.* Is he altogether lovely; let all the world see and know that he is so, by your delight in him and communion with him, your zeal for him, and readiness to part with any other lovely thing upon his account; convince them how much your beloved is better than any other beloved; display his glorious excellencies in your heavenly conversation; hold him forth to others as he is in himself, altogether lovely. See that you "walk worthy of the Lord unto all pleasing." Col. 1 : 10. Show forth the praises of Christ. 1 Pet. 2 : 9. Let not that worthy name be blasphemed through you. James 2 : 7. He is glorious in himself, and will put glory upon you : take heed ye put not shame and dishonor upon him; he hath committed his honor to you, do not betray that trust.

5. *Never be ashamed to own Christ.* He can never be a shame to you; it will be your great sin to be ashamed of him. Some men glory in their shame; be not you ashamed of your glory : if you are ashamed of Christ now, he will be ashamed of you when he shall appear in his own glory and the glory of all his holy angels. Be ashamed of nothing but sin; and among other sins, be ashamed especially for this sin, that you have no more love for him who is *altogether lovely.*

6. *Be willing to leave every thing that is lovely upon earth, that you may be with the altogether lovely Lord Jesus Christ in heaven.* Lift up your voices with the church, Rev. 20 : 20, "Come, Lord Jesus, come quickly." It is true, you must pass through the pangs of death into his bosom and enjoyment; but it is worth suffering much more than that to be

with Jesus. "The Lord direct your hearts into the love of God, and into the patient waiting for Christ." 2 Thes. 3:5.

7. *As you would be lovely in the sight of God and man, strive to be like Christ.* Certainly it is the Spirit of Christ within you, and the beauty of Christ upon you, which only can make you lovely ; the more you resemble him in holiness, the more will you manifest of true excellence ; and the more frequent and spiritual your communion with Christ, the more of the loveliness of Christ will be stamped upon your spirits, changing you into the same image, from glory to glory.

8. *Let the loveliness of Christ draw all men to him.* Is loveliness in the creature so attractive ? And can the transcendent loveliness of Christ draw none ? O the blindness of man ! If you see no beauty in Christ that you should desire him, it is because the god of this world hath blinded your minds.

CHAPTER XIII

FOURTH TITLE OF CHRIST — "THE DESIRE OF ALL NATIONS."

"And the Desire of all nations shall come." HAGGAI 2:7

THE chapter preceding our text is mainly spent in reproving the negligence of the Jews, who, being discouraged from time to time, had delayed rebuilding the temple, and in the mean time employed their care and cost in building and adorning their own houses; but at last being persuaded to set about the work, they met with this discouragement, that such was the poverty of the time that the second structure would no way correspond with the magnificence and splendor of the first. In Solomon's days the nation was wealthy, now it was poor; so that there would be no proportion between the second and the first. To this discouragement the prophet applies the relief, that whatever was wanting in external pomp and glory should be more than recompensed by the presence of Jesus Christ in this second temple, for "the Desire of all nations," said he, shall come into it; which, by the way, may give us this useful lesson, that the presence of Jesus Christ gives a more real and excellent glory to places of worship than any external beauty whatsoever can bestow upon them. Our eyes, like the disciples, are apt to be dazzled with the goodly stones of the temple, and in the mean time to neglect and overlook that which gives it the greatest honor and beauty.

In these words we have both a description of Christ and an index pointing at the time of his incarnation: he is called "the Desire of all nations;" and the time of his coming in the flesh is plainly intimated to be while the second temple should be standing. Here then we find just cause to bemoan the blindness that is happened to the Jews, who, owning the truth of this prophecy, and not able to deny the destruction of the second temple many hundred years since, yet will not be persuaded to acknowledge the incarnation of the true Messiah.

Christ, called *"the Desire of all nations,"* was to come into the world in the time of the second temple, and after grievous concussions and revolutions which were to make way for his coming; for so our prophet here speaks, "I will shake all nations, and the Desire of all nations shall come," to which the apostle alludes, Heb. 12 : 26, applying this prophecy to Jesus Christ, here called the "Desire of all nations ;" putting the act for the object, desire for the thing desired. As in Ezek. 24 : 16, "the desire of thine eyes," is the desirable wife of thy bosom ; so here the "Desire of all nations" is Christ, the object of the desires of God's people in all nations of the world. From this we learn that

The desires of God's people in all kingdoms, and among all nations of the earth, are and shall be drawn out and fixed upon the Lord Jesus Christ.

The merciful God, beholding the universal ruin of the world by sin, has provided a universal remedy for his own elect in every part of the earth. Christ is not given to any one nation in the world, but intended to be God's salvation to the ends of the earth : "There is neither Greek nor Jew, Barbarian, Scythian, bond nor free ; but Christ is all, and in all." Col. 2 : 11. In the explication of this point two things must be inquired into : why Christ is called the Desire of all nations ; and upon what account the people of God, in all nations, desire him.

I. WHY HE IS CALLED THE DESIRE OF ALL NATIONS, and what that phrase may import ; and there are divers things that are supposed or included in it.

1. That God the Father has appointed him as a remedy

for the sins and miseries of his people *in all parts of the world*. So in the covenant of redemption between the Father and the Son the Lord expresses himself, "It is a light thing that thou shouldest be my servant to raise up the tribes of Jacob, and to restore the preserved of Israel : I will also give thee for a light to the Gentiles, that thou mayest be my salvation unto the end of the earth." Isa. 49 : 6. So that prophecy, "He shall sprinkle many nations." Isa. 52 : 15. If God had not appointed him for, he could not be desired by all nations.

And indeed, herein the grace of God admirably shines forth in the freeness of it, that even the most barbarous nations are not excluded from the benefits of redemption by Christ. This is what the apostle admires, that Christ should be "preached unto the Gentiles," 1 Tim. 3 : 16, to people who seemed to be lost in the darkness of idolatry. Even for them Christ was given by the Father. "Ask of me, and I shall give thee the heathen for thine inheritance, and the uttermost parts of the earth for thy possession." Psalm 2 : 8.

2. Christ, the Desire of all nations, plainly indicates *the sufficiency* there is in him to supply the wants of the whole world. As the sun in the heavens suffices all nations for light and influence, so does the Sun of righteousness suffice for the redemption, justification, sanctification, and salvation of the people of God all over the world. "Look unto me, and be ye saved, all the ends of the earth." Isa. 45 : 22.

3. It implies the *reality of godliness*. It shows that religion is no fancy, as the atheistical world would persuade us ; for this appears in the uniform effects of it upon the hearts of all men, in all nations of the world, that are truly religious. All their desires, like so many needles touched by one and the same loadstone, move towards Jesus Christ. Were it possible for the people of God of all nations, kindreds, and languages in the world to meet

in one place, and there compare the desires and workings of their hearts, though they never saw each other's faces, nor heard each other's names, yet, as face answers to face in a glass, so would their desires after Christ answer to each other. All hearts work after him in the same manner; what one says, all say: these are my troubles and burdens, these my wants and miseries; these my desires and fears: one and the same Spirit works in all believers throughout the world; which could never be if religion were but a fancy, as some call it.

4. Christ, the Desire of all nations, implies *the vast extent of his kingdom* in the world. Out of every nation under heaven some shall be brought to Christ, and to heaven by him; and though the number of God's people, compared with the multitudes of the ungodly in all nations, be but a remnant, a little flock, and in that comparative sense there are few that shall be saved; yet considered absolutely and in themselves, they are a vast multitude which no man can number. "Many shall come from the east, and from the west, and shall sit down with Abraham, and Isaac, and Jacob, in the kingdom of heaven." Matt. 8 : 11. In order to this, the gospel, like the sun in the heavens, encircles the world. It arose in the east and takes its course towards the western world; rising by degrees upon the remote, idolatrous nations of the earth; out of all which a number is to be saved. Even "Ethiopia shall stretch out her hands unto God." Psalm 68 : 31. And this consideration should move us to pray earnestly for the poor heathen who yet sit in darkness and the shadow of death; there is yet hope for them.

5. It shows that when God opens the eyes of men to see their sin and danger, *nothing but Christ can give them satisfaction:* it is not the fertility, riches, and pleasures the inhabitants of any kingdom of the world enjoy that can satisfy the desires of their souls. When God touches their

hearts with the sense of sin and misery, Christ and none other is desirable and necessary in the eyes of such persons. Many kingdoms of the world abound with riches and pleasures, and to many of them scarcely any thing is left to desire that the world can afford. Yet all this can give no satisfaction without Jesus Christ, the Desire of all nations, when once they come to see the necessity and excellence of him : then take the world who will, they must have Christ, the desire of their souls.

But there lies an *objection* against this truth, which must be solved. "If Christ be the Desire of all nations, how comes it to pass that Jesus Christ finds no entertainment in so many nations of the world, among whom Christianity is hissed at and Christians are not tolerated?"

We must remember, the nations of the world have their times and seasons of conversion. Those that once embraced Christ have now lost him, and idols are now set up in the places where he was once worshipped. The sun of the gospel is gone down upon them, and now shines in another hemisphere ; and so the nations of the world have their distinct days and seasons of illumination. The gospel, like the sea, gains in one place while it loses in another ; and in the times and seasons appointed by the Father, they come successively to be enlightened in the knowledge of Christ ; and then shall the promise be fulfilled, "Thus saith the Lord, the Redeemer of Israel, and his Holy One, to him whom man despiseth, to him whom the nation abhorreth, to a servant of rulers, Kings shall see and arise, princes also shall worship, because of the Lord that is faithful." Isa. 49 : 7.

Let it also be remembered, that though Christ is rejected by the rulers and body of many nations, yet he is the desire of all the people of God dispersed and scattered among those nations.

II. We are to inquire UPON WHAT ACCOUNT CHRIST BECOMES THE DESIRE OF ALL NATIONS, or of all those in all the nations of the world that belong to the election of grace. And the true reason is, because Christ only has that in himself which relieves their wants and answers to all their need.

1. They are all, by nature, under condemnation, Rom. 5 : 16, 18, under the curse of the law ; against which nothing is found in heaven or earth able to relieve their consciences but the blood of sprinkling, the pure and *perfect righteousness* of the Lord Jesus : and hence it is that Christ becomes so desirable in the eyes of poor sinners all the world over. If any thing in nature could be found to pacify and relieve the consciences of men from guilt and fear, Christ would never be desirable in their eyes ; but finding no other remedy but the blood of Jesus, to him shall all the ends of the earth look for righteousness and for peace.

2. All nations of the world are polluted with sin both by nature and practice, which they shall see and bitterly bewail when *the light of the gospel* shall shine among them; and the same light by which this shall be discovered will also discover the only remedy of this evil to lie in the Spirit of Christ, the only fountain opened to all nations for sanctification and cleansing ; and this will make the Lord Jesus incomparably desirable in their eyes. O how welcome will he be that cometh unto them, not by blood only, but by water also. 1 John 5 : 6.

3. When the light of the gospel shall shine upon the nations, they shall see that by reason of sin they are all barred out of heaven ; that those doors are chained against them, and none but Christ can *open an entrance for them into the kingdom of God :* that no man cometh to the Father but by him, John 14 : 6, neither is there any name under heaven given among men whereby they must be saved, but the name of Christ. Acts 4 : 12. Hence the hearts of sinners shall pant after him as a hart panteth for the water-brooks.

INFERENCE 1. Is Christ the desire of all nations ? *how vile a sin is it then in any nation, upon whom the light of the gospel has shone, to reject Jesus Christ!* These say, "Depart from us, for we desire not the knowledge of thy ways." Job 21 : 14. They thrust away his worship, government, and servants from among them ; and in effect say, "We will not have this man to reign over us." Luke 19 : 14. Thus did the Jews, they put away Christ from among them, and thereby judged themselves unworthy of eternal life. Acts 13 : 46. This is at once a fearful sin and a dreadful sign. How soon did vengeance overtake them like the overthrow of Sodom. O let it be for a warning to all nations to the end of the world. He would have gathered the children of Israel under his wings as a hen doth her brood, even when the Roman eagle was hovering over them, but they would not : therefore their houses were left unto them desolate, their city and temple made a heap.

2. If Jesus Christ be the desire of all nations, *how incomparably happy must that nation be that enjoys Christ in the power and purity of his gospel ordinances!* If Christ under a veil made Canaan a glorious land, Dan. 11 : 41, what a glorious place must that nation be which beholds him with open face in the bright sunshine of the gospel. O my country, know thy happiness and the day of thy visitation : what others desired thou enjoyest : provoke not the Lord Jesus to depart from thee by corrupting his worship, longing after idolatry, abusing his messengers and oppressing his people, lest his soul depart from thee.

3. If Christ be the desire of all nations, *examine whether he be the desire of your soul in particular*, else you shall have no benefit by him. Are your desires after Christ true spiritual desires ? Reflect, I beseech you, upon the frame and temper of your heart. Can you say of your desires after Christ as Peter did of his love to Christ ? Lord, thou knowest all things ; thou knowest that I desire thee. Try your desires, as to their sincerity, by the following tests :

Are they *ardent?* Has Christ the supreme place in your desires? Do you esteem all things but dross in comparison of the excellency of Jesus Christ your Lord? Phil. 3 : 8. Is he to you as the refuge-city to the manslayer? Heb. 6 : 18 ; as a spring of water in a dry place; as the shadow of a great rock in a weary land? Isaiah 32 : 2. Such vehement desires are true desires.

Are your desires after Christ *universal;* is every thing in Christ desirable in your eyes? The hypocrite is for a divided Christ ; he would be called by his name, but trusts in himself. If his holiness and government, his cross and sufferings are desirable for his sake, such universal desires are right desires.

Do your desires after Christ lead you to *effort,* to use all the means of accomplishing what you desire? You say you desire Christ, but what will you do to obtain your desire? If you seek him carefully and incessantly in all the ways of duty ; if you will strive in prayer, labor to believe, cut off right hands and pluck out right eyes, that is, be willing to part with the most profitable and pleasant ways of sin that you may enjoy Christ, the desire of your souls, then are your desires right.

Are your desires after Christ *permanent,* or only a sudden fit which goes off again without effect? If your desires after Christ abide in your heart, if your longings are at all times for him, then are your desires right. Christ always dwells in the desires of his people ; they can feel him in their desires when they cannot discern him in their love or delight.

Will your desires after Christ *admit no satisfaction,* nor find rest anywhere but in the enjoyment of Christ? then are your desires right. The soul that desires Christ can never be at rest till it come home to Christ. 2 Cor. 5 : 2, 6 ; Philippians 1 : 23. The devil can satisfy others with the riches and pleasures of this world, as children are quieted with toys ; but if nothing but Christ can satisfy and terminate your desires, surely such desires are right.

Do your desires after Christ spring from *a deep sense of your need* of Christ? Has conviction opened your eyes to see your misery, to feel your burdens, and to make you sensible that your remedy lies only in the Lord Jesus? then are your desires right. Bread and water are made necessary and desirable by hunger and thirst. By these things try the truth of your desires after Christ.

4. Do you indeed, upon serious trial, find in you such desires after Christ as above described? O bless the Lord for that day wherein Christ, the desire of all nations, became the desire of your souls; and for your comfort, *know that you are happy and blessed souls at present.*

Blessed in this, that your eyes have been opened to see both the want and worth of Christ. Had not Christ applied his precious eye-salve to the eyes of your mind, you would never have desired him; you would have said, "He hath no form nor comeliness; and when we shall see him, there is no beauty that we should desire him," Isaiah 53 : 2; or as they to the spouse, "What is thy beloved more than another beloved?" Song 5 : 9. O blessed souls, enlightened of the Lord to see those things that are hid from them that perish! You are blessed, in that your desires after Christ are a sure evidence that the desire of Christ is towards you. We may say of desires as it is said of love, we desire him because he first desired us: your desires after Christ are inflamed from the desires of Christ after you. You are blessed, in that your desires shall surely be satisfied: "Blessed are they which hunger and thirst after righteousness, for they shall be filled." Matt. 5 : 6. "The desires of the righteous shall be granted." Prov. 10 : 24. God never raised such desires as these in the souls of his people to be a torment to them for ever.

You are blessed, in that God hath guided your desires

to make the best choice that ever was made, while the desires of others are eagerly set upon gaining riches, pleasure, and honor in the world. Any good will satisfy some men. Happy soul, if none but Christ can satisfy thee. Psalm 4 : 6. You are blessed, in that there is a work of grace certainly wrought upon thy soul; and these very desires after Christ are a part thereof. Blessed, in that these desires after Christ keep thy soul active and working after him continually in the way of duty. One thing have I desired, that will I seek after. Psalm 27 : 4. Desire will be a continual spring to diligence and industry in the way of duty; the desire of the end quickeneth to the use of means. Prov. 18 : 1. Others may fall asleep and cast off duty, but it will be hard for those to do so whose souls burn with desire after Christ. You are also blessed, in that your desires after Christ will make death much the sweeter and easier to you. I desire to be dissolved and to be with Christ, which is far better. Phil. 1 : 23. When a Christian was once asked whether he was willing to die, he returned this answer : Let him be unwilling to die who is unwilling to go to Christ. And much like it was that of another, I refuse this life, to live with Christ.

5. *Let me exhort and persuade all to make Jesus Christ the desire and choice of their souls.* This is the main scope and design of the gospel. And Oh that I could effectually press home this exhortation upon your hearts. Every creature naturally desires its own preservation ; do not you desire the preservation of your precious and immortal souls ? If you do, then make Christ your desire and choice, without whom they can never be preserved. Jude 1. Do not your souls earnestly desire the bodies they live in ? How tender are they of them, how careful to provide for them, though they pay a dear rent for these tenements they live in. And is not union with Christ infinitely more desirable than the union of soul and body ? O covet union with

him ; then shall your souls be happy when your bodies drop from them at death, 2 Cor. 5 : 1, 3 ; yea, soul and body shall be happy with him for evermore.

How do the men of this world desire the enjoyments of it. They rise early, sit up late, eat the bread of carefulness ; and all this for very vanity. Shall a worldling do more for earth than you for heaven? Shall the creature be so earnestly desired, and Christ neglected? What do all your desires in this world benefit you, if you go Christless? Suppose you had the desire of your hearts in these things, how long should you have comfort in them if you have not Christ ?

Does Christ desire you, who have nothing lovely or desirable in you ? And have you no desires after Christ, the most lovely and desirable one in both worlds? How absolutely necessary is Jesus Christ to your souls ! Bread and water, breath and life, are not so necessary as Christ. "One thing is needful," Luke 10 : 42, and that one thing is Christ. If you fail in your desires in other things, you may yet be happy ; but if you have not Christ, you are undone for ever. How great are the benefits that will redound to you by Jesus Christ ! In him you have a rich inheritance settled upon you : all things are yours when you are Christ's. 1 Cor. 3 : 22. All your well-grounded hopes of glory are built upon your union with Him. 2 Cor. 1 : 21. If you have not Christ, you must die without hope. Suppose you were at the judgment-seat of God, where you must shortly stand, and saw the terrors of the Lord in that day ; the sheep divided from the goats ; the sentences of absolution and condemnation passed by the great and awful Judge upon the righteous and wicked ; would not Christ be then desirable in your eyes? As ever you expect to stand with comfort at that bar, let Christ be the desire and choice of your souls now.

6. Do these considerations put thee upon this inquiry, *How shall I get my desires kindled and inflamed towards Christ ?*

Alas, my heart is cold and dead, not a serious desire stirring in it after Christ. To such I offer the following directions:

Redeem some time every day for meditation; get out of the noise of the world, Psalm 4 : 4, and seriously bethink yourself how the present state of your soul stands, and how it is likely to go with you for ever: here all sound conversion begins. Psalm 119 : 59.

Consider seriously that lamentable state in which you came into the world; children of wrath by nature, under the curse and condemnation of the law; so that either your state must be changed, or you must inevitably be damned. John 3 : 3. Consider the course you have taken since you came into the world, proceeding from iniquity to iniquity. What command of God have you not violated a thousand times over? What sin is committed in the world that you are not one way or other guilty of before God? How many secret sins lie against you, unknown to the most intimate friend you have? Either this guilt must be separated from your souls, or your souls from God to all eternity.

Think upon the severe wrath of God due to every sin: "The wages of sin is death." Rom. 6 : 23. And how intolerable must be the fulness of that wrath, when a few drops sprinkled upon the conscience in this world are so insupportable, that it has made some choose strangling rather than life; and yet this wrath must abide for ever upon you, if you have no interest in Jesus Christ. John 3 : 36.

Ponder well the happy state they are in who have obtained pardon and peace by Jesus Christ, Psalm 32 : 1, 2; and seeing the grace of God is free, and you are set under its means, why may not you also enjoy it?

Seriously consider the great uncertainty of your time, and the preciousness of the opportunities of salvation, never to be recovered when once past. John 9 : 4. Let this provoke you to lay hold upon those golden seasons while they are yet with you, that you may not bewail your folly and madness when they are out of your reach.

Associate yourselves with serious Christians ; get acquainted with them, and beg their assistance ; beseech them to pray for you ; and see that you rest not here, but be frequently upon your knees begging of the Lord a new heart.

In conclusion of the whole, let me beseech and beg all the people of God, as upon my knees, to take heed and beware lest by the carelessness and scandal of their lives they quench the weak desires beginning to kindle in the hearts of others.   O shed not soul-blood by stifling the hopeful desires of any after Christ.

Blessed be God for Jesus Christ, the Desire of all nations.

CHAPTER XIV

FIFTH TITLE OF CHRIST—"THE LORD OF GLORY "

"Which none of the princes of this world knew; for had they known it, they would not have crucified the Lord of glory." 1 Cor. 2:8

In this chapter the apostle discourses to the Corinthians of the excellence of his ministry, both to obviate the contempt which some cast upon it for want of human ornaments, and to give the greater authority to it among all ; and as the spiritual simplicity of his ministry brought it under the contempt of some, he removes that by showing,

That it was not suitable to the design and end of his ministry, his determination being to know nothing among them, save Jesus Christ, and him crucified. Verses 1, 2.

Neither was it for the advantage of their souls ; it might please their fancy, but could be no solid foundation of their faith and comfort. Verses 4, 5.

Though his discourses seemed dry to carnal hearers, yet they had a depth and excellency which spiritual and judicious Christians saw and acknowledged. Verses 6, 7.

Therefore this excellent wisdom which he preached far transcended all the natural wisdom of this world, yea, the wisdom of those that were most renowned and admired in that age. "Which none of the princes of this world knew." Verse 8.

In these words we have, first, a negative proposition : none of the princes of this world knew that spiritual wisdom which he taught. By *princes of this world*, or rather, the princes of that age, he means the learned rabbies, scribes, and Pharisees, renowned for wisdom and learning among them, and honored upon that account as so many princes. But he adds a diminutive term which darkens all their glory: they are but the *princes of this world*, utterly unacquainted with the wisdom of the other world. To which he adds a clear and full proof: "For had they known it, they would not have crucified the Lord of glory." In which words we find one of Christ's glorious and royal titles, *the Lord of glory*, on which title my present discourse will be founded. The words being clear, with nothing of ambiguity in them, give us this doctrine:

Christ crucified is the Lord of glory.

Great and excellent is the glory of Jesus Christ. The Scriptures everywhere proclaim his glory; yea, we may observe a notable *climax* or gradation in those scriptures that speak of his glory. The prophet Isaiah, speaking of him, calls him *glorious:* "In that day shall the branch of the Lord be beautiful and glorious." Isaiah 4 : 2. John, speaking of his glory, rises a step higher, and ascribes to him a "glory as of the only begotten of the Father," John 1 : 14, that is, a glory becoming the Son of God; proper to him, and incommunicable to any other. The apostle James rises yet higher, and not only calls him glorious, or glorious as the only begotten of the Father, but *the glory*—glory in the abstract: "My brethren, have not the faith of our Lord Jesus Christ, the glory, with respect of persons," James 2 : 1; for the word *Lord* in our translation is a supplement. Christ is glory itself, yea, the glory emphatically so styled; the glory of heaven; the glory of Sion; the glory of our souls for ever. The epistle to the Hebrews goes yet higher, and calls him the brightness of the Father's glory, Heb. 1 : 3; as though he should say, he is the beaming forth of his Father's glory—the very splendor or refulgency of divine glory. O what a glorious Lord is Jesus Christ; the bright, sparkling diamond of heaven, who shines in glory there above the glory of angels and saints, as the glory of the sun excels the lesser twinkling stars. The glory of Christ must be unspeakable, who reflects glory upon all that are with him, John 17 : 24, and stamps glory upon all that belong to him. His works on earth were glorious works, Luke 13 : 17 ; the purchased liberty of his people a glorious liberty, Rom. 8 : 21 ; the church, his mystical body, a glorious church, Eph. 5 : 27 ; the gospel which reveals him is a glorious gospel. 1 Tim. 1 : 11.

But more particularly let us consider the glory of Christ as it is distinguished into his essential, or his mediatorial glory.

I. THE ESSENTIAL GLORY OF CHRIST, which he has, as God, from everlasting, is unspeakable and inconceivable glory ; for he "being in the form of God, thought it not robbery to be equal with God," Phil. 2 : 6 ; that is, he has equality with the Father in glory : "I and my Father are one." John 10 : 30. And again, "All things that the Father hath are mine," John 16 : 15 ; the same name, the same nature, the same essential properties, the same will, and the same glory.

II. THE MEDIATORIAL GLORY OF CHRIST is proper to him as the head of the church which he hath purchased with his own blood. Of this glory the apostle speaks : "Wherefore God also hath highly exalted him, and given him a name which is above every name," Phil. 2 : 9 ; the original means, exalted above all exaltation. Now the mediatorial glory of our Lord Jesus Christ consists,

1. *In the fulness of grace inherent in him.* The humanity of Christ is filled with grace as the sun with light : "Full of grace and truth." John 1 : 14. Never was any creature filled by the Spirit of grace as the man Christ Jesus is filled ; for God gives not the Spirit to him by measure. John 3 : 34. By reason of this fulness of grace inherent in him, he is "fairer than the children of men," Psalm 45 : 2 ; excelling all the saints in spiritual lustre and gracious excellencies.

2. *In the dignity and authority put upon him.* He is

crowned king in Sion; all power in heaven and earth is given unto him. Matt. 28 : 18. He is a lawgiver to the church, James 4 : 12; all acts of worship are to be performed in his name—prayer, preaching, censures, ordinances, all to be administered in his name. Church officers are commissioned by him. Eph. 4 : 11. The judgment of the world in the great day will be administered by him. Matt. 25 : 31.

3. Jesus Christ shall have *glory and honor ascribed to him for evermore by angels and saints* on account of his mediatorial work. "And when he had taken the book, the four beasts, and four and twenty elders fell down before the Lamb, having every one of them harps, and golden vials full of odors, which are the prayers of saints. And they sung a new song, saying, Thou art worthy to take the book, and to open the seals thereof; for thou wast slain, and hast redeemed us to God by thy blood out of every kindred, and tongue, and people, and nation; and hast made us unto our God kings and priests." Rev. 5 : 8–10.

INFERENCE 1. *How wonderful was the love of Christ the Lord of glory, to be so abased and humbled for us vile and sinful dust!* It is astonishing to conceive that ever Jesus Christ should strip himself of his robes of glory to clothe himself with the mean garment of our flesh. If the sun had been turned into a wandering atom, if the most glorious angel in heaven had been transformed even into a fly, it had been nothing to the abasement of the Lord of glory. This act is everywhere celebrated in Scripture as the great mystery, the astonishing wonder of the whole world. 2 Tim. 3 : 16; Phil. 2 : 8; Rom. 8 : 3. The Lord of glory looked not like himself when he came in the habit of a man—"we hid, as it were, our faces from him," Isaiah 53 : 3; nay, became "a reproach of men, and despised of the people." Psalm 22 : 6. The birds of the air and beasts of the earth were provided with better accommodations than the Lord of glory. Matt. 8 : 20. O stupendous abasement! O love unspeakable! "Though he was rich, yet for our sakes he became poor, that we through his poverty might be rich." 2 Cor. 8 : 9. He put off the crown of glory to put on the crown of thorns. And as said Bernard, "The lower he humbled himself for me, the dearer he shall be to me."

2. *How transcendently glorious is the advancement of believers by their union with the Lord of glory!* This also is an admirable and astonishing mystery; it is the highest dignity and glory of which our persons are capable, to be mystically united to this Lord of glory; to be bone of his bone, and flesh of his flesh. Christian, dost thou know and believe all this, and does not thy heart burn within thee in love to Christ? This is the great mystery which the angels stoop down to look into. Such an honor as this could never have entered into the heart of man. It would have seemed blasphemy in us to have thought or spoken of such a thing, had not Christ made first the motion thereof. Wilt thou not say, Lord, what am I, and what is my father's house, that so great a King should stoop so far beneath himself to such a worm; that strength should unite itself to weakness, infinite glory to such baseness? O grace, grace for ever to be admired!

3. Is Jesus Christ the Lord of glory? *Then let no man count himself dishonored by suffering the vilest indignities for his sake.* The Lord of glory puts glory upon the very suffering you undergo in this world for him. Moses esteemed the reproach of Christ greater riches than the treasures of Egypt, Heb. 11 : 26; he left a kingdom to be crowned with reproaches for the name of Christ. The diadem of Egypt was not half so glorious as self-denial for Christ. This Lord of glory freely degraded himself for thee, and wilt thou stand hesitating with him as to what he requires of thee? It is certainly your honor to be dishonored for Christ. Acts 5 : 41. To you it is given in behalf of Christ,

not only to believe, but also to suffer for his sake. Phil. 1 : 29. The gift of suffering is there matched with the gift of faith: it is given as a badge of honor to suffer for the Lord of glory. As all have not the honor to wear the crown of glory in heaven, so few have the honor to wear the chain of Christ upon earth. Thuanus reports of Ludovicus Marsacus, a knight of France, that being led to suffer with other martyrs who were bound, and he unbound because a person of honor, he cried out, "Why don't you honor me with a chain too, and create me a knight of that noble order?" "My brethren, count it all joy when ye fall into divers temptations," James 1 : 2 ; that is, trials by sufferings.

4. Is Christ the Lord of glory? *How glorious then shall the saints one day be*, when they shall be made like this glorious Lord, and partake of his glory in heaven. "The glory which thou gavest me I have given them." John 17 : 22. Yea, the vile bodies of believers shall be made like to the glorious body of Christ. Phil. 3 : 21. What glory then will be communicated to their souls! True, his essential glory is incommunicable ; but there is a glory which Christ will communicate to his people. When he comes to judge the world, he will come "to be glorified in his saints, and to be admired in all them that believe." 2 Thess. 1 : 10. Thus he seems to account his social glory which shall result from his saints, a great part of his own glory. As we have now fellowship with him in his sufferings, so we shall have fellowship or communion with him in his glory : when he shall appear, then shall we also appear with him in glory ; then the poorest believer shall be more glorious than Solomon in all his royalty. It was a pious saying of Luther, that he had rather be a Christian *clown* than a pagan *emperor*. The righteous is more excellent than his neighbor, though he live next door to a graceless nobleman. But it does not yet appear what they shall be. The day will come, for

the Lord hath spoken it, when they shall shine forth as the sun in the kingdom of their Father.

5. *How hath the devil blindfolded and deluded them that are affrighted off from Christ by the fears of being dishonored by him!* Many persons have half a mind to religion, but when they consider the generality of its professors as persons of the lowest rank in the world, and that reproaches and sufferings attend that way, they shrink back as men ashamed, and as Salvian says, they choose rather to remain wicked than to be esteemed vile. But to them that believe, Christ is precious—an honor, as the word might be rendered. 1 Peter 2 : 7. Till God open men's eyes, they will put evil for good, and good for evil. But O, dear-bought honors, for which men stake their souls and everlasting happiness ! Paul was not of your mind : in birth he was a Hebrew of the Hebrews ; in dignity and esteem a Pharisee ; in moral accomplishments touching the law blameless ; yet all this he trampled under his feet, counting all but dross in comparison of Jesus Christ. Moses had more honor to lay down for Christ than you, yet it was no temptation to him to conceal or deny the faith of Christ. Noble Galeacius would not be withheld from Christ by the splendor and glory of Italy ; but O, how does the glory of this world dazzle and blind the eyes of many. "How can ye believe, who receive honor one of another?" John 5 : 44. Saints and sinners are, on this account, wonders one to the other. It is the wonder of the world to see Christians glorying in reproaches ; they wonder that the saints run not with them into the same excess of riot ; and it is a wonder to believers how such poor toys and empty titles should keep the world from Jesus Christ and their everlasting happiness in him.

6. If Christ be the Lord of glory, *how careful should all be who profess him, that they do not dishonor him whose name is called upon by them.* Christ is a glory to you ; be not you a shame and dishonor to him. The more glorious Christ

is, the more circumspect and watchful ye had need to be. How lovely would Jesus Christ appear to the world, if the lives of Christians adorned the doctrine of God their Saviour in all things! Remember, you represent the Lord of glory to the world; it is not your honor only, but the honor of Christ, which is involved and concerned in your actions. O let not the carelessness or scandal of your life make Jesus Christ ashamed to be called your Lord. When Israel had grievously revolted from God, he commanded Moses, "Arise, get thee down quickly from hence; for *thy* people, which thou hast brought forth out of Egypt, have corrupted themselves," Deut. 9 : 12 ; as if the Lord were ashamed to own them for his people any longer. It was a cutting question, apt to startle the consciences of loose professors, "Do not they blaspheme that worthy name by which ye are called?" James 2 : 7. Your duty is to adorn the gospel by your conversation, Titus 2: 10 ; the words signify to deck or adorn the gospel, to make it neat and lovely to the eyes of beholders. When there is a beautiful harmony and lovely proportion between Christ's doctrine and our practice, as there is in the works of creation, in which the comeliness and elegance of the world much consists, then do we walk suitably to the Lord of glory.

7. *What delight should Christians take in their daily converse with Jesus Christ in the way of duty.* Your interviews in prayer, hearing, and meditation are with the Lord of glory. The greatest peers in the kingdom count it more honor to be in the presence of a king bareheaded, or upon the knee at court, than to have thousands standing bare to them in the country. When you are called to the duties of communion with Christ, you are called to the greatest honor and dignified with the noblest privilege creatures are capable of in this world. Had you but a sense of the honor God puts upon you by this means, you would not need so much pressing and striving to bring a

dead and backward heart into the special presence of Jesus Christ. When he saith, Seek ye my face, your hearts would echo to his call, Thy face, Lord, will we seek. But, alas, the glory of Christ is much hid and veiled by ignorance and unbelief from the eyes of his own people; it is but seldom the best of saints by the eye of faith do see the King in his glory.

8. If Christ be so glorious, *how should believers long to be with him, and behold him in his glory above.* Most men need patience to *die;* a believer should need patience to *live.* Paul thought it well worth enduring the pangs of death to get a sight of Jesus Christ in his glory. Phil. 1 : 23. "The Lord direct your hearts into the love of God, and into the patient waiting for Christ," says the apostle, 2 Thess. 3 : 5, intimating that the saints have great need of patience to enable them to endure separation from Christ so long in this world. "The Spirit and the bride say, Come; and let him that heareth say, Come; and let him that is athirst come : even so, come, Lord Jesus."

Blessed be God for Jesus Christ, the Lord of glory.

CHAPTER XV

SIXTH AND LAST TITLE OF CHRIST—"THE CONSOLATION OF ISRAEL"

"Waiting for the Consolation of Israel." LUKE 2:25

SEVERAL glorious titles of Christ have been considered, out of each of which much comfort flows to believers. It is comfortable to a wounded soul to regard him as a physician; comfortable to a condemned and unworthy soul to look upon him under the idea of mercy. The loveliness, the desirableness, and the glory of Christ are all so many springs of consolation. But now I am to show from this scripture that the saints have not only much consolation from Christ, but that Christ himself is *the Consolation* of believers.

In the context you have an account of Simeon's prophecy concerning Christ, and in the text a description of the person and character of Simeon himself. His *life* was heavenly and holy—he was a just and devout man; and *the principle* from which his righteousness and holiness flowed was his faith in Christ—"He waited for the Consolation of Israel."

That *the Consolation of Israel* is a phrase descriptive of Jesus Christ is beyond all doubt, if you consult verse 26, where Simeon is satisfied by receiving Christ into his arms, *the Consolation* for which he had so long waited.

And that *waiting for Christ* is a phrase describing the believers of the times which preceded the incarnation of Christ is past doubt. They all waited for that blessed day; but it was Simeon's lot to fall just upon that happy point of time wherein the prophecies and promises of his incarnation were fulfilled.   Simeon and others that waited with him were sensible that the time of the promise was come, which could not but raise a general expectation of him.   But Simeon's faith was confirmed by a particular revelation, ver. 26, that he should see Christ before he saw death; which could not but greatly raise his expectation to look out for him, whose coming would be the greatest consolation to the whole Israel of God.   The Spirit is frequently called in Scripture παρακλητης, the *Comforter;* but Christ in this place is called comfort, or consolation itself. The reason of both is given : "He shall receive of mine, and shall show it unto you."   John 16 : 14.   Here Christ is said to be the consolation, and the Spirit the applier of it to the people of God.

This consolation is here expressed with a singular emphasis, *the consolation;* intimating that there is nothing of consolation is any thing besides him—that all other comforts compared with this are not worth naming ; and as it is emphatically expressed, so it is also limited within the compass of God's *Israel,* that is, true believers, styled the *Israel of God,* whether Jews or Gentiles.   Gal. 6 : 16. Hence the doctrine is,

Jesus Christ is the only Consolation of believers, and of none besides them.

So speaks the apostle : "For we are the circumcision, which worship God in the spirit, and rejoice in Christ Jesus, and have no confidence in the flesh."   Phil. 3 : 3. Those that worship God in the spirit are sincere believers ; to such sincere believers Christ is consolation : "Our rejoicing is in Christ Jesus."   And they have no consolation in any thing besides him ; nothing in the world can give them comfort without Christ: "We have no confidence in the flesh."   The gospel is glad tidings of great joy ; but that which makes it to be so is Jesus Christ, whom it reveals to us.

Four things here require attention : what is meant by

consolation ; that Christ, and he only, is consolation to believers ; that believers only have consolation in Christ ; and how it comes to pass that any believer should be dejected, since Christ is consolation to all believers.

I. THE NATURE OF CONSOLATION, which is nothing else but the cheerfulness of a man's spirit, whereby he is upheld and fortified against all evils felt or feared. Consolation is to the soul what health is to the body after wasting sickness, or the reviving spring to the earth after a long and hard winter.

Natural comfort is the refreshment of our spirits by the good creatures of God, "filling our hearts with food and gladness." Acts 14 : 17. *Sinful comfort* is the satisfaction and pleasure men take in the fulfilling of their lusts by the abuse of the creatures of God. "Ye have lived in pleasure upon earth," James 5 : 5 ; that is, your life hath been a life of sensuality and sin.

But *spiritual comfort* is the peace and joy gracious souls have in Christ by the exercise of faith, hope, and other graces, Rom. 5 : 2 ; and this only deserves the name of true, solid consolation ; to which four things are requisite :

1. That the matter thereof be some *spiritual*, eminent, and durable good ; else our consolation in it will be but as the crackling of thorns under a pot, a sudden blaze, quickly extinct. Christ only gives solid, durable consolation ; the righteousness of Christ, the pardon of sin, the favor of God, the hope of glory, are the substantial materials of a believer's consolation. Rom. 5 : 2 ; Matt. 9 : 2 ; Psa. 4 : 6, 7 ; 2 Pet. 1 : 8.

2. *Interest* in these comfortable things is requisite to our consolation by them : "My spirit hath rejoiced in God my Saviour." Luke 1 : 47. It is no consolation to him that is hungry to see a feast, to him that is poor to see a treasure, if the one may not taste or the other partake thereof.

3. *Knowledge* and evidence of interest is in some degree requisite to actual consolation, though without it a man may be in the state of consolation; for that which appears not, is, in point of actual comfort, as if it were not.

4. In order to this, the *work of the Spirit* upon our hearts is requisite, both to give and make clear our interest in Christ and the promises; and in both these ways he is the Comforter: the fruit of the Spirit is joy. Gal. 5 : 22.

II. CHRIST, AND HE ONLY, IS MATTER OF CONSOLATION TO BELIEVERS.

1. Jesus Christ *brings whatsoever is precious to the souls of believers.* Is pardon desired by a person condemned? this Christ brings to all believers : "And this is his name whereby he shall be called, the Lord our righteousness." Jer. 23 : 6. This cannot but give strong consolation; righteousness is the foundation of peace and joy in the Holy Ghost. Rom. 14 : 17. "The work of righteousness shall be peace; and the effect of righteousness, quietness and assurance for ever." Isa. 32 : 17. Come to a dejected soul laboring under the burden of guilt, and say, Cheer up; I bring you good tidings : such an estate has fallen to you, or such a trouble is ended; alas, this will not reach the heart. If you can bring me, says he, good news from heaven that my sins are forgiven and God is reconciled, how soon should I be comforted! And therefore, as one well observes, this was the usual receipt with which Christ cured the souls of men and women when he was here on earth : Son, daughter, "be of good cheer, thy sins are forgiven thee." And indeed it is as easy to separate light and warmth from the beams of the sun, as cheerfulness and comfort from the voice of pardon.

Are the hopes and expectations of heaven and glory cheering? Yes, nothing is if this be not. We "rejoice in hope of the glory of God." Rom. 5 : 2. Christ brings to the souls of men all the solid grounds and foundations upon which they build their expectations of glory: "Christ in you, the hope of glory." Col. 1 : 27. Name any thing else that is solid matter of comfort to the souls of men, and the grounds thereof will be found in Christ, and in none but Christ.

2. *Jesus Christ removes from believers whatever is uncomfortable;* therein relieving them against all their affliction and sorrow. Is *sin* a burden and trouble to believers? Christ, and none but Christ, removes that burden. "O wretched man that I am! who shall deliver me from the body of this death? I thank God through Jesus Christ our Lord." Rom. 7 : 24, 25. The satisfaction of his blood, Eph. 5 : 2 ; the sanctification of his Spirit, 1 John 5 : 6 ; his perfect deliverance of his people from the very being of sin at last. Eph. 5 : 26, 27. This relieves at present and removes finally the matter and ground of all their troubles and sorrows for sin.

Do the *temptations* of Satan burden believers? Temptation is an enemy under the walls ; it greatly endangers, and therefore cannot but greatly afflict the souls of believers, but Christ brings the only relief against temptations. The intercession of Christ is a singular relief at present : "But I have prayed for thee, that thy faith fail not." Luke 22 : 32. And the promises of Christ are a full relief for the future : "The God of peace shall bruise Satan under your feet shortly." Rom. 16 : 20.

Is *spiritual desertion* and the hiding of God's face the ground of affliction and distress to believers? "Thou didst hide thy face, and I was troubled." Psa. 30 : 7. Christ brings to believers substantial consolation against the troubles of desertion. He himself was deserted of God for a time, that they might not be deserted for ever. In him also the promises are made to believers, that notwithstanding God may desert them for a time, yet the union between him and them shall never be dissolved. Heb. 13 : 5 ; Jer. 32 : 40. Though he forsake them for a moment in respect to the manifestation of his favor, yet he will return again and comfort them. Isa. 54 : 7. Though Satan pull hard, yet he will never be able to pluck them out of his Father's hand. John 10 : 28. O what relief is this; what consolation is Christ to a deserted believer !

Are *outward afflictions* the ground of dejection and trouble? How do our hearts fail and our spirits sink under the many smarting rods of God upon us ! But our relief and consolation under them all is in Christ Jesus ; for the rod that afflicts us is in the hand of Christ that loveth us. "As many as I love I rebuke and chasten." Rev. 3 : 19. His design in affliction is our profit. Heb. 12 : 10. That design of his for our good shall certainly be accomplished, Rom. 8 : 28 ; and after that no more afflictions for ever. "God shall wipe away all tears from their eyes." Rev. 21 : 3. Thus two things are most evident: 1. Nothing can comfort the soul without Christ. He is the soul that animates all comforts ; they would be dead without him. Temporal enjoyments, riches, honors, health, relations, yield not a drop of true comfort without Christ. Spiritual enjoyments, ministers, ordinances, promises, are fountains sealed and springs shut up till Christ open them ; a man may go comfortless in the midst of them all. 2. No troubles or afflictions can deject the soul that Christ comforts. "As sorrowful, yet always rejoicing." 2 Cor. 6 : 10. A believer may walk with a heart full of comfort amidst all the troubles of the world. Christ makes darkness and troubles to be light round about his people. So that the conclusion stands firm, that Christ, and Christ only, is the consolation of believers.

III. I am to show you that BELIEVERS, AND NONE BUT BELIEVERS, can have consolation in Christ ; which will convincingly appear from the consideration of those things which we laid down before as the requisites to all true spiritual consolation. For,

1. No unbeliever has the *materials* out of which spirit-

ual comfort springs, which must be some solid spiritual and eternal good, as Christ and the covenant are. What do unregenerate men rejoice in, but "a thing of naught?" Amos 6 : 13. See how their mirth is described in Job 21 : 12 : "They take their timbrel and harp, and rejoice at the sound of the organ." He does not say, they take the Bible, turn to the promises, and rejoice in Christ and the covenant : it is not the melody of a good conscience, the joy of the Holy Ghost : no, no, they have no acquaintance with such music as that ; but the rejoicing of believers is in those things, 2 Cor. 1 : 12, and this is well built consolation, which reaches the heart.

2. Interest in Christ and the promises is requisite to all spiritual consolation ; but no unbeliever has any title or interest in Christ and the promises, and so they cannot support him. It is not another man's Saviour, but my own that must justify, save, and comfort my soul.

3. Evidence of a man's peace with God is necessary to his actual consolation, which no unbeliever can possibly have ; he has neither grace within him to make him the subject of any special promise, nor any witness or seal of the Spirit to confirm his interest in Christ, for he never seals but where he first sanctifies.

IV. One inquiry remains to be satisfied : SEEING JESUS CHRIST IS CONSOLATION TO BELIEVERS, HOW IS IT THAT SO MANY BELIEVERS SHOULD WALK SO DEJECTEDLY AS THEY DO, WITHOUT ANY SPIRITUAL CONSOLATION ?

1. This need not be wondered at if we consider that the consolations of Christ are of two kinds : those *prepared and reserved* for the believer, and those *in present possession* Every believer has the root and seed of comfort planted and sown for him : "Light is sown for the righteous, and gladness for the upright in heart." Psalm 97 : 11. They have Christ and the promises, which are the seeds of consolation, and will bring forth joy at last, though at present they have no actual consolation ; the seed of

all joy is sown, and in due time they shall reap the full ripe fruit.

2. It must be remembered *that interest and evidence are distinct blessings:* every believer has interest in Christ; but every believer has not the evidence of it. "Who is among you that feareth the Lord, that obeyeth the voice of his servant; that walketh in darkness, and hath no light?" Isaiah 50 : 10. Every child of God is not of sufficient age to know his Father, or take comfort in that blessed inheritance whereunto he is begotten again. 1 Pet. 1 : 3, 4.

3. All believers do not *walk with like strictness* and exact holiness; all do not exercise faith in a like degree. Among Christians some are strong in grace, rich in faith, strict in obedience, tender of sin to an eminent degree; these usually have much consolation: but others are weak in grace, poor in faith, comparatively careless of their hearts and ways, frequently grieving the good Spirit of God, and wounding their own consciences—the vessel into which spiritual consolation is poured; and these are usually denied the joy and comfort with which others abound.

4. The consolations of Christ are *dispensed by the Spirit,* who is the Comforter, and giveth to every man in such proportions and at such seasons as pleaseth him : whence it comes to pass, that he that is rich in comfort to-day may be poor to-morrow; and, on the contrary, the heart that is quite full of sorrow one hour, is filled with peace and joy in believing in the next. Things that are necessary to the being of a Christian are fixed and stable; but things belonging only to the consolation of a Christian come and go, according to the good pleasure and appointment of the Spirit.

INFERENCE 1. *The state of unbelievers is a most sad and uncomfortable state, having no interest in Christ, the consolation of Israel.* It is true, they may live in pleasure upon earth; joy may display its colors in their faces; but for all this there is nct the least drop of true consolation in any of their hearts. They have some comfort in the world, but none in Christ; the little they gather from the world now is all their portion of joy. "Ye have received your consolation." Luke 6 : 24. And as this is all they have, so they shall enjoy it but a little while, Job 21 : 13, 17; and while they do enjoy it, it is mixed with many pangs of conscience. "Even in laughter the heart is sorrowful, and the end of that mirth is heaviness." Prov. 14 : 13. Whatever consolation any unbeliever speaks of besides this, is delusive; for when the day of his distress cometh, and the terrors of conscience shall awake him out of his pleasant dreams, all his sensual joys will vanish, and the doors of true consolation will be shut against him. Let him then go to Jesus Christ and say, "Lord Jesus, thy name is Consolation: my heart is ready to burst within me; hast thou no consolation for me? O Lord, for one drop of spiritual comfort now." But alas, there will be none, no, not in Christ himself, for any unbeliever. It is children's bread, the saints' privilege; comfort and grace are undivided. Let him return into himself, search his own conscience for comfort, and say, "O conscience, thou art more than a thousand witnesses, and thousands have been comforted by thee; where thou speakest comfort none can speak trouble; hast thou no consolation for me in my deepest distress?" Alas, no; if God condemn thee, wherewithal shall I comfort thee? I can speak neither more nor less than the Scriptures put into my mouth, and I find not one word in all the book of God warranting me to be thy comforter. Believe it as an undoubted truth, that the state of unbelievers, even at the best, is a sad and dismal state.

2. *Let all believers draw their comfort from Christ, who is the consolation of his people.* We rejoice, says the apostle, in Christ Jesus, and have no confidence in the flesh. That is the true temper of a believing soul: take heed

that you live not partly upon Christ and partly upon the creature for your comfort; and beware that you forsake not Christ, the fountain of living waters, and hew out cisterns for yourselves which can hold no water. Jer. 2 : 13. If you make any creature the fountain of your comfort, assuredly God will dry up that spring. If your souls draw their comfort from any creature, you know they must outlive that creature, and what then will you do for comfort? Besides, as your comforts are, so are you. The food of every creature is suitable to its nature. Sensual men feed upon sensual things, spiritual men upon spiritual things; as your food is, so are you. If carnal comforts can content thy heart, it must then be a very carnal heart. Yea, and let Christians themselves take heed that they draw not their consolations from themselves instead of Christ. Your graces and duties are excellent means, but not the foundation of your comfort: they are useful buckets to draw with, but not the well itself in which the springs of consolation rise. If you put your duties in the room of Christ, Christ will put your comforts out of the reach of your duties.

3. *If Christ be the consolation of believers, what a joyful life should all believers live in the world!* Certainly, if the fault be not your own, you may live the happiest lives. If you would not be a discomfort to Christ, he would be a comfort to you every day, and in every condition, to the end of your lives. Your condition abounds with all the helps and advantages of consolation. You have the command of Christ to warrant your comforts. Phil. 4 : 4. You have the Spirit of Christ for a spring of comfort; you have the Scriptures of Christ for the rules of comfort; you have the duties of religion for the means of comfort. Why is it then that you go comfortless? If your afflictions are many in the world, your encouragements are more in Christ. Your troubles in the world have been turned into joy, but your comforts in Christ can never be turned into

trouble. Why should troubles obstruct your comfort, when the blessing of Christ upon your troubles makes them subservient to promote your happiness? Rom. 8 : 28. Shake off despondency then, and live up to the principles of religion. Your dejected life is uncomfortable to yourselves, and of little use to others.

4. *If Christ be the consolation of believers, let all that desire comfort embrace Jesus Christ and get union with him.* The same hour you shall be in Christ you shall also be at the fountain-head of all consolation : thy soul shall be then a pardoned soul, and a pardoned soul has all reason to be a joyful soul. In that day thy conscience shall be sprinkled with the blood of Christ, and a sprinkled conscience has all reason to be a comforting conscience. In that day you become the children of your Father in heaven, and he that has a Father in heaven has all reason to be the most joyful man upon earth. In that day you are delivered from the sting of death : and he that is delivered from the sting of death has the best reason to be happy in life. O come to Christ; till you come to him no true comfort can come to you.

CHAPTER XVI

FIRST BENEFIT PURCHASED BY CHRIST—THE FOR-GIVENESS OF SINS

"In whom we have redemption through his blood, the forgiveness of sins, according to the riches of his grace."   EPH. 1 : 7

SIX great motives have been presented from the titles of Christ to draw the hearts of sinners to him ; more are now to be offered from the *benefits* purchased for believers by Christ, by all means to win the hearts of men to him. To this end I shall, in the first place, open that glorious *privilege of gospel-remission* freely and fully conferred upon all that come to Christ by faith, "in whom we have redemption through his blood."

1. In these words we have a singular benefit or choice mercy bestowed, namely, *redemption,* or *the remission of sins :* this is a privilege of the first rank, none more desirable among all the benefits that come by Christ.   And therefore,

2. We have the *price* of this mercy, even the *blood of Christ :* "In whom we have redemption, through his blood." Precious things are of great price ; the blood of Christ is the meritorious cause of remission.

3. We have here also the *impulsive cause,* moving God to grant pardon to sinners, and that is said to be "the riches of his grace ;" where, by the way you see that the freeness of the grace ot God and the fulness of the satisfaction of Christ meet together without the least jar in the remission ot sin, contrary to the vain cavil ot the Socinian adversaries, "In whom we have redemption through his blood, the forgiveness of sins, according to the riches of his grace."

4. We have the *subjects* of this blessed privilege, namely, believers, in whose name he here speaks : " *We* have redemption ;" that is, the saints and faithful in Christ Jesus, verse 1 ; we whom God hath chosen in Christ before the foundation of the world, and predestinated unto the adoption of children, verse 4, 5 ; we that are made accepted in the Beloved, verse 6. Such, and such only have redemption through his blood. Hence,

All believers, and none but believers, receive the remission of their sins through the riches of grace, by the blood of Jesus Christ.

In the illustration of this point we shall show that all who are in Christ are in a pardoned state ; that their pardon is the purchase of the blood of Christ ; and that the riches of grace are manifested in remission.

I. ALL WHO ARE IN CHRIST ARE IN A PARDONED STATE. And here I will first show what pardon or remission of sin is, and then that this is the privilege of none but believers.

1. Remission of sin is *the gracious act of God, in and through Christ, discharging a believing sinner from all the guilt and punishment of his sin, both temporal and eternal.*

It is the *act of God.* None can forgive sins but God only. Mark 2 : 7. Against him only, that is, principally and especially, the offence is committed. Psalm 51 : 4. To his judgment guilt binds over the soul ; and who can remit the debt but the creditor ? Matt. 6 : 12

It is an act of God discharging the sinner. God's loosing one that stood bound, the cancelling of his obligation is therefore called remission or releasing in the text ; the blotting out of our iniquities, or the removing of our sins from us, as it is called in other scriptures. See Psalm 103 : 12 ; Micah 7 : 18, 19.

It is a *gracious* act of God, the effect of pure grace done for his own name's sake. Isaiah 43 : 25. Discharging us without any satisfaction at all by us ; there is much grace in this. Providing a surety for us every way able to pay our debt ; there is still more grace in that.

It is the gracious act of God *in and through Christ.* The satisfaction of Christ is the procuring cause of our remission, and so God declares himself just in the remission of our sin. Rom. 3 : 25. "Gracious is the Lord, and righteous." Psalm 116 : 5. Justice and mercy meet here and embrace each other, "in whom we have redemption;" no other price could purchase this privilege, not rivers of oil or of human blood. Micah 6 : 6, 7. And this gracious act of God discharges the pardoned soul both from guilt and punishment. Acts 13 : 38, 39.

2. That this remission of sin is *the privilege of believers* is most apparent, for all the causes of remission are in union to procure it for them : the love of God, which is the impulsive cause of pardon ; the blood of Christ, which is the meritorious cause of pardon ; and saving faith, which is the instrumental cause of pardon, all coöperate for their remission, as is plain in the text. Besides, all the promises of pardon are made to them. Jer. 31 : 34 ; Micah 7 : 19. And lastly, all the signs of pardon are found in them, and in them only, that love God, Luke 7 : 47 ; such as mercy to others, Matt. 6 : 14, a blessed peace in the conscience. Rom. 5 : 1. It is a truth beyond controversy, that all that are in Christ are in a pardoned state.

II. The pardon of believers is THE PURCHASE OF THE BLOOD OF CHRIST. Nothing but the blood of Christ is equivalent to the remission of sin, for this blood was innocent, the blood of a Lamb without spot, 1 Peter 1 : 19 ; this blood was precious blood, of infinite worth and value, the blood of God. Acts 20 : 28. It was prepared for this very purpose, Heb. 10 : 5 ; prepared by God's eternal appointment ; by Christ's miraculous production through the operation of the Spirit ; by his voluntary sanctification of himself to this very use and purpose.

The blood of Jesus is not only innocent, precious, and

prepared, but it is blood actually shed and sacrificed to the justice of God for the expiation of guilt and procurement of our discharge. Isaiah 53 : 5. The justice of God could put in no exception against the blood of Christ; it is unexceptionable, being untainted by sin, and dignified above all estimation by the person whose blood it was. Justice required no less, and could demand no more; and this is the price at which our pardon is purchased, and without which no sin could be pardoned; for "without shedding of blood there is no remission." Heb. 9 : 22.

III. God has manifested THE RICHES OF HIS GRACE in the remission of our sins. So says the apostle, "Where sin abounded, grace did much more abound." Rom. 5 : 20. "The grace of our Lord was exceeding abundant," 1 Tim. 1 : 14; which will appear, if we bring our thoughts to the matter, in several particulars.

1. From the *nature* of the mercy, which is the richest of all mercies, except Christ the purchaser of it. No mercy sweeter than a pardon to a condemned sinner; no pardon like God's pardon to a man condemned at his bar; all the goodness of God is made to pass before our eyes in his pardoning acts of grace. Exod. 33 : 19.

2. The very riches of grace must be in the pardon of sin, if we consider the *method* in which pardons are dispensed, which is, as the text speaks, "through his blood." Herein God commends his love to us. Rom. 5 : 8. He commends it more than if he had pardoned sin without such a sacrifice; for then he had only displayed his mercy, but not caused mercy and justice to meet and triumph together.

3. The riches of his grace shine forth in the *peculiarity* of the mercy. Remission is no common favor; it is never extended to the fallen angels, nor to the greater part of the children of men, but only to a little flock, a small remnant of mankind. Luke 12 : 32; John 17 : 3.

4. The riches of grace are manifested in remission, if

we consider the *subjects* of this privilege, who are not only equally plunged into sin and misery with others by nature, Eph. 2 : 3, but many of them, in sins after conversion, have been guilty of a deeper-dyed abomination than many unpardoned ones. "To me," saith Paul, "who was before a blasphemer, and a persecutor, and injurious; but I obtained mercy." 1 Tim. 1 : 13. "And such were some of you, but ye are washed." 1 Cor. 6 : 11. Yes; God singles out the most base, despised, poor, and contemptible ones among men to be the subjects of this glorious privilege. 1 Cor. 1 : 26.

5. Still more of the riches of grace appear, if we view the *extent* of this act of grace. O how innumerable are our transgressions! "Who can understand his errors?" Psalm 19 : 12. Yet the blood of Christ cleanses us from all sin. 1 John 1 : 7. Small and great sins, open and secret sins, old and new sins, all pardoned without exception. O the riches of grace! O the unsearchable goodness of God! "With the Lord there is mercy, and with him there is plenteous redemption; and he shall redeem Israel from all his iniquities." Psalm 130 : 7, 8.

6. The riches of grace shine forth in the *perpetuity* of remission. As grace pardons all sins without exception, so the pardons it bestows are without revocation. The pardoned soul shall "never come into condemnation." John 5 : 24. "As far as the east is from the west, so far hath he removed our transgressions from us." Psalm 103 : 12. The east and the west are the two opposite points of heaven, which can never come together; neither shall the pardoned soul and its sins ever meet any more. Thou hast cast, says Hezekiah, all my sins behind thy back. The penitent believer sets his sins before his face, but the merciful God casts them all behind his back, never to behold them more, so as to charge them upon his pardoned people. Thus you see what the pardon of sin is, what the price that purchaseth pardon is, and what riches

of grace God manifests in the remission of a believer's sins ; which were the things to be explained.

INFERENCE 1. If it be so that all believers, and none but believers, receive the remission of their sins through the riches of grace by the blood of Christ, *what a happy condition are believers in!* Those that never felt the load of sin may make light of pardon ; but so cannot you who have been in the deeps of trouble and fear about it : those that have been upon the rack of a condemning conscience, as David, Heman, and many of the saints have been, can never sufficiently value a pardon. "Blessed is he whose transgression is forgiven, whose sin is covered ; blessed is the man unto whom the Lord imputeth not iniquity ;" or, as in the Hebrew, O the blessedness and felicities of the pardoned man ! Psalm 32 : 1, 2.

Remission cannot but appear the wonder of mercies, if we consider through what difficulties the grace of God makes way for it to our souls—what strong bars the love of God breaks asunder to open our way to this privilege ; for there can be no pardon without a Mediator—no other Mediator but the Son of God. The Son of God cannot discharge our debts, but by taking them upon himself as our surety, and making full payment by bearing the wrath of God for us ; and when all this is done, there can be no actual pardon except the Spirit of grace open our blind eyes, break our hard hearts, and draw them to Christ in the way of believing. And as the mercy of remission comes to us through wonderful difficulties, so it is in itself a complete and perfect mercy : God would not be at such vast expense of the riches of his grace ; Christ would not lay out the invaluable treasures of his precious blood, to procure a cheap and common blessing for us. Rejoice then, ye pardoned souls ; God has done great things for you, for which you have cause to be glad. Hence it follows,

2. *That interest in Christ by faith brings the conscience of a*

believer into a state of peace. "Being justified by faith, we have peace with God." Rom. 5 : 1. I say not that every believer is presently brought into actual peace of conscience; there may be many fears and much trouble even in a pardoned soul; but this is an undoubted truth, that faith brings the pardoned soul into the condition and state where he may find perfect rest in his conscience with respect to the guilt and danger of sin. The blood of Christ sprinkles us from an evil, that is, an accusing, condemning conscience. We are apt to fear that this or that special sin which has most terrified our conscience is not forgiven; but if there are riches enough in the grace of God, and efficacy enough in the blood of Christ, the sins of believers, without limitation or exception, are pardoned.

If Christ remits no sin to any man but with respect to his blood, then all sins are pardoned, as well as any one sin; because the dignity and worth of that blood is infinite, and as much deserves pardon for all sins, as the particular pardon of any, even the least sin. Moreover, remission is an act of God's fatherly love in Christ; and if it be so, certainly no sin of any believer can be excluded from pardon; for then the same soul would be in the favor of God so far as it is pardoned, and out of favor with God so far as it is unpardoned, and all this at one and the same time, which is a thing repugnant to itself and to the whole strain of the gospel. What is the design and end of remission, but the saving of the pardoned soul? But if any sin be excluded from pardon, the retaining of that sin must make void the pardon of all other sins; and so the acts of God must cross and contradict each other, and the design and end of God miscarry and be lost, which can never be. So then we conclude, faith brings the believing soul into a state of rest and peace. Hence,

3. *No remission is to be expected by any soul without an interest by faith in Jesus Christ.* No Christ, no pardon; no faith, no Christ. Yet how apt are many poor deluded souls

to expect pardon in a way in which never any soul yet did or ever can meet it. Some look for pardon from the absolute mercy of God, without any regard to the blood of Christ: "We have sinned, but God is merciful!" Some expect remission of sin by virtue of their own duties: "I have sinned, but I will repent, restore, reform, and God will pardon!" Little do such men know how they therein diminish the evil of sin, undervalue the justice of God, slight the blood of Christ, and cheat their own souls for ever. To expect pardon from absolute mercy, or from our own duties, is to knock at the wrong door, which God has shut up to all the world. Rom. 3 : 20. While these two principles abide firm, that the price of pardon is only in the blood of Christ, and the benefit of pardon only by the application of his blood to us, this must remain a sure conclusion, that no remission is to be expected by any soul without an interest by faith in Jesus Christ. Repentance, restitution, and reformation are excellent duties in their proper place, but they were never meant for saviors, or a satisfaction to God for sin.

4. If the riches of grace be thus manifested in the pardon of sin, *how vile an abuse is it of the grace of God to take the more liberty to sin, because grace abounds in the pardon of it.*

"Shall we continue in sin, that grace may abound? God forbid." Rom. 6 : 1, 2. Will nothing else than the grace of God serve to make a cloak for sin? O vile abuse of the most excellent thing in the whole world! Did Christ shed his blood to expiate our guilt, and dare we make that a plea to extenuate our guilt? God forbid. If it be intolerable ingratitude among men to requite good with evil, sure that sin must want a name bad enough to express it, which puts the greatest dishonor upon God for the greatest mercy that ever was given to the world. "There is forgiveness with thee, that thou mayest be feared," Psalm 130 : 4, not that thou mayest be the more

abused. Nay, let me say, the devils never sinned at this
rate; they cannot abuse the pardoning grace of God, because such grace was never offered them. And certainly,
if the abuse of the common mercies of God, as meat and
drink, by gluttony and drunkenness, be a heinous sin, and
highly provoking to God, the abuse of the riches of his
grace, and the precious blood of his Son, must be out of
measure sinful.

5. *If this be so, as ever you expect pardon and mercy from
God, come to Christ in the way of faith; receive and embrace
him now in the tenders of the gospel.*

To enforce this exhortation, I beseech you, as in the
bowels of Christ Jesus, and by all the regard and value
you have for your souls, let the following considerations
sink down in your hearts.

That all Christless persons are actually *under the condemnation of God.* "He that believeth not is condemned
already," John 3 : 18; and it must be so, for every soul
is concluded under the curse of the law till Christ make
him free. John 8 : 36. Till we are in Christ we are
dead by law; and when we believe unto justification,
then we pass from death to life. A blind mistaken conscience may possibly acquit you, but be assured, God condemns you.

Consider what a *terrible thing it is* to lie under the
condemnation of God. The most terrible things in nature
cannot shadow forth the misery of such a state : put all
sickness, poverty, reproaches, the torments invented by
all tyrants into one scale, and the condemnation of God
into the other, and they will be all found lighter than a
feather. Condemnation is the sentence of the great and
terrible God; it is a sentence shutting you up to everlasting wrath; it is a sentence never to be reversed but
by application to Christ in season. O souls, you cannot
bear the wrath of God. You do not understand it if you
think it tolerable. One drop of it upon your conscience

now is enough to distract you in the midst of all the pleasures and comforts of this world; yet all that are out of Christ are sentenced to the fulness of God's wrath for ever.

There is yet *a possibility of escaping* the wrath to come; a door of hope is opened to the worst of sinners; a day of grace is offered to the children of men. Heb. 3 : 15. God declares himself unwilling that any should perish. 2 Pet. 3 : 9. O what a mercy is this! Who that is on this' side eternity fully understands the worth of it?

The door of mercy will be shortly shut. Luke 13 : 25. God has many ways to shut it: he sometimes shuts it by withdrawing the means of grace and removing the candlesticks; a judgment at this time to be greatly feared. Sometimes he shuts it by withdrawing the Spirit from the means, whereby all ordinances lose their efficacy. 1 Cor. 3 : 7. But if he shut it not by removing the means of grace from you, certain it is it will be shortly shut by your removal from all the opportunities of salvation by death.

When once the door of mercy is shut, *you are gone beyond all the possibilities of pardon and salvation* for evermore. The night is then come, in which no man can work. John 9 : 4. All the golden seasons you now enjoy will be irrecoverably gone out of your reach.

Pardons are now daily granted to others. Some who were once as far from mercy as you now are, are reading their pardons with tears of joy. The world is full of instances of the riches of pardoning grace. O therefore lift up your cries to heaven; give the Lord no rest, take no denial till he open the blind eye, break the stony heart, bow the stubborn will, effectually draw thy soul to Christ, and deliver thy pardon signed with his blood.

CHAPTER XVII

SECOND BENEFIT PURCHASED BY CHRIST—ACCEPT-ANCE WITH GOD

"To the praise of the glory of his grace, wherein he hath made us accepted in the Beloved." EPH. 1: 6

IN our last discourse we showed the blessed privilege of remission of sin, from the verse following our text: in this verse lies another glorious privilege, namely, the *acceptance* believers have with God through Jesus Christ; both which comprise, as the two main branches, our justification before God. In these words three things are observable.

1. The privilege itself, which is exceeding rich in its nature: "He hath made us accepted;" the word in the original means he hath ingratiated us, or brought us into the grace, favor, and acceptance of God the Father; endeared us to him, so that we find grace in his sight.

2. The meritorious cause, procuring this benefit for us, declared in the words, "in the Beloved;" which words refer to Christ, who is here emphatically styled "the Beloved," the great favorite of heaven, the delight of God, the prime object of his love: it is he who obtains this benefit for believers: he is accepted for his own sake, and we for his.

3. The ultimate end of conferring this benefit upon believers: "to the praise of the glory of his grace;" or, to the end that his grace might be made glorious in praises. There are riches of grace in this act of God; and the work of believers, both in this world and in that to come, is to search and admire, acknowledge and magnify God for his abundant grace herein. The doctrine taught is, that

Jesus Christ has procured special favor and acceptance with God for all who are in him.

This point is plainly taught in Scripture : "But now, in Christ Jesus, ye who sometime were far off are *made nigh* by the blood of Christ." The original is a term of endearedness : nothing is thus taken into the very bosom but what is very dear, precious, and acceptable. Believers are said to be made by Jesus Christ "kings and priests unto God and his Father," Rev. 1 : 5, 6 ; that is, dignified favorites, upon whom the special marks of honor are set by God.

In illustrating this point three things must be doctrinally discussed : what the acceptance of our persons with God is ; how it appears that believers are so accepted with God ; and how Christ the Beloved procures this benefit for believers.

I. WHAT THE ACCEPTANCE OF OUR PERSONS WITH GOD IS : to understand which it may be proper to remember that there is a twofold acceptance of persons mentioned in Scripture.

Accepting of persons is noted in Scripture as *the sinful act of a corrupt man;* a thing which God abhors, being the corruption and abuse of the authority which men have in judgment ; overlooking the merit of the cause through respect to the quality of the person whose cause it is ; so that the cause does not commend the person, but the person the cause. This God everywhere brands in men as a vile perverting of judgment, and he utterly disclaims it himself. "God accepteth no man's person." Gal. 2 : 6. "There is no respect of persons with God." Rom. 2 : 11.

There is also an accepting of persons, which is *the gracious act of a merciful God;* whereby he receives both the persons and duties of believers into special grace and favor, for Christ's sake ; and of this my text speaks.

1. This act of favor supposes *a state of alienation* and enmity : those only are accepted that were out of favor ;

and indeed so stood the case with us. Ye were aliens and strangers, "but now, in Christ Jesus, ye who sometime were far off are made nigh by the blood of Christ." Eph. 2 : 12, 13. So the apostle Peter, "Which in time past were not a people, but are now the people of God; which had not obtained mercy, but now have obtained mercy." 1 Pet. 2 : 10. The fall made a fearful breach between God and man. Sin, like a thick cloud, intercepted all the beams of divine favor from us. The satisfaction of Christ dissolves that cloud : "I have blotted out as a thick cloud thy transgressions, and as a cloud thy sins." Isa. 44 : 22. This dark cloud thus dissolved, the face of God shines forth again with cheerful beams of favor and love upon all who by faith are interested in Jesus Christ.

2. It includes *the removing of guilt* from the persons of believers by the imputation of Christ's righteousness to them : "Being justified by faith, we have peace with God through our Lord Jesus Christ, by whom also we have access by faith into this grace wherein we stand." Rom. 5 : 1, 2. The face of God cannot shine upon the wicked; the person must be first made righteous before he can be made accepted.

3. It includes the *offering* or tendering of our persons and duties to God by Jesus Christ. Believers indeed present themselves to God, Rom. 12 : 1; but Christ's presenting them makes their tender of themselves acceptable to the Lord : "In the body of his flesh through death, to present you holy and unblamable and unreprovable in his sight." Col. 1 : 22. Christ leads every believer as it were by the hand into the gracious presence of God, after this manner bespeaking acceptance for him : "Father, here is a poor soul that was born in sin, has lived in rebellion against thee all his days; he has broken all thy laws, and deserved all thy wrath; yet he is one of those which thou gavest me before the world was. I have

atoned by my blood for all his sins; I have opened his
eyes to see the sinfulness and misery of his condition;
broken his heart for his rebellion against thee; bowed his
will in obedience to thy will; united him to myself by
faith as a living member of my body; and now, Lord,
since he is become mine by regeneration, let him be thine
also by special acceptance; let the same love with which
thou lovest me embrace him also who is now become
mine."

II. I must show you HOW IT APPEARS that believers are
thus ingratiated or brought into the special favor of God
by Jesus Christ. And this will be evinced divers ways.

1. By the *titles* of love with which the Lord graceth
and honoreth believers, who are sometimes called the
household of God, Eph. 2 : 19; the friends of God, James
2 : 23; the dear children of God, Eph. 5 : 1; the peculiar
people of God, 1 Pet. 2 : 9; a crown of glory and a royal
diadem in the hand of their God, Isa. 62 : 3; the objects
of his pleasure, Psa. 147 : 11. Oh, what terms of endear-
ment does God use towards his people! Does not all this
show them to be in special favor with him?

2. The gracious *manner* in which he treats them upon
the throne of grace, to which he allows them to come
with boldness. Heb. 4 : 16. This also shows them to be
in the special favor of God; he allows them to come to
him in prayer, with the liberty, confidence, and filial boldness of children to a father. "Because ye are sons, God
hath sent forth the Spirit of his Son into your hearts, crying, Abba, Father," Gal. 4 : 6, the familiar voice of a dear
child: yea, which is a wonderful condescension of the
great God to poor worms of the earth, he says, "Thus
saith the Lord, the Holy One of Israel and his Maker,
Ask me of things to come concerning my sons, and concerning the work of my hands command ye me," Isa.
45 : 11; an expression so full of grace and special favor to
believers that it needs great caution in reading and under-

standing it : the meaning is, that God has as it were subjected the works of his hands to the prayers of his saints ; and it is as if he had said, If my glory and your necessity shall require it, do but ask me in prayer, and whatever my almighty power can do I will do it for you. However, let no favorite of heaven forget the infinite distance between himself and God. Abraham was a great favorite of heaven, and was called "the friend of God ;" yet see with what humility of spirit and reverential awe he addresses God, "Behold now I have taken upon me to speak unto the Lord, which am but dust and ashes." Gen. 18 : 27.

3. *God's readiness to grant*, as well as their liberty to ask, proves them the special favorites of God. The heart of God is so ready to grant the desires of believers that it is but to ask and have. Matt. 7 : 7. The door of grace is opened by the key of prayer. That is a favorite indeed to whom the king gives a blank to insert what request he will : "If ye abide in me, and my words abide in you, ye shall ask what ye will, and it shall be done unto you." John 15 : 7. O blessed liberty of the sons of God ! David did but say, "Lord, I pray thee, turn the counsel of Ahithophel into foolishness," 2 Sam. 15 : 31, and it was done as soon as asked. Joshua did but say, "Thou sun, stand still in Gibeon," and a miraculous stop was presently put to its swift motion in the heavens ; nay, which is indeed wonderful, a prayer conceived in the heart and not yet uttered by the lips of believers is often anticipated by the readiness of free grace : "And it shall come to pass, that before they call, I will answer ; and while they are yet speaking, I will hear." Isa. 65 : 24. The prayers of others are rejected as an abomination. Prov 15 : 8. God casts them back into their faces. Mal. 2 : 3. But free grace signs the petitions of the saints more readily than they are presented ; we have not the readiness to ask, that God has to give. It is true, the answer of a be-

liever's prayers may be a long time hid from his knowledge ; but every prayer according to the will of God is presently granted in heaven, though for wise and holy ends believers may be held in doubtful suspense about them on earth.

4. The free *discoveries of the secrets of God's heart* to believers show them to be his special favorites.   Men open not the counsels of their hearts to enemies or strangers, but to their most intimate friends.   "The secret of the Lord is with them that fear him, and he will show them his covenant."   Psa. 25 : 14.   When God was about to destroy Sodom, he would do nothing in that work of judgment until he had acquainted Abraham his friend with his purpose therein.   "And the Lord said, Shall I hide from Abraham that thing which I do?"   Gen. 18: 17.   So when a king was to be elected for Israel, and the person whom God had chosen was yet unknown to the people, God as it were whispered the secret unto Samuel the day before. "Now the Lord had told Samuel in his ear a day before Saul came," according to the manner of princes with some special favorite.   1 Sam. 9 : 15.

5. The Lord's *receiving every small thing that comes from them with grace and favor* when he rejects the greatest things offered by others, certainly bespeaks believers the special favorites of God.   There was but one good word in a whole sentence from Sarah, and that very word is noted and commended by God, 1 Pet. 3 ; 6 : "She called him lord."   There were but some small beginnings or buddings of grace in young Abijah, and the Lord took special notice thereof.   "Because in him there is found some good thing toward the Lord God of Israel in the house of Jeroboam."   1 Kings 14 : 13.   Let this be an encouragement to young people in whom there are found any breathing desires after Christ ; God will not reject them if any sincerity be found in them ; a secret groan uttered to God in sincerity shall not be despised.   Rom.

8 : 26.   The very bent of a believer's will when he has no more to offer unto God is an acceptable present. 2 Cor. 8 : 11.   The very purpose that lies secretly in the heart of a believer not yet executed is accepted with him : "Whereas it was in thy heart to build a house unto my name, thou didst well that it was in thy heart." 1 Kings 8 : 18.   Thus small things offered to God by believers find acceptance with him, while the greatest presents, even solemn assemblies, sabbaths, and prayers from others are rejected : "They are a trouble unto me, I am weary to bear them." Isa. 1 : 14.   Incense from Sheba, the sweet cane from a far country, are not acceptable, nor sacrifices sweet from other hands. Jer. 6 : 20.

III. How Christ the Beloved procures this benefit for believers.   And this he does,

1. By *the satisfaction of his blood :* "When we were enemies, we were reconciled to God by the death of his Son." Rom. 5 : 10.   No friendship without reconciliation, no reconciliation but by the blood of Christ ; therefore the new and living way by which believers come unto God with acceptance is said to be consecrated for us through the veil of Christ's flesh ; and hence believers have boldness to enter into the holiest by the blood of Jesus. Heb. 10 : 19, 20.

2. The favor of God is procured for believers *by their mystical union with Christ,* whereby they are made "members of his body, of his flesh, and of his bones." Eph. 5 : 30.   So that as Adam's posterity stood upon the same terms that he their natural head did, so believers, Christ's mystical members, stand in the favor of God by the favor which Christ their spiritual head has : "I in them, and thou in me, that they may be made perfect in one ; and that the world may know that thou hast sent me, and hast loved them as thou hast loved me." John 17 : 23.

3. Believers are brought into favor with God *by Christ's becoming their altar,* upon which their persons and duties

are all offered up to God. The altar sanctifies the gift; and this was typified by the legal rite mentioned, Luke 1 : 9, 10. Christ is that golden altar from whence all the prayers of the saints ascend to the throne of God perfumed with the odors and incense of his merits : "And another angel came and stood at the altar, having a golden censer ; and there was given unto him much incense, that he should offer it with the prayers of all saints upon the golden altar which was before the throne : and the smoke of the incense which came with the prayers of the saints, ascended up before God out of the angel's hand." Revelation 8 : 3, 4.

INFERENCE I. If all believers be in favor with God, *how great a mercy is it to have the prayers of such on our behalf.* Would we have our desires succeed in heaven, let us seek the favor of God ourselves, and engage the prayers of his people, the favorites of heaven, for us. One believer can do much, many can do more. When Daniel designed to get the knowledge of the secret hinted in the obscure dream of the king, which none but the God of heaven could make known, it is said, "Then Daniel went to his house and made the thing known unto Hananiah, Mishael, and Azariah, his companions, that they would desire mercies of the God of heaven concerning this secret." Dan. 2 : 17, 18. The benefit of such assistance in prayer by the help of Christians is plainly intimated by Jesus Christ : "If two of you shall agree on earth as touching any thing that they shall ask, it shall be done for them of my Father which is in heaven." Matthew 18 : 19. God sometimes specially regards a number of voices for the granting of some public mercy, because he delights in the harmony of many praying souls, and to gratify many in the answer of the same prayer. I know this usage is grown too formal among professors, but certainly it is a great advantage to be united with those whose prayers prevail with God. Bernard, prescribing rules for effectual prayer, closes them with this wish, When thy heart is in this frame, remember me.

2. If believers are such favorites in heaven, *in what a desperate condition are that cause and those persons against whom believers are daily engaged in prayers and cries to heaven.*

Certainly Rome shall feel the force of the many millions of prayers that are gone up to heaven from the saints for many generations ; the cries of the blood of the martyrs of Jesus, joined with the cries of thousands of believers, will bring down vengeance at last upon the man of sin. It is said, "The smoke of the incense, which came with the prayers of the saints, ascended up before God out of the angel's hand. And the angel took the censer and filled it with fire of the altar, and cast it into the earth ; and there were voices, and thunderings, and lightnings, and an earthquake. And the seven angels, which had the seven trumpets, prepared themselves to sound." Rev. 8 : 4–6. The prayer of a single saint is sometimes followed with wonderful effects : " In my distress I called upon the LORD, and cried unto my God : he heard my voice out of his temple, and my cry came before him, even into his ears : then the earth shook and trembled ; the foundations also of the hills moved and were shaken, because he was wroth." Psalm 18 : 6, 7. What then can a thundering legion of praying souls do ? It was said of Luther, that he could have of God what he would ; his enemies felt the weight of his prayers, and the church of God reaped the benefit. The queen of Scots professed she was more afraid of the prayers of John Knox than of an army of ten thousand men. These were mighty wrestlers with God, however vilified among their enemies. A time will come when God will hear the prayers of his people, who are continually crying in his ears, " How long ? Lord, how long ?"

3. *Let not believers be dejected at the contempt of men, so long as they stand in the favor of God.* It is the lot of the best

men to have the worst usage in the world : those of whom the world was not worthy were not thought worthy to live in the world. Heb. 11 : 38. Paul and his companions were men of a choice spirit ; yet saith he, " Being defamed, we entreat ; we are made as the filth of the earth, and are the offscouring of all things unto this day." 1 Cor. 4 : 13. These are words signifying the most contemptible and abhorred things among men. How are heaven and earth divided in their judgments and estimations of the saints. Those whom men call filth and dirt, God calls a peculiar treasure, a crown of glory, a royal diadem. But trouble not thyself, believer, for the unjust censures of the blind world ; they speak evil of the things they know not : "He that is spiritual judgeth all things, yet he himself is judged of no man." 1 Cor. 2 : 15. You can discern the baseness of their spirit ; they want a faculty to see the excellence of your spirit : he that carries a dark lantern in the night can discern him that comes against him, and yet is not discerned by him. A courtier regards not a slight in the country, so long as he has the ear and favor of his prince.

4. *Never let believers fear the want of any good thing necessary for them in this world.* The favor of God is the fountain of all blessings, even of all that you need. He has promised that he will withhold no good thing from them that walk uprightly. Psalm 84 : 11. He that is bountiful to his enemies will not withhold what is good from his friends. The favor of God will not only supply your needs, but protect your persons : " Thou wilt bless the righteous ; with favor wilt thou compass him as with a shield." Psalm 5 : 12.

5. Hence also it follows *that the sins of believers are very displeasing to God.* The unkindness of those whom he has received into his bosom, upon whom he has set his special delight, who are more obliged to him than all the people of the earth besides, O this grieves the blessed God.

What a melting expostulation was that which the Lord used with David : "I anointed thee king over Israel, and I delivered thee out of the hand of Saul ; and I gave thee thy master's house, and thy master's wives into thy bosom, and gave thee the house of Israel and of Judah ; and if that had been too little, I would moreover have given unto thee such and such things.   Wherefore hast thou despised the commandment of the Lord ?" 2 Sam. 12 : 7–9. But, reader, if thou be a reconciled person, and hast grieved him by any eminent transgression, how should it melt thy heart to hear the Lord thus expostulating with thee : "I delivered thee out of the hand of Satan ; I gave thee into the bosom of Christ ; I have pardoned thy millions of sins ; I have bestowed upon thee the riches of mercy ; my favor has made thee great ; and as if all this were too little, I have prepared heaven for thee : for which of all these favors dost thou thus requite me ?"

6. *How precious should Jesus Christ be to believers, by whose blood they are ingratiated with God, and by whose intercession they are and shall be continued in his favor.* When the apostle mentions the believer's translation from the sad state of nature to the blessed state of grace, see what a title he bestows upon Jesus Christ, the purchaser of that privilege, calling him the "dear Son." Col. 1 : 13. Not only dear to God, but exceeding dear to believers. Christ is the favorite in heaven ; to him you owe all your preferment there.   Take away Christ, and you have no ground on which to stand in the favor of God.   O then let Jesus Christ, the fountain of your honor, be also the object of your love and praise.

7. *Estimate by this the condition of a deserted saint upon whom the favor of God is eclipsed.*   If the favor of God be better than life, the hiding of it must be more bitter than death.   Deserted saints have reason to take the first place among all the mourners in the world : the darkness before conversion had indeed more danger, but this has more sor-

row. Darkness after light is dismal darkness. Since therefore the case is so sad, let your care be the more; grieve not the good Spirit of God; you prepare for your own grief in so doing.

8. *Let this persuade all men to accept Jesus Christ as they hope to be accepted with the Lord themselves.* It is a fearful case for a man's person and duties to be rejected of God, to cry and not be heard; and much more terrible to be denied audience in the great and terrible day. Yet, as sure as the Scriptures are the faithful sayings of God, this is no more than what every Christless person must expect in that day. Matt. 7 : 22; Luke 13 : 26. Trace the history of all times, even as early as Abel, and you shall find that none but believers ever found acceptance with God; all experience confirms this great truth, that "they that are in the flesh cannot please God." Reader, if this be thy condition, let me beg thee to ponder the misery of it.

Consider how sad it is to be rejected of God and forsaken by all creatures at once; what a day of straits thy dying day is like to be, when heaven and earth shall cast thee out together. Be assured, however thy vain hopes for the present may quiet thee, this must be thy case; the door of mercy will be shut against thee; no man cometh to the Father but by Christ. Sad was the case of Saul when he told Samuel, "The Philistines make war against me, and God is departed from me." 1 Sam. 28 : 15. The saints will have boldness in the day of judgment, 1 John 4 : 17; but thou wilt be confounded. There is yet, blessed be the God of mercy, opportunity for reconciliation. 2 Cor. 5 : 19; Isa. 27 : 5. But this cannot be of long continuance. O therefore, by all the regard and love you have for the everlasting welfare of your own souls, come to Christ; embrace him in the offers of the gospel, that you may be "made accepted in the Beloved."

CHAPTER XVIII

THIRD BENEFIT PURCHASED BY CHRIST—THE LIBERTY OF BELIEVERS

"If the Son therefore shall make you free, ye shall be free indeed."
John 8: 36

From the thirtieth verse of this chapter to my text you have an account of the different effects which the words of Christ had upon the hearts of his hearers. Some believed; these he encourages to continue in his word, giving them this assurance, "Ye shall know the truth, and the truth shall make you free." At this the unbelieving Jews take offence, and commence a contention with him: "We be Abraham's seed, and were never in bondage to any man." We are of no slavish extraction; the blood of Abraham runs in our veins. This scornful boast of the proud Jews Christ confutes, and discourses on a twofold bondage—one to men, another to sin: "Whosoever committeth sin is the servant of sin." He then tells them, "The servant abideth not in the house for ever, but the Son abideth ever;" wherein he intimates two great truths: 1, that the slaves of sin may for a time enjoy the external privileges of the house or church of God; but it would not be long before the Master of the house would reject them. But, 2, if they were once the adopted children of God, then they should abide in the house for ever; and this privilege is only to be had by their believing in and union with the Son of God, Jesus Christ; which brings us to the text, "If the Son therefore shall make you free, ye shall be free indeed." In which words we have

A *supposition:* "If the Son therefore shall make you free." As if he should say, The womb of nature cast you forth into the world in a state of bondage : in that state you have lived all your days, servants to sin, slaves to your lusts ; yet freedom is to be obtained, and this freedom it is the prerogative of the Son of God to bestow : "If the Son shall make you free." And also

Christ's *concession* upon this supposition : "Ye shall be free indeed ;" that is, you shall have a real, an excellent, and everlasting freedom ; no mere fancy, as that which you now boast of is. If therefore you would be freemen indeed, believe in me. Hence, learn that

An interest in Christ sets the soul at liberty from the bondage to which it was subject in its natural state.

Believers are the children of the new covenant, the denizens of Jerusalem which is above, which is free, and the mother of them all. Gal. 4 : 26. The glorious liberty, that which is spiritual and eternal, is the liberty of the children of God, Rom. 8 : 21 ; Christ, and none but Christ, delivers his people out of the hand of their enemies. Luke 1 : 74. I must show what believers are not freed from by Jesus Christ in this world ; what that bondage is from which every believer is freed by Christ ; what kind of freedom it is which commences upon believing ; and the excellence of spiritual freedom.

I. WHAT BELIEVERS ARE NOT FREED FROM IN THIS WORLD. We must not think that our spiritual liberty by Christ presently brings us into an absolute liberty in all respects ; for,

1. *Christ does not free believers from obedience to the moral law.* It is true, we are no more under it as a covenant for our justification ; but we are and must still be under it as a rule for our direction. The matter of the moral law is unchangeable, as the nature of good and evil is, and cannot be abolished except that distinction be destroyed. Matt. 5 : 17, 18. The precepts of the law are still urged under the gospel. Eph. 6 : 2. It is therefore a vain distinction, invented by libertines, to say it binds us as crea-

tures, not as Christians ; or that it binds the unregenerate part, but not the regenerate. It is a sure truth, that they who are freed from its penalties are still under its precepts. Though believers are no more under its curse, yet they are still under its government. The law sends us to Christ to be justified, and Christ sends us to the law to be regulated. Let the heart of every Christian join, therefore, with David in the holy wish, " Thou hast commanded us to keep thy precepts diligently ; O that my ways were directed to keep thy statutes." Psalm 119 : 4, 5. It is excellent when Christians begin to obey the law from life which others obey for life—because they are justified, not that they may be justified. It is also excellent when duties are done in the strength and for the honor of Christ, which is evangelical ; and not in our own strength and for our own ends, which is servile obedience. Had Christ freed us from obedience, such a liberty had been to our loss.

2. Christ has not freed believers in this world from *the temptations and assaults of Satan;* even those that are freed from his dominion are not free from his molestation. It is said indeed, God shall shortly bruise Satan under your feet, Rom. 16 : 20 ; but in the meantime he has power to bruise and buffet us by his injections. 2 Cor. 12 : 7. He now bruises Christ's heel, Gen. 3 : 15 ; that is, bruises him in his tempted and afflicted members. Though he cannot kill them, yet he can and does afflict and terrify them by shooting his fiery darts of temptation among them. Eph. 6 : 16. It is true, when the saints get safe into heaven there will be perfect freedom from all temptation ; a believer may then say, O thou enemy, temptations are come to a perpetual end ; I am now arrived where none of thy fiery darts can reach me. But this freedom is not yet

3. Christ has not yet freed believers in this world from *the motions of indwelling sin;* these are continually acting

and distressing the holiest men. Rom. 7 : 21, 23, 24. Corruptions, like the Canaanites, are still left in the land to be thorns in our eyes and goads in our sides. Those that boast most of freedom from the motions of sin have most cause to suspect themselves still under its dominion. All Christ's freemen are troubled with the same complaint : who among them does not complain, as the apostle did, "O wretched man that I am ! who shall deliver me from the body of this death?" Rom. 7 : 24.

4. Jesus Christ does not free believers in this world from *inward troubles of soul* on account of sin. God may let loose Satan, and conscience too, in the way of terrible accusations, which may greatly distress a believer, wofully eclipse the light of God's countenance, and break the peace of the soul. Job, Heman, and David were all made free by Christ, yet each of them has left upon record his bitter complaint upon this account. Job 7 : 19, 20 ; Psa. 88 : 14–16 ; 38 : 1–11.

5. Christ has not freed believers in this world from *affliction*. God in giving us our liberty does not abridge his own. Psalm 89 : 32. All the children of God are made free, yet what son is there whom the father chasteneth not? Heb. 12 : 7. Exemption from affliction is so far from being the mark of a free man, that the apostle makes it the mark of a slave. Bastards, not sons, want the discipline and blessing of the rod : to be free from affliction would be no benefit to believers, who receive so many benefits by it.

6. No believer is freed by Christ from *death*, though they are all freed from the *sting* of death. Rom. 8 : 10. The bodies of believers are under the same law of mortality as other men. Heb. 9 : 27. We must come to the grave as well as others, through the same agonies that other men do. Believers, indeed, are distinguished by mercy from others, but the distinguishing mercy lies not here. Thus you see what believers are not freed from

in this world. If you shall now say, What advantage then hath a believer, or what profit is there in regeneration? I answer that,

II. BELIEVERS ARE FREED FROM MANY GREAT EVILS BY JESUS CHRIST.

1. All believers are freed from the *rigor and curse of the law*. The yoke of the law is broken off from their necks, and the easy yoke of Jesus Christ put on. Matt. 11:28. The law required perfect obedience, under the pain of a curse. Gal. 3:10. It accepted of no short endeavors, admitted no repentance, gave no strength. Under the gospel, proportionable strength is given. Phil. 4:13. Transgression brings not under condemnation. Rom. 8:1. O blessed freedom! Duty becomes light, and imperfections hinder not acceptance. This is one part of the blessed freedom of believers.

2. All believers are freed from the *condemnation of sin;* it may trouble, but it cannot condemn them. Rom. 8:33. The handwriting which was against us is cancelled by Christ, nailed to his cross. Col. 2:14. When the seal and handwriting are torn off from the bond, the debtor is free. Believers are freed, "justified from all things," Acts 13:39; and finally freed, "they shall not come into condemnation." John 5:24. O blessed freedom!

3. Jesus Christ frees all believers from the *dominion* as well as the condemnation of sin. "Sin shall not have dominion over you; for ye are not under the law, but under grace." Rom. 6:14. "The law of the Spirit of life in Christ Jesus hath made me free from the law of sin and death." Rom. 8:2. Who can estimate such a liberty as this? What an intolerable drudgery is the service of divers lusts, from all which believers are freed by Christ; not from the residence, but from the reign of sin. It is with sin in believers as it was with those beasts mentioned Dan. 7:12, "They had their dominion taken away; yet their lives were prolonged for a season and a time."

4. Jesus Christ sets all believers free from *the power of Satan*, in whose dominion they were by nature : they are translated from the power of darkness into the kingdom of Christ. Col. 1 : 13. Satan had the possession of them, as a man of his own goods ; but Christ dispossesses that strong man armed, and recovers them out of his hand. Luke 11 : 21, 22. There are two ways by which Christ frees believers out of Satan's power and possession.

By *price*. The blood of Christ purchases believers out of the hands of justice by satisfying the law for them, which being done, Satan's authority over them falls as the power of a jailer over the prisoner when he has a legal discharge. "Forasmuch then as the children are partakers of flesh and blood, he also himself likewise took part of the same ; that through death he might destroy him that had the power of death, that is, the devil." The cruel tyrant burdens the poor captive no more after the ransom is once paid, and he is actually freed. Heb. 2 : 14.

Christ also delivers his people by *power*. Satan is exceedingly unwilling to let go his prey. He is a strong and malicious enemy ; every deliverance out of his hand is a glorious effect of the almighty power of Christ. Acts 26 : 18 ; 2 Cor. 10 : 5. How did our Lord Jesus Christ grapple with Satan at his death and triumph over him. Col. 2 : 15. O glorious salvation ! blessed liberty of the children of God !

5. Christ frees believers from the *sting of death*. Kill us it can, but hurt us it cannot. "O death, where is thy sting? O grave, where is thy victory? The sting of death is sin ; and the strength of sin is the law. But thanks be to God, which giveth us the victory through our Lord Jesus Christ." 1 Cor. 15 : 55–57. It is guilt that arms death with its terrifying power : to die in our sins, John 8 : 24 ; to have our bones full of the sins of our youth, which shall lie down with us in the dust, Job 20 : 11 ; to have death, like a dragon, seizing a poor guilty

creature as its prey, Psalm 49 : 14 ; in this lies the danger and horror of death.   But from death as a curse, and from the grave as a prison, Christ has set believers at liberty, by submitting to death in their stead ; and by his victorious resurrection from the grave, as the first-born of the dead, death is disarmed of its hurting power.   The death of believers is but a sleep in Jesus.

III. The nature of the freedom purchased by Christ for believers.

Believers in their *civil* capacity are not freed from the duties they owe to their superiors ; servants, though believers, are still to be subject to their masters according to the flesh, with fear and trembling.   Eph. 6 : 5.   Nor are we delivered from obedience to lawful magistrates, whom we are to obey in the Lord.   Rom. 13 : 1, 4.   Religion dissolves not the band of civil relations ; nor is it to be used as a cloak of maliciousness.   1 Pet. 2 : 16.   It is not a carnal, but a *spiritual* freedom Christ has purchased for us.   And the spiritual liberty believers have at present is but the beginning ; they are freed but in part from their spiritual enemies ; but it is growing every day, and will be complete at last.   By this liberty they are also not only freed from many miseries, burdens, and dangers, but invested by Jesus Christ with many royal privileges and invaluable immunities.

IV. The excellence of this blessed freedom which the saints enjoy by Jesus Christ.   It is,

1. A *wonderful* liberty, never enough to be admired. For those who owed God more than they could pay by their eternal sufferings ; those that were under the dreadful condemnation of the law, in the power of Satan, the strong man armed ; those that were bound with so many chains in their spiritual prison—their understanding bound with ignorance, their wills with obstinacy, their hearts with impenetrable hardness, their affections with a thousand bewitching vanities, and who slighted their state of

slavery so much as industriously to oppose all means of deliverance—for such persons to be set at liberty is the wonder of wonders, and will be marvellous in the eyes of believers for ever.

2. The freedom of believers is a *peculiar* freedom, which few obtain; the mass of men abiding still in bondage to Satan, who, from the number of his subjects, is styled "the god of this world." 2 Cor. 4 : 4. Believers in Scripture are often called a remnant, a small part of the whole. The more cause have the people of God to admire distinguishing mercy. How many nobles and great ones of the world are but royal slaves to Satan and their own lusts!

3. The liberty of believers is a liberty dearly purchased by the blood of Christ. What that captain said, Acts 22 : 28, "With a great sum obtained I this freedom," may much more be said of the believers' freedom: it was not silver or gold, but the precious blood of Christ that purchased it. 1 Pet. 1 : 18.

4. The freedom of believers is an *increasing* liberty; they get more out of the power of sin and nearer to their complete salvation every day. Rom. 13 : 11. The body of sin dies daily in them; they are said to be crucified with Christ; the strength of sin abates continually in them, after the manner of crucified persons, who die a slow but certain death; and in the same degree in which the power of sin abates, their spiritual liberty increases.

5. The freedom of believers is a *comfortable* freedom. The apostle comforts Christians of the lowest rank, poor servants, with this consideration, "He that is called in the Lord, being a servant, is the Lord's freeman." 1 Cor. 7 : 22. As if he had said, Let not the meanness of your outward condition, which is a state of subjection and dependence, of poverty and contempt, at all trouble you: you are the Lord's freemen, of precious account in his eyes. O, it is a comfortable liberty!

6. It is a *perpetual* and final freedom. They that are freed by Christ have their manumission and final discharge from the state of bondage they were in before. Sin shall never have dominion over them any more ; it may tempt and trouble them, but shall never more govern them. Acts 26 : 18.

INFERENCE 1. *How rational is the joy of Christians above the joy of all others.* Shall not the captive rejoice in his recovered liberty ? The very birds of the air had rather be at liberty in the woods, though hungry, than in a golden cage with the richest fare : every creature naturally prizes it ; none more than believers, who have felt the burden and bondage of corruption, and who in the days of their first illumination poured out many groans and tears for this mercy. What was said of the captive people of God in Babylon excellently shadows forth the state of God's people under spiritual bondage, with the way of their deliverance from it. "By the blood of thy covenant I have sent forth thy prisoners out of the pit wherein is no water." Zech. 9 : 11. Believers are delivered by the blood of Christ out of a worse pit than that of Babylon ; and how were the tribes in their return from thence overwhelmed with joy and astonishment : "When the Lord turned again the captivity of Zion, we were like them that dream. Then was our mouth filled with laughter, and our tongue with singing." Psalm 126 : 1, 2.

They were overwhelmed with a sense of the mercy ; so should it be with the people of God. It is said, when the prodigal son was returned again to his father's house, that there was heard music and dancing, mirth and feasting, in that house. Luke 15 : 24. The angels in heaven rejoice when a soul is recovered out of the power of Satan. And shall not the souls immediately concerned in the mercy greatly rejoice ? Yea, let them rejoice in the Lord, and let no earthly trouble ever have power to interrupt their joy after such a deliverance.

2. *How unreasonable and inexcusable is the sin of apostasy from Jesus Christ.* What is it but for a delivered captive to put his feet again into the shackles; his hands into the manacles; his neck into the iron yoke from which he has been delivered? It is said, Matt. 12 : 43–45, "When the unclean spirit is gone out of a man, he walketh through dry places, seeking rest, and findeth none. Then he saith, I will return into my house from whence I came out; and when he is come, he findeth it empty, swept, and garnished. Then goeth he and taketh with himself seven other spirits more wicked than himself, and they enter in and dwell there; and the last state of that man is worse than the first"—even as a prisoner, that has escaped and is again taken, is loaded with double irons. Let the people of God be willing to endure any difficulties in the way of religion, rather than return again into their former bondage to sin and Satan. O, Christian, if ever God gave thee a sense of the misery and danger of thy natural state, if ever thou hast felt the pangs of a distressed conscience, and after all this tasted the unspeakable sweetness of peace in Christ, thou wilt rather choose to die ten thousand deaths, than to forsake him and go back again into that sad condition.

3. *How suitable is a free spirit in believers to their state of freedom.* Christ has made your condition free, O let the temper and frame of your hearts be free also; do all that you do for God not by constraint, but willingly. Methinks, Christians, the new nature that is in you should be as a command, and instead of all arguments addressed to the hopes and fears of other men. See how all creatures act according to their natures. You need not command a mother to draw forth her breasts to a sucking child; nature itself teaches and prompts to that. You need not bid the sea ebb and flow at the stated hours. O, Christian, why should thy heart need any other argument than its own spiritual inclination to keep its stated

seasons of communion with God? Let none of God's commandments be grievous to you: let not thy heart need forcing to its own benefit and advantage. Whatever you do for God, do it cheerfully; and whatever you suffer for God, suffer it cheerfully. It was this spirit which actuated Paul: "I am ready not to be bound only, but also to die at Jerusalem for the name of the Lord Jesus." Acts 21: 13.

4. *Let no man wonder at the opposition of Satan to the preaching of the gospel.* It is by the gospel that souls are recovered out of his power. Acts 26 : 18. It is the work of ministers to turn men from darkness to light, and from the power of Satan unto God. Satan is a great and jealous prince: he will never endure to have liberty proclaimed by the ministers of Christ within his dominions. And indeed, what is it less, when the gospel is preached in power, but as it were by sound of trumpet to proclaim spiritual, sweet, and everlasting liberty to every soul sensible of the bondage of corruption and the cruel servitude of Satan, and who will now come over to Jesus Christ? And O, what numbers of prisoners have broken loose from Satan at one proclamation of Christ! Acts 2 : 41. But Satan owes the servants of Christ a spite for this, and will be sure to pay them, if ever they come within his reach. Persecution is the evil genius of the gospel, and follows it as the shadow does the body.

5. How careful should Christians be to *maintain their spiritual liberty in every point.* "Stand fast therefore in the liberty wherewith Christ hath made us free, and be not again entangled with the yoke of bondage." Gal. 5 : 1. "Ye are bought with a price," "be not ye the servants of men." It is Christ's prerogative to prescribe the rules of his own house; he has given no man dominion over your faith. 2 Cor. 1 : 24. One man is no rule to another, but the word of Christ is a rule to all: follow not the holiest of men one step farther than they follow Christ. 1 Cor. 11 : 1. Man is ambitious, affecting dominion; and

that over the mind rather than the body. To give law to others feeds pride in himself: so far as any man brings the word of Christ to warrant his injunctions, so far we are to obey, and no farther. Christ is your Lord and Lawgiver.

6. *Let this persuade sinners to come to Christ;* for with him is liberty for poor captives. Oh that you did but know what a blessed state Jesus Christ would bring you into! "Come unto me, all ye that labor and are heavy-laden:" and what encouragement doth he give? "My yoke is easy, and my burden is light." The devil persuades you that the ways of godliness are a bondage; but if ever God regenerate you, you will find his ways ways of pleasantness, and all his paths peace: you will rejoice in the way of his commandments as much as in all riches. You will find the work to which Christ calls you, even suffering work, sweeter than all the pleasures you found in sin. O open your hearts at the call of the gospel; come unto Christ: *then shall you be free indeed.*

CHAPTER XIX

FOURTH BENEFIT PURCHASED BY CHRIST—BRINGING
US TO GOD BY RECONCILIATION AND GLORIFICA-
TION

"For Christ also hath once suffered for sins, the just for the unjust, that
he might bring us to God." 1 Pet. 3: 18

THE scope of the apostle in this place is to fortify Christians for a day of suffering; in order to their cheerful sus-
taining of which, he prescribes two excellent rules: first,
to get a good conscience within them; and secondly, to
set the example of Christ's sufferings before them, "For
Christ hath once suffered for sins;" the sufferings of
Christ for us is the great motive engaging Christians to
suffer cheerfully for him.

In these words we have the sufficiency and fulness
of Christ's sufferings intimated in the particle once: Christ
needs to suffer no more, having completed that whole
work at once; the cause of the sufferings of Christ, and
that is sin: "Christ once suffered for sins," not his own
sins, but ours; the admirable grace and unexampled love
of Christ to us sinners, "the just for the unjust," in which
words the substitution of Christ in the room and place of
sinners is plainly expressed; the design of the sufferings
of Christ, which was, *to bring us to God;* and the issue
of the sufferings of Christ, which was, the death of Christ
in the flesh, and the quickening of Christ after death by
the Spirit. The doctrine we now propose to illustrate
is, that

*The end of Christ's death and sufferings was to bring all
those for whom he died unto God.*

In the explication, two things must be considered:

what Christ's bringing us to God imports; and what influence the death of Christ has upon this design of bringing us to God.

I. WHAT CHRIST'S BRINGING US TO GOD IMPORTS. And certainly there are many excellent things contained in this expression. Generally it denotes our state of reconciliation and our state of glorification. By reconciliation we are brought nigh unto God. Ye are made nigh, that is, reconciled by the blood of Christ. Eph. 2:13. We are said to come to God the Judge of all. Heb. 12:22, 23. By reconciliation, we are brought nigh unto God now; by glorification, we shall be brought home to God hereafter. We shall be ever with the Lord. 1 Thess. 4:17. But more particularly this phrase, "that he might bring us to God," imports,

1. That the *chief* happiness of man *consists in the enjoyment of God*. The creature has as necessary a dependence upon God for happiness as the stream has upon the fountain, or the image in the glass upon the face of him that looks into it. For as the sum of the creature's misery lies in this, "Depart from me," separation from God being the principal part of damnation; so on the contrary the chief happiness of the creature consists in the enjoyment and blessed vision of God. 1 John 3:2. "I shall be satisfied, when I awake, with thy likeness." Psalm 17:15.

2. It implies *man's apostasy from God*. "But now, in Christ Jesus, ye who sometime were far off are made nigh by the blood of Christ." Eph. 2:13. Those whom Christ brings unto God were before far off from him, both in condition and in disposition. We were lost, and had no desire to return to God. The prodigal was said to go into a far country. Luke 15:13.

3. Christ's bringing us to God implies *our inability of ourselves to return to God*. We must be brought back by Christ, or perish for ever in separation from God. The lost sheep is made the emblem of the lost sinner. Luke

15 : 5. The shepherd seeks it, finds it, and carries it back upon his shoulders. The apostle plainly tells us that "when we were without strength," that is, to save ourselves, "in due time Christ died for the ungodly." Rom. 5 : 6.

4. Christ's bringing us to God implies that *God's justice was once the great bar between him and man.* Man can have no access to God but by Christ; and he brings us to God in no other way but that of satisfaction by his blood : "He hath suffered for sins, the just for the unjust, that he might bring us to God." Better ten thousand worlds should perish for ever than that God should lose the honor of his justice. This great bar to our enjoyment of God is effectually removed by the death of Christ, whereby God's justice is not only fully satisfied, but highly honored and glorified. Rom. 3 : 24. And so the way by which we are brought to God is again opened, to the wonder and joy of all believers, by the blood and sufferings of Christ.

5. It shows us *the happiness of believers above all people.* These only shall be brought to God by Jesus Christ in a reconciled state. Others indeed shall be brought to God as a Judge, to be condemned; believers only are brought to God in the Mediator's hand as a reconciled Father, to be made blessed for ever in the enjoyment of him. Every believer is brought singly to God at his death, Luke 16 : 22; and all believers shall be jointly and solemnly presented to God in the great day. Col. 1 : 22. They shall be all presented faultless before the presence of his glory with exceeding joy. Jude 24. The privilege of believers in that day will lie in divers things.

(1.) They shall be all brought to God *together*. This will be the general assembly mentioned, Heb. 12 : 23. There shall be a collection of all believers in all ages of the world into one blessed assembly; they shall come from the east and west, the north and south, and shall sit

down in the kingdom of God.   Luke 13 : 29.   Oh what
a glorious train will be seen following the Redeemer in
that day !

(2.) As all the saints shall be collected into one body,
so they shall be all brought or presented unto God *fault-less* and without blemish.   Jude 24.   "A glorious church,
not having spot, or wrinkle, or any such thing."   Eph.
5 : 27.   This is the general assembly of the spirits of
just men made perfect.   Heb. 12 : 23.   All sin was perfectly separated from them when death had separated
their souls and bodies.

(3.) As believers shall be all brought together, and
that in a state of absolute purity and perfection, so they
shall be all brought *to God :* they shall see his face, in the
vision whereof is fulness of joy, and at whose right hand
are pleasures for evermore.   Psalm 16 : 11.   The blessedness of the saints consists in their fruition of God.
Psalm 73 : 25.   To see God in his word and works is the
happiness of the saints on earth ; but to see him face to
face will be the fulness of their blessedness in heaven.
1 John 3 : 2.   This is that transforming and sanctifying
vision of which the Scriptures frequently speak.   Psalm
17 : 15 ; 1 Cor. 15 : 28 ; Rev. 7 : 17.

(4.) To be brought to God implies a state of perfect
joy and highest delight.   Christ shall present or bring
them to God with exceeding joy.   Jude 24.   And more
fully the joy of this day is expressed, Psalm 45 : 15 :
"With gladness and rejoicing shall they be brought ; they
shall enter into the king's palace."   It will be a day of
universal joy when all the saints are brought home to God
in a perfected state.   For,

God the Father will rejoice when Christ brings home
that precious number of his elect whom he redeemed by
his blood : he rejoices in them now, though imperfect and
under many corruptions and weaknesses.   Zeph. 3 : 17.
How much more will he rejoice in them when Christ pre-

sents them without spot or wrinkle to him.   Ephesians 5 : 27.

Jesus Christ will exceedingly rejoice ; it will be the day of the gladness and satisfaction of his heart ; for now, and not till now, he receives his mystical fulness, Col. 1 : 24, beholds all the blessed issues of his death, which cannot but give him unspeakable joy.   "He shall see of the travail of his soul, and shall be satisfied."   Isa. 53 : 11.

The day in which believers are brought home to God will be a day of unspeakable joy to *the Holy Spirit* himself ; for unto this all his sanctifying designs had respect ; to this day he sealed them and stirred up desires in their hearts that cannot be uttered.   Eph. 4 : 30 ; Rom. 8 : 26. Thus the blessed persons, Father, Son, and Spirit, will rejoice in the bringing home of the elect to God.   For as it is the greatest joy to a man to see the designs which he has been long projecting and anticipating at last brought to a happy issue, much more will it be so here, each person of the Holy Trinity being deeply concerned in this blessed design.

The angels of God will rejoice at the bringing home of believers to him ; the spirits of just men made perfect will be united in one general assembly with an innumerable company of angels.   Heb. 12 : 22, 23.   Great is the love of angels to redeemed ones ; they rejoiced at the incarnation of Christ for them, Luke 2 : 13 ; they delight to pry into the mystery of their redemption, 1 Pet. 1 : 12 : they were delighted at their conversion, which was the day of their espousals to Christ, Luke 15 : 10 ; they have been careful over them and serviceable to them in this world, Heb. 1 : 14, and cannot but rejoice exceedingly to see them all brought home in safety to their Father's house.

Christ's bringing home all believers to God will be matter of unspeakable joy *to themselves;* for whatever acquaintance they had with God here, whatever anticipations they had of heaven and the glory to come, yet the sight of God and Christ the Redeemer will be an unspeakable surprise to them in that day.   It will be the full satisfaction of all their desires.

II. Let it be considered what influence THE DEATH OF CHRIST hath upon this design, and you shall find it much every way.

1. The death of Christ *removes all obstacles out of the way* of this mercy.   The bars hindering our access to God were such as nothing but the death of Christ could remove.   The guilt of sin barred us from his gracious presence.   Rom. 5 : 2, 3 ; Hos. 14 : 2.   The pollution of sin excluded us from God.   Hab. 1 : 23 ; Heb. 12 : 14.   The enmity of our nature stopped up our way to God.   Col. 1 : 21 ; Rom. 8 : 7.   By reason hereof fallen man hath no desire to come to God.   Job 21 : 14.   The justice of God, like a flaming sword turning every way, kept all men from access to him ; and Satan, that malicious adversary, lay as a lion in the way to God.   1 Pet. 5 : 8.   O with what bars were the gates of heaven shut against our souls ! The way to God was filled with difficulties that none but Christ was able to remove ; and he has effectually removed them all.   The way is now open, even the new and living way, consecrated for us by his blood.   The death of Christ effectually removes the guilt of sin, 1 Pet. 2 : 24 ; washed away the pollution of sin, 1 John 5 : 6 ; takes away the enmity of nature, Col. 1 : 20, 21 ; satisfies all the demands of justice, Rom. 3 : 25, 26 ; has broken all the power of Satan, Col. 2 : 15 ; Heb. 2 : 14 ; and consequently the way to God is fully opened to believers by the blood of Jesus.   Heb. 10 : 20.

2. The blood of Christ *purchased for believers their right* to this privilege.   "But when the fulness of the time was come, God sent forth his Son, made of a woman, made under the law, to redeem them that were under the law, that we might receive the adoption of sons," Gal. 4 : 4, 5 ;

that is, both the relation and inheritance of sons. There was worth enough in the precious blood of Christ to pay all our debts to justice, and to purchase for us this invaluable privilege. We must put this unspeakable mercy of being brought to God to the account of the death of Christ: no believer had ever tasted the sweetness of such a mercy, if Christ had not tasted the bitterness of death for him.

INFERENCE 1. *Great is the preciousness and worth of souls,* that the life of Christ should be given to redeem and recover them to God. As God laid out his counsel from eternity upon them to project the way of their salvation, so the Lord Jesus, in pursuance of that blessed design, came from the bosom of the Father and shed his invaluable blood to bring them to God. No wise man expends vast sums to obtain trifling commodities: how cheap soever our souls are in our estimation, it is evident they are of precious esteem in the eyes of Christ.

2. *Redeemed souls must expect no rest or satisfaction on this side heaven.* The life of believers in this world is a life of expectation—they are now *coming* to God. 1 Peter 2 : 4. God, you see, is the centre and rest of their souls. Heb. 4 : 9. As the rivers cannot rest till they pour themselves into the sea, so neither can renewed souls find rest till they come into the bosom of God. There are four things which disturb the souls of believers in this world—afflictions, temptations, corruptions, and absence from God. If the three former causes of disquietude were totally removed, so that a believer were placed in a condition upon earth where no affliction could disturb him, no temptation trouble him, no corruption defile or grieve him, yet his very absence from God must still keep him unsatisfied. "While we are at home in the body we are absent from the Lord." 2 Cor. 5 : 6.

3. *What pleasant thoughts should all believers have of death.* When they die they shall be fully brought home

to God. Death to the saints is the door by which they enter into the enjoyment of God. The dying Christian is almost home ; yet a few pangs more and he is come to God, in whose presence is fulness of joy. "Having a desire to depart," said Paul, "and to be with Christ, which is far better." Phil. 1 : 23. It should not affright us to be brought to death, the king of terrors, so long as it is his office to bring us to God. The opinion of the soul's sleeping after death is as ungrounded as it is uncomfortable : the day we loose from this shore we shall be landed upon the blessed shore where we shall see and enjoy God for ever. O if the friends of deceased believers did but understand with whom their souls are while they are mourning over their bodies, they would dry up their tears and fill the house of mourning with praise and thanksgiving.

4. *How comfortable and sweet should the communications of Christians be with one another.* Christ is bringing them all to God through this vale of tears : they are now in the way to him—all bound for heaven—going home to God, their everlasting rest in glory : every hour, every duty brings them nearer and nearer to their journey's end. "Now is our salvation nearer than when we believed." Rom. 13 : 11. O what manner of heavenly communications and ravishing discourses should believers have with each other as they walk by the way ! O what pleasant and delightful converse should they have about the place and state whither Christ is bringing them, and where they shall shortly be ! What transporting, transforming visions they shall have when they are brought home to God ! How surprisingly glorious to them the sight of Jesus Christ will be, who died for them to bring them to God ! How should such discourse sweeten their passage through the world, strengthen and encourage the dejected and feeble-minded, and honor and adorn their profession ! Thus lived the believers of old : "By faith he sojourned in the

land of promise, as in a strange country, dwelling in tabernacles with Isaac and Jacob, the heirs with him of the
same promise ; for he looked for a city which hath foundations, whose builder and maker is God." Heb. 11 : 9, 10.
But alas, most Christians are either so entangled in the
cares or so ensnared by the pleasures which almost continually take up their thoughts by the way, that there. is
little room for discourse of Christ and heaven among
them.   When the apostle had entertained the Thessalonians with a discourse of their meeting the Lord in the air,
and being ever with the Lord, he charges it upon them as
their great duty *to comfort one another with these words.*
1 Thess. 4 : 17, 18.

5. *How unreasonable are the dejections of believers on account of the troubles they meet with in the world.*   It is true,
afflictions of all kinds attend believers in their way to
God ; through many tribulations we must enter into that
kingdom.   But what then? must we despond and droop
under them as other men ?   Surely not.   If afflictions be
the way through which you must come to God, then never
be discouraged at affliction ; troubles are of excellent use,
under the blessing of the Spirit, to further Christ's great
design in bringing you to God.   How often would you
turn out of the way which leads to God, if he did not
hedge up your way with thorns.   Hosea 2 : 6.   Doubtless, when you come home to God you shall find you have
been more beholden to your troubles than to your comforts for bringing you thither.   The sweetness of the end
will infinitely more than recompense the sorrows of the
way, nor are they worthy to be compared with the glory
that shall be revealed in you.   Rom. 8 : 18.

6. *How much are all believers under obligation to follow
Jesus Christ whithersoever he goes.*   Thus are the saints
described : "These are they which follow the Lamb
whithersoever he goeth.   These were redeemed from
among men, being the first-fruits unto God, and to the

Lamb." Rev. 14 : 4. If it be the design of Christ to bring us to God, it is our duty to follow Christ in all the paths of obedience through which he now leads us, as ever we expect to be brought home to God at last. "We are made partakers of Christ, if we hold the beginning of our confidence steadfast unto the end." Heb. 3 : 14. If we have followed him through many sufferings, and turn away from him at last, we lose all that we have done and suffered in religion, and shall never reach home to God. The crown of life belongs only to them who are faithful unto death.

7. *Let all that desire to come to God hereafter, come to Christ by faith now.* There is no other way to the Father but by Christ; no other way to Christ but faith. How vain then are the hopes and expectations of all unbelievers. Be assured that death shall bring you to God as an avenging Judge, if Christ do not bring you now to God as a reconciled Father. Without holiness no man shall see God. The door of hope is shut against all Christless persons. "No man cometh unto the Father but by me." John 14 : 6. O what a sweet voice cometh down from heaven to your soul this day, saying, "As ever you hope to come to God and enjoy the blessing that is here, come unto Christ, obey his calls, give up yourselves to his government, and you shall certainly be brought to God. As sure as you shall now be brought to Jesus Christ by spiritual union, so sure shall you be brought to God in full fruition."

Blessed be God for Jesus Christ, the new and living way to the Father.

Thus I have finished the *motives drawn from the titles and benefits* of Christ, serving to enforce the great gospel exhortation of coming to and effectually applying the Lord Jesus Christ in the way of faith. O that the blessing of the Spirit may follow these calls, and fix these considerations as nails in a sure place !

And now, since the great hinderance to faith is the false persuasion of most unregenerate men that they are already in Christ, my next work shall be, in a further improvement for *conviction*, to undeceive men in this matter ; and that by showing them the undoubted certainty of these two things : That there is no coming ordinarily to Christ without *the application of the law to our consciences in a way of effectual conviction.* Nor by that, without *the teachings of God in the way of spiritual illumination.*

COMING TO CHRIST IMPLIES TRUE CONVICTION OF SIN, BEING SLAIN BY THE LAW AND TAUGHT OF GOD

CHAPTER XX

NECESSITY OF BEING SLAIN BY THE LAW

"For I was alive without the law once; but when the commandment came, sin revived, and I died." Rom. 7: 9

THE scope of the apostle in this epistle, and more particularly in this chapter, is to state the due use and excellency of the law: which he does, first, by denying to it a power to justify us, which is the peculiar honor of Christ; and secondly, by ascribing to it a power to convince us, and so prepare us for Christ, by showing us our need of him.

Neither attributing to it more honor than belongs to it, nor detracting from it that honor and usefulness which God has given it. It cannot make us righteous, but it can convince us that we are unrighteous; it cannot heal, but it can discover the wounds that sin has given us; which he proves in this place by an argument drawn from his own experience, confirmed also by the general experience of believers, in whose names we must here understand him to speak: "For I was alive without the law once; but when the commandment came, sin revived, and I died." Wherein three particulars are observable:

1. The opinion Paul had, and all unregenerate men have of themselves before conversion: *I was alive once.*

By *life*, understand here cheerfulness and confidence of his good state. He was full of vain hope, false joy, and presumptuous confidence.

2. The opinion he had, and all others will have of themselves, if ever they come under the regenerating work of the spirit: *I died.* The death he here speaks of stands opposed to the life before mentioned, and signifies the fears and tremblings that seized upon his soul when his state was on the change: the apprehensions he then had of his condition struck him home to the heart, and damped all his carnal mirth.

3. The ground and reason of this wonderful change of his judgment and apprehension of his own condition: the commandment came, and sin revived; it came home to my conscience, it was fixed with a divine and mighty efficacy upon my heart. The commandment came before by promulgation and the literal knowledge of it, but it never came till now in its spiritual and convincing power to his soul; though he had often read the law before, he never clearly understood its meaning and extent, he never felt its efficacy upon his heart: it so came at this time as it never came before. Hence we learn:

DOCTRINE 1. *That unregenerate persons are generally full of groundless confidence and cheerfulness, though their condition be sad and miserable.*

DOCTRINE 2. *That there is a mighty efficacy in the law of God to kill vain confidence and quench carnal mirth in the hearts of men, when God sets it home upon their consciences.*

DOCTRINE 1. *Unregenerate persons are generally full of groundless confidence and cheerfulness, though their condition be sad and miserable.* "Because thou sayest I am rich, and increased with goods, and have need of nothing; and knowest not that thou art wretched, and miserable, and poor, and blind, and naked." Rev. 3 : 17. *This is the life that unregenerate men live.* In illustrating this point, I shall show what is the life of the unregenerate ; what maintains that life ; how it appears that this is the life men generally live ; and the danger of living such a life.

I. WHAT IS THE LIFE OF THE UNREGENERATE. There are three things in which the life of the unregenerate principally consists.

1. There is in unregenerate men a great deal of *carnal security;* they dread no danger. "When a strong man armed keepeth his palace, his goods are in peace." Luke 11 : 21. There is generally a great silence in the consciences of such men: when others, in a better state, are watching and trembling, they sleep securely ; so they live, and so ofttimes they die. They have no bands in their death. Psa. 73 : 4. It is true, the consciences of few men are so perfectly stupefied that they do not sometimes make them uneasy ; but their anxiety seldom rises to such a height, or continues so long as to cause any considerable interruption to their carnal peace and quietness.

2. The life of the unregenerate consists in *presumptuous hope:* this is the foundation of their carnal security. So Christ tells the Jews : "Of whom ye say that he is your God ; yet ye have not known him." John 8 : 54, 55. The world is full of hope without a promise, which is but as a spider's web. Unregenerate men are said indeed to be without hope, Ephes. 2 : 12 ; but the meaning is, they are without any solid, well-grounded hope ; for in Scripture account, hope is no hope except it be a lively hope, 1 Pet. 1 : 3 ; a hope flowing from union with Christ, Col. 1 : 27 ; a hope nourished by experience, Rom. 5 : 4 ; a hope for which a man can give a reason, 1 Pet. 3 : 15 ; a hope that excites men to heart-purifying endeavors, 1 John 3 : 3—it is in the account of God a cypher, not deserving the name of hope ; and yet such a groundless, dead, christless, irrational hope is that on which the unregenerate live.

3. The life of the unregenerate consists in *false joy,* the immediate offspring of ungrounded hope. The stony-ground hearers received the word with joy. Matt. 13: 20.

They rejoice in corn, wine, and oil; in their estates and children; in the pleasant things of this world; yea, perchance they rejoice also in Christ and the promises; in heaven and glory: with all which they have just such a kind of communion as a man has in a dream with a full feast and enchanting music; and just so their joy will vanish when they awake.

II. WHAT MAINTAINS AND SUPPORTS THIS SECURITY, HOPE, AND JOY in the hearts of unregenerate men.

1. *Church privileges* lay the foundation of this strong delusion in many. Thus the Jews deceived themselves, saying in their hearts, "We have Abraham for our father." Matt. 3 : 9. It propped up this vain hope, that Abraham's blood ran in their veins, though Abraham's faith and obedience never wrought in their hearts.

2. *Natural ignorance;* this keeps all in peace: they that see not, fear not. There are but two ways to quiet the hearts of men about their spiritual and eternal concerns: the way of assurance and faith, or the way of ignorance and self-deceit; by the one we are put beyond danger, by the other beyond fear, though the danger be greater. Satan could never quiet men, if he did not first blind them.

3. *False evidences* of the love of God is another spring feeding this security and vain hope and false joy in the hearts of men. "Many will say to me in that day, Lord, Lord, have we not prophesied in thy name? and in thy name have cast out devils? and in thy name done many wonderful works?" Matt. 7 : 22. The things upon which they build their confidence were external things in religion; yet they had a quieting power upon them, as if they had been the best of evidences.

4. *Slight influences of the gospel:* such are transient affections under the word, Heb. 6 : 5; feeble and inconstant desire about spiritual objects, John 6 : 34; Matt. 25 : 8; and the external reformation of their ways, Matt. 12 : 43;

all which serve to nourish the vain hopes of the unregenerate.

5. *Self-love* is an apparent ground of security and false hope. Matt. 7 : 3. It makes a man overlook great evils in himself, while he is sharp-sighted to discover and censure lesser evils in others. Self-love takes away the sight of sin, by bringing it too near the eye.

6. Men's *comparing themselves with the more profane and grossly wicked* serves to hush the conscience asleep : "God, I thank thee," said the Pharisee, "that I am not as other men, or as this publican." Oh, what a saint did he seem to himself when he stood by those externally more wicked.

7. *The policy of Satan* to manage all these things to the blinding and ruining of the souls of men, is another great reason that they live securely as they do in a state of so much danger and misery. "The god of this world hath blinded the minds of them that believe not." 2 Cor. 4 : 4.

III. That this is the life men generally live will appear, if we consider,

1. *The activity and liveliness of men's spirits in pursuit of the world.* O how lively and vigorous are their hearts in the management of earthly designs ! "Who will show us any good?" Psa. 4 : 6. The world eats up their hearts, time, and strength. This could not be if their eyes were open to see the danger and misery of their souls. How few designs for the world run in the thoughts of a condemned man. O, if God had ever made the light of conviction shine into their consciences, the temptation would lie the contrary way, even in too great a neglect of things of this life. But this briskness and liveliness plainly show the great security of most men.

2. The marvellous *quietness in the consciences* of men about their everlasting concerns, plainly shows this to be the life of the unregenerate. How few doubts or fears do you hear from them ! How many years may a man live

in a worldly family before he shall hear the question seriously propounded, "What shall I do to be saved?" There are no questions in their lips, because there is no fear or sense of danger in their hearts.

3. The *professed willingness of carnal men to die* gives clear evidence that they live such a life of security and vain hope. "Like sheep they are laid in the grave." Psa. 49 : 14. O, how quiet are their consciences when there are but a few breaths more between them and everlasting burnings! Had God opened their eyes to apprehend the consequences of death, and what follows the pale horse, Rev. 6 : 8, it were impossible but that every unregenerate man should make the bed on which he dies tremble under him.

4. *The low esteem men have of Christ,* and the trifling with those duties in which he is to be found, discover this to be the life that the generality of the world live; for were men sensible of the disease of sin, there could be no quieting them without Christ the Physician. Phil. 3:8. All the business they have to do in this world could never keep them from their knees, or make them strangers to their closets.

IV. THE DANGER OF SUCH A LIFE as has been described.

1. Souls are thus inevitably *betrayed into eternal ruin.* "If our gospel be hid, it is hid to them that are lost, in whom the god of this world hath blinded the minds of them that believe not." 2 Cor. 4 : 3, 4. Those that are given over to eternal death are generally thus blinded. "And he said, Go, and tell this people, Hear ye indeed, but understand not; and see ye indeed, but perceive not. Make the heart of this people fat, and make their ears heavy, and shut their eyes; lest they see with their eyes, and hear with their ears, and understand with their heart, and convert, and be healed." Isa. 6 : 9, 10.

2. Nothing makes hell a more *terrible surprise* to the soul: by this means the wrath of God is felt before its

danger is apprehended; a man is past all hope before he begins to have any fear; his eternal ruin, "as a breach ready to fall, cometh suddenly at an instant." Isaiah 30 : 13.

3. *Nothing more aggravates a man's damnation than to sink suddenly into it* from amid so many hopes and such high confidence of safety. For a man to find himself in hell when he thought himself within a step of heaven, O what a hell will it be! The higher vain hopes lifted men up, the more dreadful must their fall be. Matthew 7: 22, 23.

4. This life of security and vain hope *frustrates all the means of recovery and salvation* in the only season in which they can be beneficial to us. By reason of these things the word has no power to convince men's consciences, nothing can bring them to a sense of their condition. Therefore Christ told the self-confident and blind Jews that the publicans and harlots would go into the kingdom of God before them. Matt. 21: 31. And the reason is, because their hearts 1'e more open to conviction and compunction for sin than those do who are blinded by vain hope and confidence.

INFERENCE 1. Is this the life that the unregenerate world live? *then it is not to be wondered at that the preaching of the gospel has so little success:* "Who hath believed our report? and to whom is the arm of the Lord revealed?" Isaiah 53 : 1. Ministers study for truths to awaken and convince the consciences of those that hear, but their words return again to them. They turn to God and mourn, "We have labored in vain, and spent our strength for naught." And this security is the cause of all; vain hopes bar fast the doors of men's hearts against all the persuasions of the word. The greater cause have they to admire the grace of God, who have found the convictions of the word sharper than any two-edged sword, piercing to the dividing asunder of the soul and spirit; to whose hearts God brings home the commandment by an effectual application.

2. If this be the life of the unregenerate world, *what deadly enemies are they that nourish and strengthen in men the vain hopes of salvation!* This the Scripture calls healing the hurt of souls slightly, by crying, "Peace, peace, when there is no peace," Jer. 6 : 14 ; the sewing of pillows under their arm-holes, Ezek. 13 : 18, that they may lie soft and easy under the ministry. And this is the doctrine which the people love ; but O, what will the end of these things be? and what an account have those men to give to God for the blood of souls by them betrayed to the everlasting burnings! Such flattery is the greatest cruelty. Those whom you bless upon earth will curse you in hell, and curse the day in which they trusted their souls to your care.

3. *How great a mercy is it to be awakened out of the general security which is fallen upon the world!* You cannot estimate the value of this peculiar mercy. O that the Spirit of the Lord should have touched thy soul under the ministry of the word, and roused thy conscience while others were left in security round about thee ; when the Lord dealt with thy soul much after the same manner he did with Paul in the way to Damascus, who not only saw a light shining from heaven, which those that travelled with him saw as well as he, but heard that voice from heaven which did the work upon his heart, though his companions heard it not. Besides, it is a mercy leading to all other spiritual mercies that follow it to all eternity. If God had not done this for thee, thou hadst never been brought to faith, to Christ, or heaven. From this act of the Spirit all other saving acts take their rise ; so that you have cause for ever to admire the goodness of God in such a favor as this.

4. *Hence it follows that men generally are in the direct way to eternal ruin;* whatever their vain confidences are, they

cannot be saved. Narrow is the way and strait is the gate that leadeth unto life, and few there be that find it. Hear me, all you that live this dangerous life of carnal security, whatever your persuasions and confidences are, except you give them up, and get better grounds for your hope, you cannot be saved. Such hopes are directly contradictory to the established order of the gospel, which requires repentance, Acts 5 : 31; faith, Acts 13 : 39; and regeneration, John 3 : 3, in all that shall be saved. If such as you are saved, all the threatenings in Scripture must be reversed, which lie in full opposition to your vain hopes. Mark 16 : 16; John 3 : 16; Rom. 3 : 8, 9. New conditions must be set to all the promises; for there is no condition of any special promise found in any unregenerate person. Compare your hearts with these scriptures, Matt. 5 : 3–6; Psa. 24 : 4; 84 : 11; Gen. 17 : 1. If such a hope as yours bring you to heaven, the saving hope of God's elect is not rightly described to us in the Scriptures. Scripture hope is the effect of regeneration. 1 Pet. 1 : 3. And purity of heart is the effect of that hope. 1 John 3 : 3. Nay, the very nature of heaven is mistaken in Scripture if such as you are subjects qualified for its enjoyment; for assimilation, or the conformity of the soul to God in holiness, is, in the Scripture account, a principal ingredient of that blessedness. By all these things it appears that the hopes of most men are vain, and will never bring them to heaven.

CHAPTER XXI

NECESSITY OF BEING SLAIN BY THE LAW—CONTINUED

"For I was alive without the law once; but when the commandment came, sin revived, and I died." Rom. 7 : 9

DOCTRINE 2. *There is a mighty efficacy in the law of God to kill vain confidence and quench carnal mirth in the hearts of men when God sets it home upon their consciences.*

The weapons of the word " are not carnal, but mighty through God to the pulling down of strong-holds, casting down imaginations and every high thing that exalteth itself against the knowledge of God, and bringing into captivity every thought to the obedience of Christ." 2 Cor. 10 : 4, 5. In illustrating this point, I shall demonstrate the efficacy of the word or law of God ; show wherein its efficacy lies ; and inquire whence it has this mighty power and efficacy.

I. THE POWER AND EFFICACY OF THE WORD OR LAW OF GOD. This will appear,

1. From *the various subjects* upon whom it works. The hearts and consciences of men of all orders and qualities have been reached and wounded to the quick by the two-edged sword of God's law. Some among the *great* and *honorable* of the earth have been made to stoop and tremble under the word. Acts 17 : 12 ; Mark 6 : 20 ; 1 Samuel 15 : 24. The wise and learned of the world have felt its power and been brought to embrace the humbling and self-denying ways of Christ. Acts 17 : 34. Thus Origen, Jerome Tertullian, Bradwardine, and many more came into Canaan laden with the Egyptian gold, as one speaks ; that is, they came into the church of God furnished with

the learned arts and sciences, devoting them all to the service of Christ. Yea, which is as strange, *the most simple, weak, and illiterate* have been wonderfully changed and wrought upon by the power of the word. The testimonies of the Lord make wise the simple. Men of weak understandings in other matters have been made wise to 'salvation by the power of the word. Matt. 11 : 25 ; 1 Cor. 1 : 27. Nay, the most malicious enemies of Christ have been converted by the word. 1 Tim. 1 : 13 ; Acts 16 : 25. Those that have been under the prejudice of the most idolatrous education have been the subjects of its mighty power, Acts 19 : 26, and men of the most profligate lives have been wonderfully changed by the power of the word. 1 Cor. 6 : 10, 11.

2. The efficacy of the law of God appears in the *manner of its operation.* It works suddenly; it strikes like a dart through the hearts and consciences of men. Acts 2 : 37. A wonderful change is made in a short time, and as it works quickly and suddenly, so it works with an uncontrolled power upon the spirits of men. 1 Thess. 1 : 5 ; Rom. 1 : 16. Let the soul be armed against conviction with the thickest ignorance, strongest prejudice, or most obstinate resolution, the word of God will wound the breast even of such a man when God sends it forth in his authority and power.

3. The power of the law or word of God is seen in *the strange effects produced by it* in the hearts and lives of men. It changes the frame and temper of the mind ; it moulds a man into a quite contrary temper : " He which persecuted us in times past, now preacheth the faith which once he destroyed." Gal. 1 : 23. Thus a tiger is transformed into a lamb by the power of the word of God. It makes the soul forego the dearest interests it has in this world for Jesus Christ. Phil. 3 : 7–9. Riches, honors, self-righteousness, relations are forsaken. Reproach, poverty, and death itself are embraced for Christ's sake, when

once the efficacy of the word has wrought on the hearts of men. 1 Thess. 1 : 6. Companions in sin are renounced and cast off with abhorrence. 1 Pet. 4 : 3. 4.

II. WHEREIN THE EFFICACY OF THE WORD UPON THE SOULS OF MEN CONSISTS. We find in Scripture it exerts its power in five distinct acts upon the soul ; by all which it strikes at the life and kills the very heart of vain hopes.

1. It has an *awakening* efficacy upon secure and slumbering sinners. It rouses the conscience, and brings a man to a sense and apprehension. Eph. 5 : 13, 14. The first effectual touch of the word startles the drowsy conscience. A poor sinner lies in his sins, as Peter did in his chains, fast asleep, though a warrant was signed for his execution the next day. But the Spirit by the word awakens him, as the angel did Peter. And this awakening power of the word is in the order both of time and nature before all its other operations and effects.

2. The law of God has an *enlightening* efficacy upon the minds of men. It is eye-salve to the blind, Rev. 3 : 18 ; a light shining in a dark place, 2 Pet. 1 : 19 ; a light shining into the very heart of man, 2 Cor. 4 : 6. When the word comes in power, all things appear with another face ; the sins that were hid from our eyes, and the danger which was concealed by Satan from our souls, now lie clear and open before us. Eph. 5 : 8.

3. The word of God has a *convincing* efficacy. It sets sin in order before the soul. Psalm 50 : 21. As an army is drawn up in exact order, so are the sins of nature and practice, the sins of youth and age, even a great and terrible army drawn up before the eye of the conscience. The convictions of the word are clear and full. 1 Cor. 14 : 24. The very secrets of a sinner's heart are made manifest ; his mouth is stopped ; his conscience yields to the charge of guilt and to the equity of the sentence of the law, so that the soul stands self-condemned at the bar of conscience : it has nothing to say why the wrath of

God should not come upon it to the uttermost.   Romans
3 : 19.

4. The law of God has a *soul-wounding* efficacy; it
pierces into the very soul and spirit of man. "When they
heard this they were pricked in their hearts, and said unto
Peter, and to the rest of the apostles, Men and brethren,
what shall we do?"   Acts 2 : 37.   A dreadful sound is in
the sinner's ears; his soul is in deep distress; he knows
not which way to turn for ease; no remedy but the blood
of Christ can heal these wounds.   No outward affliction,
disgrace, or loss ever touched the quick as the word of
God does.

5. The word hath a *heart-turning, soul-converting* efficacy in it: it is a regenerating as well as a convincing
word.   1 Pet. 1 : 23; 1 Thess. 1: 9.   The law wounds, the
gospel cures; the law discovers the evil there is in sin
and the misery that follows it; and the Spirit of God,
working in fellowship with the word, effectually turns the
heart from sin.   Thus we see in what glorious acts the
efficacy of the word discovers itself upon the hearts of
men; and all these acts lie in order to each other.   Until
the soul be awakened it cannot be enlightened.   Eph.
5 : 14.   Till it be enlightened it cannot be convinced,
Eph. 5 : 13, conviction being nothing else but the application of the light that shines in the mind to the conscience
of a sinner.   Until it be convinced it cannot be wounded
for sin.   Acts 2 : 37.   And until it be wounded for sin it
will never be converted from sin and brought effectually
to Jesus Christ.

III. Whence has the word of god all this power?   It
is most certain that it is not a power inherent in itself,
nor derived from the instrument by which it is managed,
but from the Spirit of the Lord, who communicates to it
all the power and efficacy it has upon our souls.

1. *Its power is not inherent in itself.*   It works not in a
physical way as natural agents do, for then the effect

would always follow, except it were miraculously hindered. But this spiritual efficacy is in the word as the healing virtue was in the waters of Bethesda: "An angel went down at a certain season into the pool, and troubled the water; whosoever then first after the troubling of the water stepped in, was made whole of whatsoever disease he had." John 5 : 4. It is not a power naturally inherent in it at all times, but communicated to it at special seasons. How often is the word preached and no man awakened or convinced by it.

2. The power of the word is *not communicated to it by the instrument that manageth it.* "Neither is he that planteth any thing, neither he that watereth." 1 Cor. 3 : 7. Ministers are nothing to such an effect as this. The apostle does not mean that they are useless and unnecessary, but insufficient of themselves to produce such mighty effects. The word works not as it is the word of man. 2 Thess. 2 : 13. Ministers may say of the ordinary, as Peter said of the extraordinary effects of the Spirit, "Ye men of Israel, why marvel ye at this? or why look ye so earnestly on us, as though by our own power or holiness we had made this man to walk?" Acts 3 : 12. If the effects of the word were in the command of him that preacheth it, the blood of all the souls that perish under our ministry must lie at our door.

3. If you say, Whence then hath the word all this power? our answer is, *It derives it all from the Spirit of God.* "For this cause also thank we God without ceasing, because when ye received the word of God which ye heard of us, ye received it not as the word of men, but as it is in truth, the word of God, which effectually worketh also in you that believe." 1 Thess. 2 : 13. It is a successful instrument only in the hand of the Spirit, without whose influence it never did, nor can convince, convert, or save any soul.

The Spirit has a glorious sovereignty over *the word,*

whose instrument it is, to make it successful or not, as it pleaseth him. "For as the rain cometh down, and the snow from heaven, and returneth not thither, but watereth the earth, and maketh it bring forth and bud, that it may give seed to the sower and bread to the eater ; so shall my word be that goeth out of my mouth," Isaiah 55 : 10, 11; as the clouds, so the word is carried and directed by divine pleasure. The Lord makes them both give down their blessings, or pass away fruitless and empty : yea, it is from the Spirit that this part of the word works, and not another. Discourses upon which ministers bestow greatest labor in their preparation, and from which they have the greatest expectation, do nothing ; when something that dropped occasionally from them, like a chosen shaft, strikes the mark and does the work.

The Spirit of the Lord has a glorious sovereignty over *the souls wrought upon.* It is his peculiar work to take away the stony heart out of our flesh and give us a heart of flesh. Ezek. 36 : 26. We may reason and reprove, but nothing will succeed till the Lord sets it home. The Lord opened the heard of Lydia under Paul's ministry ; he opens every heart that is effectually opened to receive Christ in the word. If the word can get no entrance, if your hearts remain dead under it, we may say as Martha concerning her brother Lazarus, "Lord, if thou hadst been here, my brother had not died ;" so, Lord, if thou hadst been in this sermon, in this prayer, or in that counsel, these souls had not remained dead under them.

The Spirit has dominion over the *times of conviction and conversion.* Therefore the day in which souls are wrought upon is called, "the day of his power." Psalm 110 : 3. That shall work at one time which had no efficacy at all at another, because this was the time appointed.

This word of God, when it is thus set home by the Spirit, is mighty to humble and break the hearts of sinners. The Spirit when it cometh shall convince the world of sin. John 16 : 9. The word signifies conviction by such demonstration as compels assent : it not only convinces men that they are sinners, but particularly of their own sins and their aggravations. So in the text, "sin revived," that is, the Lord revived his sins and the circumstances and aggravations with which they were committed ; and so it will be with us when the commandment comes : sins that we had forgotten, committed in our youth or childhood—sins that lay slighted in our consciences, shall be roused up as so many lions to terrify us, for now the soul hears the voice of God in the word, as Adam heard it in the cool of the day and was afraid. The Lord is come in the word ; sin is held up before the conscience in its aggravations and fearful consequences as committed against the holy law, clear light, warnings of conscience, manifold mercies, God's long-suffering, Christ's precious blood, many warnings of judgment, the wages whereof by the verdict of a man's own conscience is death, eternal death. Rom. 6: 23 ; 1: 32 ; 2: 9. Thus the commandment comes, sin revives, and vain hope gives up the ghost.

INFERENCE 1. Is there such a power in the word? *then certainly the word is of divine authority.* There cannot be a more satisfying proof that it is no human invention, than the common sense that all believers have of the almighty power in which it works upon their hearts. So speaks the apostle, "When ye received the word of God which ye heard of us, ye received it not as the word of man, but, as it is in truth, the word of God, which effectually worketh also in you that believe." 1 Thess. 2 : 13. Can the power of any creature so convince the conscience, terrify the heart, and discover the secret thoughts of the soul, as to put a man into such tremblings? No, a greater than man must be here ; none but God can so open the eyes of the blind, so quicken the conscience that was seared, so bind over the soul of a sinner to the judgment to come, so change the temper of a man's spirit, or so powerfully refresh and comfort a drooping soul; certainly the power of God is in all this : and this alone were sufficient to make full proof of the divine authority of the Scriptures.

2. *Judge from hence what an invaluable mercy the preaching of the word is to the world.* It is a blessing far above our estimation of it; little do we know what a treasure God commits to us in the ordinances. "To you is the word of this salvation sent." Acts 13 : 25. It is the very power of God to salvation, Rom. 1 : 16 ; and salvation is ordinarily denied where the preaching of the word is withheld. Rom. 10 : 14. It is called "the word of life," Phil. 2 : 16, and deserves to be valued by every one of us as our life. The eternal decree of God's love is executed by it upon our souls ; as many as he ordained to eternal life shall believe by the preaching of it. Great is the ingratitude of this generation which so undervalues this treasure ; a sad presage of the most terrible judgment, even the removing of our candlestick out of its place, except we repent.

3. *How terrible a judgment lies upon the souls of the men to whom no word of God is made powerful enough to convince them!* Yet so stands the case with thousands who constantly sit under the preaching of the word : many arrows are shot at their consciences, but all fall short of the end ; the commandment has come to them many times by way of promulgation and ministerial inculcation, but never came home to their souls by the Spirit's effectual application. O, friends, you have often heard the voice of man, but you never yet heard the voice of God ; your understandings have been instructed, but your consciences to this day were never thoroughly convinced. "We have mourned unto you, but ye have not lamented." Matt. 11 : 17. "Who hath believed our report ? and unto whom is the arm of the Lord revealed ?" Alas, we have labored in vain, we have spent our strength for naught ; our word returns unto us empty ; but O, what a stupendous judg-

ment is here! "The earth which drinketh in the rain that cometh oft upon it, and bringeth forth herbs meet for them by whom it is dressed, receiveth blessing from God; but that which beareth thorns and briars is rejected, and is nigh unto cursing; whose end is to be burned." Heb. 6 : 7, 8. What a sign of God's displeasure would you account it, if your fields were cursed; if you should plough and sow them, but never reap the fruit of your labor, the increase being blasted. And yet this were nothing compared with the word, which should be a savor of life unto life unto you, becoming the savor of death unto death. 2 Cor. 2 : 16.

4. I shall conclude this point with a few words of *exhortation to three classes of men.*

(1.) *Those that never felt any power in the word.* I beg you in the name of him who made you, and by all the regard and value you have for those precious souls within you, that such considerations as these may find place in your souls, and that you will bethink yourselves,

Whose word it is that cannot gain entrance into your hearts. Is it not the word of God which you despise and slight? Thou castest my word behind thy back. Psalm 50 : 17. O, what an affront and provocation to God is this! You despise not man, but the great and terrible God in whose hand your breath and soul are. This contempt runs higher than you imagine.

Consider again, that however the word hath no power upon you, yet it comes home with power to the hearts of *others*. While you are hardened, others are melted under it; while you sleep, others tremble; while your hearts are locked up, others are opened. How can you but reflect with fear and trembling upon these contrary effects of the word?

Consider also, that no judgment of God on this side hell is greater than *a hard heart* under the word. It were better that the providence of God should blast thy estate, take away thy children, or destroy thy health, than harden thy heart and sear thy conscience under the word. So much as thy soul is better than thy body, so much as eternity is more valuable than time, so much is this spiritual judgment more dreadful than all temporal ones.

O then as you love your own souls attend upon every opportunity that God affords you. Lay aside your prejudices against the word, or the infirmities of them that preach it ; for the word works not as it is the word of man, but as it is the word of God. Pray for the blessing of God upon the word ; for except his blessing go with it, it can never come home to your soul. Meditate upon what you hear, for without meditation it is not likely to have any effectual operation upon you. Search your souls by it, and consider whether that be not your state which it describes, your danger whereof it gives warning. Take heed lest, after you have heard it, the cares of the world choke what you have heard, and cause those budding convictions which begin to put forth to wither.

(2.) Let those seriously consider *who have only felt some transient and ineffectual operations of the gospel upon their souls.* The Lord has come nigh to some of our souls ; we have felt a power in the ordinances, sometimes terrifying and sometimes transporting our hearts : but, alas, it proves but a morning cloud, or the early dew. Hos. 6 : 4. We rejoice in the word, but it is only for a season. John 5 : 35 ; Gal. 4 : 14, 15. Where the new creature is perfectly formed in one soul, there are many miscarriages in others ; for which three reasons may be assigned.

One is *the subtlety and deep policy of Satan,* who never more effectually deceives and destroys the souls of men than by such an artifice as this ; for when men have once felt their consciences terrified under the word, and their hearts at other times affected with the blessings of it, they seem to have attained all that is necessary to conversion. These things look so like the regenerating effects of the

Spirit, that many are deceived by them. It is frequently seen that unrenewed hearts have their meltings and transports as well as spiritual hearts. Heaven and hell are affecting, and an unrenewed heart is apt to melt in view of them. Now here is the cheat of Satan, to persuade a man that these must be spiritual affections, because the objects about which they are conversant are spiritual; whereas it is certain the *objects* of the affections may be heavenly, and the workings of man's affections about them may be in a mere natural way.

The dampening influence of *the world* is also a cause of these miscarriages under the word. Luke 8 : 12–14. There are hopeful beginnings of affection in some persons, especially in their youth; but when they come to be engaged in the world, how soon are they quenched. As the cares of a family grow on, so does the care of salvation wear off. It is not as it was wont to be, What shall I do to be saved? How shall I get an interest in Christ? But what shall I eat and drink, and wherewith shall I and mine be maintained? The present drowns all thoughts of the future. Good had it been for many men had they never been engaged so deep in the world; their life is but a constant hurry of business, and a diversion from Christ and things that are eternal.

And again, *the deceitfulness and treachery of the heart*, which too easily gives way to the designs of Satan and suffers itself to be imposed upon by him, is not the least cause why so many hopeful beginnings come to nothing, and the effects of the word vanish. Oh, that such men would consider that the dying away of their convictions threatens the life of their souls for ever; now is the bud withered, and what expectation is there of fruit after this, except the Lord revive them again. The Lord open men's eyes to discern such dangers as these. Jude 12; Heb. 10 : 38. There are many pauses in the work of conviction: it seems to die away, and then revives again;

and revive it must, or we are lost. But how many are there who never recover it more! This is a sore judgment to the souls of men.

(3.) Let me speak a word of counsel *to them on whom the word works effectually*—to whose hearts the commandment is come home to revive sin and kill vain hopes; and these are of two classes.

Some are under the first workings of the Spirit in the word. O let it not seem a misery or unhappiness to you that the commandment comes, and sin revives, and your former hopes are overthrown. Had you gone on in your security, you had certainly been lost for ever: God has stopt you in the path that leads down to hell, and none that go in there ever return again, or take hold of the paths of life. O, it is better to weep, tremble, and be distressed now, than to mourn without hope for ever. Let it not trouble you that sin has found you out; you could never have found out the remedy in Christ, if you had not found out the disease and danger by the coming of the commandment. And I beseech you carefully to observe whether the operations of the word upon your hearts be deeper and more powerful than they are found to be in such souls as miscarry under it. Does it come to you and show you not only this or that particular sin, but all the evils of your heart and life; the corruption of your nature as well as the transgression of your life? If so, it promises well and looks hopefully for you. The commandment comes to others and startles them with the fears of damnation; but does it come to thee and discover *the infinite evil of thy sin as it is committed against the great, holy, and righteous God,* and so melt thy heart into tears for the wrong thou hast done him, as well as in view of the danger into which thou hast brought thyself? If it so revive sin as to kill all vain hopes in thee, and send thee to Christ alone as thy only door of hope, these troubles will prove the greatest mercy upon thy soul.

Others there are upon whom the word has had its full effect in conversion. O bless God for ever for this mercy; you cannot sufficiently value it. God has not only made it a convincing, but a converting word to your souls. How many have sat under the same word, but never felt such effects of it! As Christ said in another case, There were many widows in Israel in the time of Elijah, but unto none of them was the prophet sent, save unto Sarepta, a city of Sidon, to a certain widow there, Luke 4 : 25, 26; so I may say, there were many souls in the same congregation, but unto none of them was the word sent with a commission to convince and save, but thyself; one as improbable to be wrought upon as any soul there. O let this excite thankfulness in your soul; and let it make you love the word as long as you live. "I will never forget thy precepts, for with them thou hast quickened me." Psalm 119 : 93.

But above all, I beseech you make it appear that the commandment has come home to your hearts with power to convince you of the evil of sin, *by your care to shun it as long as you live.* If you have seen sin in the glass of the law of God; if your heart has been broken for it in the days of your trouble, you will choose the worst affliction rather than sin. It would be the greatest folly to return again to iniquity. Psalm 85 : 8. You that have seen so much of the evil of sin, and the danger that follows it; you that have had such inward terrors and fears of spirit about it, will be loath to feel those stings of conscience again for the best enjoyment in this world.

Blessed be God if any word has been brought home to our hearts to bring us to Christ.

CHAPTER XXII

NECESSITY OF BEING TAUGHT OF GOD

"It is written in the prophets, And they shall be all taught of God. Every man therefore that hath heard, and hath learned of the Father, cometh unto me." JOHN 6:45

How necessary to our union with Jesus Christ the application of the law to the heart of a sinner is, we have seen in the last discourse. We now proceed to consider how impossible it is either for the commandment to come to us, or for us to come to Christ, without *instruction from above*.

This scripture has much of the mind of God in it; and he that is to expound it, had need himself to be taught of God. In the foregoing verses Christ offers himself as the bread of life unto the souls of men: against this doctrine they oppose their carnal reason. Christ strikes at the root of all their objections in his reply: "Murmur not among yourselves: no man can come to me, except the Father, which hath sent me, draw him;" as though he had said, "You slight me because you do not know me, and you do not know me because you are not taught of God: of these divine teachings the prophets of old have spoken, and what they foretold is at this day fulfilled in our sight; so many as are taught of God, and no more, come unto me in the way of faith: it is impossible to come without the teachings of God, and it is as impossible to fail in coming unto me under the influence of these divine teachings."

The words selected consist of two parts, namely,

1. *An allegation out of the prophets:* "It is written in the prophets, And they shall be all taught of God." The places in the prophets to which Christ seems to refer, are Isa. 54 : 13, "And all thy children shall be taught of the

Lord ;" and Jer. 31 : 34, "And they shall teach no more every man his neighbor, and every man his brother, saying, Know the Lord ; for they shall all know me, from the least of them unto the greatest of them, saith the Lord." These promises contain the great blessing of the new covenant, namely, divine instruction, without which no man can obtain an interest in Christ.

2. We have the *application of these testimonies* out of the prophets made by Christ himself : "Every man therefore that hath heard, and learned of the Father, cometh unto me." In which words we have both the necessity and the efficacy of these divine teachings ; without them no man can come, and with them no man can fail. Hence we draw two propositions :

DOCTRINE 1. *The teachings of God are absolutely necessary to every man that cometh unto Christ in the way of faith.*

DOCTRINE 2. *No man can miss of Christ, or fail in the way of faith, that is under the special teaching of the Father.*

DOCTRINE 1. *The teachings of God are absolutely necessary to every man that cometh unto Christ in the way of faith.*

Of the necessity of divine teaching in order to believing, the apostle speaks in Eph. 4 : 20, 21 : "But ye have not so learned Christ ; if so be that ye have heard him, and been taught by him, as the truth is in Jesus ;" that is, your faith must be effectual both to the reformation of your lives and your perseverance in the ways of holiness, if it be such a faith as is introduced into your hearts by divine teaching. In explaining this point, I shall speak to the following inquiries : How does God teach men, or what is implied in our being taught of God ? What are those special lessons which all believers are taught of God ? In what manner does God teach these things to men in the day of their conversion to Christ ? What influence has God's teaching upon our believing ? And why is it impossible for any man to believe or come to Christ without the Father's teaching ?

I. How DOTH GOD TEACH MEN, or what is implied in our being taught of God?

1. *The teaching of God is not to be understood of any extraordinary appearances or immediate voice of God to men.* God did indeed in former times so appear unto some, Num. 12 : 8 ; but now these extraordinary ways are ceased, Heb. 1 : 1, 2, and we are no more to expect them. We may sooner meet with satanical delusions than divine illuminations in this way. I remember the learned Gerson tells us that the devil once appeared to a holy man in prayer, personating Christ and saying, I am come in person to visit thee, for thou art worthy. But he shut his eyes, saying, I will not see Christ here ; it is enough for me to see him in glory. We are now to attend only to *the voice of the Spirit in the Scriptures:* this is a more sure word than any voice from heaven. 2 Pet. 1: 19.

2. *The teachings of God are not to be understood as opposite to, or exclusive of the teachings of men.* Divine teachings do not render the ministry vain or useless. Paul was taught of God, Gal. 1 : 12, and his conversion had something extraordinary in it, yet the ministry of Ananias was used and honored in that work. Acts 9 : 4, 17. Divine teachings excel, but do not exclude human teachings. I know the scripture to which Christ here refers is objected against the necessity of a standing ministry in the church : "They shall teach no more every man his neighbor, and every man his brother." Jer. 31 : 34. But if these words should be understood absolutely, they would not only overthrow God's own institution, 1 Cor. 12 : 28, and deprive us of a principal fruit of Christ's ascension, Eph. 4 : 11, 12, but would destroy all private instructions and admonitions. Such a sense would make the prophet contradict the apostle, and destroy the unity and harmony of the Scriptures : the sense therefore cannot be negative, but comparative ; it shows the excellency of divine, but does not destroy the usefulness of human teaching. The

teachings of men are made effectual by the teachings of the Spirit ; and the Spirit in his teachings will use and honor the ministry of man.

3. *The teaching of God is the spiritual and heavenly light, by which the Holy Spirit shines into the hearts of men,* to give them "the light of the knowledge of the glory of God in the face of Jesus Christ." 2 Cor. 4 : 6. And though this is the proper work of the Spirit, yet it is called the teaching of the Father, because the Spirit who enlightens us is commissioned and sent by the Father so to do. John 14 : 26. Now these teachings of the Spirit of God consist in two things :

(1.) *In his sanctifying impressions* or regenerating work upon the soul, by virtue of which it receives insight into spiritual things ; and that not only as illumination is the first act of the Spirit in our conversion, Col. 3 : 10, but as his whole work of sanctification is illuminative and instructive to the converted soul. "The anointing which ye have received of him abideth in you ; and ye need not that any man teach you ; but as the same anointing teacheth you." 1 John 2 : 27. The meaning is, that sanctification gives the soul experience of the mysterious things contained in the Scriptures, and that experience is the most excellent key to unlock and open those scripture mysteries : no knowledge is so distinct, so clear, so sweet, as that which the heart communicates to the head. "If any man will do his will, he shall know of the doctrine." John 7 : 17. A man that never read the nature of love in books, may yet truly describe it by the sense of it in his own soul ; yea, he that has felt, much better understands, than he that has only read or heard. O what a light does spiritual experience cast upon a great part of the Scriptures ; for indeed sanctification is the very copy or transcript of the word of God upon the heart of man : I will write my law in their hearts. Jer. 31 : 33. So that the Scriptures and the experience of believers answer to each other, as the lines in the press answer to the impressions upon the paper, or the figure in the wax to the engraving in the seal. When a sanctified man reads David's Psalms or Paul's epistles, how is he surprised with wonder to find the very workings of his own heart so exactly expressed there ! O, says he, these holy men speak what my heart has felt.

(2.) The Spirit of God teaches us, moreover, by *his gracious assistances* which he gives us as our need requires: "It shall be given you in that same hour what ye shall speak." Matt. 10 : 19. He "shall bring all things to your remembrance." John 14 : 26. He assists both the understanding in the apprehension of truth, and the heart in the improvement of it.

II. We inquire, WHAT ARE THOSE SPECIAL TRUTHS which believers learn of the Father when they come to Christ? There are many great and necessary truths in which the Spirit enlightens men in that day. I cannot say they are all taught to every believer in the same degree and order; but it is certain that believers are taught of God such lessons as these, which they never so understood before.

LESSON 1. They are taught of God *that there is abundantly more evil in their nature and actions than ever they had discerned.* The Spirit when he cometh shall convince the world of sin. John 16 : 8, 9. Men had a general notion of sin before ; so had Paul when a Pharisee : but how different were his apprehensions of sin from all he had in his natural state, when God brought home the commandment to his very heart. There is as great a difference between such an intuitive knowledge of sin, whereby God makes a soul to discern the nature and evil of it in a spiritual light, and the mere traditional or speculative knowledge of it, as there is between the sight of a painted lion on the wall, and the sight of a living lion roaring in the way. The intuitive sight of sin is another thing than men imagine it to be : it is a sight that wounds a man to the very heart, Acts 2 : 37 ; for God not only shows a man this or that particular sin, but in the day of conviction he *sets all his sins in order before him.* Psalm 50 : 21. Conviction lays open the original corruption whence spring the innumerable evils of the life, James 1 : 14, 15 ; and the Lord shows the man whom he is bringing to Christ the sinful and miserable state which he is in by reason of both. John 16 : 9. And now all excuses and defences of sin are gone ; he shows him how his iniquities have exceeded, Job 36 : 8, 9 ; exceeded in number and in aggravations of sinfulness ; exceeding many and exceeding vile : "No such sinner in the world as I ! Can such sins as mine be pardoned ? The greatness of God magnifies my sin ; the holiness of God makes it beyond measure vile ; the goodness of God adds inconceivable weight to my guilt. O, can there be mercy for such a wretch as I ? If there be, then there will not be a greater example of the riches of free grace in all the world than I am." Thus God teacheth the evil of sin.

Lesson 2. God teaches the soul whom he is bringing to Christ *the misery which hangs over it because of sin.* Scripture threatenings were formerly slighted ; now the soul trembles at them. Isa. 28 : 15 ; Psalm 50 : 21. Men thought, as they heard no more of their sins after the commission of them, that they should never hear more ; that the effect had been as transient as the act of sin was ; or if trouble must follow sin, they should fare no worse than others, men generally being in the same case ; besides, they hoped to find God more merciful than many preachers represented him. But when light from God enters the soul to discover the nature of God and of sin, it sees that whatever wrath is treasured up for sinners in the dreadful threatenings of the law, is but the just demerit of sin : "The wages of sin is death." Rom. 6 : 23. The *penal* evil of damnation is but equal to the *moral* evil of sin : so that in the whole ocean of God's wrath there is not one drop of injustice; yea, the soul doth not only see the justice of God in its eternal damnation, but the wonderful mercy of God in its being delayed so long. How is it that I am not in hell? Now do the fears of eternity seize the soul, and the worst of men are supposed to be in a better condition than one's self. Never do men tremble at the threatenings of God, nor rightly apprehend the danger of their condition, until sin and the wages of sin are discovered to them by a light from heaven.

LESSON 3. God teaches the soul whom he brings to Christ that *deliverance from sin and the wrath to come is the greatest and most important business it hath to do in this world.* "What must I do to be saved?" O direct me to some effectual way, if there be any, to secure my wretched soul from the wrath of God. Sin, and the wrath that follows it, are things that swallow up the soul and drink up the spirits of men. These things float not upon their fancies as matters of speculation, but settle upon their hearts day and night as the deepest of all concerns. They now know much better than any mere scholar the sense of the text, "What is a man profited, if he shall gain the whole world, and lose his own soul? or what shall a man give in exchange for his soul?" Matt. 16 : 26.

Five things show how weighty the cares of salvation are upon their hearts. 1. Their continual solicitude about these things : if earthly affairs divert them for a while, yet they return again to this solemn business. 2. Their careful redeeming of time, saving the very moments thereof to employ about this work. Those that were prodigal of hours and days, now look upon every moment of time as precious and valuable. 3. Their fears lest they should come short at last, show how much their hearts are set upon this work. 4. Their readiness to embrace all the assistance they can get from others ; and, 5. The little notice they take of all other troubles, tells you their hearts are taken up about greater things.

Lesson 4. The Lord teaches souls that are coming to Christ, *that though it be their duty to strive to the uttermost for salvation, yet all strivings in their own strength are insufficient to obtain it.* This work is quite above the power of nature: "It is not of him that willeth, nor of him that runneth, but of God that showeth mercy." The soul is brought to a full conviction of this by the discovery of the heinous nature of sin and the severity of the law of God. No repentance or reformation can possibly amount to a just satisfaction, nor are they within the compass of our will. It was a saying of Dr. Hill to his friends, speaking about the power of man's will—he would lay his hand upon his breast and say, Every man hath something here to confute the erroneous doctrine. This takes off the soul from expectations of deliverance in that way: it cannot but strive, that is its duty ; but to expect deliverance as the purchase of its own strivings would be its sin.

Lesson 5. The soul that is coming to Christ by faith is taught of God, *that though its state be sad, yet it is not desperate.* There is a way of escape for poor sinners, how dark and fearful soever their own apprehensions are ; there is usually at this time a dawn of hope in the soul that is under the Father's teachings ; and this commonly arises from the general promises of the gospel, which, though they do not presently secure the soul from danger, mightily support it against despair. For though they be not certain that deliverance shall be the event of their trouble, yet the possibilities and probabilities of deliverance are a great stay to a sinking soul. The troubled soul cannot but acknowledge itself to be in a far better case than the damned are, whose hopes are perished from the Lord. And herein the merciful nature of God is discovered, in opening the door of hope almost as soon as the evil of sin is seen. It was not long after Adam's eyes were opened to see his misery, that God showed Christ in the first promise. Gen. 3 : 15. And the same method of grace is still continued to his elect offspring.   Gal. 3 : 21, 22 ; Rom. 3 : 21, 22.   These hopes the Lord sees necessary, to encourage the use of means ; hope sets all the world at work ; if all hope were cut off, every soul would sit down in sullen despair.

LESSON 6.   The Lord teaches those who come to Christ, *that there is a fulness of saving power in him to deliver the soul that receives him from all its sin and misery.*   Heb. 7 : 25 ; Col. 1 : 19 ; Matt. 28 : 18.   This is a necessary point for every believer to learn from the Father ; for unless the soul be satisfied of the fulness of Christ's saving power, it will never move towards him.   And herein also the goodness of God is most seasonably manifested, for at this time it is the design of Satan to fill the soul with despairing thoughts of a pardon ; but all those thoughts vanish before the discovery of Christ's all-sufficiency.   Now the sin-sick soul saith with the woman, "If I may but touch his garment I shall be whole."   Matt. 9 : 21.   How deep soever the guilt of sin be, the soul which acknowledges the infinite dignity of the blood of Christ, the offering it up to God in our stead, and God's declared satisfaction in it, must be satisfied that Christ is "able to save to the uttermost all that come unto God by him."

LESSON 7.   Every man that cometh to Christ is taught of God, *that he can never reap any benefit by the blood of Christ, except he have union with Christ.*   1 John 5 : 12 ; Eph. 4 : 16. Time was when men thought nothing was necessary to their salvation but the death of Christ ; but now the Lord shows them that their union with Christ by faith is as necessary to their salvation as the death of Christ.   The purchase of salvation is an act of Christ without us while we are yet sinners ; the application thereof is by a work wrought within us when we are believers.   Col. 1 : 27. In the purchase, all the people of God are redeemed together by way of price ; in the application, they are redeemed, each individually, by way of power.   As the sin

of Adam could never hurt us unless he had been our head
by way of generation ; so the righteousness of Christ can
never benefit us unless he be our head by way of regeneration. In teaching this lesson, the Lord in mercy un-
teaches and blots out that dangerous principle by which
the greatest part of the christianized world do perish,
namely, that the death of Christ is in itself effectual to salvation, though a man he never regenerated or united to
him by saving faith.

LESSON 8. God teaches the soul whom he is bringing
to Christ, *that whatever is necessary to be wrought in us, or
done by us, in order to our union with Christ, is to be obtained
from him by prayer.* Ezek. 36 : 37. And the soul no sooner
comes under the effectual teachings of God, but the Spirit
of prayer begins to breathe in it, "Behold he prayeth."
Acts 9 : 11. Those that were before taught to pray by
men, are now taught of the Lord to pray. To pray, did I
say? Yea, and to pray fervently too, as men concerned
for their eternal happiness ; to pray not only with others,
but to pour out their souls before the Lord in secret ; for
their hearts are as bottles full of new wine, which must
vent or break. Now the soul returns to its God often in
the same day ; now it can express its burdens and wants in
words and groans which the Spirit teacheth. They pray,
and will not give over till Christ come with complete salvation.

LESSON 9. All that come to Christ are taught of God
to abandon their former ways and companions in sin. Isaiah
55: 7 ; 2 Cor. 5: 17. Sins that were profitable and pleasant as the right hand and right eye must now be cut off.
Companions in sin, once the delight of their lives, must
now be cast off. Christ says to the soul concerning these,
as in another case, "If therefore ye seek me, let these go
their way." John 18 : 8. And the soul says, "Depart
from me, ye evil-doers ; for I will keep the commandments
of my God." Psa. 119 : 115. And now pleasant sins and

companions in sin become the very burden and shame of a man's soul. Objects of delight become objects of pity. No endearments, no earthly interests whatever are found strong enough to hold the soul any longer from Christ. Nothing but the effectual teachings of God are found sufficient to dissolve such bonds of iniquity as these.

Lesson 10. All that come unto Christ are taught of God *that there is unequalled beauty and excellence in the ways and people of God.* Psa. 16:3. When the eyes of strangers to Christ begin to be enlightened in his knowledge, you may see the change of judgment wrought in them with respect to the people of God: towards them especially whom God has any way made instrumental for the good of their souls: they then call the spouse of Christ the fairest among women. Song 5:9. Now, and never before, the righteous appears more excellent than his neighbor. Change of heart is always accompanied with change of judgment with respect to the people of God: thus the jailer washed the apostle's stripes, to whom he had been so cruel before. Acts 16:33. The godly now seem to be the glory of the places where they live; and the glory of any place seems to be darkened by their removal. It is esteemed a choice mercy to be in their company. "We will go with you; for we have heard that God is with you." Zech. 8:23. Whatever low thoughts they had of the people of God before, now they are the excellent of the earth, in whom is all their delight.

Lesson 11. All that come to Christ are taught of God *that whatever difficulties they apprehend in religion, they must not, on pain of damnation, be discouraged thereby, or return again to sin.* "No man having put his hand to the plough, and looking back, is fit for the kingdom of God." Luke 9:62. Ploughing work is hard work; a strong and steady hand is required for it: he that ploughs must keep on, and make no balks in the hardest ground he meets.

Religion is running a race, 1 Cor. 9 : 24 ; there is no standing still, much less turning back, if we hope to win the
prize.

The devil, indeed, labors every way to discourage the
soul by representing the insuperable difficulties of religion ; and young beginners are but too apt to fall into
despondency ; but the teachings of the Father encourage
them, and they are carried on from strength to strength
against all the oppositions they meet from without, and
the discouragements they find within them.   To this conclusion they are brought by the teaching of God : "We
must have Christ, we must get pardon, we must strive
for salvation, let the difficulties and sufferings be never
so great or many."   As one said, It is necessary that I
go on, it is not necessary that I live ; so says the soul
that is taught of God, It is easier for me to dispense with
ease, honor, relations, yea, with life itself, than to part with
Christ and the hopes of eternal life.

LESSON 12.   They that come to Christ are taught of
God *that whatever unworthiness they discover in themselves, and
whatever their fears as to acceptance, yet it is their wisdom to
venture themselves upon Jesus Christ, whatever be the issue.*
Three great discouragements are usually found in the
hearts of those that come to Christ in the way of faith.

The *greatness of guilt and sin.*   How can I go to Christ,
that have been so vile a wretch?   And here measuring
the grace and mercy of Christ by what it finds in itself or
in other creatures, the soul is ready to sink under the
weight of its own discouraging thoughts.   1 Sam. 24 : 19.

The sense they have of *their own insufficiency* to do what
God requires.   "My heart is harder than adamant ; how
can I break it?   My will is stubborn and obstinate ; the
frame and temper of my spirit is altogether carnal and
earthly, and it is not in the power of my hand to change
it ; alas, I cannot subdue any one corruption, nor perform
one spiritual duty, nor bear one of those burdens which

religion lays upon all that follow Christ." This also proves a great discouragement in the way of faith.

And which is more than all, the soul that is coming to Jesus Christ has *no assurance of acceptance* with him, if it should venture itself upon him. It is much more probable, if I look to myself, that Christ will shut the door of mercy against me.

But under all these discouragements the soul learns this lesson from God, that, ungodly as it is, it is every way its duty and concern to go on in the way of faith, and make the great venture of itself upon Jesus Christ: and of this the Lord convinces the soul by two things:

(1.) The soul sees *an absolute necessity of coming*. Necessity is laid upon it, there is no other way. Acts 4 : 12. God has shut it up by a blessed necessity to this only door of escape. Gal. 3 : 23. Damnation lies in the neglect of Christ. Heb. 2 : 3. The soul has no choice in this case; angels, ministers, duties, cannot save me; Christ, and none but Christ can deliver me from present guilt and the wrath to come. Why do I delay when certain ruin must inevitably follow the neglect or refusal of gospel-offers?

(2.) The Lord shows those under his teaching *the probabilities of mercy*, for their encouragement in believing. And these probabilities the soul is enabled to gather from the general and free invitations of the gospel, Isa. 55:1, 7; Rev. 22 : 17; from the conditional promises of the gospel, John 6 : 37; Matt. 11 : 28; Isa. 1 : 18; from the vast extent of grace beyond all the thoughts of men, Isa. 55 :8, 9; Heb 7 : 25; from the encouraging examples of other sinners who have found mercy in as bad a condition as they, 1 Tim. 1: 13; 2 Chron. 33 : 13; 2 Cor. 6 : 10, 11; from the command of God, which answers all the objections of unworthiness and presumption in them that come to Christ, 1 John 3 : 23; and from the changes already made upon the temper of the heart. "Time was when I had no sense of sin, nor sorrow for it; no desire after Christ, no heart to duties.   But it is not so with me now : I now see the evil of sin so as I never saw it before ; my heart is now broken in the sense of that evil ; my desires begin to be inflamed after Jesus Christ ; I am not at rest, nor where I would be, till I am in secret mourning after the Lord Jesus : surely these are the dawnings of the day of mercy ; let me go on in this way." It saith, as the lepers at the siege of Samaria, 2 Kings 7 : 3, 4, "If I stay here, I perish :" If I go to Christ, I can but perish. Hence believers bear up against all discouragements. Thus you have the lessons which all who come to Christ are taught by the Father.

CHAPTER XXIII

NECESSITY OF BEING TAUGHT OF GOD—CONTINUED

"It is written in the prophets, And they shall be all taught of God. Every man therefore that hath heard, and hath learned of the Father, cometh unto me." JOHN 6 : 45

IN the last chapter we considered the great truth, that *the teachings of God are absolutely necessary to every soul that cometh unto Christ in the way of faith.* I have shown, 1, what is implied in the teachings of God; and 2, what those special lessons are which believers hear and learn of the Father. It remains to show, 3, what are the properties of divine teaching; 4, what influence they have in bringing souls to Christ; and 5, why it is impossible for any man to come to Christ without these teachings of the Father.

III. What are THE PROPERTIES OF DIVINE TEACHING? Concerning the teachings of God we affirm in general, that though they do not exclude, yet they vastly differ from all human teachings : as the power of God transcends all human power, so the wisdom of God in teaching transcends all human wisdom.

1. God teacheth *powerfully.* He speaks to the soul. When the word comes accompanied with the Spirit, it is mighty, through God, to cast down all imaginations. 2 Cor. 10 : 4. Now the gospel comes not in word only, as it was wont to do, but in power, 1 Thess. 1 : 4, 5—a power that makes the soul fall down before it and acknowledge that God is in that word. 1 Cor. 14 : 25.

2. The teachings of God are *sweet.* Men never relish the sweetness of truth till they learn it from God. His name is an ointment poured forth. Song 1 : 3. "His mouth is most sweet." Song 5 : 16. O how powerfully

and how sweetly does the voice of God slide into the hearts of poor broken-hearted sinners! how dry and taste-less are the discourses of men, compared with the teach-ings of the Father!

3. God teacheth *plainly*. He not only opens truths to the understanding, but he opens the understanding also to perceive them. In that day the veil is taken away from the heart, 2 Cor. 3 : 16 ; a light shines into the soul, a beam from heaven is darted into the mind. Luke 24 : 45. Divine teachings are satisfying ; the soul doubts and hesitates no more, but acquiesces in what God teaches, and is so satisfied that it can venture all upon the truth of what it has learned from God : as that martyr said, *I cannot dispute, but I can die for Christ*. See Prov. 8 : 8, 9.

4. The teachings of God are *infallible*. The wisest of men may mistake, and lead others into mistakes ; but it is not so in the teachings of God. If we can be sure that God teaches us, we may be as sure of the truth of what he teaches ; for his Spirit guideth us into all truth, John 16 : 3, and into nothing but truth.

5. The teachings of God are *abiding;* they make ever-lasting impressions upon the soul ; they are ever with it. Psalm 119 : 98. The words of men vanish, but the words of God abide : what God teaches he writes upon the heart, Jer. 31 : 33, and that will abide. It is usual with those whose understandings have been opened by the Lord, to say, many years afterwards, I shall never forget such a scripture which once convinced, such a promise which once encouraged me.

6. The teachings of God are *saving*, they make the soul wise unto salvation. 2 Tim. 3 : 15. There is much of other knowledge that goes to hell with men ; but "this is life eternal, that they might know thee the only true God, and Jesus Christ whom thou hast sent." John 17 : 3. This is deservedly styled the light of life. John 8 : 12. In this light we shall see light. Psa. 36 : 9.

7. The teachings of God make their way into the *weakest capacities*. "The heart also of the rash shall understand knowledge, and the tongue of the stammerers shall be ready to speak plainly." Isa. 32 : 4. Upon this account Christ said, "I thank thee, O Father, Lord of heaven and earth, because thou hast hid these things from the wise and prudent, and hast revealed them unto babes." Matt 11 : 25. It is admirable to see what clear illuminations some illiterate Christians have in the mysteries of Christ and salvation, which others, of great abilities, deep and searching heads, can never discover with all their learning and study.

8. The teachings of God are *transforming*, they change the soul into the same image, 2 Cor. 3 : 18 ; God casts them whom he teacheth into the very mould of those truths which they learn of him. Rom. 6 : 17.

IV. Let us see what INFLUENCE DIVINE TEACHINGS HAVE UPON SOULS in bringing them to Christ, and we shall find a threefold influence in them.

1. They have an influence upon the *means* by which we come to Christ. The best ordinances are but a dead letter, except the teaching and quickening Spirit of God work with them. 2 Cor. 3 : 6. The best ministers, like the disciples, cast forth the net, but take not one soul till God teach as well as they. Paul is nothing, and Apollos nothing, but God that giveth the increase. 1 Cor. 3 : 7. Let the most learned and powerful orator be in the pulpit, yet no man's heart is persuaded till it hear the voice of God.

2. They have influence upon the mind to *remove what hindered it* from Christ. Except the minds of men be first led from those errors by which they are prejudiced against Christ, they will never be persuaded to come to him ; and nothing but the Father's teachings can cure those evils of the mind. The mind of man slights the truths of God until he teach them, and then they tremble with reverence

of them. Sin is but a trifle till God shows it to us in the law, and then it appears *exceeding sinful.* Rom. 7 : 13. We think God to be such a one as ourselves, Psalm 50 : 21, until he discover himself to us in his infinite greatness, holiness, and justice ; and then we cry, Who can stand before this great and dreadful Lord God ! We thought there was time enough hereafter to mind the concerns of another world, till the Lord opened our eyes to see in what danger we stood on the very brink of eternity ; and then nothing alarmed us more than the fears that our time would end before the great work of salvation be finished. We thought ourselves in a converted state till God made us see the necessity of another manner of conversion, upon pain of eternal damnation. We readily caught hold upon the promises when we had no right to them ; but the teachings of God make the presumptuous sinner let go his hold, that he may take a better and surer hold of them in Christ. We once thought that the death of Christ had been enough to secure our salvation ; but under the teachings of God we discern the necessity of a change of heart, or else the blood of Christ can never profit us. Thus the teachings of God remove the errors of the mind by which men are withheld from Christ.

3. The teachings of God powerfully *attract the will of a sinner to Christ.* Hos. 2 : 14. But of these drawings of the Father I have largely spoken before, and therefore shall say no more of them in this place, but hasten to consider,

V. WHY IT IS IMPOSSIBLE FOR ANY MAN TO COME TO CHRIST WITHOUT THE FATHER'S TEACHINGS, and this will appear from three considerations :

1. The impossibility of coming to Christ without the teachings of the Father, will appear from *the power of sin*, which has so strong a hold upon the hearts of all unregenerate men that no human persuasion whatever can separate them ; for sin is *natural* in the soul ; it is born and bred with a man. Psalm 51 : 4 ; Isaiah 48 : 8.

It is as natural for fallen man to sin as it is to breathe. Again, the power of sin has been strengthening itself from the beginning by long-continued *custom*, which gives it the force of a second nature, and makes regeneration naturally impossible. "Can the Ethiopian change his skin, or the leopard his spots? Then may ye also do good that are accustomed to do evil?" Jer. 13 : 23. Sin is also the *delight* of a sinner. "It is as sport to a fool to do mischief." Prov. 10 : 23. Carnal men have no other pleasure but what arises from their lusts : to cut off their corruptions by mortification, were at once to deprive them of all the pleasure of their lives. Sin being thus natural, customary, and delightful, bewitches their hearts to madness, so that they rather choose damnation than separation from sin. Their hearts are fully set in them to do evil, Eccles. 8 : 11 ; they rush into sin "as the horse rusheth into the battle." Jer. 8 : 6. And now, what can separate a man from his beloved lusts, except the powerful teaching of God? Nothing but a light from heaven can rectify the enchanted mind ; no power but that of God can change the sinful inclination of the will.

2. The impossibility of coming to Christ without the Father's teaching appears from the *indisposedness* of man, the subject of this change. The natural man receives not the things which are of God. 1 Cor. 2 : 14. Three things must be wrought upon man before he will come to Christ. His understanding must be enlightened ; his hard heart must be broken ; his obstinate will must be subdued : all these are effects of a supernatural power. The illumination of the mind is the work of God. 2 Cor. 4 : 6 ; Rev. 3 : 17 ; Eph. 5 : 8. The breaking of the heart is the Lord's work ; it is he that giveth repentance. Acts 5 : 31. It is the Lord that "taketh away the heart of stone, and giveth a heart of flesh." Ezek. 36 : 26. It is he that poureth out the spirit of contrition upon man. Zech. 12 : 10. The changing of the natural bent and inclination of the

will is the Lord's prerogative. Phil. 2 : 13. All these things are effectually done in the soul of man when God teaches it, and never till then.

3. *The nature of faith*, by which we come to Christ, shows the impossibility of coming without the Father's teaching. It is not of ourselves, but the gift of God. Eph. 2 : 8. It is not acquired by industry, but imparted by grace. Phil. 1 : 29. The light of faith by which spiritual things are discerned is from above. Heb. 11 : 1, 27. It seeth things that are invisible. The adventures of faith are so ; for against hope a man believeth in hope, giving glory to God. Rom. 4 : 18. By faith a man goes to Christ against all the discouragements of reason. The self-denial of faith is from above ; the cutting off the right hand and plucking out of the right eye must be so. Matt. 5 : 29. The victories of faith all speak it to be from God ; it overcomes the strongest oppositions from without. Hebrews 11 : 33, 34. It subdues and purges the most obstinate and deep-rooted corruptions within. Acts 15 : 9. It overcomes all the blandishments of the bewitching world. 1 John 5 : 4. All which considered, how evident is the conclusion that none can come to Christ without the Father's teachings.

INFERENCE 1. *How false and absurd is the doctrine which asserts the possibility of believing without divine grace.* The desire of self-sufficiency was the ruin of Adam, and the conceit of self-sufficiency is the ruin of his posterity. This doctrine is not only contradictory to the current of Scripture, Phil. 2 : 13, John 1 : 13, with many other texts, but to the experience of believers ; yet the pride of nature will strive to maintain what Scripture and experience plainly contradict.

2. *Hence, we may also inform ourselves how it comes to pass that so many wise and learned men miss Christ, while many simple and illiterate persons obtain salvation by him.* The reason is plainly given us by Christ. "It is given to you

to know the mysteries of the kingdom of heaven, but to them it is not given." Matt. 13 : 11. It is the dropping of divine teaching upon one and not upon another that dries up the green tree and makes the dry tree flourish. Many natural men have searching wits, solid judgments, nimble fancies, tenacious memories ; they can search out the mysteries of nature, satisfy the inquiries of the curious, measure the earth, and discover the motions of the heavens, but after all take up their place in hell ; when in the meantime *the statutes of the Lord*, by the help of his teachings, *make wise the simple*. Psalm 19 : 17. It is no matter how dull the scholar be, if God undertake to be the teacher. I remember Austin speaks of one who was commonly reputed a fool, and yet he judged him to be truly godly, and that by two signs of grace which appeared in him : one was his seriousness when he heard any thing of Christ ; the other his indignation against sin. It was truly said by two cardinals riding to the council of Constance, who overheard a poor shepherd in the fields with tears bewailing his sins, The unlearned will rise and take heaven, while we, with all our learning, shall descend into hell.

3. *This also informs us the true reason of the various success of the gospel in the souls of men.* Here we see why the ministry of one man becomes fruitful, and of another barren ; yea, why the labors of the same man prosper at one time and not at another ; these things are according as God accompanies our teachings. We often see a plain discourse blessed with success, while that which is more neat and labored comes to nothing. Austin has a similitude to illustrate this. Suppose, says he, two conduits, the one very plain, the other curiously carved and adorned with images of lions, eagles, etc., the water does not refresh and nourish as it comes from such a conduit, but as it is water. Where we find most of man, we frequently find least of God. I do not speak this to encourage care-

lessness and indolence, but to provoke the dispensers of the gospel to more earnest and fervent prayer for the blessing of the Spirit upon their labors, and to make men less fond of their own gifts and abilities.

4. *Learn hence the transcendent excellence of saving, spiritual knowledge, above that which is natural.* One drop of knowledge taught by God is more excellent than the whole ocean of human knowledge and acquired gifts. Phil. 3 : 8 ; John 17 : 3 ; 1 Cor. 2 : 2. Let no man therefore be dejected at the want of those gifts with which unsanctified men are adorned. If God has taught thee the evil of sin, the worth of Christ, the necessity of regeneration, the mystery of faith, the way of communion with him, trouble not thyself on account of ignorance in natural things : thou hast that, reader, which will bring thee to heaven ; and he is truly wise that knows the way of salvation, though he be ignorant in other things. Thou knowest those things which all the learned doctors and libraries in the world could never teach thee, but God has revealed them to thee ; bless God, and take courage.

5. If there is no coming to Christ without the teachings of the Father, it greatly concerns us to *examine our hearts* whether we have had the saving teachings of God under the preaching of the gospel. Let not the question be mistaken. I do not ask what books you have read, what ministers you have heard, what stock of speculative knowledge you have acquired ; but the question is, whether God ever spoke to your hearts, and has effectually taught you such lessons as were mentioned in our last discourse. There is a vast difference between that speculative and traditional knowledge which man learns from men, and that spiritual and transforming knowledge which a man learns from God. If you ask how the teachings of God may be distinguished from all mere human teachings, I answer, they may be discerned and distinguished by these signs :

SIGN 1. The teachings of God are *very humbling to the soul.* Human knowledge puffeth up, 1 Cor. 8 : 1, but the teachings of God greatly abase the soul. "I have heard of thee by the hearing of the ear; and now mine eye seeth thee. Wherefore I abhor myself, and repent in dust and ashes." Job 42 : 5, 6. The same light which discovers to us the holiness, justice, greatness, and goodness of God, discovers also the vileness and total unworthiness of the best and holiest of men. Isaiah 6 : 5.

SIGN 2. The teachings of God are *deeply impressive;* they fully reach the heart of man. "I will allure her, and bring her into the wilderness, and speak comfortably unto her," Hosea 2 : 14; or as it is in the Hebrew, I will speak to her heart. When God shows man the evil of sin, he so convinces the soul that no creature comforts have any sweetness in them; and when he shows man his right-eousness and peace in Christ, he so comforts the heart that no outward afflictions have any bitterness in them. One drop of consolation from heaven sweetens a sea of trouble upon earth. "In the multitude of my thoughts within me, thy comforts delight my soul." Psalm 94 : 19.

SIGN 3. The teachings of God are *sanctifying and re-newing;* they reform and change the heart. "If so be that ye have heard him, and have been taught by him, as the truth is in Jesus: that ye put off concerning the for-mer conversation the old man, which is corrupt according to the deceitful lusts; and be renewed in the spirit of your mind." Eph. 4 : 21, 22, 23. See here what holiness and purity are the effect of divine teaching. Holiness, both external and internal, of every kind follows the Fa-ther's teachings. All the discoveries God makes to us of himself in Christ have an assimilating quality, and change the soul into their own likeness. 2 Cor. 3 : 18.

SIGN 4. All God's teachings are *practical, producing obe-dience.* Idle and useless speculations are not learned from God. As God's creating words, so his teaching words are with effect: as when he said, "Let there be light, and there was light;" so when he says to the soul, Be comforted, be humbled, it is effectually comforted, Isa. 66 : 13, and humbled, Job 40 : 4, 5. As God has made no creature in vain, so he speaks no word in vain; every thing which men hear or learn from the Father is for use and benefit to the soul.

SIGN 5. All teachings of God are *agreeable with the written word.* The Spirit of God and his word do never jar. "He shall receive of mine, and shall show it unto you." John 16 : 14. When God speaks to the heart of man, whether in conviction, consolation, or instruction, he always either makes use of the express words of Scripture, or speaks to the heart in language every way agreeable to Scripture. So that the written word becomes the *standard* to weigh and try all divine teachings. "To the law, and to the testimony: if they speak not according to this word, it is because there is no light in them." Isa. 8 : 20. What disagrees with the Scripture must not pass for an inspiration of God, but a deluding insinuation of Satan.

SIGN 6. The teachings of God are *satisfying to the soul of man.* The understanding, like a dial, is enlightened with the beams of divine truth shining upon it: this no man's teaching can do. Men can only teach by propounding truth to the understanding; they cannot enlighten the faculty itself, as God does. 1 John 5 : 20. He gives man understanding as well as instruction. Eph. 1 : 18. Thus we may discern and distinguish the teachings of God from all other teaching.

6. The last use I shall make of this point shall be a word of *exhortation,* both to them that never were effectually taught of God, and to them that have heard his voice and are come to Christ.

(1.) To *those that never heard the voice of God* speaking to their hearts; and truly this is the case of most men.

They have heard the sound of the gospel, but it has been a confused and ineffectual sound in their ears; they have heard the voice of man, but not the voice of God. The gifts of preachers have improved their understandings, and sometimes slightly touched their affections; but all this is only the effect of man upon man. O that you would look for something beyond all this: satisfy not yourselves with what is merely human in ordinances; come to the word with more spiritual designs than to get some notions of truth which you had not before, or to judge the gifts and abilities of the speaker. If God speak not to your hearts, all the ordinances in the world can do you no good. 1 Cor. 3 : 7. O remember what a solemn thing it is to attend upon the ministration by which the purposes of heaven are to be executed upon your souls, which must be to you the "savor of life unto life," or of "death unto death." Wrestle with God by prayer for a blessing upon the ordinances. Say, "Lord, speak thyself to my heart; let me hear thy voice and feel thy power in this prayer or in this sermon: others have heard thy voice, cause me to hear it; it had been much better for me if I had never heard the voice of preachers, except I hear thy voice in them."

(2.) Let *all those that have heard the voice of God* and are come to Christ in the virtue of his teachings, admire the condescension of God to them. O that God should speak to thy soul and be silent to others! There are thousands this day under ordinances, to whom the Lord has not given an ear to hear or a heart to obey. Deut. 29 : 4. "It is given unto you to know the mysteries of the kingdom of heaven, but to them it is not given." Matthew 13 : 11. And I beseech you, walk as those that have been taught of God. When Satan and your corruptions tempt you to sin, and to walk in the ways of the carnal and careless world, remember then that scripture, "But ye have not so learned Christ, if so be that ye have heard him,

and have been taught by him, as the truth is in Jesus."
Eph. 4 : 20, 21. To conclude, see that you are humble
and lowly in spirit. Humility qualifies you for divine teachings. The meek he will teach his way, Psalm 25 : 9 ; and
the more you are taught of God, the more humble you
will be.

Thus you see that no man can come to Christ without
the *application of the law and the teachings of the Father;*
which being considered, may be very useful to convince
us, which indeed is the design of it, that among the multitudes living under the ordinances of God and the general profession of religion, there are but few to be found
who have effectually received the Lord Jesus Christ by
saving faith.

———————

And now, reader, I suppose by this time thou art de-
sirous to know *by what signs and evidences* thy union with
Christ by faith may be made evident to thee ; and how
that great question, *whether thou hast yet effectually applied
Christ to thy soul,* may be clearly decided ; which brings
me to the third general use of the whole, *the examination
of our interest in Christ.*

EVIDENCES OF UNION WITH CHRIST

CHAPTER XXIV

THE INDWELLING OF THE SPIRIT

"And hereby we know that he abideth in us, by the Spirit which he hath given us." 1 John 3:24

The apostle in this chapter is engaged in a very trying discourse: his design is to discriminate the spirit and state of sincere believers from that of merely nominal Christians; which he attempts not to do by any thing that is external, but by the operations of the Spirit of God upon their hearts. His inquiry is not into the things which men profess or the duties they perform, but about the tempers of their hearts and the principles by which they are governed in religion. According to this test, he puts believers upon the study of their own hearts; calls them to reflect upon the operations of the Spirit of God wrought within their own souls, assuring them that these gracious effects and fruits of the Spirit in their hearts will be a solid evidence of their union with Jesus Christ, amounting to more than a general, conjectural ground of hope, under which there may lurk a dangerous and fatal mistake. The gracious effects of the Spirit of God within them are a foundation upon which they may build the certainty of their union with Christ: *Hereby we know that he abideth in us, by the Spirit which he hath given us.* In which words we have to consider,

1. *The thing to be tried;* which is indeed the weightiest matter that can be brought to trial in this world or in that

to come, namely, our union with Christ, expressed here by
his abiding in us; a phrase clearly expressing the difference between those who by profession pass for Christians
among men, though they have no other union with Christ
but in the external duties of religion, and those whose
union with Christ is real, vital, and permanent by the indwelling of the Spirit of Christ in their souls. In John
15 : 5, 6, Christ explains the force and importance of this
phrase : "I am the vine, ye are the branches ; he that
abideth in me, and I in him, the same bringeth forth much
fruit ; for without me ye can do nothing. If a man abide
not in me, he is cast forth as a branch, and is withered."
The thing to be tried is, whether we stand in Christ as
dead branches in a living stock, which are only bound to
it by external bonds that hold them for a while together ;
or whether our souls have a vital union with Christ, by
the participation of the living sap of that blessed root.

2. *The trial of this union,* which is by the *giving of the
Spirit to us.* The Spirit of Christ is the very bond of union
between him and our souls.   I mean not, that the person
of the Spirit dwells in us, imparting his essential properties to us ; it were blasphemy so to speak ; but his saving
influences are communicated to us as sanctifying operations, as the sun is said to come into the house when his
rays and influence reach there.   Nor must we think that
the influences of the Spirit abide in us in the same measure they do in Christ, for God giveth not the Spirit to
him by measure ; in him all fulness dwells, he is anointed with the Spirit above his fellows ; but there are proportions of grace communicated to believers by the same
Spirit ; and these graces and operations in our hearts
prove the reality of our union with Christ, as the communication of the vital sap of the stock to the branch, whereby it brings forth fruit of the same kind, proves it to be a
part of the same tree.

3. *The certainty of the trial* this way.   *Hereby we know*

we so know that we cannot be deceived. There is something in grace *essential to its being;* and something that flows from grace *manifesting* such being. We cannot intuitively discern the essence of grace as it is in its simple nature : God only thus discerns it, who is the author of it ; but we may discern it *by its effects and operations.* Accordingly God has furnished us with a power of self-intuition and reflection, whereby we are able to look upon our hearts, and make a judgment upon ourselves and upon our actions. The soul has not only power to project, but reflect upon its actions ; not only to put forth a direct act of faith on Jesus Christ, but to discern that act. "I know whom I have believed." 2 Tim. 1 : 12. And this is the way in which believers attain their knowledge of their union with Christ. Hence we learn that,

An interest in Christ may be certainly inferred from the gift of the Spirit to us.

"No man hath seen God at any time. If we love one another, God dwelleth in us, and his love is perfected in us. Hereby know we that we dwell in him, and he in us, because he hath given us of his Spirit." 1 John 4 : 12, 13. God is invisible, but the operations of his Spirit in believers are discernible. The soul's union with Christ. is a mystery, yet is discoverable by the effects perceptible in and by believers. Two things here require attention : what the giving of the Spirit signifies, and how it evidences the soul's interest in Jesus Christ.

I. What is meant by the Spirit, and what by the giving of the Spirit.

The Spirit is spoken of in Scripture essentially or personally. In the first sense it is put for the Godhead : "Justified in the Spirit," 1 Tim. 3 : 16, that is, by the power of his divine nature, which raised Christ from the dead. In the second sense it denotes the third person in the blessed Trinity ; and to him the word Spirit is attributed, sometimes in the sense before mentioned, as denoting his *personality*, and at other times it is put for the graces and gifts of the Spirit communicated by him unto men. *Be ye filled with the Spirit.* Eph. 5 : 18. Now,

The fruits or gifts of the Spirit are either common and assisting gifts, or special and sanctifying gifts. In the last sense it must be taken in this place; for the common gifts of the Spirit are bestowed upon one as well as another: such gifts are found in the unregenerate, and therefore can never amount to evidence of the soul's union with Christ. But his special sanctifying gifts, being the proper effect of that union, must prove or confirm it. In this sense we are to understand the Spirit in this place; and by giving the Spirit to us, we are to understand more than the coming of the Spirit upon us. The Spirit of God is said to come upon men in a transient way for assistance in some particular service, though they are unsanctified persons. Thus the Spirit of God came upon Balaam, Num. 24 : 2, enabling him to prophesy of things to come. Though the extraordinary gifts of the Spirit have now ceased, yet the Spirit ceases not to give his ordinary assistances unto men, both regenerate and unregenerate. 1 Cor. 12 : 8–10, 31. But, whatever he gives to others, he is said to *be given, to dwell,* and *to abide* only in believers. "Know ye not that ye are the temple of God, and that the Spirit of God dwelleth in you?" 1 Cor. 3 : 6; an expression denoting both his property in them and gracious familiarity with them.

There is a great difference between the *assisting* and the *indwelling* of the Spirit; the one is *transient*, the other *permanent*, in which latter sense the Spirit is in believers: therefore they are said "to live in the Spirit," Gal. 5 : 25; to be "led by the Spirit," ver. 18; to be in the Spirit, and the Spirit to dwell in them. Rom. 8 : 9.

II. We are to inquire HOW THIS GIVING OF THE SPIRIT PROVES THE SOUL'S INTEREST IN CHRIST

1. The Spirit of God in believers is *the bond by which*

they are united to Christ. If we find in ourselves the bond of union, we may conclude that we have union with Jesus Christ. This is evidently taught in the words of Christ, " The glory which thou gavest me I have given them ; that they may be one, even as we are one : I in them and thou in me, that they may be made perfect in one ; and that the world may know that thou hast sent me, and hast loved them, as thou hast loved me." John 17 : 22, 23. It is the glory of Christ's human nature to be united to the Godhead. This thou gavest me, and the glory thou gavest me I have given them ; that is, by me they are united unto thee : so that in Christ God and believers meet in a blessed union. It is Christ's glory to be one with God ; it is our glory to be one with Christ, and with God by him. But how is this done ? Certainly no other way but by the giving of his Spirit unto us ; for so much the phrase *I in them* must import. Christ is in us by the sanctifying Spirit, which is the bond of our union with him.

2. *The Scriptures make this indwelling of the Spirit the great mark of our interest in Christ: positively,* as in the text ; and *negatively,* as in Rom. 8 : 9, " Now if any man have not the Spirit of Christ, he is none of his ;" Jude 19, " Sensual, having not the Spirit." This evidence agreeing to all believers, and to none but believers, and at all times, it proves the soul's union with Christ in whomsoever it is found.

3. That which is a mark of our *freedom from the covenant of works, and our title to the privileges of grace,* must also show our union with Christ and interest in him. But the indwelling of the Spirit in us is a certain mark of this, and consequently proves our union with the Lord Jesus. This is plain from the apostle's reasoning : " And because ye are sons, God hath sent forth the Spirit of his Son into your hearts, crying, Abba, Father. Wherefore thou art no more a servant, but a son ; and if a son, then an heir

of God, through Christ." Gal. 4 : 6, 7. The spirit of the
first covenant was a spirit of fear and bondage, and they
that were under it were not sons, but servants ; but the
spirit of the new covenant is a free spirit acting in the
strength of God, and those that do so are the children of
God ; and as such they inherit the privileges and immunities of that great charter, the covenant of grace : they
are "heirs of God," and the evidence of their inheritance,
and of freedom from the bondage of the first covenant, is
the Spirit of Christ in their hearts, crying, Abba, Father.
"If ye be led of the Spirit, ye are not under the law."
Gal. 5 : 18.

4. If the purpose of God's electing love be executed,
and the benefits of the death of Christ applied by the
Spirit unto every soul in whom he dwells *as a spirit of
sanctification*, such a giving of the Spirit must be a proof
of our interest in Christ. But such is the method of grace :
"Elect according to the foreknowledge of God the Father,
through sanctification of the Spirit unto obedience and
sprinkling of the blood of Jesus Christ," 1 Pet. 1 : 2 ;
where you see God's purpose executed, and the blood of
Jesus applied to us by the Spirit, as a Spirit of sanctification. There is a blessed order of working observed as
proper to each person in the Godhead : the Father elects,
the Son redeems, the Spirit sanctifies. What the Father
decreed and the Son purchased, the Spirit applies ; and so
completes the salvation of believers. And this some divines give as the reason why the sin against the Spirit
is unpardonable, because he being the last agent in the
order of working, if the heart of a man be filled with enmity against the Spirit there can be no remedy for such a
sin ; there is no looking back to the death of Christ or to
the love of God for remedy. This sin against the Spirit
is the bar to the whole work of salvation. And on the
other hand, where the Spirit is received, the love of God,
the benefits of the blood of Christ run freely without in-

terruption; and the interest of such a soul in Jesus Christ is beyond dispute.

5. The giving of the Spirit to us, or his residing in us as a sanctifying Spirit, is everywhere in Scripture made *the earnest of eternal salvation,* and consequently must prove the soul's interest in Christ. "In whom also, after that ye believed, ye were sealed with that Holy Spirit of promise, which is the earnest of our inheritance." Eph. 1 : 13, 14. "Who hath also sealed us, and given the earnest of the Spirit in our hearts." 2 Cor. 1 : 22.

THE IMPROVEMENT to be made of this point shall be that to which the text so palpably leads us : to EXAMINE OUR INTEREST IN, AND THE VALIDITY OF OUR CLAIM TO JESUS CHRIST. In pursuance of which design, I shall first lay down *some general rules,* and then propose *some particular trials.*

RULE 1. *Though the Spirit of God be given us, and work-eth in us, yet he works not of necessity, but freely.* He neither assists nor sanctifies, as the fire burns, as much as he can, but as much as he pleases, "dividing to every man sever-ally as he will," 1 Cor. 12 : 11 ; bestowing greater meas-ures of gifts and graces upon some than upon others, and assisting the same person more at one season than an-other ; and all this variety of operation flows from his own good pleasure.

RULE 2. *There is a great difference in the manner of the Spirit's working before and after regeneration.* While we are unregenerate, he works in those that work not at all with him, and what motion there is in our souls is opposed to the Spirit ; but after regeneration, he works upon a com-plying and willing mind—we work, and he assists. Rom. 8 : 26. Our conscience witnesses, and he bears witness with it. Rom. 8 : 16. It is therefore an error that sanc-tified persons are not bound to strive in the way of duty without a sensible impulse of the Spirit. Isa. 64 : 7.

RULE 3. *Though the Spirit of God be given to believers,*

yet they may obstruct his working in them. He deals with us in his comforting work as we deal with him in obedience to his dictates. There is a grieving, yea, a quenching of the Spirit by the lusts and corruptions of the heart in which he dwells; and though he will not forsake his habitation as a Spirit of sanctification, yet he may for a time desert it as a Spirit of consolation. Psalm 51 : 11.

RULE 4. *The things which discover the indwelling of the Spirit in believers are not so much their duties, as the springs, aims, and manner of their performing them.* It is not so much the matter of a prayer, the neat expressions in which it is uttered, as the inward sense of the soul; it is not the choice of elegant words, or the copiousness of the matter with which we are furnished, for even a poor stammering tongue and broken language may have much of the Spirit of God in it. This made Luther say he saw more excellence in the duty of a plain Christian than in all the triumphs of Cæsar and Alexander. The excellence of spiritual duties is an inward thing.

RULE 5. *All the operations of the Spirit are harmonious, and according to the written word.* " To the law, and to the testimony; if they speak not according to this word, it is because there is no light in them." Isa. 8 : 20. The Scriptures are by the inspiration of the Spirit; therefore his work on the hearts of believers must agree with the Scriptures, or the inspiration of the Spirit is contradictory to itself. It is observable that the work of grace wrought by the Spirit in the hearts of believers, is represented to us in Scripture as a transcript of the written word; I will write my law in their hearts. Jer. 31 : 33. Now as a copy answers to the original, letter for letter, so does the work of the Spirit in our souls harmonize with his dictates in the Scriptures: whatsoever motion therefore shall be found repugnant thereto must not be attributed to the Spirit of God, but to the spirit of error and corrupt nature.

Rule 6. *Though the works of the Spirit in all sanctified persons substantially agree with the written word and with one another, yet as to the manner of operation there are many circumstantial differences.* The Spirit of God has not one and the same method of working on all hearts. The work of grace is introduced into some souls with more terror and trouble for sin than in others : he wrought upon Paul one way, upon Lydia in another ; he holds some much longer under terrors than others. Inveterate and more profane sinners often have stronger troubles for sin, and are held longer under them, than those into whose heart grace is more early implanted by the Spirit's blessing upon religious education ; but as these have less trouble at first, so commonly they have more doubts about the work of the Spirit afterwards.

Rule 7. *There is a great difference between the sanctifying and the comforting influences of the Spirit upon believers in respect to constancy and permanency.* His sanctifying influences abide for ever in the soul, they never depart ; but his comforting influences come and go, and abide not long upon the hearts of believers. Sanctification belongs to the being of a Christian, consolation only to his well-being. The first is fixed and abiding, the latter various and inconstant. Sanctification brings us to heaven hereafter, consolation brings heaven to us here ; our safety lies in the former, our cheerfulness in the latter. There are times in the lives of believers in which the Spirit of God more eminently seals their spirits and ravishes their hearts with joy unspeakable ; but what Bernard says is certainly true in the experience of Christians : "It is a sweet hour, and it is but an hour—a thing of short continuance ; the relish of it is exceeding sweet, but it is not often that Christians taste it."

I now proceed to specify SOME PARTICULAR MARKS by which we may discern whether God has given us his Spirit : by which Christians in a due composed frame may, with the assistance of the Spirit of God, discern his indwelling and working in themselves.

EVIDENCE 1. *In whomsoever the Spirit of Christ is a Spirit of sanctification, he has been a Spirit of conviction and humiliation.* This is the order which the Spirit constantly observes : "And when he is come, he will reprove the world of sin, and of righteousness, and of judgment. Of sin, because they believe not on me." John 16 : 8, 9.

This, you see, is the method he observes ; he shall reprove or convince the world of sin. Conviction of sin has the same respect to sanctification as the blossoms of trees have to the fruits that follow them ; a blossom is but in order to a more perfect and noble fruit. Where there are no blossoms we can expect no fruit, and where we see no conviction of sin we can expect no conversion to Christ. Has then the Spirit of God been a Spirit of conviction to thee? Has he more particularly convinced thee of sin because thou hast not believed on Christ? That is, has he shown thee thy sin and misery as an unbeliever : not only terrified thy conscience with more notorious acts of sin, but fully convinced thee of the state of sin that thou art in by thy unbelief, which, holding thee from Christ, must also hold thee under the guilt of all thy other sins? Such a conviction gives at least a strong probability that God has given thee his Spirit, especially when it remains day and night upon thy soul, so that nothing but Christ can give it rest, and consequently the great inquiry of thy soul is after him.

EVIDENCE 2. *As the Spirit of God has been a convincing, so he is a quickening Spirit to all those to whom he is given.* "The law of the Spirit of life in Christ Jesus hath made me free from the law of sin and death." Rom. 8 : 2. He is the Spirit of life, that is, the principle of spiritual life in the souls in which he dwells, uniting them to Christ the fountain of life ; and this spiritual life in believers manifests itself in vital actions and operations. When the

Spirit of God comes into the soul of a man that was sense-less in sin, he may say, "Now I begin to feel the load of sin, Rom. 7 : 24 ; now I begin to hunger and thirst after Christ and his ordinances, 1 Pet. 2 : 2 ; now I begin to breathe after God in spiritual prayer." Acts 9 : 11. Spiritual life has its spiritual senses and suitable operations. O think upon this, you that cannot feel any burden in sin, you that have no hungerings or thirstings after Christ ; how can the Spirit of God be in you? There may at times be much deadness in the hearts of Christians, but this is not always ; and when it is so with them they complain of it as their greatest affliction, their spirits are not easy and at rest.

EVIDENCE 3. *Those to whom God gives his Spirit have a tender sympathy with all the interests of Christ.* This must be so if the Spirit which is in Christ dwells also in their heart. This is a plain case ; even in nature itself, the members of the same body being animated by the same spirit of life : "Whether one member suffer, all the members suffer with it ; or one member be honored, all the members rejoice with it. Now ye are the body of Christ, and members in particular." 1 Cor. 12 : 26, 27. For as Christ, the head of that body, is touched with a tender feeling of the troubles of his people—he is persecuted when they are persecuted, Acts 9 : 4—so they that have the Spirit of Christ in them cannot be without a deep sense of the reproach done to Christ : this is as it were a sword in their bones. Psa. 42 : 10. If his public worship cease, or the assemblies of his people are scattered, it cannot but go to the hearts of all who have the Spirit of Christ. Those that have the Spirit of Christ do not more earnestly long after any thing than the advancement of Christ's interest in the earth. Psa. 45 : 3, 4. Paul rejoiced that Christ was preached though his own afflictions were increased, Phil. 1 : 16, 18, and John, that Christ increased though he himself decreased ; therein was his joy fulfilled. John

3 : 29. So certainly the concerns of Christ will touch the heart which is the habitation of his Spirit. I cannot deny that even a good Baruch may seek great things for himself, and be too much swallowed up in his own concerns when God is plucking up and breaking down. Jer. 45:4, 5. But this is only the influence of a temptation; the true spirit of a believer inclines him to sorrow and mourning when things are in this state : " Go through the midst of the city, through the midst of Jerusalem, and set a mark upon the foreheads of the men that sigh and that cry for all the abominations that be done in the midst thereof." Ezek. 9 : 4. O reader, is it thus with thee ? Dost thou sympathize with the affairs of Christ in the world ; or carest thou not which way things go with the people of God and the gospel of Christ, so long as thine own affairs prosper and things are well with thee ?

EVIDENCE 4. *The Spirit of God mortifies and subdues the corruptions of the soul in which he resides.* The Spirit lusteth against the flesh, Gal. 5 : 17, and believers, through the Spirit, mortify the deeds of the body. Rom. 8 : 13. This is one special part of his sanctifying work. I do not say he subdues sin in believers that it shall never trouble or defile them any more ; no, that freedom belongs to the perfect state in heaven ; but its dominion is taken away, though its life be prolonged for a season. It lives in believers still, but not upon provision they willingly make to fulfil the lust of it. Rom. 13 : 14. The design of every believer is coincident with that of the Spirit, to destroy and mortify corruption. They long after the extirpation of it, and are daily in the use of all sanctified means to destroy it ; the workings of their corruption are the affliction of their souls : " O wretched man that I am ! who shall deliver me from the body of this death ?" Rom. 7 : 24. And there is no one thing that sweetens the thoughts of death to believers, except the sight and full enjoyment of God, more than their expected deliverance from sin.

Evidence 5. *Wherever the Spirit of God dwells in the way of sanctification, he is the Spirit of prayer and supplication.* "Likewise the Spirit also helpeth our infirmities: for we know not what we should pray for as we ought; but the Spirit itself maketh intercession for us with groanings which cannot be uttered." Rom. 8 : 26. Wherever he is as the Spirit of grace, he is also as the Spirit of supplication. Zech. 12 : 10. His praying and his sanctifying influences are undivided. He helps them *before* they pray by kindling their desires and affections; he helps them *in prayer* by supplying subjects of request to them, teaching them what they should ask of God : he assists them in the *manner* of prayer, supplying them with suitable affections, and helping them to be sincere in all their desires to God. He humbles their pride and dissolves the hardness of their hearts; out of deadness makes them lively; out of weakness makes them strong. He assists the spirits of believers *after prayer*, giving them faith and patience to believe and wait for returns and answers to their prayers. O reader, reflect upon thy duties : consider what spirituality, sincerity, humility, broken-heartedness, and melting affections after God are to be found in them. Is it so with thee ? Or dost thou hurry over thy duties as an interruption to thy business and pleasures ? Are they an ungrateful task imposed upon thee by God and thine own conscience ? Are there no hungerings and thirstings after God in thy soul ? Or if there is pleasure arising to thee out of prayer, is it from the ostentation of thy gifts ? If it be so, reflect upon the carnal state of thy heart; these things do not show the Spirit of grace and supplication to be given thee.

Evidence 6. *There is a heavenly, spiritual frame of mind evidencing the indwelling of the Spirit.* "For they that are after the flesh, do mind the things of the flesh; but they that are after the Spirit, the things of the Spirit. For to be carnally minded is death; but to be spiritually minded is life and peace." Rom. 8 : 5, 6. By the mind, understand the reasonings, the fears, and pleasures of the soul which follow the meditations of the mind. If these are ordinarily and habitually exercised about earthly things, then is the frame and state of the man carnal and earthly. If God, Christ, heaven, and the world to come engage the affections of the soul, and the temper of such a soul is spiritual, and the Spirit of God dwells there, this is the life of the regenerate. "Our conversation is in heaven." Phil. 3 : 20. Such a frame is *life* and *peace:* a serene, placid, and most comfortable life. No pleasures on earth, no gratifications of the senses relish as spiritual things do. Consider, therefore, which way thy heart ordinarily works, especially in thy hours of retirement. David could say, "How precious are thy thoughts unto me, O God ; how great is the sum of them ! If I should count them, they are more in number than the sand : when I awake, I am still with thee." Psa. 139 : 17, 18. Yet it must be acknowledged, for the relief of weaker Christians, that there is a great diversity in this respect among the people of God. For the strength and constancy of a spiritual mind result from the depth and improvement of sanctification : the more grace, the more evenness, spirituality, and constancy there is in the motions of the heart after God. The minds of weak Christians are more easily entangled in earthly vanities, and diverted by inward corruptions ; yet still there is a spiritual inclination and bent of their hearts towards God, and the vanity and corruption which hinder their communion with him are their greatest grief.

EVIDENCE 7. *Those to whom the Spirit of grace is given are led by the Spirit.* "As many as are led by the Spirit of God, they are the sons of God." Rom. 8 : 14. Sanctified souls give themselves up to the government of the Spirit, obey his voice, ask his direction, and deny the solicitations of flesh and blood in opposition to him, Gal. 1 : 16 ; and they that do so are the sons of God. It is the office of the Spirit to guide us into all truth, and it is our great duty to follow his guidance. Hence it is, that in all undertakings the people of God so earnestly beg counsel from him. "Lead me, O Lord, in thy righteousness because of mine enemies ; make thy way straight before my face." Psa. 5 : 8. They dare not lean to their own understandings ; they dare not neglect duty nor commit sin against the convictions of their own consciences. Though sufferings be unavoidable in that path of duty, when they have balanced duties with sufferings the conclusion will be, it is better to obey God than man, the dictates of the Spirit rather than flesh and blood.

But before I leave this point I reckon myself a debtor to weak Christians, and shall endeavor to give satisfaction to some doubts and fears with which their minds are ordinarily entangled in this matter ; for it is a very plain case that many souls have the presence and sanctification of the Spirit without the evidence and comfort thereof.

OBJECTION 1. I greatly fear the Spirit of God is not in me, because of the great *darkness* which clouds my soul ; for I read that he enlightens the soul which he inhabits. "The anointing which ye have received of him abideth in you, and ye need not that any man teach you, but as the same anointing teacheth you of all things." 1 John 2 : 27. But alas, my understanding is weak and cloudy, I have need to learn of the meanest of God's people : this only I know, that I know nothing as I ought. to know.

ANSWER. Two things are to be regarded in spiritual knowledge, namely, its quantity and its efficacy. Your condition does not so much depend upon the measure of knowledge ; for perhaps you are under many disadvantages, and want those helps and means of increasing knowledge which others enjoy. It may be you have wanted education, or been encumbered by cares of the world, which have allowed you little leisure for the improvement of your mind. But if that which you know is turned into practice, Col. 1 : 9, 10 ; if it influence your heart and transform your affections into a spiritual frame, 2 Cor. 3 : 17, 18 ; if your ignorance humble you and drive you to God for knowledge, one drop of such knowledge of Christ and yourselves is worth more than a sea of unsanctified and speculative knowledge. Though you know but little, that little, being sanctified, is of great value. Though you know but little, time was when you knew nothing of Jesus Christ or the state of your soul. In a word, though you know but little, that little will be increasing like the morning light, which shineth more and more unto the perfect day. Prov. 4 : 18. If thou knowest so much as brings thee to Christ, thou shalt shortly be where thy knowledge shall be as the light at noonday.

OBJECTION 2. I sometimes find my heart raised and my affections melted in duties, but I fear it is *not from the Spirit of God :* could I be assured those motions of my heart were from the Spirit of grace, and not merely a natural thing, it would be satisfaction to me.

ANSWER. Consider whether the ground of your doubting is that you *take pains* in the way of meditation, prayer, and other duties, to bring your hearts to relish the things of God ; whereas, it may be, you expect your spiritual comforts should flow in upon you spontaneously, without any pains of yours. Here may be a great mistake ; for the Spirit of God works in the natural method in which affections are raised, and makes use of such duties as meditation and prayer. Ezek. 36 : 37. So David was forced to chide his own heart. Psa. 42 : 5. Thy comfort may nevertheless be the fruit of the Spirit, because God makes it grow upon thy duties.

Take this also as a sure rule, Whatsoever rises from self, always terminates in self. This stream cannot be carried higher than the fountain : if therefore thy aim in striving for affection in duty be only to win applause from men, this is the fruit of a very corrupt and hypocritical nature; but if thy heart be melted in the sense of the evil of sin, in order to the mortification of it; and under the apprehensions of the free grace of God in the pardon of sin, in order to engage thy soul more firmly to him—if these be thy designs, never reject them as the mere fruits of nature. A carnal root cannot bring forth such fruits as these.

OBJECTION 3. On the contrary, *spiritual deadness* and indisposition to duties, those especially which are more secret, spiritual, and self-denying than others, is the ground upon which many who are yet truly gracious doubt the indwelling of the Spirit in them. O, says such a one, if the Spirit of God be in me, why is it thus? Could my heart be so dead and averse to spiritual duties? No; these things would be my meat and my drink, the delight and pleasure of my life.

ANSWER. These things are indeed sad, and show thy heart to be out of frame, as the body is when it cannot relish the most desirable meats or drinks. But the question is, how thy soul behaves in such a condition; whether this be easy or burdensome to be borne by thee; and if thou complain under it as a burden, then what pains thou takest to get rid of it.

Know also that there is a great difference between spiritual death and spiritual deadness; the former is the state of the unregenerate, the latter is the complaint of many thousand regenerate souls: if David had not felt it as well as thee, he would never have cried out nine times in the compass of one psalm, "Quicken me, quicken me."

Besides, it is not so always with thee; there are seasons wherein the Lord breaks in upon thy heart and sets thy soul at liberty; to which times thou wilt do well to have an eye in these cloudy days.

OBJECTION 4. But the Spirit of God is the *comforter* as well as a *sanctifier:* he not only enables men to believe, but after they believe he seals them. Eph. 1:13. But I walk in darkness, and am a stranger to the sealing and comforting work of the Spirit. How therefore can I imagine the Spirit of God dwells in me, who go from day to day in the bitterness of my soul, mourning as without the sun?

ANSWER. There is a twofold sealing and comfort. The Spirit seals both in the work of sanctification and in giving evidence of that work. Thou mayest be sealed in the first, while thou art not yet sealed in the second sense. If so, thy condition is safe, though it be at present uncomfortable. And as to comfort, that also is of two sorts, in the root, or in the fruit: "Light is sown for the righteous," Psalm 97 : 11, though the harvest to gather in that joy be not yet come. There are many other ways besides that of comfort, whereby the indwelling of the Spirit may evidence itself in thy soul: if he do not enable thee to rejoice, yet if he enable thee sincerely to mourn for sin; if he do not enlarge thy heart in comfort, yet if he humble and purify thy heart by sorrows; if he deny thee the assurance of faith and yet give thee the dependence of faith, thou hast no reason to call in question or deny the indwelling of the Spirit in thee.

OBJECTION 5. But the apostle says, they that walk in the Spirit do not fulfil the lusts of the flesh, Gal. 5 : 16; but I find myself entangled and frequently overcome by them; therefore I fear the Spirit of God is not in me.

ANSWER. It is possible the ground of your doubt may be your mistake of the true meaning of that scripture. It is not the apostle's meaning that sin in believers does not work and oftentimes overcome them; for then he would contradict himself where he complains, "But I see another law in my members warring against the law of my mind, and bringing me into captivity to the law of sin which is in my members." Rom. 7 : 23. Two things are meant by the expression, "Ye shall not fulfil the lusts of the flesh." One is, that the principle of grace will give a check to sin in its first motions before it come to its maturity; it shall never be able to gain the full consent of the will, as it does in the unregenerate. The other meaning is, that if, notwithstanding all the opposition grace makes to hinder the commission of sin, it yet prevails and breaks forth into action ; yet such acts of sin, as they are not committed without regret, so they are followed with sorrow and true repentance. And those very surprisals of sin at one time are made warnings to prevent it at another time. If it be so with thee, thou dost not fulfil the lusts of the flesh.

And now, reader, if upon examination of thy heart by these rules the Lord shall help thee to discern the saving work of the Spirit upon thy soul and thine interest in Christ, what a happy man art thou ; what pleasure will arise to thy soul from such a discovery! Look upon thy heart as it is at present, or comparatively with what once it was and others still are, and thou wilt find enough to transport thy soul within thee. Certainly this is the most glorious piece of workmanship that ever God wrought upon any man. Eph. 2 : 10. The Spirit of God is come down from heaven and hath hallowed thy soul to be a temple for himself to dwell in ; as he hath said, "I will dwell in them, and walk in them ; and I will be their God, and they shall be my people." 2 Cor. 6 : 16. Moreover, this gift of the Spirit is a sure pledge and earnest of thy future glory. Time was when there was no such work upon thy soul; and considering the frame and temper of it, the total aversion and rooted enmity in it, it is a wonder of wonders that ever such a work should be wrought in such a heart as thine ; that ever the Spirit of God, who is pure and perfect holiness, should choose such an unclean, abominable heart to frame a habitation for himself to dwell in ; to say of thy soul as he once said of the material temple at Jerusalem, "The Lord hath chosen it, he hath desired it for his habitation. This is my rest for ever: here will I dwell; for I have desired it." Psalm 132 : 13, 14.   O, what hath God done for thy soul.

Think, reader, and think again : Are there not many thousands in the world of more amiable dispositions than thyself, whom yet the Spirit of God passes by, leaving them as tabernacles for Satan to dwell in? Such a one thou wast, and hadst still remained, if God had not wrought for thee beyond all the expectations and desires of thine own heart. O bless God that you have received not the spirit of the world, but the Spirit which is of God ; that you may know the things which are freely given unto you of God.

CHAPTER XXV

THE NEW CREATURE

"Therefore if any man be in Christ, he is a new creature: old things are passed away; behold, all things are become new." 2 Cor. 5:17

You have seen one trial of an interest in Christ, in our last discourse, by the indwelling of the Spirit. We have here another from one of the greatest effects of the Spirit upon our souls, namely, his work of *new creation:* "If any man be in Christ, he is a new creature." The apostle's scope in the context is to dissuade Christians from a sinful partiality in respect to men; that they should not regard them after the manner of the world, according to external differences, but according to their real internal worth and excellence. This he presses by two arguments: one drawn from the end of Christ's death, which was to take off our minds from those selfish designs by which the world is swayed; the other drawn from the *new spirit* by which believers are actuated. They that are in Christ are to judge and measure all things by a new rule: "If any man be in Christ, he is a new creature; old things are passed away;" as if he had said, We have done with the low, selfish spirit of the world, which was wholly governed by carnal interest; we are now to judge by a new rule, to be actuated from a new principle, aim at a new and more noble end: "Behold, all things are become new."

1. We have here the great *question to be determined*, whether a man be in Christ—a question upon the determination of which we must stand or fall for ever. By being in Christ the apostle does not mean the general profession of Christianity, which gives a man the reputation of an interest in him; but an interest in him by vital union

with his person and participation of his benefits. This is the question to be determined, than which nothing can be more solemn and important.

2. We have the rule by which this great question may be determined, namely, *the new creation:* "If any man be in Christ, he is a new creature." By this rule all claims to an interest in Christ are to be examined. *If any man,* be he high or low, learned or illiterate, young or old, if he pretend interest in Christ, this is the standard by which he must be tried: if he be in Christ he is a new creature; and if he be not a new creature, he is not in Christ, let his endowments, confidence, and reputation be what they will. A new creature—not physically, he is the same person he was—but renewed by gracious principles imparted from above, which sway him and guide him in another manner and to another end than ever he acted before; and these gracious principles not being educed out of any thing preëxistent in man, but imparted from above, are called "a new creature." This is the rule by which our claim to Christ must be determined.

3. This rule is here more particularly *explained.* "Old things are passed away; behold, all things are become new." He satisfies not himself to express it in general terms, by telling us the man in Christ must be a new creature; but more particularly, he shows us what this new creature is: "Old things are passed away—all things are become new."

By old things he means all those principles and lusts belonging to the carnal state, or the old man: all these are *passed away*—not perfectly, but in part at present, and wholly in hope and expectation hereafter.

"All things are become new." He means not that the old faculties of the soul are abolished, and new ones created in their room; but as our bodies may be said to be new bodies by reason of the endowments to be bestowed upon them in their resurrection, so our souls are now renewed by the imparting of new principles to them in the work of regeneration.

These two parts, the passing away of old things and the renewing of all things, comprise the whole of sanctification, which in other scriptures is expressed by equivalent phrases : sometimes by putting off the old and putting on the new man, Eph. 4 : 24 ; sometimes by dying unto sin, and living unto righteousness, Rom. 6 : 11, which is the same thing the apostle here intends by the passing away of old things and making all things new. And because this is the most excellent and glorious work of the Spirit wrought upon man in this world, the apostle asserts it with a note of special remark and observation, "*Behold!*"— behold and admire this surprising, marvellous change which God has made upon men ; they are come out of darkness into his marvellous light, 1 Pet. 2 : 9, out of the old, as it were, into a new world. "Behold, all things are become new." Hence,

God's creating of a new supernatural work of grace in the soul of any man, is infallible evidence of a saving interest in Jesus Christ.

Suitable hereto are those words of the apostle, "But ye have not so learned Christ ; if so be that ye have heard him, and have been taught by him, as the truth is in Jesus : that ye put off concerning the former conversation the old man, which is corrupt according to the deceitful lusts ; and be renewed in the spirit of your mind ; and that ye put on the new man, which after God is created in righteousness and true holiness." Eph. 4 : 20–24. Where we have, in other words of the same import, the very selfsame description of the man that is in Christ which the apostle gives us in this text. It will be necessary to show why the regenerating work of the Spirit is called a new creation ; in what respect every soul that is in Christ is renewed or made a new creature ; what are the remarkable properties of this new creature ; the necessity of this new creation to all that are in Christ; how this new creation evidences our interest in Christ; and then apply the whole.

I. WHY THE REGENERATING WORK OF THE SPIRIT IS CALLED A NEW CREATION. And the reason of this appellation is the analogy which is found between the work of regeneration and God's work in the first creation.

1. The same almighty *Author* who created the world creates this work of grace in the soul of man. "God, who commanded the light to shine out of darkness, hath shined in our hearts, to give the light of the knowledge of the glory of God in the face of Jesus Christ." 2 Cor. 4 : 6. The same powerful word which created the natural, creates also the spiritual light. It is as absurd for any man to say, I make myself to repent or believe, as it is to say, I made myself to exist.

2. The first thing that God created in the natural world was *light*, Gen. 1 : 3; and the first thing which God creates in the new creation is *the light of spiritual knowledge.* "And have put on the new man, which is renewed in knowledge after the image of him that created him." Col. 3 : 10.

3. Creation is *out of nothing.* It requires no preëxistent matter; it does not bring one thing out of another, but something out of nothing; it gives a being to that which before had no being. So it is also in the new creation. "Who hath called you out of darkness into his marvellous light; which in time past were not a people, but are now the people of God; which had not obtained mercy, but now have obtained mercy." 1 Peter 2 : 9, 10. The work of grace is not educed out of the power and principles of nature, but is a pure work of creation. The heathen philosophers could neither understand nor acknowledge the creation of the world, because it was repugnant to the maxim, out of nothing nothing can be made. Thus did they mistake through their reasonings;

and after the same manner some great pretenders to reason among us declare it an absurdity to affirm that the
work of grace is not virtually contained in nature.

4. The efficacy of *the Spirit of God* gave the world its
being by creation, Gen. 1 : 2 ; the Spirit of God moved
upon the face of the waters ; it hovered over chaos as the
wings of a bird over her eggs, as the same word is rendered, Deut. 32 : 11, imparting to the rude mass a quickening
influence. So in the new creation a quickening influence
must come from the Spirit of God. "So is every one that
is born of the Spirit." John 3 : 8. "That which is born
of the Spirit is spirit." John 3 : 6.

5. *The word of God was the instrument* of the first creation. "By the word of the Lord were the heavens made ;
and all the host of them by the breath of his mouth. For
he spake, and it was done ; he commanded, and it stood
fast." Psalm 33 : 6, 9. The word of God is also the instrument of the new creation in man. "Being born again,
not of corruptible seed, but of incorruptible, by the word
of God, which liveth and abideth for ever" 1 Peter,
1 : 23. So James 1 : 18, "Of his own will begat he us
with the word of truth." *Of his own will,* that was the
impulsive cause ; *with the word of truth,* that was the instrumental cause. Great respect and honor, love and
delight is due to the word upon this account, that it is the
instrument of our regeneration or new creation

6. *The same power which created the world still supports it*
in being ; the world owes its preservation as well as its
existence to the power of God. So it is with the new
creation, which entirely depends upon the preserving
power which first formed it. "Preserved in Jesus Christ"
Jude 1. "Who are kept by the power of God, through faith,
unto salvation." 1 Peter 1 : 5. As we live, move, and have
our being in God, Acts 17 : 28, so in a spiritual sense we
continue believing and delighting in God, without whose
continued influence upon our souls we could do neither.

7. *God surveyed the creation with complacence;* he beheld the works of his hands, and approved them as very good. Gen. 1 : 31. So also in the second creation; nothing pleases God more than the work of grace in his people. It is not an outward privilege of nature or gift of Providence which commends any man to God; circumcision is nothing, and uncircumcision is nothing, but a new creature. Gal. 6 : 15.

II. We inquire, IN WHAT RESPECTS every soul that is in Christ is renewed, or made a new creature?

1. He is renewed in his *state*, for he passes from death to life in his justification. 1 John 3 : 14. He was condemned by the law; he is now justified freely by grace, through the redemption which is in Christ : he was under the curse of the first covenant; he is now under the blessing of the new : he was afar off, but is now made nigh unto God : once a stranger, now of the household of God. Eph. 2 : 12, 13. O blessed change from a sad to a happy condition! "There is therefore now no condemnation to them which are in Christ Jesus." Rom. 8 : 1.

2. Every man in Christ is renewed in his *affections;* all the affections of his soul are renewed by regeneration : his understanding was dark, but now is light in the Lord, Eph. 5 : 8 ; his conscience was dead, or full of guilt and horror, but is now become tender, watchful, and full of peace, Heb. 9 : 14 ; his will was rebellious and inflexible, but is now obedient to the will of God, Psalm 110 : 3 ; his desires once pursued vanities, now they are set upon God, Isaiah 26 : 8 ; his love doted upon earthly subjects, now it is swallowed up in the infinite excellencies of God and Christ, Psalm 119 : 97 ; his joy was once in trifles, now his rejoicing is in Christ Jesus, Phil. 3 : 3 ; his fears once were about worldly things, now God is the object of his reverence, Acts 9 : 31, and sin the object of his dread, 2 Cor. 7 : 11 ; his expectations were only from this world, but now are from that to come. Heb. 6 : 19. Thus the

soul in its faculties and affections is renewed, and the members and senses of the body must be employed by it in new services; no more to be the weapons of unrighteousness, but instruments of service to Jesus Christ. Rom. 6 : 19.

3. The man in Christ is renewed in his *practice*. The regenerate not being what they were, cannot act as they once did. "And you hath he quickened, who were dead in trespasses and sins; wherein in time past ye walked according to the course of this world." Eph. 2 : 1, 2, 3. They were carried away, like water by the strength of the tide, by the influence of their corrupt natures and the customs of the world; but the case is now altered. So the apostle shows believers their old companions in sin, and tells them, "Such were some of you; but ye are washed, but ye are sanctified," 1 Cor. 6 : 11; as though he had said, The world is now altered with you, thanks be to the grace of God for it. This wonderful change of practice, which is so remarkable in all the regenerate, and immediately consequent upon their conversion, sets the world wondering at them. "Wherein they think it strange that ye run not with them to the same excess of riot, speaking evil of you." 1 Peter 4 : 4. They "think it strange." The original word signifies to stand and gaze as the hen does which has hatched partridge eggs, when she sees the chickens she has brought forth fly away from her. Thus do the men of the world stand amazed to see their old companions in sin, whose language was earthly, it may be profane, now praying, speaking of God, heaven, and things spiritual, having no more to do with them except by way of admonition: this amazes the world, and makes them look with admiration upon the people of God.

III. We are to inquire into THE PROPERTIES of this new creature. O how little do we know of the nature and operations of this new creature. But so far as God has revealed it to our weak understandings, we may speak of it.

1. The Scripture speaks of it as *a thing of great diffi-culty to be conceived by man.* "The wind bloweth where it listeth, and thou hearest the sound thereof, but canst not tell whence it cometh and whither it goeth; so is every one that is born of the Spirit." John 3 : 8. The origin of winds is a great difficulty in philosophy. We hear the voice of the wind, feel its force, and see its effects; but neither know whence it comes or whither it goes. Ask a man, Do you hear the wind blow? Yes. Do you feel it blow? Yes, very sensibly. Do you see the effects of it, rending and overturning the trees? Yes, very plainly. But can you describe its nature, or declare its original? No; that is a mystery which I do not understand. Just so it is with him that is born of the Spirit. The Holy Spirit of God, of whose nature and operations we under-stand but little, comes from heaven, quickens and influ-ences our souls, and mortifies our lusts by his almighty power. These effects of the Spirit in us we experimen-tally feel; but how the Spirit of God first entered into and quickened our souls, we understand little more than how the bones do grow in the womb of her that is with child. Eccles. 11 : 5. Therefore is the life of the new creature called a hidden life. Col. 3 : 3. Its nature is not only hidden from carnal men, but is in a very great measure unknown to spiritual men, though themselves are the subjects of it.

2. But though this life be a great mystery, yet, so far as it is known to us, the new creature is the most *beau-tiful and lovely* that ever God made; for the beauty of the Lord himself is upon it. The new man is created after God. Eph. 4 : 24. As the picture is drawn after the man, so this is God himself delineated by the Spirit upon the soul of man. Holiness is the beauty and glory of God; and in holiness the new creature is created after God's own image. Col. 3 : 10. The regenerate soul hereby be-comes holy, 1 John 3 : 3; not *essentially* holy, as God is,

nor yet *efficiently* holy, for the regenerate soul can neither make itself nor others holy. But the life of the new creature resembles the life of God in this, that as God lives to himself, so the new creature lives to God; as God loves holiness, so does the new creature; it is in these things formed after the image of God that created it. When God newly creates the soul of man, we are said to be "partakers of the divine nature." 2 Pet. 1 : 4. So that nothing can be communicated to men which so beautifies and adorns the soul as this new creation. Men do not resemble God as they are noble and rich, but as they are holy. An awful majesty sits upon the brow of the new creature, commanding men to do homage to it. Mark 6 : 20. Yea, such is the beauty of the new creature, that Christ, its author, is also its admirer. Song 4 : 2.

3. This new creature is created in man, upon *the highest design* that ever any work of God was wrought—salvation to the soul. When we receive the end of our faith, we receive the salvation of our soul: as death is the end of sin, so eternal life is the end of grace. The new creature, by the steady direction of its nature, takes its course as directly to God and to heaven, the place of its full enjoyment, as the rivers do to the ocean; it shows itself made for God by its workings after him; and as salvation is the end of the new creature, so it is the design of him that created it. "Now he that hath wrought us for the selfsame thing, is God." 2 Cor. 5 : 5. By this workmanship of his upon our souls he is now preparing and making them meet to be partakers of the inheritance of the saints in light. Col. 1 : 12.

4. This new creation is the most *necessary* work that God ever wrought upon the soul of man: the eternal well-being of his soul depends upon it; and without it no man shall see God. Heb. 12 : 14; and John 1 : 3, 5. Except ye be born again, ye cannot see the kingdom of God. Can you be saved without Christ? You know you

cannot. Can you have interest in Christ without the new creature? My text expressly tells you it can never be; for, "if any man be in Christ, he is a new creature." O reader, with whatever slight thoughts of this matter, and with however careless an eye thou readest these lines, yet know, thou must either be a new creature or be miserable for ever. If civility could save thee, why are not the heathen saved? If strictness of life could save thee, why did it not save the scribes and Pharisees? If a high profession of religion can save thee, why did it not save Judas, Hymeneus, and Philetus also? Nothing is more evident than this, that no repentance, obedience, self-denial, prayers, tears, reformations, or ordinances, without the new creation, avail any thing to the salvation of thy soul. The blood of Christ himself, without the new creature, never did and never will save auy man. Oh how necessary a work is the new creation! Circumcision avails nothing, and uncircumcision nothing, but a new creature.

5. The new creature is a *wonderful* creature. There are many wonders in the first creation: "The works of the Lord are great, sought out of all men that have pleasure therein." Psalm 111 : 2. But there are no wonders in nature like those in grace. Is it not the greatest wonder ever seen in the world, except the incarnation of the Son of God, to see the nature of man changed as it is by grace? to see lascivious Corinthians and idolatrous Ephesians become heavenly Christians? to see a cruel persecutor become a glorious confessor for Christ? Gal. 1 : 23; to see the mind of man, lately set in a strong bent to the world, taken from its lusts, and set on things spiritual and heavenly? Certainly it was not a greater display of divine power to see Lazarus come out of his sepulchre, than to see the carnal mind embrace Jesus Christ; it was not a greater wonder to see the dry bones in the valley move and come together, than it is to see a dead soul moving to Christ in the way of faith.

6. The new creature is *immortal*, and shall never see death. Grace is, in the soul of man, a well of water springing up unto eternal life. John 4 : 14. The new creature has a beginning and succession; and therefore might also have an end, as to any thing in its own nature. Experience also shows us that it is capable both of increasing and decreasing, and may be brought nigh unto death. Rev. 3 : 2. The work of the Spirit in believers may be ready to die; but its perpetuity flows out of God's covenant and promises, which make it immortal. When all other excellencies in man go away, as at death they will, Job 4 : 21, this remains : our gifts, our friends, our estates may leave us, but our graces will never die; they ascend with the soul into glory when death separates it from the body.

7. The new creature is *heavenly*. It is not born of flesh, nor of blood, nor of the will of man, but of God, John 1 : 13; its origin is heavenly, it is spirit born of Spirit, John 3 : 6; its centre is heaven, and thither are all its tendencies, Psalm 63 : 8; the food on which it lives are heavenly things, Psalm 4 : 6, 7; the object of all its delight is in heaven, "Whom have I in heaven but thee?" Psalm 73 : 25. The expectations of the new creature are all from heaven; it looks for little in this world, but waits for the coming of the Lord. The life of the new creature upon earth is a life of patient waiting for Christ; his desires and longings are after heaven. Phil. 1 : 23. The flesh indeed lingers, but the new creature hastens, and would fain be gone. 2 Cor. 5 : 2. It is not at home while here; it came from heaven, and cannot find rest until it comes there again.

8. The new creature is *active*. No sooner is it born but it is acting. "Behold, he prayeth." Acts 9 : 10. Activity is its very nature. "If we live in the Spirit, let us also walk in the Spirit." Gal. 5 : 25. Nor is it to be wondered at that it should be always active, seeing activity

in obedience was the end for which it was created. "For we are his workmanship, created in Christ Jesus unto good works," Eph. 2 : 10 ; and he that acts in religion from this principle of the new nature, will delight to do the will of God, and find the sweetest pleasure in the paths of duty.

9. The new creature is *thriving;* growing from strength to strength, 1 Pet. 2 : 2, and changing from glory to glory. 2 Cor. 3 : 18. The vigorous and constant striving of this new creature is to attain its just perfection and maturity. Phil. 3 : 11. It can endure no limits short of perfection ; every degree of strength it attains but sharpens its desires after higher degrees. Upon this account it greatly delights in the ordinances of God, the duties of religion, and the society of the saints, as they are helps in its great design.

10. The new creature is *wonderfully preserved.* There are many wonders of providence in the preservation of our natural lives, but none like those whereby the life of the new creature is preserved. There are times of temptation and desertion in which it is ready to die, Rev. 3 : 2 ; the degrees of its strength and liveliness are sometimes sadly abated and its comfortable workings intermitted, Rev. 2 : 4 ; the evidences of its being in us may be and often are darkened, 2 Pet. 1 : 9 ; and the soul may draw sad conclusions about the issue, concluding its life not only to be hazarded; but quite extinguished, Psalm 51 : 10–12 ; but though it be only to die, God wonderfully preserves it from death : it has its reviving as well as its fainting seasons.

IV. We will demonstrate THE NECESSITY OF THIS NEW CREATION to all that are in Christ, and by him expect to attain salvation.

1. From *the express will of God* revealed in Scripture. Search the Scriptures, and you shall find God has laid the whole stress of your eternal happiness by Jesus Christ upon this work of the Spirit in your soul. So our Saviour

told Nicodemus: "Verily, verily I say unto thee, except a man be born of water and of the Spirit, he cannot enter into the kingdom of God." John 3:5. Agreeable whereunto are those words of the apostle, "Without holiness no man shall see the Lord." Heb. 12:14. And though some may think that birthright privileges, ordinances, and the profession of religion may commend them to God's acceptance without this new creation, he shows them how ungrounded are all such hopes. "For in Christ Jesus neither circumcision availeth any thing, nor uncircumcision, but a new creature." Gal. 6:15. Christ and heaven are the gifts of God; he is at liberty to bestow them upon what terms he please; and this is the way, the only way, in which he will bring men by Christ unto glory.

2. This new creation is *the first part of the great salvation* we expect through Christ, and therefore without this all expectations of salvation must vanish. Salvation and renovation are inseparably connected. Our glory in heaven, if we rightly understand its nature, consists in two things—our assimilation to God, and our fruition of him; and both these begin with our renovation in this world. Here we begin to be changed into his image, 2 Cor. 3:18, for the new man is created after God. In the work of grace, God is said to begin that good work which is to be finished in the day of Christ. Phil. 1:6. Nothing can be more irrational than to imagine that the design or work should be finished which never had a beginning

3. So necessary is the new creation to all that expect salvation by Christ, that *without it heaven would be no heaven*, by reason of the unsuitableness of our carnal minds thereto. "The carnal mind is enmity against God," Rom. 8:7, and enmity excludes all complacency and delight. There is a necessity of a suitable frame of heart towards God in order to the complacent rest of our souls in him, and this temper is wrought by our new creation. "He that hath wrought us for the selfsame thing is God."

2 Cor. 5 : 5. Renovation, you see, is the moulding of a man's spirit into an agreeable temper, or making us meet for the inheritance of the saints in light. Col. 1 : 12.

From all which it follows, that since there can be no complacency in God without conformity to him, as is plain from 1 John 3 : 2, and from the nature of the thing itself, either God must become like us, which it would be blasphemy to imagine, or we must be made agreeable to God, which is what I am proving the necessity of.

4. There is an absolute necessity of this change to all that expect interest in Christ, since *all the marks and signs of such an interest belong to the new creature.* Look over all the signs of interest in Christ or salvation by him dispersed through the Scriptures, and you will still find purity of heart, Matt. 5 : 8 ; holiness both in principle and practice, Heb. 12 : 14 ; mortification of sin, Rom. 8 : 13 ; longing for Christ's appearance, 2 Tim. 4 : 8, with multitudes more of the same nature, constantly made the marks of our salvation by Christ. So that either we must have a *new Bible* or a *new heart;* for if these Scriptures be the true and faithful words of God, no unrenewed creature can see his face.

V. The last thing to be considered is, HOW THE NEW CREATION IS AN INFALLIBLE PROOF of the soul's interest in Christ.

1. Where all *the graces of the Spirit* are, interest in Christ must be certain ; and where the new creature is, there are all the saving graces of the Spirit ; for what is the new creature but the union of all special saving graces ? It is not this or that particular grace, as faith, or hope, or love to God, which constitutes the new creature, for these are but as so many branches of it ; but the new creature comprehends all the graces of the Spirit : "The fruit of the Spirit is love, joy, peace, long-suffering, gentleness, goodness, faith, meekness, temperance." Gal. 5 : 22, 23. Any one of the graces of the Spirit gives proof

of our interest in Christ; how much more, then, the new creature, which is the union of all the graces?

2. Where all *the causes* of an interest in Christ and all *the effects* of such an interest *appear*, there undoubtedly a real interest in Christ is found. But in the new creature you find the cause, the electing love of God, from which the new creature is inseparable, 1 Pet. 1 : 2, as it is from interest in Christ and union with him. Eph. 2 : 10 ; 1 : 4–6. And you also find the effects of an interest in Christ in the new creature. There are all the fruits of obedience, for we are created in Christ Jesus unto good works. Eph. 2 : 10 ; Rom. 7 : 4. There is opposition to sin, "He that is begotten of God keepeth himself, and that wicked one toucheth him not." 1 John 5 : 18. There is love to the people of God, "Every one that loveth is born of God." 1 John 4 : 7. There is a conscientious respect to the duties of both tables, for the new creature is created after God in righteousness and true holiness. Eph. 4 : 24. There is perseverance in the ways of God and victory over all temptations, "for whosoever is born of God overcometh the world." 1 John 5 : 4.

CHAPTER XXVI

THE NEW CREATURE—CONTINUED

"Therefore if any man be in Christ, he is a new creature: old things are
passed away; behold, all things are become new." 2 COR. 5:17

IN the previous discourse we drew from this scripture
the doctrine, that *God's creating of a new supernatural work
of grace in the soul of any man, is infallible evidence of a saving interest in Jesus Christ.* We have seen why the regenerating work of the Spirit is called a new creation; in
what respect every soul in Christ is renewed; what are
the properties of this new creature; the necessity of this
new creation; and how it evidences our interest in Christ.
We now come to make A PRACTICAL IMPROVEMENT of the
subject. Is the "new creature" the sure and infallible
evidence of our saving interest in Christ? Then,

INFERENCE 1. *In how miserable a state are all unrenewed
souls!* They can lay no claim to Christ while in that state,
and therefore are under an impossibility of salvation. O
reader, if this be the state of thy soul, better had it been
for thee not to have been God's natural workmanship as a
man, except thou be also his workmanship as a new man.
So Christ speaks of Judas, that son of perdition, "Good
were it for that man if he had never been born," Mark
14 : 21; for what is being without the comfort of it; what
is life without the joy and pleasure of it? A lost being is
without comfort; no glimpse of light shines into that
darkness: they shall indeed see the light and joy of the
saints in glory; they shall see Abraham and Isaac and
Jacob in the kingdom of God, but they themselves shall
be shut out. Luke 13 : 28. Such a sight is so far from
giving comfort, that it will be the aggravation of torment.

O it is better to have no being at all, than to have a being only to capacitate a man for misery ; to desire death while death flies from him. Rev. 4 : 6. Think on it, reader, and lay it to thy heart : better thou hadst died from the womb, better the knees had prevented thee, and the breasts which thou hast sucked, than that thou shouldst live and die a stranger to the new birth.

2. On the contrary, we may hence learn *what cause regenerate souls have to bless God for the day wherein they were born.* O what a privileged state does the new birth bring men into ! It is possible for the present they understand it not ; for many believers are like a great heir lying in the cradle, that knows not to what an estate he is born : nevertheless, on the day wherein we become new creatures by regeneration, we have a firm title to all the privileges of the sons of God. John 1 : 12, 13. God becomes our Father not only by nature, but by adoption and by regeneration, a much dearer relation. In that day the image of God is restored, Eph. 4 : 24, that is, both the health and beauty of the soul. In that day we are begotten again to a lively hope, 1 Pet. 1 : 3, a hope worth more than ten thousand worlds in life and in death. Some have kept their birthday as a day of rejoicing, but none have more cause to rejoice that ever they were born, than those that are new-born.

3. *Learn from hence, that the work of grace is wholly supernatural ;* it is a creation, and creation-work is above the power of the creature. No power but that which gave being to the world can give being to the new creature. This creature is not born of flesh, or of blood, nor of the will of man, but of God. John 1 : 13. The character of this new creature speaks its origin to be above the power of nature. When God, therefore, puts the question, Who maketh thee to differ ; and what hast thou that thou hast not received ? let thy soul, reader, answer it with all humility and thankfulness : It is thou, Lord, thou only that

hast made me to differ from another; and what I have received, I have received from thy free grace.

4. If the work of grace be a new creation, *let not the parents and friends of the unregenerate despair of their conversion, how great soever their present discouragements.* If it had been possible for a man to have seen the rude chaos before the Spirit of God moved upon it, would he not have said, Can such a beautiful order of beings spring out of this dark lump? Surely it would have been very hard for a man to imagine it. It may be, you see no encouraging inclinations in your friends towards God and spiritual things; nay, possibly they are filled with enmity against them; they deride serious piety wherever they behold it: this indeed is very sad; but yet remember, the work of grace is from above. God, that commanded the light to shine out of darkness, can shine into their hearts, to give them the light of the knowledge of the glory of God in the face of Jesus Christ. He can say to the dry bones, Live; to the proud and stubborn heart, Yield thyself to the will of God. God can yet make thee rejoice over thy most hopeless relations; to say, with the father of the prodigal, "This my son was dead, and is alive again; he was lost, and is found. And they began to be merry." Luke 15:24. Difficulties are with men, not with God: he works in conversion by a power which is able to subdue all things unto itself.

5. If none but new creatures be in Christ, *how small a remnant among men belong to him.* Among the multitude of rational creatures inhabiting this world, how very few are new creatures; how few are for Jesus Christ. Look over our cities, towns, and villages around you, and how few will you find that speak the language or do the works of new creatures. How few have ever had any awakening convictions; and how many of those that have been convinced have never come to the new birth. The more cause have they whom God has indeed regenerated, to admire the riches of his distinguishing mercy to them.

6. If the change by grace be a new creation, *how marvellous a change does regeneration make upon men!* The new creation denotes a change both in the state and temper of men; they come out of gross darkness into marvellous and heavenly light, 1 Peter 2 : 9 ; Eph. 5 : 8 ; their condition, disposition, and conversation are new.

And yet this marvellous change, great as it is, is not alike evident and *clearly discernible* in all new creatures ; for the work of grace is wrought in the people of God with much diversity of manner. Some are changed from a state of notorious profaneness to serious godliness. In these the change is very evident—all the neighborhood rings with it; while in others it is more insensibly distilled in their tender years by the blessing of God upon religious education. Though a great change be wrought, yet much natural corruption remains, which is a ground of fear and doubting ; they see not how such corruptions are consistent with the new creature. In some, too, the new creature shows itself mostly in the affections, in desires after God, and but little in the clearness of the understanding and strength of the judgment ; for want of which many are entangled and kept in darkness most of their days. Some Christians are also more tried by temptations from Satan than others, and these clouds darken the work of grace in them. And there is great variety in the natural temper of the regenerate : some are of a more melancholy, fearful, and suspicious temper than others, and are therefore much longer held under doubtings and trouble of spirit. Nevertheless, what differences soever these things make, the change made by grace is a marvellous change.

7. *How inconsistent are carnal ways with the spirit of Christians,* who being new creatures, can never delight in their former sinful companions and practices. Those things seem now most unsuitable and detestable, how pleasant soever they once were ; that which they counted their liberty is now reckoned their greatest bondage ; that which

was their glory is now their shame : "What fruit had ye then in those things whereof ye are now ashamed? for the end of those things is death." Romans 6 : 21. They will freely confess what madmen they once were. None can censure their former conversation more freely than they themselves do. 1 Tim. 1 : 13, 14.

8. If none be in Christ but new creatures, and the new creation makes such a change as has been described, we may be convinced *how many deceive themselves and run into dangerous and fatal mistakes.*

But before I urge this reflection, I desire none may make a perverse use of it. Let not the wicked conclude from hence that there is no such thing as true religion in the world, or that all who profess it are hypocrites ; neither let the godly injure themselves by that which is designed for their benefit. Let none conclude, that as there are so many mistakes about the new creature, assurance must be impossible, as the papists affirm it to be. The proper use of this doctrine is to undeceive pretenders, and to awaken all to a more thorough search of their own state. These cautions being remembered, let all men be convinced of the following truths :

(1.) *That the reformation of the profane is a different thing from the new creature:* moral virtue is one thing, the influence of the regenerating Spirit is quite another, however some have studied to confound them. Some of the heathen excelled in moral virtues : Plato, Aristides, Seneca, and multitudes more, outvied many professed Christians in justice, temperance, patience, etc., yet were perfect strangers to the new creation. A man may be very strict and temperate, and yet be a perfect stranger to regeneration. John 3 : 10.

(2.) *Many strong convictions of sin may be found where the new creature is never formed.* Conviction is preparative for the new creature, as the blossoms of the tree are to the fruit ; but as fruit does not always follow where blossoms appear, so neither doth the new creature follow all convictions of sin. Conviction is a common work of the Spirit; but the new creature is formed only in God's people. Convictions may vanish away, and the man under trouble for sin may return again, with the dog to his vomit, and the sow that was washed to her wallowing in the mire, 2 Pet. 2 : 22 ; but the new creature never perishes, nor can consist with such a return to sin.

(3.) *Excellent gifts, fitting men for service in the church of God, may be where the new creature is not;* for these are dispensed by the Spirit both to the regenerate and unregenerate. "Many will say to me in that day, Lord, Lord, have we not prophesied in thy name?" Matt. 7 : 22. Gifts are attainable by study ; prayer and preaching may be reduced to an art; but regeneration is wholly supernatural. Sin, in dominion, may consist with excellent gifts, but is wholly incompatible with the new creature. In a word, these things are so different from the new creature that they often prove the greatest obstacles to the regenerating work of the Spirit. Let no man, therefore, trust to things whereby multitudes deceive and destroy their souls. Reader, it may cost thee many an aching head to attain gifts, but thou wilt find an aching heart for sin if ever God makes thee a new creature.

(4.) *Multitudes of religious duties may be performed by men in whom the new creature was never formed.* Though all new creatures perform the duties of religion, all that perform those duties are not new creatures ; regeneration is not the only root from which the outward duties of religion spring. "Yet they seek me daily, and delight to know my ways, as a nation that did righteousness, and forsook not the ordinance of their God : they ask of me the ordinances of justice ; they take delight in approaching to God." Isa. 58 : 2. These are but slippery foundations for men to build their hopes upon.

9. Let me, therefore, persuade every man to *try the*

state of his heart in this matter, and closely consider this great question : Am I indeed a new creature ; or am I an old creature still, in a new creature's dress? Some light may be drawn from the following considerations :

(1.) Weigh and consider well the *antecedents* of the new creation : Have those things passed upon your souls which ordinarily make way for the new creature in whomsoever the Lord forms it? Has the Lord opened the eyes of your understanding in the knowledge of sin and of Christ? Has he showed you both your disease and remedy, by a light shining from heaven into your soul? Acts 26 : 18. Has he brought home the word with power and efficacy upon your heart to convince and humble you? Rom. 7 : 9; 1 Thess. 1 : 5. Have these convictions overthrown your vain confidences, and brought you to a great concern and inward distress of soul, making you cry, What shall I do to be saved? These are the ways of the Spirit in the formation of the new creature. Acts 16 : 29; 2 : 37. If no such work of the Spirit have passed upon your heart, you have no ground for confidence that the new creature is formed in you.

(2.) Consider the workings of spirit which ordinarily *accompany* the production of the new creature, and judge impartially between God and your own soul whether they have been the workings of your heart. Has your spirit been composed to the greatest *seriousness* and most solemn consideration of things eternal, as the hearts of all are whom God regenerates ? When the Lord is about this work upon the soul of man, whatever levity was there before, it is banished ; for now heaven and hell, life and death, are before a man's eyes, and these are the most awful subjects that ever our thoughts conversed with. A man of the most airy mind, when brought to the sense of these things, "says of laughter, It is mad ; and of mirth, What doeth it?" Eccl. 2 : 2. *A meek and humble* frame of heart accompanies the new creation ; the soul is weary and heavy-laden. Matt. 11 : 28. Convictions of sin bring down the pride of man and empty him of his vain conceits. It is with such as it was with Jerusalem, that lofty city, "Woe to Ariel, to Ariel, the city where David dwelt! Thou shalt be brought down, and shalt speak out of the ground, and thy speech shall be low out of the dust." Isaiah 29 : 1, 4. Ariel signifies the lion of God: so Jerusalem was in her prosperity, other cities trembled at her voice; but when God brought her down by humbling judgments, then she whispered out of the dust. So it is in this case. A *longing*, *thirsting* frame of spirit accompanies the new creation; the desires of the soul are ardent after Christ; never did the hireling long for the shadow as the weary soul does for Christ, and rest in him. If no such frames have accompanied that which you take for your new birth, you have the greatest reason to suspect yourself under a delusion.

(3.) Weigh well *the effects and consequents of the new creature*, and consider whether such fruits as these are found in your heart and life.

Wherever the new creature is formed, a man's *course of life* is changed. "That ye put off concerning the former conversation the old man, which is corrupt according to the deceitful lusts; and be renewed in the spirit of your mind." Eph. 4 : 22, 23. The new creature cannot but blush and be ashamed of the old creature's conversation. Rom. 6 : 21.

The new creature continually opposes and *conflicts with sin* in the heart. The Spirit lusteth against the flesh. Gal. 5 : 17. Grace can no more mix with sin than oil with water. If there be no conflict with sin in thy soul, or if that conflict be only between the conscience and affections, light in the one struggling with lust in the other, thou wantest that fruit which should evidence thee to be a new creature.

The affections of the new creature are set upon *heaven-*

ly and spiritual things.   Col. 3 : 1, 2; Eph. 4 : 23; Rom. 8 : 5.
If therefore thy heart be habitually earthly, and driving
eagerly after the world as the great business of thy life,
deceive not thyself, this is not the fruit of the new creature,
nor consistent with it.

The new creature is *prayerful,* living by its daily communion with God.   Zech. 12 : 10 ; Acts 9 : 11.   If therefore thou art a prayerless soul, or if, in thy prayers, thou
art a stranger to communion with God—if there be no
brokenness of heart for sin in thy confessions, no melting
affections for Christ and holiness in thy supplications, surely
Satan does but delude thy soul in persuading thee that
thou art a new creature.

The new creature is *restless,* after falls into sin, until it
has recovered peace and pardon ; it cannot endure a state
of defilement.   Psa. 51 : 8–12.   It is with the conscience
of a new creature under sin, as with the eye when any
thing offends it, it cannot cease weeping till it has wept
it out ; and in the same restless state is the soul under
the hiding of God's face.   If therefore thou canst sin and
sin again without a burdensome sense of sin or solicitude
to recover purity and peace, with the light of God's countenance shining, as in days past, upon thy soul, thou hast
not the signs of a new creature in thee.

10. If the new creation be evidence of our interest in
Christ, *let me persuade all that are in Christ to prove themselves
such by walking as becomes new creatures.*   The new creature
is born from above, all its tendencies are heavenward ; set
your affections then on things that are above, and let your
conversation be in heaven.   If you live earthly and sensual lives as others do, you must oppose your new nature
therein : and can those actions be pleasant to you which
are done with so much regret ; wherein you must offer a
kind of violence to your own hearts ?   Earthly delights
and sorrows are expected in the unregenerate and sensual,
but exceedingly contrary to that Spirit by whom you are

renovated. If ever you would act becoming the nature of new creatures, seek earthly things with submission, enjoy them with caution, resign them with cheerfulness; and thus "let your moderation be known unto all men." Philemon 4, 5. Let your hearts daily meditate and your tongues discourse about heavenly things; be exceeding tender of sin, punctual in duty, and convince the world that you are of another spirit.

11. Let every new creature be *cheerful and thankful:* if God has renewed you, and thus changed the frame and temper of your hearts, he has bestowed the richest mercy upon you that heaven or earth affords. A new creature may be called one among a thousand: it is also an everlasting work never to be destroyed, as all natural works of God must be. It is carried on by almighty power, through unspeakable opposition. Eph. 1 : 19. The exceeding greatness of God's power produces it; indeed, no less is required to enlighten the mind, break the heart, and bow the will of man; and the same almighty power which at first created it, is necessary to be continued every moment to preserve it. 1 Pet. 1 : 5. The new creature is a mercy which draws a train of invaluable mercies after it. Eph. 2 : 13, 14 ; 1 Cor. 3 : 20. When God has given us a new nature, he dignifies us with a new name, Rev. 2 : 17 ; brings us into a new covenant, Jer. 31 : 33 ; begets us again to a new hope, 1 Pet. 1 : 3 ; and entitles us to a new inheritance. John 1 : 12, 13. The new creature, through Christ, makes our persons and duties acceptable with God. Gal. 6 : 15. In a word, it is the wonderful work of God, of which we may say, "This is the Lord's doing, and it is marvellous in our eyes." There are unsearchable wonders in its generation, operation, and preservation. Let all therefore whom the Lord has thus renewed, fall down at his feet in humble admiration of the unsearchable riches of free grace, and never open their mouths to complain under any adverse providences of God

CHAPTER XXVII

CRUCIFYING THE FLESH, OR THE MORTIFICATION OF SIN

"And they that are Christ's have crucified the flesh, with the affections and lusts." GAL. 5:24

Two great trials of our interest in Christ have been considered; we now proceed to a third, crucifying the flesh, or the mortification of sin. "They that are Christ's have crucified the flesh." The design of the apostle in the context was to heal the unchristian collisions among the Galatians, prevailing, by the instigation of Satan, to the breach of brotherly love. To cure this, he urges four weighty arguments.

1. The great commandment to love one another; upon which the whole law, that is, the duties of the second table, depend.

2. He dissuades them from the consideration of the sad result of their bitter contests and detractions, their mutual ruin.

3. From the contrariety of these practices to the Spirit of God, by whom they all professed to be governed.

4. From the inconsistency of these or any other lusts of the flesh with an interest in Christ: "They that are Christ's have crucified the flesh." As if he had said, You all profess to be members of Christ, followers of him; but how inconsistent are these practices with such a profession. Is this the fruit of the dovelike Spirit of Christ? Are these the fruits of your faith and professed mortification? Shall the sheep of Christ fight like furious beasts of prey? "They that are Christ's have crucified the flesh, with the affections and lusts." So much for the order of

the words, which are themselves a proposition, wherein we consider,

1. The *subject* of the proposition, they that are Christ's, namely, true Christians, real members of Christ; such as have given themselves up to be governed by him and are actuated by his Spirit: such, all such persons, and none but such.

2. The *predicate*, they "have crucified the flesh, with the affections and lusts." By flesh, we are here to understand the workings of corrupt nature; and by the affections, not the natural, but the inordinate affections, for Christ does not destroy, but regulates the affections of those that are in him; and by crucifying the flesh, we are not to understand the perfect subduing of corrupt nature, but the deposing of corruption from its dominion in the soul—its dominion is taken away, though its life be prolonged for a season. But as death surely though slowly follows crucifixion, it is so in the mortification of sin, and therefore what the apostle in this place calls *crucifying*, he calls elsewhere mortifying, "If ye, through the Spirit, do *mortify*"—the Greek word means *put to death*—"the deeds of the body," Rom. 8 : 13 ; but in this place he calls it crucifying, to show not only the conformity between the death of Christ and the death of sin in respect of shame, pain, and lingering slowness, but to denote also the principal means of mortification, namely, the death or cross of Jesus Christ, in virtue whereof believers mortify the corruptions of their flesh, the great persuasives to mortification being drawn from the sufferings of Christ for sin. In a word, he does not say, They that believe Christ was crucified for sin, are Christ's ; but, They, and they only, are his who feel as well as profess the efficacy of the sufferings of Christ, in the mortification of their lusts and sinful affections. The doctrine taught is, that

A saving interest in Christ may be inferred from the crucifying or mortifying of the flesh, with its affections and lusts.

This is fully confirmed by those words of the apostle,

"For if we have been planted together in the likeness of his death, we shall be also in the likeness of his resurrection: knowing this, that our old man is crucified with him, that the body of sin might be destroyed, that henceforth we should not serve sin; for he that is dead is free from sin. Now if we be dead with Christ, we believe that we shall also live with him." Rom. 6 : 5, 6, 8.

Mark the force of the apostle's reasoning: if we have been planted into the likeness of his death, namely, by the mortification of sin, which resembles the manner of Christ's death, we shall be also in the likeness of his resurrection; because the mortification of sin is an undoubted evidence of the union of such a soul with Christ, the very groundwork of that blessed and glorious resurrection. Therefore he says, "Reckon ye also yourselves to be dead indeed unto sin, but alive unto God, through Jesus Christ our Lord." As if he had said, Reason thus with yourselves: these mortifying influences of the death of Christ are unquestionable presages of your future blessedness, God never taking this course with any but those who are in Christ and are to be glorified with him. The death of your sin is as clear evidence as any thing can be of your spiritual life for the present, and of your eternal life with God hereafter. Mortification is the evidence of your union, and that union is the groundwork and pledge of your glorification; and so you ought to reckon or reason the case with yourselves. In illustrating this point, I shall open and confirm these five things: what the mortification or crucifixion of sin imports; why this work of the Spirit is expressed by crucifying; why all that are in Christ must be so crucified or mortified unto sin; what is the evangelical principle of mortification; and how the mortification of sin evinces our interest in Christ.

1. What the mortification or crucifixion of sin IMPORTS. And for clearness, I shall first show what *is not* intended by the Spirit of God in this expression.

1. The crucifying of the flesh does not imply *the total abolition of sin in believers*, or the destruction of its being and existence in them for the present; sanctified souls put off their corruptions with their dead bodies at death. This will be the effect of our future glorification, not of our present sanctification. Sin exists in the most mortified believer in the world, Rom. 7 : 17; it still acts in the regenerate soul, Gal. 5 : 17; yea, notwithstanding its crucifixion in believers, it may, in respect to single acts, surprise and captivate them. Psalm 65 : 3; Rom. 7 : 23. This therefore is not the intention of the Spirit of God in this expression.

2. Nor does the crucifixion of sin consist in the suppression of the *external acts* of sin only; for sin may reign over the souls of men, while it does not break forth in open actions. 2 Pet. 2 : 20; Matt. 12 : 43. Many a man shows a white hand who has a very foul heart.

3. The crucifixion of the flesh does not consist in the *cessation* of the external acts of sin; for in that respect the lusts of men may die of their own accord, a kind of natural death. The members of the body are the weapons of unrighteousness, as the apostle calls them; age or sickness may so blunt or break those weapons, that the soul cannot use them to such sinful purposes as it was wont to do in the vigorous seasons of life: not that there is less sin in the heart, but that there is less strength in the body. Like an old soldier, who has as much skill and delight as ever in military actions; but age and hard service have so enfeebled him that he can no longer follow the camp.

4. The crucifixion of sin does not consist in the *castigation of the body* by penances, stripes, fasting, and tiresome pilgrimages. This may pass for mortification among papists, but never was any lust of the flesh destroyed by this rigor. Christians indeed are bound not to indulge and pamper the body, which is the instrument of sin; nor yet must we think that the spiritual corruptions of the

soul feel the stripes inflicted upon the body. See Col. 2 : 23. It is not superstition but religion which destroys corruption ; it is faith in Christ's blood, not the spilling of our own, which gives sin the mortal wound.

But if you inquire, what then *is implied* in the mortification or crucifixion of sin, I answer,

1. It necessarily implies the soul's *implantation into Christ* and union with him : "They that are Christ's have crucified the flesh." Without this all attempts are ineffectual : "When we were in the flesh, the motions of sins which were by the law did work in our members to bring forth fruit unto death." Rom. 7 : 5. Sin was then in its full dominion ; no abstinence or outward severity, no purposes or solemn vows could mortify or destroy it ; there must be an implantation into Christ, before there can be any crucifixion of sin. What believer has not in the days of his first conviction tried all external means of mortifying sin, and found all to be to as little purpose as the binding of Samson with green withes? But when he has come to act faith upon the death of Christ, the design of mortification has succeeded.

2. Mortification of sin implies the *agency of the Spirit of God* in that work, without whose aid all our endeavors must be fruitless. Of this work we may say, "Not by might, nor by power, but by my Spirit, saith the Lord." Zech. 4 : 6. When the apostle would show by what hand this work is performed, he thus speaks : "If ye through the Spirit do mortify the deeds of the body, ye shall live." Rom. 8 : 13. The duty is ours, but the power whereby we perform it is God's. The Spirit is the only successful combatant against the lusts that war in our members. Gal. 5 : 17. It is true, this excludes not our endeavors, for it is *we through the Spirit* who mortify the deeds of the body ; but all our endeavors without the Spirit's aid avail nothing.

3. The crucifixion of sin necessarily implies *the subver-*

sion of its dominion in the soul : a mortified sin cannot be a reigning sin. Rom. 6 : 12–14. Two things constitute the dominion of sin—the fulness of its power, and the soul's subjection to it. The fulness of its power rises from the pleasure it gives to the corrupt heart of man. It seems to be as necessary as the right hand, as useful as the right eye, Matt. 5 : 29 ; but the mortified heart is dead to the profits of sin ; it has no pleasure in it ; it becomes its daily complaint. Mortification presupposes the illumination of the mind and conviction of the conscience ; by reason whereof sin cannot blind the mind, or bewitch and ensnare the will and affections as it was wont to do, consequently its dominion over the soul is destroyed.

4. The crucifying of the flesh implies a *gradual weakening of the power of sin* in the soul. The death of the cross was a slow and lingering death, and the crucified person grew weaker and weaker every hour ; so it is in the mortification of sin, the soul is still cleansing itself from all filthiness of the flesh and spirit, and perfecting holiness in the fear of God. 2 Cor. 7 : 1. And as the body of sin is weakened, so the inward man, or the new creature is "renewed day by day." 2 Cor. 4 : 16. Sanctification is a progressive work of the Spirit ; and as holiness roots itself deeper in the soul, so the power of sin abates and sinks until at length it is swallowed up in victory.

5. The crucifying of the flesh denotes the believer's *application of spiritual means* and instruments for the destruction of it. There is nothing which a gracious heart more vehemently desires than the death of sin and perfect deliverance from it, Rom. 7 : 24 ; the sincerity of which desires manifests itself in the application of all God's remedies : such are daily watching against the occasions of sin, "I have made a covenant with mine eyes," Job 31 : 1 ; more than ordinary vigilance over their special sin, "I kept myself from mine iniquity," Psa. 18 : 23 ; earnest cries to heaven for preventing grace, "Keep back thy ser-

vant also from presumptuous sins, let them not have dominion over me," Psa. 19 : 13 ; deep humblings of soul for sins past, an excellent preventive of future sins : in "that ye sorrowed after a godly sort, what carefulness it wrought," 2 Cor. 7 : 11 ; care to give no advantage to sin by making provision for the flesh to fulfil the lusts thereof, as others do, Rom. 13 : 13, 14 ; willingness to bear due reproofs for sin, "Let the righteous smite me, it shall be a kindness." Psalm 141 : 5. These and such like means of mortification regenerate souls are daily using for the death of sin.

II. We shall examine the reasons why this work of the Spirit is expressed under the expression of CRUCIFYING THE FLESH. The reason is, the resemblance which the mortification of sin bears to the death of the cross, which appears in five particulars.

1. The death of the cross was a *painful death,* and the mortification of sin is a very painful work, Matt. 5 : 29 ; it is as the cutting off our right hands and plucking out our right eyes ; it will cost many tears and groans, prayers, and strong cries to heaven, before one sin will be mortified. On account of the difficulty of this work, the Scripture says, "Strait is the gate, and narrow is the way, that leadeth unto life, and few there be that find it," Matt. 7 : 14 ; and that the righteous themselves are "scarcely saved."

1. The death of the cross was *universally painful ;* every member, every sinew, every nerve was subject to tormenting pain. So in the mortification of sin, it is not this or that particular member, but the whole body of sin that is to be destroyed, Rom. 6 : 6 ; and accordingly the conflict is in every faculty of the soul ; for the Spirit of God, by whose aid sin is mortified, combats with sin as sin, and for that reason with every sin in every faculty of the soul.

3. The death of the cross was *lingering,* denying to them that suffered it the favor of a quick dispatch ; so it

is in the death of sin. Though the Spirit of God be mortifying it day by day, it is a truth sealed by the experience of all believers, that sin is long in dying. And if we ask a reason of this dispensation of God, this seems to be one: corruptions in believers, like the Canaanites in the land of Israel, are left to prove the people of God, to keep us watching, praying, and believing; wondering at the riches of pardoning and preserving mercy all our days.

4. The death of the cross was very *shameful;* they that died thus were loaded with ignominy; their crimes were exposed to public view: after this manner dieth sin—a very shameful and ignominious death. Every true believer draws up a charge against it in every prayer, condemns it in every confession, bewails the evil of it with tears, making sin as odious as he can find words to express it. "O my God, I am ashamed, and blush to lift up my face to thee." Ezra 9:6. So Daniel in his confession, "O Lord, righteousness belongeth unto thee; but unto us confusion of face, as at this day," Dan. 9:7 Nor can it grieve any believer in the world to accuse and be filled with shame for sin, while he remembers that all the shame and confusion of face which he takes to himself goes to the vindication and honor of God. As David was content to be more vile still for God, so it pleases the heart of a Christian to advance the glory of God by exposing his own shame in humble confessions of sin.

5. The death of the cross was not natural, but *violent.* Such is the death of sin: it dies not of its own accord, as nature dieth in the aged; for if the Spirit of God did not kill it, it would live to eternity. Sin can live to eternity in the fire of God's wrath; so that either it must die a violent death by the hand of the Spirit, or it never dies at all.

III. WHY ALL THAT ARE IN CHRIST MUST BE SO CRUCIFIED OR MORTIFIED UNTO SIN. And the necessity of this will appear divers ways.

1. From the *contrariety between Christ and unmortified lust*. "These are contrary the one to the other." Gal. 5 : 17. There is a threefold inconsistency between Christ and such corruptions. They are contrary to the holiness of Christ : "Whosoever abideth in him sinneth not : whosoever sinneth hath not seen him, neither known him," 1 John 3 : 6 ; that is, whosoever is thus plunged into the lust of the flesh can have no communion with the pure and holy Saviour. There is also an inconsistency between such sin and the honor of Christ : "Let every one that nameth the name of Christ depart from iniquity," 2 Tim. 2 : 19 ; as Alexander said to a soldier of his name, Remember thy name is Alexander, and do nothing unworthy of that name. Unmortified lusts are also contrary to the government of Christ : "If any man will come after me, let him deny himself, and take up his cross daily, and follow me." Luke 9 : 23. These are the self-denying terms upon which men are admitted into Christ's service ; and without mortification and self-denial he allows no man to call him Lord and Master.

2. The necessity of mortification appears from the *necessity of conformity between Christ the Head, and the members of his mystical body;* for how uncomely would it be to see a holy, heavenly Christ leading a company of unclean and sensual members. "Take my yoke upon you, and learn of me, for I am meek and lowly." Matt. 11 : 29. As though he had said, It would be monstrous to the world to behold a company of lions and wolves following a meek and harmless lamb—men of raging and unmortified lusts owning me for their head of government. And again, 1 John 2 : 6, "He that saith he abideth in him, ought himself also so to walk, even as he walked." As if he had said, Either imitate Christ in your practice, or never make pretensions to Christ in your profession. This was what the apostle complained of : For many walk, of whom I have told you often, and now tell you, even weep-

ing, that they are the enemies of the cross of Christ. Phil.
3 : 18. Men cannot put a greater dishonor upon Christ
than by making his name a cloak to their lusts.

3. The necessity of crucifying the flesh appears from
the method of salvation as stated in the gospel. God everywhere requires the practice of mortification, under pain of
damnation. "Wherefore if thy hand or thy foot offend
thee, cut them off, and cast them from thee ; it is better
for thee to enter into life halt or maimed, rather than having two hands or two feet to be cast into everlasting fire."
Matt. 18 : 8. The gospel allows no hopes of salvation
unaccompanied with serious endeavors of mortification.
" Every man that hath this hope in him purifieth himself,
even as he is pure." 1 John 3 : 3. It was one special
end of Christ's coming into the world, to save his people
from their sins, Matt. 1 : 21 ; nor will he be a Saviour to
any who remain under the dominion of their lusts.

4. *The whole current of the gospel* puts us under the necessity of mortification. Gospel precepts have respect to
this : "Mortify therefore your members which are upon
the earth," Col. 3 : 5 ; "Be ye holy, for I am holy." 1 Pet.
1 : 15. Gospel precedents have respect unto this : "Wherefore, seeing we also are compassed about with so great a
cloud of witnesses, let us lay aside every weight, and the
sin which doth so easily beset us." Heb. 12 : 1. Gospel
threatenings are written for this end, and press mortification : "If ye live after the flesh, ye shall die." Romans
8 : 13. " The wrath of God is revealed from heaven against
all ungodliness and unrighteousness of men." Rom. 1 : 18.
The promises of the gospel are written designedly to promote it : " Having therefore these promises, dearly beloved,
let us cleanse ourselves from all filthiness of the flesh and
spirit, perfecting holiness in the fear of God." 2 Cor.
7 : 1. But in vain are all these things written in the
Scriptures, except mortification be the daily practice of
professors.

5. Mortification is the very *design* of our regeneration and the imparting of the principles of grace. "If we live in the Spirit, let us walk in the Spirit." Gal. 5 : 25. In vain were the habits of grace planted, if the fruits of holiness and mortification be not produced. Yea, mortification is not only the design, but a special part of our sanctification.

6. If mortification be not the daily endeavor of believers, *the way to heaven* does not answer to Christ's description of it. He tells us, "Wide is the gate and broad is the way that leadeth to destruction, and many there be which go in thereat ; because strait is the gate and narrow is the way which leadeth unto life, and few there be that find it." Matt. 7 : 13, 14. Either Christ must be mistaken in the account he gave of the way to glory, or all unmortified persons are out of the way ; for what makes the way of salvation narrow, but the difficulties and severities of mortification?

7. He that denies the necessity of mortification confounds all *discriminating marks between saints and sinners*, pulls down the pale of distinction, and lets the world into the church. It is a great design of the gospel to preserve the boundaries between the one and the other. Romans 2 : 7, 8 ; 8 : 1–13. But if men may be Christians without mortification, we may as well go into the worst places among the sottish crew of sinners, and say, Here are those that are redeemed by the blood of Christ, here are his disciples and followers, as to seek them in the purest churches or most strictly religious families.

IV. We inquire into THE TRUE PRINCIPLE of mortification. There are many ways attempted for the mortification of sin, and many rules laid down to guide men in that great work, some of which are very trifling and impertinent : such are those prescribed by Popish votaries. But the sanctifying Spirit is the only effectual principle of mortification ; and without him, no resolutions, vows, or any other external endeavors can avail to the mortification of one sin. The heathen have prescribed many rules for the suppression of vice; Aristides, Seneca, and Cato were renowned among them on this account. Formal Christians have also gone far in the reformation of their lives, but could never attain true mortification: formality pares off the excrescences of vice, but never kills the root of it; it usually recovers again, and their souls relapse into a worse condition than before. Matt. 12: 43, 44; 2 Peter 2: 20.

This work of mortification is peculiar to the Spirit of God, Rom. 8:13; Gal. 5:17; and the Spirit becomes a principle of mortification in believers in two ways.

1. The Spirit of God *implants habits of a contrary nature* which are destructive to sin. 1 John 5:4; Acts 15:9. Grace is to corruption what water is to fire, between which there is a contrariety both in nature and operation. Gal. 5:17. There is a threefold remarkable advantage given us by grace for the destruction and mortification of sin. Grace gives the heart of man a contrary *inclination*, by which spiritual things become natural to the regenerate soul. "For I delight in the law of God after the inward man." Rom. 7:22. Sanctification is in the soul as a living spring running with a kind of central force heavenward. John 4:14. Moreover, holy principles destroy the interest sin once had in the *love* of the soul; the sanctified soul cannot take pleasure in sin, or in that which grieves God, as it was wont to do; but that which was the object of delight, hereby becomes the object of grief and hatred. What I hate, that I do. Rom. 7:15. From these follow a third advantage for the mortification of sin, inasmuch as sin being contrary to the new nature, and the object of hatred, cannot be committed without very sensible regret; and what is done with regret is neither done frequently nor easily: the case of a regenerate soul under the surprisals of temptation, being like that of a captive in war who marches by constraint among his enemies.

So the apostle expresses himself: "But I see another law in my members warring against the law of my mind, and bringing me into captivity to the law of sin which is in my members." Rom. 7 : 23. Thus the Spirit of God promotes the design of mortification by the implantation of contrary habits.

2. *By assisting gracious habits* in all times of need, which he does many ways : sometimes awakening and arousing grace, and drawing forth its activity and power to actual and successful resistance of temptation. "How then can I do this great wickedness, and sin against God ?" Gen. 39 : 9. Holy fear awakens and raises all the grace in the soul to make a vigorous resistance of temptation ; the Spirit also strengthens weak grace in the soul. "My grace is sufficient for thee ; for my strength is made perfect in weakness." 2 Cor. 12 : 9. And by reason of grace thus implanted and thus assisted, he that is born of God keepeth himself, and the wicked one toucheth him not.

V. How mortification of sin EVINCES THE SOUL'S INTEREST IN CHRIST.

1. Whatever shows the *indwelling of the Holy Spirit* in us, must be evidence of a saving interest in Christ, as has been fully proved ; but the mortification of sin plainly shows the indwelling of the Spirit, for, as we have also seen, it can proceed from no other principle. There is as inseparable a connection between mortification and the Spirit, as between the effect and its proper cause, and the same connection between the inbeing of the Spirit and union with Christ. So that to reason from mortification to the inhabitation of the Spirit, and from the inhabitation of the Spirit to our union with Christ, is a scriptural way of reasoning.

2. That which proves a soul to be under the *covenant of grace*, proves its interest in Christ ; for Christ is the head of that covenant, and none but believers are under

its blessings and promises ; and mortification of sin is a sound evidence of the soul's being under the covenant of grace, as is plain from those words of the apostle, "Let not sin therefore reign in your mortal body, that ye should obey it in the lust thereof. Neither yield ye your members as instruments of unrighteousness unto sin; but yield yourselves unto God, as those that are alive from the dead, and your members as instruments of righteousness unto God. For sin shall not have dominion over you ; for ye are not under the law, but under grace," Rom. 6 : 12-14 ; where the apostle presses believers to mortification by this encouragement, that it will be a good evidence to them of a new covenant interest, for all duties and endeavors can never mortify sin. It is the Spirit in the new covenant which produces it. Whoever therefore has his corruptions mortified, has his interest in the covenant, and consequently in Christ, so far made clear to him.

3. The evidence of *saving faith* must needs be a good evidence of our interest in Christ; and mortification of sin is the fruit and evidence of saving faith. " Purifying their hearts by faith." Acts 15 : 9. " This is the victory that overcometh the world, even our faith." 1 John 5 : 4. Faith overcomes the allurements of the world on the one hand, and the terrors of the world on the other, by mortifying the affections to all earthly things. A mortified heart is not easily ensnared with the pleasures of the world, or much moved with the losses and sufferings it meets from it : so the force of its temptations are broken, and the mortified soul becomes victorious over it, and all this by the instrumentality of faith.

4. In a word, there is an indissoluble connection between the mortification of sin and the life of grace : " Reckon ye also yourselves to be dead indeed unto sin, but alive unto God through Jesus Christ," Rom. 6 : 11 ; and the life of Christ must needs involve a saving interest in Christ.

CHAPTER XXVIII

CRUCIFYING THE FLESH, OR THE MORTIFICATION OF SIN—CONTINUED

"And they that are Christ's have crucified the flesh, with the affections and lusts." GAL. 5:24

In the previous discourse we have shown from this text that *a saving interest in Christ may be inferred from the crucifying or mortifying of the flesh with its affections and lusts.* Having considered the nature and necessity of mortification, and shown how a saving interest in Christ may be inferred from it, we now proceed to a PRACTICAL IMPROVEMENT of the whole.

INFERENCE 1. If they that are Christ's have crucified the flesh, *the life of the Christian is no idle life.* The corruptions of his heart continually fill his hands with work of the most difficult nature—sin-crucifying work, which the Scripture calls cutting off the right hand and plucking out the right eye. Sin-crucifying work is hard work, and it is constant work throughout the life of a Christian; there is no time nor place freed from this conflict; every occasion stirs corruption, and every stirring of corruption calls for mortification : corruptions work in our very best duties, Rom. 7:23, and call the Christian to mortifying labors. The world and the devil are great enemies and sources of many temptations to believers, but not like the corruptions of their own hearts; they only tempt externally, but these tempt internally, and are much more dangerous; they only tempt at times, these continually. Besides, whatever Satan or the world attempts upon us would be altogether ineffectual were it not for our own corruptions, John 14:30; so that the corruptions of our own hearts, as they create most danger, must give us more labor. Our life and this labor must end together; for sin is long dying in the best heart: those who have been many years exercised in the study of mortification, may feel the same corruption troubling them now which drew forth their tears and brought them to their knees twenty or forty years ago. It may be said of sin as of Hannibal, that active enemy, that it will never be quiet, whether conquering or conquered; and until sin cease working, the Christian must not cease mortifying.

2. If mortification be the great work of a Christian, *those that give the corruptions of Christians an occasion to revive, do them a very ill office.* They are not our best friends who stir the pride of our hearts by the flattery of their lips. The grace of God in others is thankfully to be owned, and under discouragements to be wisely spoken of; but the strongest Christians scarcely show their own weakness in any one thing more than in hearing their own praises. Christian, thou carriest gunpowder about thee, desire those that carry fire to keep at a distance : it is a dangerous crisis when a proud heart meets with flattering lips : take away the fire, said a holy divine of Germany, when his friend commended him upon his death-bed, for I have yet combustible matter about me. Faithful, seasonable, discreet reproofs are much more safe to us, and advantageous to our mortifying work; but alas, how few have the wisdom duly to administer them? It is said of Alexander, that he told a philosopher who had been long with him to be gone ; for, said he, so long thou hast been with me and never reproved me, which must be thy fault; for either thou sawest nothing in me worthy of reproof, which argues thy ignorance ; or thou durst not reprove me, which argues thy unfaithfulness. A wise and faithful reprover is of singular use to him that is heartily engaged in the design of mortification ; such a faithful friend, or some enemy, must be helpful to us in that work.

3. Hence it follows *that manifold and successive afflictions are necessary for the best Christians.* The mortification of our lusts requires them all, be they never so many. "If need be, ye are in heaviness." 1 Pet. 1 : 6. It is no more than need that one loss should follow another, to mortify an earthly heart ; for so intensely are our affections set on the world, that it is not one, or two, or many checks of providence that will suffice to wean them. Alas, the earthliness of our hearts requires all this, it may be much more than this, to purge them. The wise God sees it but necessary to permit frequent discoveries of our own weakness, and to let loose the tongues of many enemies upon us, and all little enough to destroy the vanity in our hearts. Christian, how difficult soever it be for thee to bear it, yet the pride of thy heart requires all the scoffs and calumnies that the tongues or pens of thy enemies or mistaken friends have at any time thrown upon thee. Such weeds as grow in our hearts will require hard frosts to rot them ; the straying bullock needs a heavy clog, and so does a Christian whom God will keep within the bounds of his commandments. Psalm 119 : 67 ; Dan. 11 : 35.

4. If they that are Christ's have crucified the flesh, *the number of real Christians is small.* It is true, if all that seem to be meek and heavenly might pass for Christians, the number would be great ; but if none must be accounted Christians but those who crucify the flesh with its affections and lusts, O how small is the number ! For how many are there under the Christian name that indulge their lusts, that secretly hate all who faithfully reprove them, and love none but such as feed their lusts, by praising and admiring them. How many that make provision for the flesh to fulfil its lusts, and cannot endure to have their corruptions crossed. How many that seem very meek and humble until an occasion be given to stir up their passion, and then you shall see in what degree they are mortified : the flint is a cold stone till it be struck, and then it is all fiery. I know the

best Christians are mortified but in part; and strong corruptions are often found in very eminent Christians; but they love them not so well as to purvey for them; to protect, defend, and countenance them; nor dare they hate such as faithfully reprove them. On account of mortification it is said, "Strait is the gate, and narrow is the way, that leadeth unto life, and few there be that find it." Matt. 7 : 14.

5. If they that are Christ's have crucified the flesh, if mortification is their daily work, *how falsely are Christians charged as troublers of the world and disturbers of the civil peace and tranquillity.* Justly may they retort the charge, as Elijah did to Ahab, "It is not I that trouble Israel, but thou and thy father's house." It is not meek and humble Christians that put the world into confusion, but the profane and atheistical, or the designing and hypocritical, who lay it at the door of innocent Christians : as all the public calamities, which, from the hand of God or by foreign or domestic enemies befell Rome, were constantly charged upon Christians, who were condemned and punished for what the righteous hand of God inflicted on the heads of the enemies of that state. The apostle James propounds and answers a question very pertinent to this discourse : "From whence come wars and fightings among you? come they not hence, even of your lusts that war in your members?" James 4 : 1. O, if men did but study self-denial, and live as much at home in the constant discipline of their own hearts as some do, what tranquillity and peace, what blessed halcyon days should we quickly see! It is true, Christians are always contending, but it is with themselves and their own corrupt hearts and affections : they hate no enemy but sin; they thirst for the blood and ruin of no other enemy; they are ambitious of no victory but over the corruptions of their own hearts; they carry no grudge except it be against sin; and yet these are the men who are charged with disturbing the times they live in, just as the wolf accused the lamb below him for defiling the stream.

But there will be a day when God will clear up the innocence and integrity of his abused servants ; and the world shall see it was not preaching and praying, but drinking, swearing, and enmity to true godliness, which disturbed the quietness of the times. In the mean time let innocence commit itself unto God, who will protect and in due time vindicate it.

6. If they that are Christ's have crucified the flesh, *whatever religion or doctrine countenances sin is not of Christ.* The doctrine of Christ everywhere teaches mortification : the whole stream of the gospel runs against sin ; it is holy and heavenly ; it has no tendency to extol corrupt nature and feed its pride by magnifying its freedom and power, or stamping the merit of the blood of Christ upon its works : it never makes the death of Christ a cloak to cover sin, but an instrument to destroy it.

7. If mortification is the great business of a Christian, *that condition is most desirable which is least exposed to temptation.* "Give me neither poverty nor riches, but feed me with food convenient." Prov. 30 : 8. The holy Agur was well aware of the danger lurking in both extremes ; and how near they border upon deadly temptations and approach the very precipice of ruin, that stand upon either ground. Few Christians have a head strong enough to stand upon the pinnacle of wealth and honor, nor is it every one that can grapple with poverty and contempt. A mediocrity is the Christian's best security, and is therefore most desirable ; and yet how do the corruption, the pride and ignorance of our hearts covet the condition which only serves to nourish our lusts and make the work of mortification more difficult. It is well for us that our wise Father leaves not to our own choice, that he frequently dashes our earthly projects and disappoints our fond expectations. If children were left to carve for themselves, how often would they cut their own fingers.

8. If mortification is the great business of a Christian,

Christian fellowship duly improved must be of special advantage to the people of God. For thereby we have the friendly help of others to carry on our great design and help us in our most difficult business; if corruption be too hard for us, others come in to our assistance. "Brethren, if a man be overtaken in a fault, ye which are spiritual restore such a one in the spirit of meekness." Gal. 6:1. If temptations prevail, that we fall under sin, it is a special mercy to have the reproofs and counsels of our brethren, who will not suffer sin to rest upon us. Lev. 19:17. While we are sluggish, others are vigilant for our safety. The humility of another reproves and mortifies my pride. The activity of another quickens my deadness. The gravity of another detects and cures my levity. The spirituality of another may be exceedingly useful to reprove and heal the earthliness and sensuality of my heart. Two are better than one, but woe unto him that is alone. The devil is well aware of this great advantage, and therefore strikes with special malice against associated Christians, who are as a well-disciplined army, whom he therefore more especially endeavors to rout and scatter by persecutions, that thereby Christians may be deprived of the sweet advantages of mutual society.

9. *How deeply has sin fixed its roots in our nature, that it should be the constant work of a Christian's life to mortify and destroy it!* God has given us many excellent helps: his Spirit within us, and a variety of ordinances and duties appointed as instruments of mortification. From the very day of regeneration to the last moment of dissolution the Christian is at work in the use of all sanctified means, external and internal, yet can never destroy corruption at the root all his life long. The most eminent Christians of long standing in religion, who have shed floods of tears for sin, and poured out many thousand prayers for the mortification of it, after all, find the remains of their old disease, and that there is still life in the corruptions to

which they have given so many wounds. O the depth and strength of sin, which nothing can separate from us but that which separates our souls and bodies. And upon that account the day of a believer's death is better than the day of his birth. Never till then do we put off our armor, sheath our sword, and cry, Victory, victory.

10. If they who are Christ's have crucified the flesh, as we hope to make good our claim to Christ, let us GIVE ALL DILIGENCE TO MORTIFY SIN; in vain else are all our pretences to union with him. This is the great work of a believer. And seeing it is the main business of life and the great evidence for heaven, I shall therefore press you to it by the following MOTIVES:

MOTIVE 1. Methinks the *comfort resulting from mortification* should persuade every believer to diligence in this duty. There is a double sweetness in mortification: one as it is a sweet Christian *duty*. Dost thou not feel a blessed calm in thy conscience when thou hast repelled temptation, resisted and overcome thy corruptions? Does not God smile upon thee, and conscience encourage thee? Hast thou not a heaven within thee, while others feel a kind of hell in the bitter accusations of their own conscience? But consider it also as *an evidence* of the soul's interest in Christ, as my text considers it; and what a heaven upon earth must then be found in mortification. These endeavors to subdue and mortify my corruptions speak the Spirit of God in me, and my being in Christ. What heart has largeness and strength enough to contain the joy which flows from a clear interest in Jesus Christ. Certainly, Christian, the comfort of your life depends upon it. "If ye through the Spirit do mortify the deeds of the body, ye shall live," Rom. 8 : 13 ; you shall live a placid, comfortable life ; for it is corruption unmortified which clouds the face of God and breaks the peace of his people, and consequently imbitters the life of a Christian.

MOTIVE 2. As the comfort of your life, which is much,

so *your fitness for the service of God*, which is much more, depends upon the mortification of your sins. "If a man therefore purge himself from these, he shall be a vessel unto honor, sanctified and meet for the Master's use, and prepared unto every good work." 2 Tim. 2 : 21. Where is the enjoyment of life, but in its usefulness in the service of God? It is not worth while to live sixty or seventy years in the world to eat and drink, to buy and sell, and then go down to the grave. So far as any man lives to God a useful life to his honor, so far only does he answer the end of his being. But it is the mortified soul which is the vessel of honor prepared and meet for the Master's use. Let a proud earthly heart be employed in any service for God, and you will find it will spoil the work by managing it for self, as Jehu did; and then claim the praise of it by a proud boast, "Come see my zeal." When the Lord would employ the prophet Isaiah in his work, his iniquity was first purged, and after that he was employed. Isa. 6 : 6–8. Sin is the soul's sickness, a consumption of the inner man; and we know that languishing consumptive persons are unfit to be employed in strenuous labors. Mortification cures the disease, restores our strength, and enables us to serve God in our generation.

MOTIVE 3. *Your safety in the hour of temptation* depends upon the success of your mortifying endeavors. Is it a mercy to be kept upright and steadfast in the critical season of temptation, when Satan shall be wrestling with you for the crown and the prize of eternal life? Then give diligence to mortify your corruptions. Temptation is a siege : Satan is the enemy without the walls, laboring to force an entrance ; natural corruptions are the traitors within, that hold correspondence with the enemy without, and open the gate of the soul to receive him. It was the covetousness of Judas' heart which overthrew him in the hour of temptation. They are our fleshly lusts which go over unto Satan in the day of battle, and fight against our souls. 1 Pet. 2 : 11. The corruptions or infectious atoms which fly up and down the world in times of temptation, as the word translated "pollutions" in 2 Pet. 2 : 20 imports, are through lusts. 2 Pet. 1 : 4. It is the lust within which gives a lustre to the vanities of the world without, and thereby makes them strong temptations to us. 1 John 2 : 16. Mortify therefore your corruptions, as ever you expect to maintain your station in the day of trial : cut off the advantages of your enemy, lest by them he cut off your souls and all your hopes from God.

MOTIVE 4. As temptations will be irresistible, so *afflictions will be insupportable* to you without mortification. My friends, you live in a mutable world. You that have husbands or wives to-day may be left desolate to-morrow. You that have estates and children now may be bereaved of both before you are aware. Sickness will tread upon the heel of health, and death will assuredly follow life as night does the day. Consider, are you able to bear the loss of your enjoyments with patience ? Can you think upon the parting hour without trembling ? O get a heart mortified to all these things, and you will bless a taking as well as a giving God. It is the living world, not the crucified world, that raises tumults in our souls in the day of affliction. How cheerful was Paul under all his sufferings ! and what, think you, gave him that peace but his mortification to the world ? "I know both how to be abased, and I know how to abound : everywhere and in all things I am instructed both to be full and to be hungry, both to abound and to suffer need." Phil. 4 12. Job was the mirror of patience in the greatest shock of calamity, and what made him so but the mortified state of his heart amidst the full enjoyment of all earthly things ? Job 31 : 25.

MOTIVE 5. The *honor of religion* is concerned in the mortification of the professors of it ; for unmortified professors will be the scandal and reproach of it. The profession of religion may give credit to you, but you will never bring credit to it. All the scandals and reproaches that fall on the name of Christ in this world, flow from the fountain of unmortified corruption. Judas and Demas, Hymeneus and Philetus, Ananias and Sapphira ruined themselves and became rocks of offence to others by this means.

MOTIVE 6. What *hard work will you have in your dying hour*, except you get a heart mortified to the world and all that is in it! Your parting hour will be a dreadful hour without the help of mortification. Your corruptions, like glue, fasten your affections to the world, and how hard will it be for such a man to be separated by death! O what a bitter parting have carnal hearts from carnal things; whereas the mortified soul can receive the messenger death without alarm, and as cheerfully put off the body as a man does his clothes at night. Death need not compel: such a man goes half way to meet it. I desire to be dissolved, and to be with Christ, which is far better. Phil. 1 : 23. Christian, wouldst thou have thy death-bed soft and easy; wouldst thou have an easy death? then get a mortified heart: the surgeon's knife is scarcely felt when it cuts off a mortified member

11. Are you fully satisfied of the excellence and necessity of mortification, and inquisitive after the means in the use of which it may be attained? then, for your help and encouragement, I will offer my best assistance in some RULES for this work.

RULE 1. If you would succeed in the work of mortification, *get and daily exercise more faith*. Faith is the great instrument of mortification. This is the victory, or sword by which the victory is won, the instrument by which you overcome the world, even your faith. 1 John 5 : 4. By faith alone eternal things are discovered to your souls in their reality and excelling glory, and these are the great things for the sake of which self-denial and mortification become easy to believers. By opposing things eternal to things temporal, we resist Satan. 1 Pet. 5 : 8. This is the shield by which we quench the fiery darts of the wicked one. Eph. 6 : 16.

RULE 2. *Walk in daily communion with God,* if you would mortify the corruptions of nature. That is the apostle's prescription : "This I say then, walk in the Spirit, and ye shall not fulfil the lusts of the flesh." Gal. 5 : 16. Spiritual and frequent communion with God gives manifold advantages for the mortification of sin, as it is a bright glass wherein the holiness of God, and the sinfulness of sin as opposite thereto, are most clearly discovered, than which scarcely any thing can set a keener edge of indignation upon the spirit of a man against sin. Besides, all communion with God assimilates and transforms the soul into his image ; it leaves a heavenly savor upon the soul ; it darkens the glory of all earthly things by presenting to the soul a glory which excelleth ; it improves and deepens sanctification in the soul : by all which means it becomes singularly useful in the work of mortification.

RULE 3. *Keep your conscience in the fear of God* continually, as you hope to be successful in the mortification of sin. The fear of God is the great preservative from sin, without which all rules and helps signify nothing. "By the fear of the Lord men depart from evil," Prov. 16 : 6: not only from external evils, which the fear of men as well as the fear of God may prevent ; but from the most secret and inward evils, which is a special part of mortification. Lev. 19 : 14. It keeps men from the evils which no eye nor ear of man can possibly discover. The fear of the Lord breaks temptations baited with pleasure, with profit, and with secresy. If ever you are cleansed from all filthiness of flesh and spirit, it must be by the fear of God. 2 Cor. 7 : 1.

RULE 4. *Study the vanity of earth,* and labor to get true

notions of its emptiness, if ever you would attain to the mortification of your affections towards it. It is the false image of the world in our fancy that crucifies us with so many cares and solicitudes about it; and it is the true image of the world, represented to us in the glass of the word, which greatly helps to crucify our affections to the world. O, if we did but believe three things about the world we should never be so fond of it as we are, the fading, defiling, and destroying nature of it. The best and sweetest enjoyments in the world are but fading flowers and withering grass, Isa. 40 : 6; Jas. 1 : 10, 11; yea, it is of a defiling as well as a fading nature, 1 John 5 : 19; it "lies in wickedness," it spreads universal infection among all mankind, 2 Pet. 1 : 4; yea, it destroys as well as defiles multitudes of souls, drowning men in perdition. 1 Tim. 6 : 9. Millions of souls will wish to eternity they had never known its riches, pleasures, or honors. Were this believed, how would men slacken their pace in the eager pursuit of the world.

Rule 5. Be careful to *cut off all occasions of sin*, and keep at the greatest distance from temptation, if you would mortify the deeds of the body. The success of sin mainly depends upon the stratagems it uses to ensnare the soul; therefore the apostle bids us keep at the greatest distance. "Abstain from all appearance of evil." 1 Thess. 5 : 22. "Come not nigh the door of her house." Prov. 5 : 8. He that dares venture to the brink of sin, has but little light in his understanding and less tenderness in his conscience; he neither knows sin, nor fears it as he ought. It is usual with God to chastise self-confidence by allowing men to fall into sin.

Rule 6. If you would successfully mortify the corruptions of your nature, never engage against them *in your own strength*. When the apostle draws forth Christians into the field against sin, he bids them "be strong in the Lord, and in the power of his might." Eph. 6 : 10. O remember what a feather thou art in the gusts of temptation ; call to mind the height of Peter's confidence : "Though all men forsake thee, yet will not I ;" and the depth of his fall, shame, and sorrow. A weak Christian, trembling in himself, depending by faith upon God and graciously assisted by him, shall be able to stand against the shock of temptation, when the bold and confident resolutions of others shall melt away as wax before the flames.

Rule 7. Concur with the chastening design of God in *the day of thine affliction.* Sanctified afflictions are prescribed in heaven for purifying our corruptions : "By this therefore shall the iniquity of Jacob be purged ; and this is all the fruit to take away his sin." Isa. 27 : 9. It is a glass to represent the evil of sin and the vanity of the creature, to imbitter the world and draw thy affections from it. Fall in, therefore, with the gracious design of God ; connect every affliction with prayer that God would follow it with his blessing. God kills thy comforts from no other design but to kill thy corruptions ; wants are ordained to kill wantonness, poverty is appointed to kill pride, reproaches are permitted to destroy ambition. Happy is the man who understands, approves, and heartily concurs with the design of God in afflicting providences.

Rule 8. Bend the strength of your endeavors against *your easily besetting sin.* It is in vain to lop off branches while this root of bitterness remains untouched. This was David's practice : "I was also upright before him, and I kept myself from mine iniquity." Psalm 18 : 23. We observe in men that one faculty is more vigorous than another ; we find in nature that one soil suits some sorts of seeds rather than others ; and every believer may find his constitution inclining him to one sin rather than another. As graces, so corruptions exceed one another, even in the regenerate. The power of special corruption arises from our constitution, education, company, custom, calling, and such like occasions; but from wherever it comes, this is the sin that most endangers us; and according to the progress of mortification in this sin, we may safely estimate the degrees of mortification in other sins. Strike, therefore, at the root of your own iniquity.

RULE 9. Study the *nature and importance of the things to be won or lost*, according to the issue of this conflict. Your life is a race, eternal glory is the prize, grace and corruption are the antagonists, and as either finally prevails, eternal life is won or lost. "Know ye not that they which run in a race run all, but one receiveth the prize? So run, that ye may obtain." 1 Cor. 9 : 24. This will make mortification appear the most necessary thing to you. Shall I lose heaven for indulging a wanton appetite? God forbid. "I keep under my body, and bring it into subjection; lest that by any means, when I have preached to others, I myself should be a castaway." 1 Cor. 9 : 27.

12. Accustom your thoughts to MEDITATIONS proper to mortify sin in your affections, else all endeavors will be but faint and languid. To this purpose I recommend the following meditations as proper means to mortify sin.

MEDITATION 1. Consider *the evil of sin*, and how terrible the revelations of God will one day be against those that obey it in the lusts thereof. "The wrath of God is revealed from heaven against all ungodliness and unrighteousness of men." Rom. 1 : 18. "The Lord Jesus shall be revealed from heaven with his mighty angels, in flaming fire taking vengeance on them that know not God, and that obey not the gospel of our Lord Jesus Christ: who shall be punished with everlasting destruction from the presence of the Lord, and from the glory of his power." 2 Thess. 1 : 7–9. Dwell much on the consideration of the consequences of sin. It shows its fairest side in the hour of temptation; but consider how it will look to you in the day of affliction; in that day your sin will find you out. Think what its aspect will be in a dying hour: "The sting of death is sin." 1 Cor. 15 : 56.   Think what the remembrance of it will be at the bar of judgment, when Satan shall accuse, conscience upbraid, God condemn, and everlasting burnings avenge the evil of it.   Such thoughts as these are mortifying thoughts.

MEDITATION 2.   Think *what it cost the Lord Jesus to expiate the guilt of sin* by suffering the wrath of God for it in our room.   Meditations on a crucified Christ are very crucifying meditations unto sin, Gal. 6 : 14 ; he suffered unspeakable things for sin ; divine wrath lay upon his soul for it, that wrath of which the prophet saith, "The mountains quake at him, and the hills melt.   Who can stand before his indignation ? and who can abide in the fierceness of his anger ? his fury is poured out like fire, and the rocks are thrown down by him." Nahum 1 : 5, 6.   It was unmixed wrath, poured out in the fulness of it ; and shall we be so easily drawn to the commission of sins which put Christ under such sufferings?   Read such scriptures as Luke 22 : 44 ; Matt. 26 : 36, 37 ; Mark 14 : 33 ; and see what sorrow sin brought upon the Lord of glory ; how the wrath of God brought him into a sore amazement, a bloody sweat, and made his soul heavy unto death.

MEDITATION 3.   Consider *what a grief the sins of believers are to the Spirit of God.*   Eph. 4 : 30 ; Ezek. 16 : 43 ; Isa. 63 : 10.   O how it grieves the Holy Spirit of God.   Nothing is more contrary to his nature.   "O do not this abominable thing that I hate," saith the Lord.   Jeremiah 44 : 4. Nothing obstructs the sanctifying design of the Spirit as sin does—defacing the most admirable workmanship that God ever wrought in the world ; violating all the engagements laid upon us by the love of the Father, by the death of his Son, and the operations of his Spirit.   Lay this meditation upon thy heart, believer, and say, Dost thou thus requite the Lord, O my ungrateful heart, for all his goodness ?   Is this the fruit of his temporal and spiritual mercies, which are without number?

MEDITATION 4. Consider that *no real good can result from sin.* You can have no pleasure in it, whatever others may have, it being against your new nature ; and as for the pleasure which others have in sin, it can be but for a moment ; for either they must repent or not repent : if they then repent, the pleasure of sin will be turned into the gall of asps here ; if they do not repent, it will terminate in everlasting wailings hereafter. That is a solemn question, "What fruit had ye in those things whereof ye are now ashamed? For the end of those things is death." Rom. 6 : 21. You who are believers must never expect pleasure in sin ; for you can neither commit it without regret, nor reflect upon it without shame. Expect no better consequences of sin than wounds of conscience and dismal cloudings of the face of God.

MEDITATION 5. Consider *what the damned suffer for the sins the devil now tempts you to commit.* It has deprived them of all outward good, Luke 16 : 25 ; all spiritual good, Matt. 25 : 41 ; and of all hope of enjoying good for ever : and as it has deprived them of all good, so it has plunged them into all misery—misery from without, the wrath of God being come upon them to the uttermost ; and misery from within, for their worm dieth not. Mark 9 : 44. The memory of things past, the sense of things present, and the fearful expectation of things to come, are the gnawings of the worm of conscience, under which damned souls cry out, O the worm ! the worm ! Would any man who is not forsaken by reason, run the hazard of those eternal miseries for the pleasures of a moment?

MEDITATION 6. Bethink yourselves *what inexcusable hypocrisy it will be in you to indulge your lusts,* under a contrary profession of religion. You that profess holiness, and to be under the government of Christ, must the worthy name of Christ be only used to cloak and cover your lusts, which are so hateful to him ? God forbid. You profess daily to pray against sin, and to confess and bewail it ; you pour out supplications for pardoning grace; are you in jest or earnest, in these solemn duties of religion? If all these duties produce no mortification, you do but flatter God with your lips, and put a dreadful cheat upon your own souls. Nay, do you not frequently censure these things in others, and dare you allow them in yourselves? What horrid hypocrisy is this! Christians are dead to sin, Rom. 6 : 2— dead to it by profession, by obligation, by relation to Christ, who died for them; and how shall they that are in so many ways dead to sin, live any longer therein? O think not that God hates sin the less in you because you are his people; nay, that very consideration aggravates it the more. Amos 3 : 2.

MEDITATION 7.   Consider *what hard things some Christians have chosen to endure rather than defile themselves with guilt;* and shall every small temptation ensnare and take your souls? Read over the eleventh chapter to the Hebrews, and see what the saints endured to escape sin: no torments were so terrible to them as the displeasure of God and the wounding of conscience; and did God favor them more than he has you? O Christians, how can you, that have found mercies as free and pardons as full as ever any souls found, show less care, less tenderness of grieving the Spirit of God than others have done? Certainly, if you saw sin as they saw it, you would hate it as deeply, watch against it as carefully, and resist it as vigorously as any of the saints have done before you.

MEDITATION 8.   Consider *what pleasure is to be found in the mortification of sin.*   The fulfilling of your lusts cannot give you the thousandth part of the comfort and contentment that the resistance of them and victory over them will give you. Who can express the comfort to be found in the testimony of an absolving conscience? 2 Cor. 1 : 12.   Remember what satisfaction it was to Hezekiah upon his supposed death-bed, when he turned to the wall and said, "Remember now, O Lord, I beseech thee, how I have walked before thee in truth, and with a perfect heart, and have done that which is good in thy sight." Isa. 38 : 3.

13. This naturally puts us upon the EXAMINATION OF OUR HEARTS, whether we who so confidently claim a special interest in Christ have crucified the flesh with its affections and lusts. And because two sorts of persons will be concerned in this trial, namely, the weaker and the stronger Christians, I shall lay down two classes of evidences of mortification—one respecting the sincerity and truth of that work in all who are savingly converted, the other respecting its strength and progress in confirmed and grown Christians.

(1.) There are some things that are evidences of *the sincerity* of mortification, even in the weakest Christians : as,

True tenderness of conscience as to *all known sins,* is a good sign sin has lost its dominion in the soul. O it is a special mercy to have a heart that shall smite and reprove us for the things that others make nothing of—that shall check and admonish us for our secret sins, which can never turn to our reproach among men : this is a good sign that we hate sin, however through the weakness of the flesh we may be ensnared by it. "What I hate, that do I." Rom. 7 : 15.

The earnest desires of our souls to God in prayer for *sin mortifying grace,* is a good sign our souls have no love for sin. Canst thou say, poor believer, in thy heart, that if God would give thee thy choice, it would please thee better to have sin cast out than to have the world brought in—that thy heart is not so earnest with God for daily bread as it is for heart-purifying grace? This is a comfortable evidence that sin is nailed to the cross of Christ.

Do you make conscience of guarding against *the occasions* of sin? keeping a daily watch over your hearts and senses, according to 1 John 5 : 18 ; Job 31 : 1. This speaks a true purpose of mortification.

Do you rejoice and bless God from your hearts when

his providence orders any means for the *prevention* of sin? Thus did David : "And David said to Abigail, Blessed be the Lord God of Israel, which sent thee this day to meet me ; and blessed be thy advice, and blessed be thou, which hast kept me this day from coming to shed blood, and from avenging myself with mine own hand." 1 Sam. 25 : 33.

In a word, though the thoughts of death may be terrible, yet if the hope of your *deliverance from sin* thereby sweeten the thoughts of it to your souls, it will turn unto you for a testimony that you are not the servants of sin.

(2.) There are other signs of *a more deep and thorough* mortification of sin in confirmed believers. The more submissive any man is under the will of God in afflicting providences, the more his heart is mortified to sin. Psa. 119 : 67, 71 ; Col. 1 : 11. The more able any one is to bear reproaches and rebukes for his sin, the more mortification there is in him. Psa. 141 : 5. The more easily any man can give up his dearest earthly comforts at the call of God, the more progress he has made in the work of mortification. Heb. 11 : 17 ; 2 Sam. 15 : 25. The more power a man has to resist sin in the first motions of it and stifle it in the birth, the greater degree of mortification he has attained. Rom. 7 : 23, 24. If great changes in our outward condition make no change for the worse in our spirits, but we can bear prosperous and adverse providences with an equal mind, then mortification is advanced far in our souls. Phil. 4 : 11, 12. And the more steady our hearts are with God in duty, and the less they are infested with wandering thoughts, the more mortification there is in the soul.

14. It only remains that I add a few words of *consolation* to all that are under the mortifying influence of the Spirit. In brief, mortified sin shall never be your ruin : it is only reigning sin that is ruining sin. Rom. 8 : 13. Mortified and pardoned sin shall never lie down with us in the dust. If sin be dying, your souls are living ; for dying

unto sin and living unto God are inseparably connected. Rom. 6 : 11. If sin be dying in you, it is certain that Christ died for you, and you cannot desire a better evidence of it. Rom. 6 : 5, 6. If sin be dying under the mortifying influences of the Spirit, and it be your daily labor to overcome it, you are in the direct way to heaven and eternal salvation, which few in the world shall find. Luke 13 : 24. Finally, if you, through the Spirit, are daily mortifying the deeds of the body, the death of Christ is effectually applied by the Spirit to your souls, and your interest in him is unquestionable. For "they that are Christ's have crucified the flesh with the affections and lusts ;" and they that have so crucified the flesh with its affections and lusts are Christ's.

Blessed be God for a crucified Christ.

CHAPTER XXIX

THE IMITATION OF CHRIST

"He that saith he abideth in him ought himself also so to walk, even as he walked." 1 John 2:6

The principal design of the apostle in this chapter is to propound marks for the examination of men's claims to Christ, among which my text is a principal one; a trial of men's *interest* in Christ by their *imitation* of Christ. It is supposed by some expositors that the apostle, in laying down this mark, had a special design to overthrow the wicked doctrine of the Carpocratians, a sect of ancient heretics, who taught that men might have as much communion with God in sin as in duty. In opposition to which the apostle asserts the necessity of a Christlike conversation in all that claim union with him, or interest in him. In these words we have then,

1. *A claim to Christ supposed:* if any man say he abideth in him. Abiding in Christ is an expression denoting real interest in Christ and communion with him; for it is put in opposition to those temporary and transient effects of the gospel which are called a morning dew or an early cloud; such a receiving of Christ as that, Matt. 13:21, which is but a present flash, sudden and vanishing. Abiding in Christ implies a solid and effectual work of the Spirit, thoroughly joining the soul to Christ. Let no man, whosoever he be, think his claim to be valid, except he takes this course to adjust it.

2. We have *the only way to have this claim warranted*, by *so walking even as he walked;* which words carry in them the necessity of our imitation of Christ. But it is not to be un-

derstood universally of all the works or actions of Christ, some of which were extraordinary and miraculous, and some purely mediatory, and not imitable by us. In these paths no Christian can follow Christ, nor may so much as attempt to walk as he walked. But the words point at the ordinary and imitable ways and works of Christ. In these it must be the care of all that profess and claim interest in him to follow him; they must "so walk as he walked." This "*so*" is a very important word in this place; the emphasis of the text seems to lie in it. It is certain, however, that so walking does not imply an equality with Christ in holiness and obedience; for, as he was filled with the Spirit without measure, and anointed with that oil of gladness above his fellows, so the purity, holiness, and obedience of his life are never to be equalled by any of the saints. But this so walking denotes a sincere intention and endeavor to imitate and follow him in all the paths of holiness and obedience according to the measure of grace received. The life of Christ is the believer's copy, and though the believer cannot draw one letter exact as his copy is, yet his eye is still upon it; he is looking unto Jesus, Heb. 12 : 2, and laboring to draw all the lines of his life as agreeably as he is able to Christ his pattern. Hence,

Every man is bound to the imitation of Christ, under penalty of forfeiting his claim to Christ.

The imitation of Christ is solemnly enjoined by many express commands of the gospel. "But as he which hath called you is holy, so be ye holy in all manner of conversation." 1 Peter 1 : 15. "Be ye therefore followers of God as dear children, and walk in love, as Christ also hath loved us." Eph. 5 : 1, 2. Christians, says Bernard, receive this name from Christ, and it is very meet that as they inherit his name, so they should also imitate his holiness.

It will be needful to discuss three things : what the saints' imitation of Christ implies ; in what particulars they are especially bound to imitate Christ; and why no claim to Christ is valid without this imitation of him.

I. What the saints' imitation of Christ, or walking as he walked, IMPLIES.

1. It supposes that *no Christian is a rule to himself* to act according to the dictates of his own pleasure; for as no man has wisdom enough to direct and govern himself, so, if his own will were made the rule of his actions, it would be the highest invasion of the divine prerogative that could be imagined. "I know, O Lord, that the way of man is not in himself; it is not in man that walketh to direct his steps." Jer. 10 : 23. We may as well pretend to be our own makers as our own guides. It is an observation of Aquinas, that if the workman's hand were the rule of his work, it were impossible he should ever err in working. And if the will of man were the only guide of his way, we might say no man would sin in his walking. The apostle indeed saith of the heathen, that they "are a law to themselves," Rom. 2 : 14; but he does not mean that their will is their law, but the law of God engraven upon their hearts : the light and dictates of their consciences bind them as a law.

2. This imitation of Christ implies, that as no man is his own guide, so *no man may pretend to be a rule to other men;* but Christ is the rule of every man's walking. It is true indeed, the apostle says, we should be followers of them who through faith and patience inherit the promises. Heb. 6 : 12. And again, "Take, my brethren, the prophets who have spoken in the name of the Lord, for an example of suffering affliction, and of patience." James 5 : 10. But we must always remember that the wisest among men may pretend no higher than a ruled rule. The apostle, though filled with as great a measure of the Spirit of wisdom and holiness as ever was possessed by any mere man, goes no higher than this : "Be ye followers of me, as I also am of Christ." 1 Cor. 11 : 1. The best of men

are but men at best; they have their errors and defects, which they freely acknowledge; and where they differ from Christ, it is our duty to differ from them. It was the commendation Paul gave of the Thessalonians, "And ye became followers of us and of the Lord." 1 Thess. 1: 6. The noble Bereans were also commended for searching the Scripture, and examining the apostles' doctrine by it; and it was a good reply of one to a clamorous disputant, who cried, "Hear me, hear me!" "I will neither hear thee, nor do thou hear me; but let us both hear Christ."

3. The imitation of Christ implies *the necessity of sancti-fication* in all his followers, as it is impossible there should be a practical conformity in point of obedience where there is not a conformity in spirit and in principle. It is very plain, from Ezek. 11: 19, 20, that a new heart must be given us, and a new spirit put within us, before we can walk in God's statutes. We must first live in the Spirit before we can walk in the Spirit. Gal. 5: 25.

4 The imitation of Christ plainly shows *that the Christian religion is precise and strict,* no way countenancing men in their lusts, but rejecting every man's claim to Christ who labors not to tread in the footsteps of his holy example. Profaneness and licentiousness can find no protection under the wing of the gospel. This is the universal rule laid upon all the professors of religion: "Let every one that nameth the name of Christ depart from iniquity," 2 Tim. 2: 19; let him either put on the life of Christ, or put off the name of Christ. Let him show the hand of a Christian in works of holiness and obedience, or the language of a Christian should gain no belief or credit.

5 The imitation of Christ necessarily implies *the imperfection of the best men in this life;* for if the life of Christ be our pattern, the holiest men must confess they come short in every thing of the rule of their duty. Our pattern is still above us; the best of men are ashamed when they compare their lives with the life of Christ. A vain heart

may swell with pride when a man compares himself with other men : thus measuring ourselves by ourselves, and comparing ourselves among ourselves, we show our folly and nourish our pride ; but if any man will compare his life with Christ's, he will find abundant cause to be humbled. Paul was a great proficient in holiness ; yet when he looks up and sees the life of Christ and rule of duty so far above him, he reckons himself still but at the foot of the hill. "Not as though I had already attained, either were already perfect ; but I follow after, if that I may apprehend that for which also I am apprehended of Christ Jesus." Phil. 3 : 12. As though he had said, Alas, I do not come up to my duty, I am a great way behind ; but I am following after, if at last I may attain it. Perfection is in my expectation and hope at last, but it is not what I have yet attained.

6. The imitation of Christ as our rule or pattern necessarily implies *the transcendent holiness of the Lord Jesus.* His holiness is greater than that of all creatures ; for only that which is first and best in every kind is the rule and measure of all the rest. It is the height of the saints' ambition to be made conformable to Christ. Phil. 3 : 10. Christ has a double perfection, a perfection of being, and a perfection of working. His life was a perfect rule, no error could be found therein ; for he was "holy, harmless, undefiled, separate from sinners." And such a high-priest becomes us, as the apostle speaks, Heb. 7 : 26. The conformity of professors to Christ's example is the test of all their graces ; the nearer any man comes to this pattern, the nearer he approaches towards perfection.

7. The Christian's imitation of Christ, under penalty of losing his claim to Christ, necessarily implies that *sanctification and obedience are the evidences of our justification* and interest in Christ. Assurance is unattainable without obedience. "As many as walk according to this rule, peace be on them, and mercy, and upon the Israel of God." Gal.

6 : 16. A careless conversation can never be productive of peace and consolation. "Our rejoicing is this, the testimony of our conscience, that in simplicity and godly sincerity, not with fleshly wisdom, but by the grace of God, we have had our conversation in the world." 2 Cor. 1:12. Let men talk what they may of the immediate sealing and comfort of the Spirit, without regard to holiness or obedience; sure I am, whatever delusion they meet with in that way, true peace and consolation are only to be expected and found in the imitation of Christ: "The fruit of righteousness shall be peace, and the effect of righteousness quietness and assurance for ever." We have it not for our holiness, but we always have it in the way of holiness.

II. In the next place, we are to inquire IN WHAT THINGS all who profess Christ are BOUND to the imitation of him; or what those excellent graces in the life of Christ were, which are proposed as patterns to the saints. The life of Christ was a living law; all the graces of the Spirit were represented in their full glory in his conversation on earth : never man spoke as he spoke, never any lived as he lived. "We beheld his glory, the glory as of the only begotten of the Father, full of grace and truth." John 1 : 14. But to descend to the particular imitable excellencies in the life of Christ, which are high patterns and excellent rules for the life and conversation of his people, we shall, from among many others, single out the ten following.

PATTERN 1. First of all, *the purity and holiness* of the life of Christ is proposed as a glorious pattern for the saints' imitation. "As he which hath called you is holy, so be ye holy in all manner of conversation," 1 Pet. 1:15; in every point and turning of yourselves, as the Greek expresses it. There is a twofold holiness in Christ, the holiness of his nature and the holiness of his practice, his holy being and his holy working. This obliges all that profess interest in him to a twofold holiness : holiness in the principles of it in their hearts, and holiness in the practice and exercise of it in their lives. True, we cannot in all respects imitate the holiness of Christ, for he is *essentially* holy, proceeding by nature as a pure beam of holiness from the Father; and when he was incarnate, he came into the world pure from the least stain of pollution. It was said, "That holy thing which shall be born of thee shall be called the Son of God." Luke 1:35. In this we can never be like Christ, for "who can bring a clean thing out of that which is unclean? Not one." The Lord Jesus was also *efficiently* holy, that is, he makes others holy; therefore his sufferings and blood are called a fountain opened for sin and for uncleanness to cleanse men's souls. Zech. 13:1. In this Christ also is inimitable; no man can make himself or others holy. It is a great truth, though it will hardly be relished by proud nature, that we may sooner make ourselves to be men than to be saints. Besides, Christ is infinitely holy, as he is *God;* and there are no measures set to his holiness as *Mediator*, "for God giveth not the Spirit by measure unto him." John 3:34. But the holiness of Christ is propounded as a pattern for our imitation in various respects.

He was *truly and sincerely* holy, without simulation; and this appeared in the greatest trial of the truth of holiness ever made in this world. "The prince of this world cometh, and hath nothing in me." John 14:30. When he was agitated and shaken with the greatest temptations, no dregs appeared; he was like pure water in a crystal glass. The hypocrite makes show of more holiness than he has, but there was more holiness in Christ than ever appeared to the view of men. There was much inward beauty in him, and so there ought to be in all his followers: our holiness, like Christ's, must be sincere and real, Eph. 4:24, shining with inward beauty towards God rather than towards men.

Christ was *uniformly* holy, at one time as well as another—in one place and company as well as another : he was still like himself ; one and the same tenor of holiness ran throughout his whole life. So must it be with all his people, "holy in all manner of conversation." Christians, look to your copy, and be sure to imitate Christ in this ; let not one part of your life be heavenly and another earthly ; or as one expresses it, now a heavenly rapture, and by and by a worldly frolic.

Christ was *exemplarily* holy, a pattern of holiness to all that came nigh him and conversed with him. O imitate Christ in this ! It was the commendation of the Thessalonians, that they were ensamples to all that believed in Macedonia and Achaia ; and that in every place their faith to God-ward was spread abroad. 1 Thess. 1 : 7, 8. Let no man go out of your company without conviction or edification. So exemplary were the primitive Christians. Phil. 3 : 17.

Christ was *strictly* holy. "Which of you convinceth me of sin?" The most envious and observing eyes of his enemies could not find a flaw in any of his words or actions. It is our duty to imitate Christ in this. "That ye may be blameless and harmless, the sons of God, without rebuke, in the midst of a crooked and perverse nation, among whom ye shine," or as the word may be rendered imperatively, among whom shine ye, "as lights in the world." Phil. 2 : 15. Thus it becomes the followers of Christ to walk circumspectly : "For so is the will of God, that with well-doing ye may put to silence the ignorance of foolish men." 1 Peter 2 : 15.

Christ was *perseveringly* holy, even to the last breath ; as he began, so he finished his life in a constant course of holiness : in this also he is our great pattern. It becomes not any of his people to begin in the Spirit and end in the flesh ; but on the contrary, their last works should be more than their first. Let him that is holy be holy still. Rev. 22 : 11.

In a word, *the delight of Christ was in holy things and holy persons.* They were his chosen companions; even so it becomes his people to have their delight in the saints and the excellent of the earth. Psalm 16 : 3. Thus, Christians, be ye followers of Christ in his holiness; God has decreed this conformity to Christ in all that shall be saved, Rom. 8 : 29; he banishes all unholy ones from his gracious presence for ever. 1 Cor. 6 : 9; Heb. 12 : 14. The design of Christ in dying for you was to make you holy. Eph. 5 : 25, 26. Oh, then, study holiness, and as dear children, be ye followers of your most holy Lord Jesus Christ.

PATTERN 2. *The obedience of Christ to his Father's will* is a pattern for the imitation of Christians. It is said of Christ, that he learned obedience by the things which he suffered. Heb. 5 : 8. Christ learned obedience, and yet was not ignorant before of what he learned; he was perfect in knowledge, and yet the apostle speaks of him as a proficient in the school of wisdom. But we must consider, that though Christ, as God, was perfect in knowledge and nothing could be added to him, yet when he became man he came to understand or learn by sufferings, as the apostle here speaks; which, though it added nothing to his knowledge, yet it was a new way of knowing. The obedience of Christ is our pattern, to which we are obliged to conform ourselves in the following respects.

Christ's obedience was *voluntary*, not compulsory; it was so from his first undertaking the work of our redemption. "Then I was by him, as one brought up with him : and I was daily his delight, rejoicing always before him; rejoicing in the habitable part of his earth; and my delights were with the sons of men." Prov. 8 : 30, 31. And when the fulness of time was come for executing the blessed design which had been in prospect from eternity, how cheerfully did the will of Christ echo to his Father's call. "Then said I, Lo, I come; in the volume of the book it is written of me, I delight to do thy will, O my God: yea, thy law is within my heart." Psa. 40 : 7, 8. Nor was this a flourish before he came into the field and saw the enemy, for he laid down his life with the greatest readiness and spontaniety that could be. "Therefore doth my Father love me, because I lay down my life, that I might take it again. No man taketh it from me, but I lay it down of myself." John 10 : 17, 18. And indeed the voluntariness of Christ in his obedience unto death gave that death the nature of a sacrifice; for so all sacrifices ought to be offered, Lev. 1 : 3, and so Christ's sacrifice was offered unto God. Eph. 5 : 2. It was as grateful a work to Christ to die for us, as it was to Moses' mother to take him to nurse from the hand of Pharaoh's daughter. O Christians, tread in the steps of Christ's example, do nothing grudgingly for God, let not his commands be grievous. 1 John 5 : 3. If you do any thing for God willingly you have a reward; if otherwise, only a dispensation is committed to you. 1 Cor. 9 : 17. Obedience in Christ was an abasement to him, but in you it is a very great honor.

The obedience of Christ was *complete:* he was obedient to all the will of God, making no demur to the hardest service imposed by the will of God upon him; he "became obedient unto death, even the death of the cross," Phil. 2 : 8; and though the humanity of Christ recoiled when the bitter cup of the wrath of God was given him to drink, how soon was that innocent aversion overcome by a perfect submission! Nevertheless, not my will, but thine be done. Matt. 26 : 39. Christians, here is your pattern: happy art thou, reader, if thou canst say, when God calls thee to suffering and self-denying work, I am filled with the will of God. Such was Paul's obedience: "I am ready not only to be bound, but also to die at Jerusalem for the name of the Lord Jesus." Acts 21 : 13.

The obedience of Christ was *pure*, without any by-end,

aiming at the glory of God: "I have glorified thee on the earth, I have finished the work which thou gavest me to do." John 17 : 4. He sought not honor of men. This was the great desire of his soul, "Father, glorify thy name," John 12 : 28 ; and the choicest part of your obedience consists in the purity of your aims, and in this Christ is propounded as your pattern. Phil. 2 : 3–5.

The streams of Christ's obedience flowed from the fountain of *ardent love to God:* "But that the world may know that I love the Father ; and as the Father gave me commandment, even so I do." John 14 : 31. Thus let all your obedience to God turn upon the hinge of love, for "love is the fulfilling of the law." Rom. 13 : 10. Not as if no other duty but love were required in the law, but because no act of obedience is acceptable to God but that which is performed in love.

The obedience of Christ was *constant:* he was obedient unto death, he was not weary of his work to the last. Such a patient continuance in well-doing is one part of your conformity to Christ, Rom. 2 : 7 ; it is laid upon you by his command, backed with the most encouraging promise, "Be thou faithful unto death, and I will give thee a crown of life." Rev. 2 : 10.

PATTERN 3. The *self-denial* of Christ is the pattern of believers, and their conformity to it is their indispensable duty. Phil. 2 : 5, 6. "For ye know the grace of our Lord Jesus Christ, that though he was rich, yet for our sakes he became poor, that ye through his poverty might be rich." 2 Cor. 8 : 9. Jesus Christ, for the glory of God and the love he bare to his people, denied himself all the delights and pleasures of the world. "The Son of man came not to be ministered unto, but to minister, and to give his life a ransom for many," Matt. 20 : 28 ; he was all his lifetime "a man of sorrows, and acquainted with grief," Isa. 53 : 3 ; more unprovided with comfortable accommodations than the birds of the air or beasts of the earth.

"Foxes have holes, and birds of the air have nests; but the Son of man hath not where to lay his head." Luke 9 : 58. Yet this was the least part of Christ's self-denial. What did he not give up when he left the bosom of his Father with the ineffable delights he there enjoyed from eternity, to drink the bitter cup of his Father's wrath for our sake! O Christians, look to your pattern and imitate your self-denying Saviour.

Deny your natural self for him. Hate your own life, in competition with his glory, as well as your natural lusts. Luke 14 : 26; Tit. 2 : 12. Deny your civil self for Christ; whether it be gifts of the mind, Phil. 3 : 8, or your dearest relations in the world. Luke 14 : 26. Deny your moral and religious self for Christ, your own righteousness. Phil. 3 : 9. Deny sinful self absolutely. Col. 3 : 4, 5. Deny natural self conditionally, that is, be ready to forsake its interests at the call of God. Deny your religious self, even your own graces, as to any idea of righteousness in them.

To encourage you in this difficult work, consider what great things Christ denied for you, and what small matters you have to deny for him. How readily he denied all for your sakes, making no objections against the most difficult commands. How incapable you are of laying Christ under any obligation to deny himself in the least for you, and what strong obligations Christ has laid you under to deny yourselves in your dearest earthly interests for him. Remember that your self-denial is a condition consented to by yourselves if ever you received Christ aright. And consider how much your self-denial for Christ makes for your advantage in both worlds. Luke 18 : 29, 30. O therefore look not every man upon his own things, but upon the things that are of Christ; let not that be justly charged upon you which was charged upon some of old, "All seek their own, not the things which are Jesus Christ's." Phil. 2 : 21.

PATTERN 4. The *activity and diligence* of Christ in finishing the work of God committed to him, was a pattern for all believers to imitate. It is said of him, he "went about doing good." Acts 10 : 38. O what a great and glorious work did Christ finish in a little time! A work to be celebrated to all eternity by the praises of the redeemed. Six things were very remarkable in the diligence of Christ about his Father's work. That his heart was intently set upon it: "Thy law is within my heart." Psa. 40 : 8. That he never fainted under the many great discouragements he frequently met with in that work : "He shall not fail, nor be discouraged." Isa. 42 : 4. That the shortness of time led him to the greatest diligence : "I must work the works of him that sent me, while it is day ; the night cometh, when no man can work." John 9 : 4. That he improved all opportunities to further the great work under his hand. John 4 : 31–34. That nothing more displeased him than when he met with discouragements in his work : on this account it was that he gave Peter the sharp reproof, "Get thee behind me, Satan." Matt. 16 : 23. And that nothing rejoiced his soul more than the success of his work. When the disciples made the report of the success of their ministry, it is said, "In that hour Jesus rejoiced in spirit." Luke 10 : 21. And O, what a triumphant shout was that upon the cross at the accomplishment of his work, "It is finished !" John 19 : 30.

Now, Christians, look unto Jesus ; trifle not away your lives in vanity. Christ was diligent, be not you slothful. And to encourage you in your imitation of Christ in labor and diligence, consider how great an honor God puts upon you in employing you for his service ; every vessel of service is a vessel of honor. 2 Tim. 2 : 21. The apostle was ambitious of that honor. Rom. 15 : 20. It was the glory of Eliakim to be fastened as a nail in a sure place, and to have many people hang upon him. Isaiah 22 : 23. Your diligence in the work of God will be your security in the hour of temptation; for "the Lord is with you while ye be with him." 2 Chron. 15 : 2. Diligence in the work of God is an excellent help to the improvement of grace; for though gracious habits are not acquired, they are greatly improved by frequent action : to him that hath shall be given. Matt. 25 : 29. It is a good remark of Luther, Faith improves by obedience. Diligence in the work of God is the way to the assurance of his love. 2 Pet. 1 : 10. This leads to a heaven upon earth. Diligence in obedience is a great security against backsliding; small omissions in duty increase by degrees unto great apostasies. "Do the first works." Rev. 2 : 5. In a word, laborious diligence in the day of life will be your comfort when the night of death overtakes you. 2 Pet. 1 : 11 ; 2 Kings 20 : 3.

PATTERN 5. *Delight in God and his service* was eminently conspicuous in the life of Christ, and is a pattern for the believer's imitation. "But he said unto them, I have meat to eat that ye know not of; my meat is to do the will of him that sent me, and to finish his work." John 4 : 32, 34. The Son of man was in heaven, in respect to delight in God, while he conversed here among men. And if you are Christ's, heavenly things will delight your souls also. Spiritual delight is nothing but the complacency of a renewed heart in conversing with God and the things of God, resulting from their agreeableness to the temper of the mind.

Four things are desirable in respect to spiritual delight. The *nature* of it, which consists in the complacency and satisfaction of the mind in God and spiritual things. The heart of a Christian is centred, it is where it would be ; it is gratified in the highest degree in the acting forth of faith and love upon God, as the taste is gratified with a delicious relish. Psalm 63 : 5, 6 ; 119 : 14 ; 17 : 15. The *object* of spiritual delight, which is God himself and the things which relate to him. He is the blessed ocean into which all the streams of spiritual delight pour themselves. Whom have I in heaven but thee, and on earth there is none that I desire in comparison of thee. Psalm 73 : 25. The *subject* of spiritual delight, which is a renewed heart, and that only so far as it is renewed : "I delight in the law of God after the inward man." Rom. 7 : 22. The *spring* of this delight, which is the agreeableness of spiritual things to the temper of a renewed mind. Pleasure arises from the suitableness of the faculty and object. So it is here—no sweetness can be so pleasant to the taste, or color to the eye, or sound to the ear, as spiritual things to renewed souls, because spiritual senses are more delicate and the objects more excellent.

But my business here is nct so much to show the nature as to press you to *the practice* of this duty, in conformity to your great pattern, whose life was a life of delight in God, and whose work was performed in the same spirit. "I delight to do thy will, O my God." O Christians, strive to imitate your pattern in this. Scarcely any thing can be better proof of sincerity than a heart delighting in God and his will. Hypocrites go as far as others in outward duties, but here they are defective ; they have no delight in God and things spiritual, but perform whatever they do in religion from the compulsion of conscience or from selfish ends. A heart delighting in God will be a choice help and means to perseverance. The reason why many so easily part with religion is, that their souls never tasted the sweetness of it ; but the Christian who delights in the law of God will be meditating on it day and night, and shall be like a tree planted by a river of water, whose leaf fadeth not. Psalm 1 : 2, 3. This will represent religion very beautifully to such as are yet strangers to it : you will then be able to invite them to Christ by your example, and your language will be, "O taste and see that the Lord is good." Psalm 34 : 8. This will make all your services to God acceptable through Christ ; you will now begin to do the will of God on earth as it is done in heaven ; your duties are so far angelical as they are performed in the strength of delight in God.

OBJECTION. But may not a sincere Christian act in duty without delight? Yea, may he not feel some kind of weariness in duties?

ANSWER. Yes, doubtless he may; but then we must distinguish between the temper and distemper of a renewed heart; the best hearts are not always in the right frame.

PATTERN 6. The *inoffensiveness* of the life of Christ upon earth is an excellent pattern for all his people; he injured none, but was holy and harmless, as the apostle speaks, Heb. 7 : 26. He gave up his own liberty to avoid occasion of offence, as in the case of the tribute-money: The children are free; notwithstanding, lest we should offend them, go, etc. Matt. 17 : 26, 27. So circumspect was Christ, that though his enemies sought occasion against him, yet could they find none. Luke 6 : 7. Look unto Jesus, O ye professors of religion; imitate him in his life, according to the command, "That ye may be blameless and harmless, the sons of God, without rebuke, in the midst of a crooked and perverse nation." Phil. 2 : 15. You are indeed allowed the exercise of your prudence, but not a jot farther than will consist with your innocence. "Be ye wise as serpents, and harmless as doves." It is the rule of Christ that you offend none. 1 Cor. 10 : 32; 2 Cor. 6 : 3.

To engage you to the imitation of Christ in this particular, I must briefly press it with a few encouragements. For the honor of Jesus Christ, be you inoffensive, his name is called upon you, his honor is concerned in your deportment; if your deportment give just matter of offence, Christ's worthy name will be blasphemed thereby. James 2 : 7. Your inoffensive conduct is the only means to stop the mouths of detractors. 1 Pet. 2 : 15. For the sake of the precious and immortal souls of others, be careful that you give no offence. "Woe unto the world because of offences." Matt. 17 : 7.   Nothing was more commonly objected against Christ and religion by the heathen in Cyprian's time, than the loose and scandalous lives of professors: Behold, say they, these are the men who boast themselves to be redeemed from the tyranny of Satan, to be dead to the world; nevertheless, see how they are overcome by their lusts.   And much after the same rate Salvian brings in the wicked of his time, stumbling at the looseness of professors, and saying, Where is the law which they believe?   Where are the examples of piety and chastity which they have learned ?   O Christians, draw not the guilt of other men's eternal ruin upon your souls.   In a word, answer the ends of God in your sanctification ; by the holiness of your lives many may be won to Christ. 1 Pet. 3 : 1.   What the heathen said of moral virtue, that if it were but visible to mortal eyes all men would be enamoured with it, will be more true of religion when you shall represent the beauty of it in your conversation.

PATTERN 7.   The *humility and lowliness* of Christ is propounded by himself as a pattern for his people's imitation. " Learn of me ; for I am meek and lowly."   Matt. 11 : 29. He could abase and empty himself of all his glory.   Phil. 2 : 6, 7.   He could stoop to the meanest office, even to wash the disciples' feet.   We read of but one triumph in all the life of Christ ; when he rode to Jerusalem, the people strewed branches in the way, and the very children in the streets of Jerusalem cried, Hosanna to the son of David ; Hosanna in the highest ; and yet with what lowliness and humility was it performed by Christ.   "Behold, thy King cometh unto thee, meek."   Matt. 21 : 5.   The humility of Christ appeared in every thing he spoke or did.   It discovered itself in his language : " I am a worm, and no man."   Psalm 22 : 6.   In his actions, not refusing the meanest office.   John 13 : 14.   In his condescension to the worst of men, which led them to call him "a friend of publicans and sinners."   Matt. 11 : 19.   But especially in stooping from his glory to a state of the deepest contempt, for the glory of God and our salvation. Christians, here is your pattern; look to your meek and humble Saviour, and tread in his steps; be you "clothed with humility." 1 Pet. 5 : 5. Whoever are ambitious to be the world's great ones, let it be enough for you to be Christ's little ones. Convince the world, that ever since you knew God and yourselves, your pride has been dying. Show your humility in your habits, 1 Pet. 3 : 3; 1 Tim. 2 : 9, 10; in your company, not contemning the meanest and poorest that fear the Lord, Psa. 15 : 4; Rom. 12 : 16; in your language, this dialect befits your lips, "Less than the least of all saints," Eph. 3 : 8; but especially in the low value and humble thoughts you have of yourselves. 1 Tim. 1 : 15.

And to press this, I beseech you to consider from how vile a root *pride* springs. Ignorance of God and of yourselves gives being to this sin. They that know God will be humble, Isa. 6 : 5; and they that know themselves cannot be proud. Rom. 7 : 9. Consider the mischievous effects it produces: it estranges the soul from God, Psa. 138 : 6; provokes God to lay you low, Job 40 : 11, 12; goes before destruction and a dreadful fall. Prov. 16 : 18. As it is a great sin, so it is a bad sign. "Behold, his soul which is lifted up, is not upright in him." Hab. 2 : 4. How unsuitable pride is to the complaints you make of your own corruptions and spiritual wants; and above all, how contrary it is to your pattern and example. Did Christ speak, act, or think as you do? O learn humility from Jesus Christ; it will make you precious in the eyes of God. Isa. 57 : 15.

PATTERN 8. The *contentment* of Christ in a low condition in the world, is an excellent pattern for his people's imitation. His lot fell in a condition of poverty and contempt; yet how well was he contented with it! Hear him expressing himself, "The lines are fallen unto me in pleasant places; yea, I have a goodly heritage." Psa. 16 : 6.

The contentment of his heart with a suffering condition evinced itself in his silence under the greatest sufferings. "He was oppressed, and he was afflicted, yet he opened not his mouth : he is brought as a lamb to the slaughter, and as a sheep before her shearers is dumb, so he opened not his mouth." Isa. 53 : 7. O that in this the poorest Christians would imitate their Saviour, and learn to be in an afflicted condition with a contented spirit.

Let no murmurs or foolish charges against God be heard from you, whatever straits or troubles he brings you into. The most afflicted Christian is owner of many invaluable mercies. Eph. 1 : 3 ; 1 Cor. 3 : 23. Is sin pardoned and God reconciled? then never open your mouth any more. Ezek. 16 : 63. You have many precious promises that God will not forsake you in your straits. Heb. 13 : 5 ; Isa. 41 : 17. Your whole life has been an experience of the faithfulness of God in his promises. Which of you cannot say with the church, His mercies are new every morning, and great is his faithfulness? Lam. 3 : 23. How useful and beneficial are afflictions to you ; they purge your sins, prevent temptations, wean from the world, and turn to your salvation : how unreasonable then must be your discontent! Moreover, the time of your full deliverance from all trouble is at hand. If the candle of your earthly comfort be blown out, remember it is but a little while to the break of day, and then there will be no need of candles. Besides, your lot falls to you by divine direction, and it is much easier than that of Christ was. Yet he was contented, and why are not you? O that we could learn contentment from Christ in every condition.

CHAPTER XXX

THE IMITATION OF CHRIST—CONTINUED

"He that saith he abideth in him ought himself also so to walk, even as he walked." 1 John 2: 6

From these words in the previous discourse we drew the doctrine, that *every man is bound to the imitation of Christ, under penalty of forfeiting his claim to Christ.* In the discussion of this point, we have shown what the imitation of Christ imports, and what are the imitable excellencies in the life of Christ. It now remains to show,

III. Why all that profess Christ are bound to imitate his example. The necessity of this imitation of Christ will appear,

1. From *the established order of salvation,* which is fixed and unalterable. God, who has appointed the end, has also established the means by which men shall attain the end. Conformity to Christ is the method in which God will bring souls to glory. "For whom he did foreknow, he also did predestinate to be conformed to the image of his Son, that he might be the first-born among many brethren." Rom. 8 : 29. The same God who has predestinated men to salvation has, in order thereunto, predestinated them unto conformity to Christ, and this order of heaven is never to be reversed; we may as well hope to be saved without Christ, as to be saved without conformity to him.

2. The relation of believers to Christ *as his mystical body* requires this conformity ; otherwise the body of Christ must be of a nature different from the head, and how un-

comely would this be. Christ the head is holy, and therefore unsuitable to sensual and earthly members. The apostle in his description of Christ-mystical, describes the members of Christ as of the same nature with the head. "As is the heavenly, such are they also that are heavenly. And as we have borne the image of the earthly, we shall also bear the image of the heavenly." 1 Cor. 15 : 48, 49. That resemblance of Christ which shall be complete and perfect after the resurrection, must be begun in its first draught here by the work of regeneration.

3. This conformity to Christ appears necessary *from the communion which all believers have with Christ* in the same spirit of grace and holiness. Believers are called Christ's fellows, or copartners, Psalm 45 : 7, from their participation with him of the same spirit. 1 Thess. 4 : 8. God giveth the same Spirit unto us, which he more plentifully poured out upon Christ. Now where the same spirit and principle is, there the same fruits and operations must be produced, according to the measure of the Spirit of grace communicated ; and this reason is farther enforced by the very design of God in imparting the Spirit of grace : for it is plain, from Ezek. 36 : 27, that practical holiness and obedience is the design of that gift of the Spirit. The indwelling of the Spirit of God in men, is to elevate their minds and set their affections upon heavenly things ; to purge their hearts from earthly dross, and fit them for a life of holiness. Its nature also is assimilating, and changes them in whom it is into the same image with Jesus Christ their heavenly head. 2 Cor. 3 : 18.

4. The necessity of this imitation of Christ may be argued from *the design of Christ's exhibition to the world in a body of flesh.* For though we detest the doctrine of the Socinians, which makes the exemplary life of Christ to be the whole end of his incarnation, we must not run so far from an error as to lose a precious truth. The satisfaction of his blood was the principal end of his incarnation, ac-

cording to Matthew 20 : 28 ; but it was a great design of
the incarnation of Christ to set before us a pattern of holiness for our imitation ; for so speaks the apostle, "Leaving us an example that we should follow his steps." 1 Pet.
2 : 21. And this example of Christ binds believers to imitate him. "Let this mind be in you, which also was in
Christ Jesus." Phil. 2 : 5.

5. Our imitation of Christ is one of *the great articles
which every man is to subscribe* whom Christ will admit into
the number of his disciples. "Whosoever doth not bear
his cross, and come after me, cannot be my disciple." Luke
14 : 27. And again, "If any man serve me, let him follow me." John 12 : 26. To this condition we have submitted, if we are sincere believers ; and therefore are
strictly bound to the imitation of Christ, not only by God's
command, but by our own consent. But if we profess
interest in Christ when our hearts never consented to follow and imitate his example, then are we self-deceiving
hypocrites, wholly disagreeing from the Scripture character of believers. They that are Christ's are such as "walk
not after the flesh, but after the Spirit." Romans 8 : 1.
And "if we live in the Spirit, let us also walk in the
Spirit." Gal. 5 : 25.

6. *The honor of Christ* calls for the conformity of Christians to his example, else what way is there to vindicate
the name of Christ from the reproaches of the world?
How can wisdom otherwise be justified of her children?
By what means shall we cut off occasion from such as
desire it, but by regulating our lives by Christ's example?
The world has eyes to see what we practise, as well as
ears to hear what we profess. Therefore show the con-
sistency between your profession and practice, or you can
never hope to vindicate the name and honor of the Lord
Jesus.

INFERENCE 1. If all that profess interest in Christ are
bound to imitate his example, it follows *that religion is very*

unjustly charged by the world with the scandals of them that profess it.

The Christian religion severely *censures* loose and scandalous actions in all professors, and therefore is not to be censured for them. It is absurd to condemn religion for what itself condemns. Sin no way flows from Christianity, but is most contrary to it: "For the grace of God that bringeth salvation hath appeared to all men, teaching us, that denying ungodliness and worldly lusts, we should live soberly, righteously, and godly in this present world." Tit. 2 : 11, 12. It is an evidence for the Christian religion that even wicked men covet the name and profession of it, though they only cloak their evils under it. I confess it is a great abuse of such an excellent thing as religion is ; but if it had not an awful reverence paid it by the consciences of men, it would never be abused to this purpose by hypocrites. If this objection from the faults of professed Christians be valid, there can be no religion in the world ; for what religion is not scandalized by the practice of some that profess it ? So that this practice has a natural tendency to atheism ; and is, no doubt, encouraged by the devil for that end.

2. *If all men forfeit their claim to Christ who endeavor not to imitate him in the holiness of his life, then how small a number of real Christians are there in the world.* Indeed, if talking without accurate walking, if common profession without holy practice, were enough to constitute a Christian, this quarter of the world would abound with Christians. But if Christ owns none but those that copy his example, the number of real Christians is very small. The generality of men that bear the Christian name walk after the flesh. Rom. 8 : 2. According to the course of this world, they yield their members as instruments of unrighteousness unto sin. Rom. 6 : 13. Strict godliness is a bondage to them ; narrow is the way, and few there be that walk therein.

3. *What blessed times should we see, if true religion generally prevailed in the world.* How would it humble the proud and spiritualize those that are carnal. The perverse world charge religion with all the tumults and disturbances in it; whereas nothing but religion, in the power of it, can cure these epidemical evils. O if men were brought under the power of religion indeed, to walk after Christ in holiness, obedience, meekness, and self-denial, no such miseries as these would be heard of among us. "The sucking child shall play on the hole of the asp, and the weaned child shall put his hand on the cockatrice's den; they shall not hurt nor destroy in all my holy mountain; for the earth shall be full of the knowledge of the Lord, as the waters cover the sea." Isa. 11 : 8, 9.

4. Hence it also follows *that real Christians are the sweetest companions.* It is a comfortable thing to walk with them that walk after the example of Christ. The holiness, heavenliness, humility, self-denial, and diligence in obedience which was in Christ, are, in some measure, to be found in all sincere Christians. They show forth the virtues of him that calleth them; the graces of the Spirit more or less shine forth in them. And O, how endearing and engaging are these things. Upon this account the apostle invited others into the fellowship of the saints, "That ye also may have fellowship with us; and truly our fellowship is with the Father, and with his Son Jesus Christ." 1 John 1 : 3. And is it not sweet to have fellowship with them who have fellowship with Christ? O let all your delights be in the saints, and in the excellent of the earth, who excel in virtue. Psalm 16 : 3. Yet there is a great difference between one Christian and another, and even the best Christians are sanctified but in part. If there is something engaging, there is also imperfection in the best of men. If there is something to draw forth your love, there is also something to exercise your patience. Yet notwithstanding all their infirmities, they are the best company this world affords.

5. In a word, if no man's claim to Christ be warranted but theirs that walk as he walked, *how vain and groundless are the hopes and expectations of all unsanctified men, who walk after their own lusts.* None are more forward to claim the privileges of religion than those who reject the duties of it; multitudes hope to be saved by Christ, who yet refuse to be governed by him. But such hopes have no scripture warrant to support them, but have many scripture testimonies against them. "Know ye not that the unrighteous shall not inherit the kingdom of God? Be not deceived; neither fornicators, nor idolaters, nor adulterers, nor effeminate, nor abusers of themselves with mankind; nor thieves, nor covetous, nor drunkards, nor revilers, nor extortioners, shall inherit the kingdom of God." 1 Cor. 6 : 9. O how many vain hopes are laid in the dust, and how many souls are sentenced to hell by this one scripture!

6. If this be so, it calls all the professors of Christianity to *strict godliness in their life,* as ever they expect benefit by Christ. O professors, be ye not conformed unto this world, but be ye transformed by the renewing of your minds. Set the example of Christ before you, and labor to tread in his steps.

This is the great business of religion, the main scope of the gospel. Give me leave, therefore, closely to press it upon your hearts by the following MOTIVES:

(1.) *Christ hath conformed himself to you by his abasing incarnation;* how reasonable therefore is it that you conform yourselves to him in the way of obedience and sanctification. He came as near to you as it was possible for him to do, strive you therefore to come as near to Christ as it is possible for you to do; he has taken your nature upon him, Heb. 2 : 14, and with your nature your infirmities, Rom. 8 : 3, and your condition also, for he came under the law for your sakes. Gal. 4 : 4. He conformed himself to you, though he was infinitely above you; that was his abasement: do you conform yourselves to him; that will be your advancement. His conformity to you emptied him of his glory, your conformity to him will fill you with glory: he conformed himself to you, though you had no claim upon him; will you not conform yourselves to him, who lie under infinite obligations so to do?

(2.) *You shall be conformed to Christ in glory;* how reasonable is it then that you should now conform yourselves to him in holiness. The apostle says, "We shall be like him, for we shall see him as he is." 1 John 3 · 2. Not only your souls shall be like him, but your bodies, even these vile bodies of yours shall be changed, that they may be fashioned like unto his glorious body. How forcible a motive is this to bring men to conformity with Christ here, especially seeing our conformity to him in holiness is the evidence of our conformity to him in glory. Rom. 6 : 5 ; 2 Pet. 3 : 11. O professors, as ever you hope to be with Christ in glory, see that ye walk after Christ's example in holiness and obedience.

(3.) The conformity of your lives to Christ your pattern, *is your highest excellency.* The measure of your grace is to be estimated by this rule. The excellency of every creature rises higher according as it approaches nearer to its original. The more you resemble Christ in grace, the more illustrious and resplendent will your lives be in true spiritual glory.

(4.) So far as you imitate Christ in your lives, *you will be beneficial in the world.* So far as God helps you to follow Christ, you will be helpful to bring others to Christ, or build them up in him; for all men are forbidden by the gospel to follow you farther than you follow Christ. 1 Cor. 11 : 1. And when you have finished your course, the remembrance of your ways will be no farther sweet to others than they are ways of holiness and obedience to Christ. 1 Cor. 4 : 17. If you walk according to the course of this world, the world will not be the better for your walking.

(5.) To walk as Christ walked is a walk *worthy of a Christian;* this is to "walk worthy of the Lord." 1 Thess. 2:12; Col. 1:10. By worthiness the apostle does not mean meritoriousness, but the comeliness or decorum which befits a Christian. As when a man walks suitably to his calling in the world, we say he acts like himself; so when you walk after Christ's pattern, you act like yourselves, like men of your profession. I "beseech you that ye walk worthy of the vocation wherewith ye are called." Eph. 4:1 This walking accords with your obligation to live unto him who died for us. 2 Cor. 5:15. This only suits with your designation, for you are "created in Christ Jesus unto good works, which God hath before ordained that we should walk in them." Eph. 2:10. In a word, such walking as this only becomes your expectation. "Wherefore, beloved, seeing that ye look for such things, be diligent, that ye may be found of him in peace, without spot, and blameless." 2 Peter 3:14.

(6.) How comfortable will *the close of your life be,* if you have walked after Christ's example. A comfortable death is ordinarily the close of a holy life. "Mark the perfect man, and behold the upright; for the end of that man is peace." Psalm 37:37. A careless life gives terrible stings to death. As worms in the body are bred of the putrefaction there, so the worm of conscience is bred of the moral putrefaction that is in our nature and life. O then be prevailed with by all these considerations to imitate Christ in the whole course and compass of your life.

7. I would leave a few words of SUPPORT to such as sincerely endeavor to follow Christ's example, but being weak in grace, and meeting with strong temptations, are frequently carried aside from their holy purposes, to the great grief of their souls. They heartily aim at holiness, and say with David, "O that my ways were directed to keep thy statutes." Psalm 119:5. They follow after holiness, as Paul did, "if by any means they might attain

it." Phil. 3 : 12. But finding how short they come of the pattern, they mourn as he did, " O wretched man that I am! who shall deliver me from the body of this death ?" Rom. 7 : 24. If this be thy case, be not discouraged, but hearken to a few words of support with which I shall close.

(1.) *Such defects in obedience make no flaw in your justification*, for that is not built upon your obedience, but upon Christ's, Rom. 3 : 24 ; and how defective soever you are in yourselves, "ye are complete in him which is the head of all principality and power." Col. 2 : 10. Woe to Abraham, Moses, David, Paul, and the most eminent saints that ever lived, if their justification with God had depended upon the perfection of their own obedience.

(2.) *Your deep sorrow for the defectiveness of your obedience* does not argue you to be less, but more sanctified than those who make no such complaints ; for it proves you to be better acquainted with your hearts ; to have a deeper hatred of sin, and to love God with a more fervent love. The most eminent saints have made the bitterest complaints upon this account. Psa. 65 : 3 ; Rom. 7 : 23, 24.

(3.) *The Lord makes use even of your infirmities to do you good.* By these he hides pride from your eyes, beats you off from self-dependence, makes you admire the riches of grace, makes you long more ardently for heaven, and entertain sweeter thoughts of death. Does not the Lord then make blessed fruits to spring up from such a bitter root ? O the blessed chemistry of heaven, to extract such mercies out of such miseries.

(4.) *Your bewailed infirmities do not break the bond of the covenant.* That bond holds firm, notwithstanding your defects and weaknesses. Jer. 32 : 40. Iniquities prevail against me, says David ; yet he adds, as for our transgressions, thou shalt purge them away. Psalm 65 : 3. He is still thy God and thy Father.

(5.) Though the defects of your obedience are grievous to God, *your deep sorrows for them are well pleasing in his eyes.*

"The sacrifices of God are a broken spirit; a broken and a contrite heart, O God, thou wilt not despise." Psalm 51 : 17. Ephraim was never a more pleasant child to his father than when he bemoaned himself and smote upon his thigh. Jer. 31 : 20. Your sins grieve him, but your sorrows please him.

(6.) Though God has left many defects to humble you, yet *he has given many things to comfort you.* This is a comfort, that the desire of thy soul is to God, and to the remembrance of his name; that thy sins are not thy delight as once they were, but thy shame and sorrow; that thy case is not singular, the same complaints are found in all gracious souls; and in one word, this is the comfort above all others, that the time is at hand in which all these infirmities and failings shall be done away: "When that which is perfect is come, then that which is in part shall be done away." 1 Cor. 13 : 10.

For ever blessed be God for Jesus Christ.

Thus I have finished the third general use of examination whereby every man is to try his interest in Christ, and discern whether ever Christ hath been effectually applied to his soul. What remains is a use of *lamentation,* wherein the miserable and most wretched state of all those to whom Jesus Christ is not effectually applied will be yet more particularly discovered and bewailed.

LAMENTABLE STATE OF UNBELIEVERS

CHAPTER XXXI

SPIRITUAL DEATH AND ITS MISERY

"Wherefore he saith, Awake, thou that sleepest, and arise from the dead, and Christ shall give thee light." EPH. 5:14

THIS scripture represents the miserable and lamentable state of the unregenerate, as being under the power of spiritual death, the cause and inlet of all other miseries. From hence, therefore, I shall make the first discovery of the wretched state of them that apply not Jesus Christ to their souls.

The design of the apostle in the context is to press believers to a circumspect and holy life; to "walk as children of light." This exhortation is laid down and pressed from the tendency of holy principles to holy fruits and practice; from the efficacy of practical godliness on the consciences of the wicked as it awes and convinces them; and from the coincidence of such a life with the great design of the Scriptures, which is to awaken men by regeneration out of that spiritual sleep or death into which sin has cast them; and this is the argument of the text: "Wherefore he saith, Awake, thou that sleepest, and arise from the dead, and Christ shall give thee light." Some think reference is made in these words to Isaiah 26:19: "Awake, and sing, ye that dwell in dust." Others to Isaiah 60:1: "Arise, shine, for thy light is come," etc. But most probably the words refer to neither particularly, but to the scope of the whole Scriptures, which were inspired and written with the great design to awaken and quicken souls out of the state of spiritual death.

In the words selected we may notice more particularly,

1. *The miserable state of the unregenerate*, represented under the images of *sleep* and *death;* both expressions intending the same thing with some variety of illustration. The Christless and unregenerate world are in a deep sleep; a spirit of slumber and security is fallen upon them, though they lie immediately exposed to eternal wrath, ready to drop into hell every moment. A man fast asleep in a house on fire, and while the consuming flames are round about him, having his fancy sporting itself in some pleasant dream, is a very lively resemblance of the unregenerate soul. But he that sleeps has life in him, though his senses are bound and the actions of life suspended. Lest, therefore, we should think it is only so with the unregenerate, the expression is varied, and those that were said to be *asleep*, are affirmed to be *dead*, to inform us that it is not a simple *suspension* of the exercise, but a total *privation* of *the principle of spiritual life*, which is the misery of the unregenerate.

2. *The duty* of the unregenerate, which is to awake out of sleep and arise from the dead. This is their great concern; no duty in the world is of greater necessity and importance to them. "Strive to enter in at the strait gate." Luke 13 : 24. And the order of these duties is natural. First awake, then arise. Startling convictions make way for spiritual life. Till God awake us by convictions of our misery, we shall never be persuaded to arise and move towards Christ for remedy and safety.

3. But you will say, "If unregenerate men are dead, to what purpose is it to persuade them to rise and stand up? The exhortation supposes some power or ability in the unregenerate, else in vain are they commanded to arise." This difficulty is solved in the text. Though the duty is

ours, the power is God's.   God commands that in his word which only his grace can perform.   "Christ shall give thee light."   Popish commentators would build the tower of free-will upon this scripture, by an argument drawn from the order in which these things are here expressed; which is but a very weak foundation to build upon, for it is usual in Scripture to put the effect before the cause, as in Isa. 26 : 19 : "Awake and sing, ye that dwell in dust."   The plain doctrine of the text is, that

All Christless souls are under the power of spiritual death.

Multitudes of testimonies are given in Scripture to this truth : "You hath he quickened, who were dead in trespasses and sins."   Eph. 2 : 1, 5.   "And you, being dead in your sins and the uncircumcision of your flesh, hath he quickened together with him," Col. 2 : 13 ; with many other places.   The method in which I shall discuss this point will be to show in what sense Christless and unregenerate men are said to be dead ; what the state of spiritual death is ; and how it appears that all unregenerate men are in this sad state.

I. IN WHAT SENSE ARE CHRISTLESS AND UNREGENERATE MEN SAID TO BE DEAD?

To understand this, we must know there is a threefold death.   *Natural* death is the privation of the principle of natural life, or the separation of the soul from the body. "The body without the spirit is dead."   James 2 : 26. *Spiritual* death is the privation of the principle of spiritual life, or the absence of the quickening Spirit of God in the soul : the soul is the life of the body, and Christ is the life of the soul ; the absence of the soul is death to the body, and the absence of Christ is death to the soul.   *Eternal* death is the separation both of body and soul from God, which is the misery of the damned.   Christless and unregenerate men are not dead in the first sense ; they are naturally alive, though they are dead while they live ; nor are they dead in the last sense, eternally separated from

God by an irrevocable sentence as the damned are; but they are dead in the second sense, they are spiritually dead while they are naturally alive, and this spiritual death is the forerunner of eternal death.

Spiritual death is put in Scripture in opposition to a twofold spiritual life—the life of *justification*, and the life of *sanctification*. Spiritual death, in opposition to the life of justification, is nothing else but the guilt of sin bringing us under the sentence of death. Spiritual death, in opposition to the life of sanctification, is the pollution or dominion of sin. In both these senses unregenerate men are dead; but it is the last which I am now to speak to, and therefore let us consider,

II. WHAT THIS SPIRITUAL DEATH IS, the absence of the quickening Spirit of Christ from the soul of man. That soul is dead to which the Spirit of Christ is not given in the work of regeneration; and all its works are dead works, as they are called, Heb. 9 : 14. For consider how it is with the damned : they live, they have sense and motion and immortality; yet because they are eternally separated from God their life deserves not the name of life, but is everywhere in Scripture called death. So the unregenerate are naturally alive; they eat and drink, they buy and sell, they talk and laugh, they rejoice in the world; and many of them spend their days in pleasure, and then go down to the grave. This is the life they live; but the Scripture calls it death rather than life, because, though they live, it is without God in the world, Eph. 2 : 12; it is a life alienated from the life of God. Eph. 4 : 18. So that while they are naturally alive, they are in Scripture said to remain in death, 1 John 3 : 14; and to be dead while they live. 1 Tim. 5 : 6. And there is great reason why a Christless, unregenerate state should be represented in Scripture under the notion of death; for there is nothing which more aptly represents this miserable state of the soul.

The dead discern nothing, and the natural man perceiveth not the things that are of God. The dead have no beauty or desirableness in them: Bury my dead, said Abraham, out of my sight: neither is there any spiritual loveliness in the unregenerate. True it is, some of them have qualities and excellencies which are engaging, but they are so many flowers adorning the dead. The dead are objects of lamentation: "Man goeth to his long home, and the mourners go about the streets." Eccl. 12 : 5. But unregenerate and Christless souls are much more the objects of lamentation. How are all the people of God, especially those that are naturally related to them, concerned to mourn over them as Abraham did for Ishmael: "O that Ishmael might live before thee." Gen. 17: 18. Upon these and other accounts, the state of unregenerate man is represented to us under the idea of death.

III. How DOES IT APPEAR THAT UNREGENERATE MEN ARE THUS DEAD?

1. *The causes of spiritual life have not wrought upon them.*

The *principal internal* cause of spiritual life is the regenerating Spirit of Christ. "The law of the Spirit of life in Christ Jesus hath made me free from the law of sin and death." Rom. 8 : 2. It is the Spirit, as a regenerating Spirit, that unites us with Christ, in whom all spiritual life originally is. "Verily I say unto you, the hour is coming, and now is, when the dead shall hear the voice of the Son of God, and they that hear shall live. For as the Father hath life in himself, so hath he given to the Son to have life in himself." John 5 : 25, 26. As all the members of the natural body receive animation, sense, and motion by their union with their head; so all believers, the members of Christ, receive spiritual life and animation by their union with Christ their mystical head. Eph. 4 : 15, 16. Except we are united with him in the way of faith, we can have no life in us. "Ye will not come unto me, that ye might have life." John 5 : 40.

Now the Spirit of God has exerted no regenerating, quickening influences, nor begotten any saving faith in natural, unsanctified men. Whatever he hath done for them in natural or spiritual common gifts, he hath not quickened them with the life of Christ.

And as for the subordinate *external means* of life, the preaching of the gospel, which is the instrument of the Spirit in this glorious work, and is therefore called *the word of life*, Phil. 2 : 16, this word has not been made a regenerating, quickening word to their souls. Possibly it has enlightened them and convinced them : it has wrought upon their minds in the way of common illumination, and upon their consciences in the way of conviction, but not upon their hearts and wills by way of effectual conversion. To this day the Lord has not given them a heart opening itself in the way of faith to receive Jesus Christ.

2. *The effects of spiritual life do not appear in them.* For,

They have no sense of misery and danger. I mean such as thoroughly awakens them to apply Christ their remedy. That spiritual judgment lies upon them : "And he said, Go and tell this people, Hear ye indeed, but understand not ; and see ye indeed, but perceive not. Make the heart of this people fat, and make their ears heavy, and shut their eyes." Isa. 6 : 9, 10.

They have no spiritual motions towards Christ or spiritual things. No arguments can persuade them to move one step towards Christ in the way of faith. "Ye will not come unto me." John 5 : 40. Were there a principle of spiritual life in their souls, they would move towards Christ and heaven. It would be in them a well of water springing up into eternal life. John 4 : 14. The natural tendency of the spiritual life is upward.

The unregenerate have no appetite for spiritual food ; they savor not things that are spiritual. They can go from week to week and from year to year, all their lifetime, without any communion between God and their souls, and feel no need of it, nor hungerings or thirstings after it; which could never be, if a principle of spiritual life were in them; for then they would "esteem the words of God's mouth more than their necessary food." Job 23:12.

They have no heat or spiritual warmth in their affections to God and things above; their hearts are cold as a stone to spiritual objects. They are heated by their lusts and affections to the world; but O, how cold and dead are they towards Jesus Christ and spiritual excellences.

They breathe not spiritually, therefore they live not spiritually: were there a spiritual principle of life in them, their souls would breathe after God in spiritual prayer. "Behold, he prayeth." Acts 9 : 11. The lips of the unregenerate may move in prayer, but their hearts and desires do not breathe and pant after God.

They have no cares or fears for self-preservation, which is always the effect of life. The wrath of God hangs over them in the threatenings, but they tremble not; they are on the very precipice of eternal ruin, yet use no means to avoid it. How plain is the sad case I have undertaken to demonstrate, namely, that Christless and unregenerate souls are spiritually dead.

INFERENCE 1. If Christless and unregenerate souls are spiritually dead, *how little pleasure can Christians take in their society.*

Certainly it is no pleasure for the living to converse among the dead. It was a cruel torment invented by Mezentius the tyrant, to tie a dead and living man together. The pleasure of society arises from the harmony of spirit, and the hope of mutual enjoyment in the world to come; neither of which can sweeten the society of the godly with the wicked in this world. It is true, there is a necessary civil intercourse which we must have with the ungodly here; or else, as the apostle speaks, we must go out of the world.   There are also relative duties which must be faithfully discharged ; but where we have our free election, we shall be much wanting both to our duty and comfort, if we make not the people of God our chosen companions.

Excellently to this purpose speaks Gurnal, in his Christian Armor. "Art thou a godly master? when thou takest a servant into thy house, choose for God as well as thyself. A godly servant is a greater blessing than we think : he can work, and set God on work also for his master's good : 'O Lord God of my master Abraham, I pray thee send me good speed this day, and show kindness unto my master,' Gen. 24 : 12 ; and surely Eliezer did his master as much service by his prayer as by his prudence in that journey.   Holy David observed while he was at Saul's court the mischief of having wicked and ungodly servants, for with such was that unhappy king so compassed that David compares his court to the profane and barbarous heathen, among whom there was scarce more wickedness to be found.   'Woe is me that I sojourn in Meshech, that I dwell in the tents of Kedar,' Psa. 120 : 5 ; that is, among those who are as wicked as any there ; and no doubt but this made him, in his banishment before he came to the crown, resolve what he would do when God should make him the head of a royal family.   'He that worketh deceit shall not dwell within my house ; he that telleth lies shall not tarry in my sight.'   Psa. 101 : 7.

"Art thou godly? show thyself so in the choice of husband or wife.   I am sure if some could bring no other testimonials for their godliness than the care they have taken in this particular, it might justly be called into question both by themselves and others.   There is no one thing in which gracious persons have more shown their weakness, yea, given offence and scandal, than in this particular.   The sons of God saw that the daughters of men were fair.   Gen. 6 : 2.   One would have thought that the sons of God should have looked for grace in the heart, rather than beauty in the face; but we see even they sometimes turn in at the fairest sign, without much inquiry what grace is to be found dwelling within." Look to the rule, O Christian, if thou wilt keep the power of holiness: that is clear as the sun-beam written in the Scripture, "Be ye not unequally yoked together with unbelievers." 2 Cor. 6 : 14.

2. *How great and wholly supernatural is the change regeneration makes on the souls of men!* It is a change from death to life. "This my son was dead, and is alive again." Luke 15 : 24. Regeneration is life from the dead; the most excellent life from the most terrible death: it is the life of God imparted to a soul alienated from it by sin. Eph. 5 : 11. There are two changes made upon the souls of men, which challenge the highest admiration: that from sin to grace, and that from grace to glory. The change from grace to glory is acknowledged by all, and justly, to be a wonderful change. For God to take a poor creature out of the society of sinful men; yea, from under the burden of many sinful infirmities, which made him groan from day to day in this world, and in a moment to make him a perfect soul, shining in the beauties of holiness, and filling him with the inconceivable joys of his presence—to turn his groanings into triumphs, his sighings into songs of praise, is marvellous. And yet the former change from sin to grace is no way inferior to it, nay, in some respects it is beyond it. Great is this work of God; and let it for ever be marvellous in our eyes.

3. If unregenerate souls are dead, *what a fatal stroke does death give to the bodies of all unregenerate men.* A soul dead in sin, and a body dead by virtue of the curse for sin, and both soul and body remaining for ever under the power of eternal death, is so full and perfect a misery, that nothing can make it more miserable. It is the comfort of a Christian that he can say when death comes, I

shall not wholly die; there is a life which death cannot touch. "The body is dead because of sin; but the spirit is life because of righteousness." Rom. 8 : 10. Blessed and holy is he that hath part in the first resurrection : on such the second death hath no power. As death takes the believer from many sorrows, and brings him to the vision of God, to the general assembly of the perfected saints, to a state of freedom and full satisfaction; so it drags the unregenerate from all his sensual delights to the place of torment : it buries the dead soul out of the presence of God for ever; it is the king of terrors, a serpent with a deadly sting to every man who is out of Christ.

4. If every unregenerate soul be dead, *how sad is the case of hypocrites, who are twice dead!* These are those cursed trees of which the apostle Jude speaks, "Trees whose fruit withereth, without fruit, twice dead, plucked up by the roots." Jude 12. Though they were still under the power of spiritual death, yet in the beginning of their profession they seemed to be alive : they showed the fragrant leaves of a fair profession, many buddings of affection towards spiritual things; but wanting the root of regeneration, they quickly began to wither and cast their untimely fruit. Their original defect is the want of a good root, and therefore they who were always once dead for want of regeneration, are now become twice dead by the decay of their profession. Such trees are prepared for the severest flames in hell, Matt. 24 : 51; their portion is the saddest allotted for the sons of death. "For if after they have escaped the pollutions of the world, through the knowledge of the Lord and Saviour Jesus Christ, they are again entangled therein and overcome, the latter end is worse with them than the beginning. For it had been better for them not to have known the way of righteousness, than after they have known it, to turn from the holy commandment delivered unto them." 2 Pet. 2 : 20, 21. Double measures of wrath seem to be prepared for them that die this double death.

5. If this be so, *how lamentable is the state of unregenerate persons.* Were this truth heartily believed, we could not but mourn over them with the most tender compassion and sorrow. If our husbands, wives, or children are dying a natural death, how are our hearts rent with pity and sorrow for them; what cries, tears, and wringing of hands show the deep sense we have of their misery! O Christians, is all the love you have for your relatives spent upon their bodies? Are their souls of no value? Is spiritual death no misery? Does it not deserve a tear? The Lord open your eyes, and affect your hearts with the wretchedness of spiritual death.

Consider, my friends, while they remain spiritually dead, they are wholly unserviceable to God in the world, as to any acceptable service, 2 Tim. 2 : 21; they are incapable of all spiritual comforts from God; they cannot taste the least sweetness in Christ, in duties, or in promises, Rom. 8 : 6; they have no beauty in their souls, how comely soever their bodies : nothing but grace beautifies the inner man. Ezek. 16 : 6, 7. The spiritually dead have neither comfort nor beauty; they have no hope to be with God in glory, for the life of glory is began in grace, Phil. 1 : 6; their graves must be shortly made, to be buried for ever in the lowest hell, the pit digged by justice for all that are spiritually dead. Can such considerations as these draw no pity from your souls, nor excite your endeavors for their regeneration? then it is to be feared your souls are dead as well as theirs. O pity them, and pray for them; in this case only, prayers for the dead are our duty : who knows but at the last God may hear your cries, and you may say with comfort "This my son was dead, but is alive again; he was lost, but is found." Luke 15 : 24.

CHAPTER XXXII

THE CONDEMNATION OF UNBELIEVERS

"But he that believeth not is condemned already, because he hath not believed in the name of the only begotten Son of God."   JOHN 3: 18

CHRIST having discoursed with Nicodemus, in the beginning of this chapter, about the necessity of regeneration, proceeds to show the reason why regeneration and faith are so indispensably necessary, namely, because there is no other way to set men free from the curse and condemnation of the law.   The curse of the law, like the fiery serpents in the wilderness, has smitten every sinner with a deadly stroke, for which there is no cure but Christ lifted up in the gospel, "as Moses lifted up the serpent in the wilderness."   Neither does Christ cure any but those that believingly apply him to their own souls.   The result and conclusion of all we have in the text and the words preceding, "He that believeth in him is not condemned; but *he that believeth not is condemned already.*"   In this clause we find three parts:

1. The sin threatened, namely, *unbelief*—the neglecting or refusing of an exalted and offered Saviour.   Negative unbelief is the sin of the heathen, who never had the gospel nor the offers of Christ made to them; and how shall men believe on him of whom they have not heard?   Positive unbelief is the sin of men under the gospel, to whom Christ is offered, but they neglect the great salvation.   They receive not Christ into their hearts, nor consent to the self-denying terms upon which he is offered.   This is the sin threatened.

2. The punishment inflicted, that is, *condemnation;* a word of deep and dreadful signification; appearing as the

handwriting upon the wall utno Belshazzar, Daniel 5 : 5 ; a word whose deep sense and emphasis are fully understood in hell.   *Condemnation* is the judgment or sentence of God, condemning a man to bear the punishment of his eternal wrath for sin.

3. The immediate respect this punishment has to the sin of unbelief. The unbeliever is condemned already ; he is virtually condemned by the law of God ; he is condemned as *a sinner*, by the breach of the first covenant ; and that condemnation has been ratified by the sentence of God condemning him as an *unbeliever*, for slighting and rejecting the grace offered in the second covenant. So that he is already virtually condemned, both as he is a sinner and as he is an unbeliever ; as he has transgressed the law, and as he has refused the gospel ; as he has contracted sin the moral disease, and refused Christ the only effectual remedy. Unbelief is his great sin, and condemnation is his great misery. Hence,

All unbelievers are presently and immediately under the just and dreadful sentence of God's condemnation.

"He that rejecteth me, and receiveth not my words, hath one that judgeth him ; the word that I have spoken, the same shall judge him in the last day." John 12 : 48. "He that believeth not the Son shall not see life ; but the wrath of God abideth on him." John 3 : 36.

Three things are here to be illustrated : what unbelief, or the not receiving of Jesus Christ, is ; what condemnation, the punishment of this sin, is ; and why this punishment unavoidably follows that sin.

I. WHAT THE SIN OF UNBELIEF, OR NOT RECEIVING CHRIST, IS. By unbelief, we are not here to understand the remains of that sin in the people of God which is mixed with their faith ; unbelief is mingled with faith in the best hearts. He that can say, "Lord, I believe," has cause enough to cry out with tears, "help thou mine unbelief ;" but this does not bring the soul under condemnation. The unbelief here spoken of is neglecting to take Christ as he is offered in the gospel.

1. *It excludes the saving act of faith,* which is the receiving of Christ offered in the gospel, consenting to take him upon his own terms. This the unbeliever will not be persuaded to do ; he will be persuaded to accept the promises of Christ, but not his person. He is willing to accept Christ in part, a divided Christ, but not to accept Christ entirely in all his offices. He will accept the righteousness of Christ in conjunction with his own ; but he will not accept the righteousness of Christ as the sole ground of his justification, exclusive of his own righteousness. He is willing to wear the crown of Christ, but cannot be persuaded to bear his cross. God will not alter his terms, nor the unbeliever his resolution ; and so Christ is refused, salvation neglected, and in effect the unbeliever chooses rather to be damned than to comply with the terms of self-denial, mortification, and bearing the cross of Christ.

2. *It excludes the saving fruits and effects of faith.* Faith produces love to God, but the unbeliever does not truly love him. "I know you," says Christ to unbelievers, "that ye have not the love of God in you." John 5 : 42. Faith purifies the heart of a believer, but the hearts of unbelievers are full of impurity. The believer overcomes the world, the world overcomes the unbeliever. Faith makes the cross of Christ easy to the believer; unbelief makes Christ, because of the cross, bitter to the unbeliever. Thus unbelief excludes both the saving act and the fruits of faith, and consequently bars the soul from the benefits of faith, namely, justification and peace with God.

II. Consider THE PUNISHMENT OF THIS SIN, which is condemnation. Condemnation in the general is the sentence of a judge awarding a penalty to be inflicted upon the guilty person. There is a twofold condemnation. With respect to *the fault,* it is the casting of the person as guilty of the crime charged upon him. Condemnation, with respect to *the punishment*, is sentencing the convicted offender to undergo such a punishment for such a fault. This forensic or law word, condemnation, is applied to the case of a guilty sinner cast at the bar of God, where the fact is proved and the punishment awarded. Thou art an unbeliever, for this sin thou shalt die eternally. Condemnation with respect to the fault stands opposed to justification. Rom. 5 : 16. Condemnation with respect to the punishment stands opposed to salvation. Mark 16 : 16.

1. Condemnation is the sentence of *the great and terrible God*, the omniscient, omnipotent, supreme, and impartial Judge, at whose bar the sinner stands. The law of God condemns him now : he has one that judges him. It is a dreadful thing to be condemned at man's bar ; but courts of human justice, how awful soever they are, are trifles compared with this court of heaven, and conscience, by which the unbeliever is arraigned and condemned.

2. It is the sentence of God adjudging the unbeliever to *eternal death.* What is a prison to hell ? what is a scaffold and an axe to, "Go, ye cursed, into everlasting fire ?"

3. Condemnation is the *final* sentence of God the supreme Judge, from whose judgment there lies no appeal, for execution certainly follows condemnation. Luke 19: 27. If man condemn, God may justify ; but if God condemn, no man can deliver. If the law condemn a man as a sinner, the gospel may save him as a believer ; but if the gospel condemn him as an unbeliever, if a man finally reject Jesus Christ whom it offers, all the world cannot save him. O then what a dreadful word is condemnation. All the evils of this life are nothing to it. Put all afflictions and miseries of this world into one scale, and this sentence of God into the other, and they will be all lighter than a feather.

III. This condemnation must follow the sin of unbelief. As many unbelieving persons as are in the world, so many condemned persons there are in the world. For,

1. Let us consider *what unbelief excludes a man from.*

It excludes him from the *pardon* of sin. "If ye believe not that I am he, ye shall die in your sins." John 8 : 24. He that dies under the guilt of all his sins must be in a state of wrath and condemnatiou for ever ; "for the wages of sin is death." Rom. 6 : 23. If a man be saved without pardon, then may the unbeliever hope to be saved.

Unbelief excludes a man from all the saving *benefits* of the sacrifice or death of Christ.   For if faith be the instrument that brings home to the soul the benefits of the blood of Christ, as unquestionally it is, unbelief must exclude a man from those benefits and leave him in the state of condemnation.   Faith is the instrument by which we receive the saving benefit of the blood of Christ.   "Whom God hath set forth to be a propitiation through faith in his blood." Romans 3 : 25.   "By grace are ye saved through faith." Eph. 2 : 8.   So then if the unbeliever be acquitted and saved, it must be without the benefit of Christ's death and sacrifice, which is utterly impossible.

Unbelief excludes a man from the saving efficacy of *the gospel*, by shutting up the heart against it and opposing the main drift of it, to bring men to the terms of salvation. To persuade them to believe is its great design, the substance of all its commands.   1 John 3 : 23 ; Mark 1 : 14, 15 ; John 12 : 36.   It is the design of its promises ; they are written to encourage men to believe.   John 6 : 35, 37. So that if the unbeliever escapes condemnation, it must be in a way unknown to us by the gospel, yea, contrary to its established order.   For the unbeliever obeys not the great command of the gospel, 1 John 3 : 23 ; nor is he under any one saving promise of it.   Gal. 3 : 14, 22.

Unbelief excludes a man from *union with Christ*, faith being the bond of that union.   Eph. 3 : 17.   The unbeliever may as reasonably expect to be saved without Christ as to be saved without faith.

2. Let us next see *what guilt and misery unbelief includes men under*.

It is a sin which reflects the greatest *dishonor upon God :* " He that believeth on the Son of God hath the witness in himself; he that believeth not God hath made him a liar ; because he believeth not the record that God gave of his Son." 1 John 5 : 10.

Unbelief makes a man guilty of the vilest *contempt of Christ,* and the whole design of redemption by him. All the attributes of God were manifested in the work of redemption by Christ ; therefore the apostle calls him " the wisdom of God, and the power of God." 1 Cor. 1 : 24. And what does the neglect and rejection of Christ imply, but the weakness and folly of redemption by him.

Unbelief includes in it the sorest spiritual judgment that can be inflicted upon the soul of man ; even spiritual blindness and the fatal darkening of the understanding by Satan, 2 Cor. 4 : 4, of which more hereafter.

Unbelief also includes a man under the curse, and shuts him up under all the threatenings written in the book of God, among which is the terrible one, "He that believeth not shall be damned," Mark 16 : 16 ; so that nothing can be more evident than that condemnation follows unbelief. This sin and that punishment are fastened together with chains of adamant.

INFERENCE 1. If this be so, *how great a number of persons are in the state of condemnation!* So many unbelievers, so many condemned. That is a sad complaint of the prophet, " Who hath believed our report, and to whom is the arm of the Lord revealed?" Isa. 53 : 1. Many talk of faith, and many profess it, but there are few in the world unto whom the arm of the Lord has been revealed in the work of faith with power. It is put among the great mysteries, that Christ is believed on in the world. 1 Tim. 3 : 16. O what a terrible day will be the day of Christ's coming to judgment, when so many millions of unbelievers shall be brought to his tribunal to be solemnly sentenced ! They are condemned already ; but then that dreadful sentence will be solemnly pronounced by Jesus Christ, whom they have despised and rejected. Then shall that scripture be fulfilled : "Those mine enemies that would not that I should reign over them, bring hither and slay them before me." Luke 19 : 27.

2. Hence learn *how great a mercy the least measure of saving faith is;* for this unites the soul to Jesus Christ ; and "there is no condemnation to them that are in Christ Jesus," Rom. 8 : 1 ; not one sentence of God against them. "By him all that believe are justified from all things." Acts 13 : 39. The weakest believer is as free from condemnation as the strongest ; the righteousness of Christ comes upon all believers. "Even the righteousness of God, which is by faith of Jesus Christ unto all and upon all them that believe ; for there is no difference." Rom. 3 : 22. The faith that receives the righteousness of Christ may be different in degrees of strength ; but the received righteousness is equal upon all believers. O the exceeding preciousness of saving faith !

3. *How dreadful a sin is the sin of unbelief,* which brings men under the condemnation of the great God. No sin startles less or damns surer : it is a sin that does not affright the conscience as some other sins do, but it kills the soul more certainly than any of those sins. Other sins could not damn us were it not for unbelief, which fixes the guilt of them all upon our persons. "This is the condemnation." Unbelief is the sin of sins ; and when the Spirit comes to convince men of sin, he begins with this as the capital sin. John 16 : 9.

Estimate the evil of unbelief from its *object.* It is slighting the most excellent person in heaven or earth : the vision of Christ by faith is the joy of saints upon earth ; the vision of Christ above is the happiness of saints in heaven. It is despising him who is altogether lovely in himself, who hath loved us and given himself for us.

It is rejecting the only Mediator between God and man; after rejecting whom there remains no sacrifice for sin.

Let the evil of unbelief be estimated by the offer of Christ in the gospel. It is one part of the great mystery of godliness that Christ should be preached to the Gentiles, 1 Tim. 3 : 16; that the word of this salvation should be sent to us, Acts 13 : 26; a mercy denied to the fallen angels and the greatest part of mankind, which aggravates the evil of this sin beyond all imagination. In refusing or neglecting Jesus Christ are found vile ingratitude, the highest contempt of the grace and wisdom of God; and in the event, the loss of the only opportunity of salvation, never to be recovered to all eternity.

4. If this be the case of all unbelievers, *it is not to be wondered at that souls under convictions of their miserable condition are plunged into deep distress.* They at Jerusalem were pricked at the heart, and cried out, Men and brethren, what shall we do? Acts 2 : 37. And so the jailer came in trembling and astonished, and said, Sirs, what must I do to be saved? Certainly, if souls apprehend themselves under the condemnation of the great God, tears and trembling, wearisome days and restless nights are not without just cause. Those that never saw their miserable condition by the light of a clear and full conviction, may wonder to see others distressed in spirit. They may misjudge the case, and call it melancholy or madness; but spiritual troubles do not exceed the cause of them, great as they may be. And indeed, it is one of the great mysteries of grace and providence how such souls are supported under sorrows, which, in a few hours, might break the stoutest spirit in the world. Luther was a man of great natural courage; and yet, when God let in spiritual troubles upon his soul, it is said he had neither voice, nor heat, nor blood appearing in him.

5. *How groundless is the mirth of unregenerate men.* They

feast in their prison and dance in their fetters. O the
madness that is in their hearts! If men did but believe
they are condemned already, it were impossible for them
to live in vanity as they do. And is their condition less
dangerous because it is not understood? Surely not, but
much more so. O poor sinners, you have found out a
way to prevent your present troubles: it were well if you
could find out how to prevent eternal misery. But it is
easier for a man to stifle conviction than to prevent damnation. Your mirth prevents repentance and increases
your future torment. O what a hell will theirs be, who
drop into it out of all the sinful pleasures of this world!
If ever man may say of mirth that it is mad, and of laughter, what doeth it? he may say so in this case.

6. *What cause have they to rejoice and praise the Lord to
eternity who have a well-grounded confidence that they are freed
from God's condemnation!* O give thanks to the Father,
who hath delivered you from the power of darkness, and
translated you into the kingdom of his dear Son. Col.
1 : 12, 13. Rejoice, and be exceeding glad; for if freed
from condemnation, you are out of Satan's power, he has
no more dominion over you. The power of Satan over
men comes in by virtue of their condemnation, as the
power of the *jailer* or *executioner* over the bodies of condemned prisoners. Heb. 2 : 14. If you are freed from
condemnation, the sting of death shall never touch you,
for it smites men only by virtue of God's sentence : "The
sting of death is sin, and the strength of sin is the law."
1 Cor. 15 : 56. If you are freed from condemnation you
shall stand with boldness at the judgment-seat of Christ;
and verily in this is the love of God perfected. 1 John
4 : 17. O it is a privilege in which the grace and love of
God shine as clearly as the sun in its full strength. And
you will find cause to lie at the feet of God, overwhelmed
with the sense of this mercy, when you shall find yourselves free from condemnation, while many others are still

under it. Yea, yourselves freed, and others, that had the same external advantages as you had, still in chains. 2 Cor. 2 : 16. O brethren, this is a marvellous deliverance ; look on it which way you will, your ransom is paid, but not a particle of it by yourselves ; it cost you nothing to procure your pardon ; your pardon is full, and not one sin is excepted out of it that you ever committed. You are freed, Jesus Christ procured your discharge ; your pardon is sealed in his blood, so that you shall never more come into condemnation. "He that heareth my word, and believeth on him that sent me, hath everlasting life, and shall not come into condemnation, but is passed from death unto life." John 5 : 24.

Let them that are so delivered spend their days on earth in praise and obedience ; and when they die, let them not shrink from death, it can do them no harm ; yea, let them close their dying lips with,

Thanks be to God for Jesus Christ.

CHAPTER XXXIII

AGGRAVATION OF THE SIN AND PUNISHMENT OF UNBELIEF

"And this is the condemnation, that light is come into the world, and men loved darkness rather than light, because their deeds were evil." JOHN 3 : 19

FROM the verse preceding our text it has been fully proved that all unregenerate men are no better than dead men, being condemned already.   Our Saviour proceeds in this verse yet farther to describe the misery of those that refuse him, and show that those who remain in unbelief and unregeneracy must expect greater wrath than other men; not only a simple condemnation, but an aggravated and peculiar condemnation.   "This is the condemnation, that light is come into the world, and men loved darkness rather than light, because their deeds were evil." John 3 : 19.

1. We have here the aggravation of sin by *the abuse of gospel light*.   "Light is come."   By light we are to understand the knowledge of Christ, and redemption by him in the gospel.   He is the Sun of righteousness that arises in the gospel upon the nations.   Mal. 4 : 2.   When he came in the flesh, then did the day-spring from on high visit us.   Luke 1 : 78.   The light may be said to come in either the means by which it is conveyed to us, or in its efficacy, when it actually shines in our souls.   Light may come among a people in the means, and yet they actually remain in darkness.   As it is in nature ; the sun may rise and a glorious morning be far advanced while thousands are on their beds with their curtains drawn about them.   Light may be intellectual only in conviction ; or efficacious, bringing the soul to Christ by real conversion, called in 1

Cor. 4 : 6, God shining into the heart. Wherever light comes in the last sense, it is impossible that men should prefer darkness before it. But it may come in the means, and may shine into the consciences of men and convince them of their sins, and yet men may hate it, and choose darkness rather than light. And this is the sense of this text : light had come in the gospel dispensation among them ; yea, it had shone into many of their consciences and reproved them for sin, but they hated it, and had rather been without it.

In a word, by the coming of light we are to understand a more clear manifestation of Christ by the gospel than was made to the world before ; for we are not to think that there was no light in the world until Christ came, and that the gospel was first published by the apostles' ministry. Abraham saw Christ's day, John 8 : 56, and all the faithful before Christ saw the promises, that is, their accomplishment in Christ, afar off. Heb. 11 : 13. It was with Christ, the Sun of righteousness, as with the natural sun, which illuminates the hemisphere before it actually rises or shows its body above the horizon ; but when it rises and shows itself, the light is much clearer. The greater therefore was the sin of those that rebelled against it and preferred darkness to light.

2. In proportion to this sin, we have here *the aggravated condemnation of them who sinned against such clear gospel light.* " This is the condemnation," this is the judgment of all judgments ; a severer sentence of condemnation than ever passed against any in the times of ignorance and darkness : they that live and die unregenerate, how few soever the means of salvation they have enjoyed, must be condemned : yea, the pagan world, who have but natural light to help them, will be condemned by it ; but " this is the condemnation," that is, such sinning as this is the cause of the greatest condemnation and sorest punishment, as it is called, Heb. 10 : 29.

3. *The cause and occasion; drawing men into this sin and misery,* "because their deeds are evil," that is, the light of truth put vigor and activity into their consciences, which they could not endure. The accusations and condemnation of conscience are very irksome and troublesome to men. To avoid this they are willing to be ignorant. An enlightened conscience gives interruption in their sinful courses; they cannot sin so easily in the light as they did in darkness, and this made them hate the light as very troublesome. Thus you see what was the sin, what the punishment, and what the cause of both. Hence,

The clearer the light under which the unregenerate live in this world, so much the greater and heavier will their condemnation and misery be in the world to come.

"Woe unto thee, Chorazin! woe unto thee, Bethsaida! for if the mighty works, which were done in you, had been done in Tyre and Sidon, they would have repented long ago in sackcloth and ashes. But I say unto you, It shall be more tolerable for Tyre and Sidon, at the day of judgment, than for you." Matt. 11 : 21, 22. Two things require to be considered : how light aggravates sin ; and why sin so aggravated exposes men to greater condemnation.

I. WHY GREATER LIGHT AGGRAVATES THE SINS COMMITTED UNDER IT.

1. *All evangelical light is a great preservative from sin.* It is the property of light to inform the judgment, rectify its mistakes, and thereby to check the affections in the pursuit of sinful courses. Many men would never act as they do, if their understandings were better informed. "Which none of the princes of this world knew ; for had they known it, they would not have crucified the Lord of glory." 1 Cor. 2 : 8. It was want of better information which drew them under that unparalleled guilt. Our Saviour also intimates in the place before cited, that if Tyre and Sidon had enjoyed the light and means of grace that Chorazin and Beth-

saida did, they would not have been so sinful as they were; light discovers danger, and stops men from proceeding farther in those courses that lead them into it.

2. Sinning against the light *involves a greater contempt of God's authority* than sinning in ignorance and darkness. Every man that breaks the law of God does not in the same degree despise the authority of the law-maker. But when a man has light to see the evil of what he does, and yet will dare to do it, he treads God's authority under foot. Wilful sinning is despiteful sinning against God, Hebrews 10 : 26 ; it argues a low and vile esteem of the law of God, which is reverend and holy ; and by so much the more it makes sin to be exceeding sinful.

3. Sinning against the light *admits not the excuses to extenuate the offence* which sins of ignorance do. Those that live without the gospel may say, Lord, we never heard of Christ and the great redemption wrought by him ; if we had, we would not have lived as we did : and therefore Christ says, " If I had not come and spoken unto them, they had not had sin ; but now they have no cloak for their sin." John 15 : 22. The meaning is, that if the gospel light had not shone among them, their sin had not been of such deep guilt as now it is. It is heinous by reason of the light against which it is committed, and they have no excuse to extenuate it.

4. *Evangelical light is a rich favor of God to men*, one of the choicest gifts bestowed upon the nations of the world, and therefore it is said, "He showeth his word unto Jacob, and his statutes and his judgments unto Israel. He hath not dealt so with any nation ; and as for his judgments, they have not known them." Psalm 147 : 19, 20. Other nations have corn and wine, gold and silver, abundance of pleasures, but they have not a beam of heavenly light shining upon them. We may account this mercy small ; but God, who is best able to value it, accounts it great. "I have written to him the great things of my law." Hosea

8 : 12. Christ reckoned Capernaum to be exalted to heaven by the ministry of the gospel. The greater the mercy which the light of truth brings with it, so much the more heinous must be the abuse of it.

5. Sinning against the light argues *a love to sin without any disguise.* When a man, through a mistake of judgment, thinks that to be lawful which is indeed sinful, he does not close with sin as sin, but as his duty, or at least his liberty. It is hard for Satan to persuade many men to embrace a naked sin, and therefore he clothes it in the habit of a duty or liberty, and thereby draws men to the commission of it. But if a man has light shining into his conscience, convincing him that he is in the way of sin quite contrary to the revealed will of God, stripping the sin naked before the eye of his conscience, so that he has no excuse, and yet he will persist in it, it argues that his soul is in love with sin as sin. Now as for a man to love grace as grace, is a solid argument to prove the truth of his grace ; so on the contrary for a man to love sin as sin, not only argues him to be in the state of sin, but to be in the forefront and among the highest rank of sinners.

6. The clearer the light against which men continue to sin, *the more must the consciences of such sinners be violated;* for the greatest violation of conscience is the greatest sin. Conscience is a noble and tender part of the soul of man: it is in the soul, as the eye in the body, very sensible of the least injury ; and a wound in the conscience is like a blow in the eye. But nothing gives a greater blow to conscience, nothing so much injures it, as sin against the light.

II. Let us examine why sin, so aggravated by the light, makes men liable to THE GREATER CONDEMNATION. That it does so is beyond all debate, else the apostle Peter would not have said of sinners against light, "it had been better for them not to have known the way of righteousness." 2 Pet. 2 : 21. Nor would Christ have told the inhabitants of Chorazin or Bethsaida, that it should be more tolerable

for Tyre and Sidon at the day of judgment than for them.
There is a twofold reason of this.

1. *On God's part,* who is the righteous Judge of the
whole earth, and will therefore render to every man according as his work shall be. Shall not the Judge of the
whole earth do right? He will judge the world in righteousness, which requires that difference be made in the
punishment of sinners according to the different degrees of
their sins. That there are different degrees of sin is clear
from what we have lately shown, that the light under
which men sin aggravates their sins, in accordance with
which will be the degree of punishment awarded by the
Judge of heaven and earth. The Gentiles, who had no
other light but the dim light of nature, will be condemned
for disobeying the law of God written upon their hearts ;
but greater wrath is reserved for those who sin both against
the light of nature and the light of the gospel. Therefore
it is said, Rom. 2 : 9, " Tribulation and anguish upon every
soul of man that doeth evil ; of the Jew first, and also of
the Gentile." Impenitent Jews and Gentiles will be condemned at the bar of God ; but to the Jew first, that is,
especially, because the mercies which he abused were far
greater than those bestowed upon the Gentiles : "because
unto them were committed the oracles of God ;" and God
has not dealt with any nation as with them. Indeed, in
the gracious rewards of obedience, he that came into the
vineyard the last hour of the day may be equal in reward
with him that bore the heat and burden of the whole day,
because the reward is of grace, not of merit. But justice
observes an exact proportion in distributing punishments
according to the degrees and measures of sin. Therefore
it is said concerning Babylon, "How much she hath glorified herself, and lived deliciously, so much torment and
sorrow give her." Rev. 18 : 7.

2. *On the part of sinners.* It must be that the heaviest
wrath and torments should be the portion of those who

have sinned against the clearest light and means of grace. For we find in the Scripture that a principal part of the torment of the damned will arise from their own consciences: "Where their worm dieth not, and the fire is not quenched." Mark 9 : 44. And nothing is plainer than that if conscience be the tormentor of the damned, sinners against light must have the greatest torment.

The more knowledge any man had in this world, the more was his *conscience* abused by sinning against it. And O, what work will these violations make for a tormenting conscience in hell! With what fury will it then avenge itself upon the most daring sinner. The more guilt now, the more rage and fury then.

The more knowledge or means of knowledge any man has enjoyed, *the more* is laid up for conscience to upbraid him with in the place of torment. O what a peal will conscience ring in the ears of such sinners. "Did not I warn thee of the issue of such sins, undone wretch? How often did I strive with thee, to take thee off from thy course of sinning, and to escape this wrath! Did not I often cry out, Stop thy course, sinner? Hearken to my counsel, turn and live; but thou wouldst not hearken? I forewarned thee of this danger, but thou didst slight all my warnings; and now thou seest whither thy way tended, but, alas, too late!"

The more knowledge or means of knowledge any man has neglected in this world, so many *great advantages he has lost* for heaven; and the more intolerable will hell be to him : as the mercy was great which was offered by them, so the torment will be unspeakable that will arise from their loss. Sinners, you have now an open door; many blessed opportunities of salvation under the gospel; it has put you in a fair way for everlasting happiness. Many of you are not far from the kingdom of God. How sad in hell to reflect upon this loss. "O how fair was I once for heaven, to have been with God, and among yonder saints. My conscience was once convinced, and my affections melted under the gospel. I was almost persuaded to be a Christian. The treaty was almost concluded between Christ and my soul. But, wretch that I was, I could not deny my lusts, nor live under the yoke of Christ's government; and now I must live under the insupportable wrath of the righteous God for ever." And this torment will be peculiar to such as perish under the gospel. The heathen, who enjoyed no such means, can have no such reflections ; nay, the very devils themselves, who never had a Mediator in their nature, or such terms of reconciliation offered them, will not reflect upon their lost opportunities of recovery as such sinners will. This, therefore, "is the condemnation, that light is come into the world ; but men loved darkness rather than light."

INFERENCE 1. *Hence it follows that neither knowledge, nor the best means of it, are sufficient to secure men from wrath to come.* Light is a choice mercy, and therefore the means that gave it must be so ; but it is a mercy liable to abuse, and the abuse of the best mercies causes the greatest miseries. Alas, Christians, your duty is but half learnt when you know it ; obedience to light makes light a blessing indeed. "If ye know these things, happy are ye if ye do them." John 13 : 17. Happiness is not entailed on knowing, but on doing—upon obedience to our knowledge ; otherwise he that increases knowledge does but increase sorrow. "That servant which knew his Lord's will, and prepared not himself, nor did according to his will, shall be beaten with many stripes." Luke 12 : 47. "To him that knoweth to do good, and doeth it not, to him it is sin." James 4 : 17. We are bound with all thankfulness to acknowledge the bounty of heaven in furnishing us with so many excellent means of light beyond many other nations and past generations ; but we ought to rejoice with trembling when we consider the abuses of light. God has blessed us with many burning and shining lights. The

greater will our account be for abusing such light and rebelling against it. The clearer our light is now, the thick-
er will the mists of darkness be hereafter, if we abuse it
The devils have more light than we, and therefore the
more torment. Of them it is said, "The devils also believe and tremble." James 2 : 19. The horror of their
consciences is answerable to their illumination.

2. If the abuse of light thus aggravate sin and misery,
times of great temptation are like to be times of great guilt.
Woe to an enlightened generation, when strong temptations befall them. How do many, in such times, imprison
the truth to keep themselves out of prison, and offer
violence to their conscience to avoid violence from other
hands.

Plato was convinced of the unity of God, yet durst not
own his convictions ; but said, " It is a truth neither easy
to find, nor safe to own." And even Seneca, the renowned
moralist, was led by temptation to dissemble his convictions ; of whom Augustine says, " He worshipped what he
reprehended, and did what he himself reproved." And even
a great papist of later times was heard to say, as he was
going to mass, "Let us go to the common error." O how
hard it is to keep conscience pure in days of temptation.
Doubtless it is a mercy to many weak Christians to be
removed by death out of harm's way, and disbanded by
Providence before the heat of the battle. Christ and anti-
christ seem at this day to be drawing into the field, and a
fiery trial threatens the professors of this age ; but when
it comes to a close engagement, we may tremble to think
how many thousands will break their way through the
convictions of their consciences to save their lives. If
Christ hold you to himself by no other tie than the slen-
der thread of a single conviction ; if he have not interest
in your heart and affections, as well as in your understanding and conscience ; if you are men of great light
and unmortified lusts ; if you profess Christ with the

tongue and worship the world with your hearts ; I may say of you, without the gift of prophecy, what the prophet said of Hazael, I know what you will do in the day of temptation.

3. If this be so, *what a strong engagement lies on all enlightened persons to turn heartily to God and reduce their knowledge to practice and obedience*   The more men know, the more violence they do their consciences in rebelling against the light ; this is to sin with a high hand.   Num. 15 : 30. Believe it, you cannot sin at so cheap a rate as others do ; knowledge in a wicked man but the sooner precipitates him into ruin.   You may know more than others, but if you go to heaven, it must be in the same way of faith and obedience, mortification and self-denial, in which the weakest Christian goes there ; whatever knowledge you have, you have no wisdom, if you expect salvation on any easier terms than the most illiterate Christian finds it.   It was an observation of one of the fathers, The unlearned rise and take heaven.   What a pity is it that men of excellent powers should be enslaved to their lusts ; that ever it should be said that learning does but blind men in spiritual things, and prepares them for greater misery.

4. Hence also it follows *that the work of conversion is very difficult;* the soul is scarcely half won to Christ when Satan is cast out of the understanding by illumination. The devil has deeply entrenched himself, and fortified every faculty of the soul against Christ.   The understanding is the first entrance into the soul, and out of that faculty he is oftentimes cast by light and conviction, which seems to make a great change upon a man : now he becomes a professor, takes up the duties of religion, and passes for a convert.   But alas, all the while Satan keeps the fort, the heart and will are in his possession ; and the weapons of that warfare must indeed be mighty through God, which not only cast down imaginations, but bring every thought of the heart into captivity to the obedience

Method.   23

of Christ. 2 Cor. 10 : 4, 5. While the heart stands out, though the understanding be won, the soul remains in Satan's possession : it is a greater work to win one heart than to convince twenty understandings.

5. Hence also we learn *what power there is in the lusts of men's hearts, which are able to bear down before them such strong convictions of the conscience.* That is a great truth, though a very sad one, "The heart of the sons of men is fully set in them to do evil." Eccl. 8 : 11. O how common is it to see men hazarding their souls to satisfy their lusts! "Every man," says the prophet, "turneth to his course, as the horse rusheth into the battle." The horse is a fierce and warlike creature ; and when his courage is roused by the sound of drums and trumpets and shouts of armies, he breaks headlong into the ranks of armed men, though death is before him. Such boisterous and headlong lusts are found in many enlightened persons ; though their consciences represent damnation before them, onward they will rush, though God be lost and the precious soul undone for ever.

6. *As you would avoid the deepest guilt and escape the heaviest condemnation, open your hearts to obey whatever God has opened your understandings to receive of his revealed will.* Obey the light of the gospel while you have opportunity to enjoy it. This was the counsel given by Christ : "Yet a little while is the light with you. Walk while you have the light, lest darkness come upon you." John 12 : 35. The manifestation of Christ in the gospel is the light of the world ; all the nations of the earth that have not this light are benighted ; and those on whom it has risen have but a short time under it. "Yet a little while the light is with you :" whatever patience God may exercise towards ignorant souls, commonly he makes short work with the despisers of this light. The light of the gospel is a lamp fed with golden oil ; God will not always continue such a light for them that but trifle with it. The night is coming, when

no man can work. There are many sad signs upon us of a setting sun, a night of darkness approaching; many burning and shining lights are extinguished, and many *put under a bushel;* your work is great, your time short, this is the only space you have for repentance. Rev. 2 : 21. If this opportunity of salvation is lost, it will never come again. Ezek. 24 : 13. How pathetic was that lamentation which Christ made over Jerusalem. "And when he was come near, he beheld the city, and wept over it, saying, 'If thou hadst known, even thou, at least in this thy day, the things which belong unto thy peace ; but now they are hid from thine eyes." Luke 19: 41, 42. Christ is threatening this people with the removal of his gospel presence ; he hath found but cold entertainment among us. The nation has been unkind to Christ. Many thousands there are that rebel against the light, that say unto God, "Depart from us ; we desire not the knowledge of thy ways." Christ will not tarry where he is not welcome. Obey the light therefore, lest God put it out in obscure darkness.

CHAPTER XXXIV

SATAN'S BLINDING THE CAUSE OF UNBELIEF, AND FORERUNNER OF DESTRUCTION

"But if our gospel be hid, it is hid to them that are lost; in whom the god of this world hath blinded the minds of them which believe not, lest the light of the glorious gospel of Christ, who is the image of God, should shine unto them." 2 Cor. 4: 3, 4

The aversion of men from Jesus Christ, their only remedy, is to be wondered at as well as lamented; one would think the news of deliverance should make the hearts of captives leap for joy, and that the tidings of a Saviour should transport the heart of a lost sinner. A man would think a little reasoning might persuade a sinner to put on the robes of Christ's righteousness, which cost him nothing but acceptance; or the perishing, starving sinner to accept the bread of God which cometh down from heaven and giveth life unto the world. This is the great design I have had in this work, the centre to which all these lines are drawn; many arguments have been used to prevail with men to apply and put on Christ, but I fear that to multitudes I have but labored in vain, and spent my strength for naught; that to them all these discourses are but beating the air, and that few, if any, will be persuaded to come unto Christ, who is clearly revealed and freely offered in the gospel.

For alas, while I am reasoning, Satan is blinding their minds with false reasonings and contrary persuasions; the god of this world turns away the ears and the hearts of almost the whole world from Christ. "The god of this world hath blinded the minds of them which believe not, lest the light of the glorious gospel of Christ, who is the image of God, should shine unto them." Satan is a jealous prince, and is well aware that such of his subjects as are brought to see the misery of their condition, will not abide any longer in subjection to him: it is therefore his policy to put out their eyes, that he may secure their souls; to darken their understandings, that he may keep his interest firm in their wills and affections: and this makes the effectual application of Christ so great a difficulty, that it is matter of admiration that any soul is persuaded to quit the service of Satan and come to Christ.

Therefore, in closing the whole work—to show the great difficulty of conversion, and how all our endeavors are obstructed, so that we accomplish no more, with all our laboring and striving, reasoning and persuading; as also to mourn over and bewail the misery of Christless and unregenerate souls—I have chosen this scripture, which is of a most awakening nature, if haply the Lord may thereby persuade any soul to come to Christ.

The apostle hath been speaking in the former chapter of the transcendent excellence of the gospel above the law, and among other things, he prefers it to the law on account of its clearness. The law was an obscure dispensation; there was a veil upon the face of Moses and the hearts of the people, that they could not see to the end of that which is abolished; but under the gospel, we all, with open face, behold, as in a glass, the glory of the Lord. Against this the apostle foresaw and obviated the objection, "If your gospel be so clear, what is the reason that many, who live under the ministration of it, see no excellence in it?" To this he replies, "If our gospel be hid, it is hid from them that are lost, whose eyes the god of this world hath blinded;" as though he had said, It is true, multitudes see no glory in Christ or the gospel, but the fault is not in either, but in the minds of them that believe not. The sun shines forth in its glory, but the blind see no glory in it: the fault is not in the sun, but in the eye. In the words themselves we have,

1. *A very dreadful spiritual judgment inflicted on the souls of men*, the hiding of the gospel from them. "If our gospel be hid;" for these words are a concession that so it is; a very sad but undeniable truth: many see no beauty in Christ, nor necessity of him; though both are so plainly revealed in our gospel. "If *our gospel* be hid." It is called our gospel, not as if Paul and other preachers were the authors of it, but because we are the preachers and dispensers of it. We are put in trust with the gospel, and though we preach it in the demonstration of the Spirit and of power, using all plainness of speech to make men understand it, yet it is hid from many under our ministry: it is hid from their understandings, they see no glory in it; and hid from their hearts, they see no power in it. Our gospel, notwithstanding all our endeavors, is hidden from some.

2. We have *an account of that wicked instrument by whom this judgment is inflicted*, namely, Satan, called here the god of this world; not properly, but because he challenges to himself the honor of a god, rules over a vast empire, and has multitudes of souls, even the greater part of the world, in subjection and blind obedience to his government.

3. Here, also, we have *the polity of this government*, how he maintains his dominion among men and keeps them in subjection, namely, by blinding the minds of all them that believe not; darkening that noble faculty, the understanding, the thinking and reasoning power of the soul, which philosophers call the leading and directing faculty; for it is to the soul what eyes are to the body, and is therefore called "the eyes of the understanding." Eph. 1 : 18. These eyes Satan blinds, so that when men come to see and consider spiritual things, "they see indeed, but perceive not." Isa. 6 : 9. They have some confused notions, but no distinct and effectual apprehensions of those things: and this is the way, indeed none like it, to bar men effectually from Jesus Christ, and hinder the *application of the*

benefit of redemption to their souls. It is true, the righteous
God permits all this to be done by Satan upon the souls
of men; but wheresoever he finally prevails thus to blind
them, it is, as the text speaks, *in them that are lost.* The
people of God are all blinded for a time, but Christ opens
the eyes of their understandings and recovers them out of
Satan's power; but on those who continue thus blinded
the symptoms of eternal death appear upon their souls;
they are lost men. Hence we learn, that

*The understandings of unbelievers are blinded by Satan to
their everlasting perdition.*

Four things must be here illustrated: what the blinding of the understanding, or hiding of the gospel from it,
is; that the understandings of many are thus blinded, and
the gospel hidden from them; what policy Satan uses to
blind the minds of men; and that this blindness is the
sorest judgment, securing men's everlasting perdition.

I. We shall inquire WHAT THE BLINDING OF THE MIND, OR
HIDING THE GOSPEL FROM IT, IS. Two sorts of men are thus
blinded: those that want the means of illumination, and
those that have the means, but are denied the efficacy of
them. The former is the case of the pagan world, who are
in midnight darkness for want of the gospel. The latter
is the case of the Christian world: the greater part of
them that live within the sound of the gospel being blinded by the god of this world. "And he said, Go and tell
this people, Hear ye indeed, but understand not; and see
ye indeed, but perceive not. Make the heart of this people fat, and make their ears heavy, and shut their eyes;
lest they see with their eyes, and hear with their ears,
and understand with their heart, and convert and be
healed." Isa. 6: 9, 10. Thus, when the Sun of righteousness actually arose on the world, it is said, "The
light shined in darkness, but the darkness comprehended
it not." John 1: 5. So we may say of all the light
which is in the understanding of unbelievers, what Job

says of the grave, That the light there is as darkness. Job 10 : 22. But more particularly,

1. Let us examine *what spiritual blindness is not opposed to.*

It is not opposed to *natural wisdom:* a man may be of an acute and clear understanding, eagle-eyed to discern the mysteries of nature, and yet the gospel may be hid from him. Who were more sagacious and quick-sighted in natural things than the heathen philosophers? yet unto them the gospel was foolishness. 1 Cor. 1 : 20, 21. Augustine confesses, that before his conversion he was filled with contempt of the simplicity of the gospel. I scorned, says he, to become a child again. And Bradwardine, who was learned to a wonder, professed that when he first read Paul's epistles he despised them because he found not in them the metaphysical notions which he expected. On this account it was that Christ broke forth into the pathetic admiration of his Father's love to his people: "At that time Jesus answered and said, I thank thee, O Father, Lord of heaven and earth, because thou hast hid these things from the wise and prudent, and hast revealed them unto babes." Matt. 11 : 25.

It is not opposed to *all light and knowledge in spiritual truths.* A man may have a correct understanding of the Scriptures, and enlighten the minds of others by them; and yet the gospel may be hidden from himself. "Many will say to me in that day, Lord, Lord, have we not prophesied in thy name?" Matt. 7 : 22. "And art confident that thou thyself art a guide of the blind, a light to them that sit in darkness." Rom. 2 : 19. A man may show others the way to Christ and salvation, while both are hid from himself.

It is not opposed to *all kind of influence on the affections;* for it is possible the gospel may touch them, and cause some sweet motions and raptures in them, and yet be hidden from the soul. Heb. 6 : 5, 6.

2. But if these may consist with spiritual blindness, to what then *is it opposed*? To which I answer, spiritual blindness stands opposed to the saving manifestation of Jesus Christ in the gospel by the Spirit, by which the soul is regenerated and effectually changed in real conversion to God. Wherever the gospel thus comes in the demonstration of the Spirit and of power, producing such an effect in the soul, it is no longer a hidden gospel. Though such persons do not see clearly all the glory which is revealed by the gospel; though they know but in part, and see darkly as through a glass; yet the eyes of their understandings are opened, and the things which belong to their peace are not hidden from them.

II. But though this is the happiness of some men, THE EYES OF MANY ARE BLINDED by the god of this world, and the gospel is hidden from them.

1. Many that live under the gospel are so *swallowed up in the world*, that they allow themselves no time to ponder the great concern of their souls in the world to come; and judge you, whatever the gifts and knowledge of these men are, whether the god of this world has not blinded their eyes. If it were not so, it were impossible that they should thus waste the most precious opportunities of salvation on which their everlasting well-being depends, and spend time at the door of eternity about trifles which so little concern them. Yet this is the case of the greater number that go under the Christian name. The earth hath opened her mouth and swallowed up their time, thoughts, studies, and strength, as it did the bodies of Korah and his associates. The whole of their time is devoted to the service of the world; for even when they present their bodies before the Lord in his worship, their hearts are wandering after vanities, and "going after their covetousness." Ezek. 33 : 31. Judge whether the god of this world has blinded these men or not, who can see so much beauty in the world, but none in Christ, and put an abso-

lute necessity upon the vanities of this world, but none
upon their own salvation. If this be not spiritual blindness, what is?

2. The *quietness of men's consciences*, under the most
awakening truths of the gospel, proves that the god of
this world has blinded their eyes. For did men see the
dangerous condition they are in as the word represents it,
nothing would quiet them but Christ. As soon as men's
eyes are opened, the inquiry they make is, "What shall
we do to be saved?" It is not possible that a man should
hang over hell and see Christ and the hope of salvation
going, and the day of patience ending, and yet be quiet.
O it cannot be that conscience should let them be quiet in
such a case, if it were not blinded and stupefied; but
while the god of this world, that strong man armed, keepeth his palace, his goods are in peace." Luke 11 : 21. If
once your eyes were opened by conviction, you could not
sit still and let the season of salvation pass away. Suppose one should come in and whisper in your ears, that
your child is fallen into the fire and is dying; would it be
in the power of friends to quiet you, and make you sit
still after such information? much less when a man apprehends his own soul to be in immediate danger of everlasting burnings.

3. The *presumptuous hopes* men have of salvation while
they remain unregenerate, show their minds to be blinded
by the policy of Satan. This presumption is one of those
false reasonings by which Satan deludes the understanding, as the apostle calls them. James 1 : 22. It is the
cunning sophistry of the devil seconded by self-love:
"Every way of a man is right in his own eyes," Prov.
21 : 2; and partly by self-ignorance : "Thou sayest I am
rich and increased with goods, and have need of nothing;
and knowest not that thou art wretched." Rev. 3 : 17.
You have no fears, no doubts, no case to propound that
concerns your future state ; and why so, but because you

have no sight? Your consciences are quieted because your eyes are blinded.

4. *The trifling of men with the duties of religion* shows the blinding power of Satan on their understandings, else they would never trifle with the solemn ordinances of God as they do. If their eyes were opened, they would be in earnest in prayer, and apply themselves with the closest attention to hearing the gospel. There are two sorts of thoughts about any subject of meditation : some think at a distance, and others think close to the subject. Never do thoughts of men come so close to Christ, to heaven, and to hell, as they do immediately upon their illumination. When John's ministry enlightened the people, it is said, "From the days of John the Baptist until now the kingdom of heaven suffereth violence, and the violent take it by force." Matt. 11 : 12. Surely these men were in earnest who would take no denial, but force themselves through all difficulties into heaven ; and so would it be with you. If the god of this world had not blinded your minds, you would never pray with so much unconcern, nor hear with so much carelessness. It is with many of your hearts as it was with Aristotle, who, after an oration made before him, was asked how he liked it. Truly, said he, I did not hear it, for I was thinking all the while of another matter.

5. It is also an evidence that the god of this world hath blinded the eyes of many, that they *fear not to commit great sins to avoid small troubles*, which all the world could not persuade them to do, if they were not hoodwinked by the god of this world. Those that have seen sin in the glass of God's law will choose, as Moses did, to suffer any affliction with the people of God, rather than enjoy the pleasures of sin, which are but for a season. Heb. 11 : 25. Those that have felt the evil of sin in the deep troubles of their spirit for it, will account all reproaches, all losses, all sufferings from men to be but as nothing to the burden of sin.

6. *The pride and self-conceit* of many who profess Christianity, show their mind to be blinded by the sophistry of Satan, and that they do not understand themselves and the state of their souls. Those that see God in the clearest light, abhor themselves in the deepest humility. Isa. 6 : 5 ; John 42 : 6. If the Lord had effectually opened your eyes by a discovery of your state by nature, and the course of your life under the influence of continual temptations and corruptions, how would your pride fall. None would rate you lower than you yourselves would.

III. We are to consider WHAT POLICY SATAN USES to blind the minds of them that believe not, and we shall find there are three sorts of policies practised by the god of this world upon the minds of men which he darkens.

1. It is a great policy in Satan to blind the understandings of men *by hindering the reception of gospel light*, which he does,

(1.) By tempting *the dispensers* of the gospel to darken its truths in delivering them : to shoot over the heads of their hearers in lofty language and terms of art, so that common understandings can give no account, when the sermon is done, what the preacher has said ; but commend him as a good scholar and an excellent orator. The devil is very busy with ministers in their studies, tempting them, by the pride of their own hearts, to gratify his designs herein : he teaches them how to paint the glass, that he may keep out the light.

I acknowledge, a proper, grave, and comely style befits the lips of Christ's ambassadors ; they should not be rude and careless in their language or method. But the affectation of great swelling words of vanity is but too like the proud Gnostics, whom the apostle is supposed to reprove for this evil, Jude 16. This is to darken counsel by words without knowledge, Job 38 : 2, and to amuse poor ignorant souls, and nullify the design of preaching ; for every thing is accounted so far good as it is good to the end it is ordained for. A sword that has a hilt of gold set thick with diamonds is not a good sword if it has no edge to cut, or wants a good back to support the stroke. O that the ministers of Christ would choose sound rather than great words, such as are apt to pierce the heart rather than such as tickle the fancy ; and let people beware of furthering the design of Satan against their souls, in putting a temptation upon their ministers by despising plain preaching. The more popular, plain, and intelligible our discourses are, so much the more likely they are to be successful. That is the most excellent oratory which draws men to Christ.

(2.) Satan hinders the access of light to the understandings of men, by employing their minds about other things while they are attending on the ordinances of God. Thus he tempted the Jews : "And they come unto thee as the people cometh, and they sit before thee as my people; and they hear thy words, but they will not do them ; for with their mouth they show much love, but their heart goeth after their covetousness. And lo, thou art unto them as a very lovely song of one that hath a pleasant voice." Ezek. 33 : 31, 32. The prophet's voice was very pleasing to their ears, but their thoughts were wandering after their lusts ; their hearts were full of earthly projects.

(3.) Satan hinders the access of light to the understandings of men, by *raising objections* to the word, to shake its authority and hinder the assent of the understanding to it, and so it makes no more impression than a fable or romance. The devil has persuaded many that the gospel is but a cunningly devised fable ; that the ministers must say something to get a living ; that heaven and hell are but fancies, or, at most, things of great uncertainty. Thus the door of the soul is shut against truth. And this design of Satan hath prospered the more in this generation, by the corrupt doctrines of seducing spirits, which have overthrown the faith of some, 2 Tim. 2 : 18 ; and partly from the scandalous lives of loose and vain professors, by which the gospel has been brought into contempt

(4.) Satan hinders the access of light by helping erroneous minds to *draw false conclusions* from the precious truths of the gospel, thereby bringing them under contempt. Thus he assists the errors of men's minds about the doctrine of election, when he either persuades them that it is an unreasonable doctrine and not worthy of credit, that God should choose some and leave others to perish; or that, if there be any certainty in the doctrine, then men may throw the reins upon the neck of their lusts and live at what rate they list; for they argue that if God has chosen them to salvation, their wickedness will not hinder it; and if he has appointed them unto wrath, their diligence and self-denial cannot prevent it. Thus the doctrine of free grace is by the like sophistry of Satan turned into lasciviousness. If grace abound, say some, men may sin the more freely; and thus the shortness of our time upon earth, which should awaken men to diligence, is by the subtlety of Satan turned to a contrary purpose, "Let us eat and drink, for to-morrow we die."

(5.) Satan darkens the minds of men *by filling them with pride and self-conceit*, persuading them that they know all these things already, and causing them to contemn the most weighty and precious truths of God as trite and vulgar notions. The word cannot be received without meekness and humility of mind, James 1 : 21; Psalm 25 : 8, 9; and pride is the nurse of ignorance. 1 Tim. 6 : 4; 1 Cor. 8 : 7. The devil is aware of this, and therefore cherishes the pride of men's hearts all he can. And this temptation generally prevails wherever it meets with a knowing head matched with a graceless, unsanctified heart. Thus we see by what wiles Satan keeps out the light, and prevents the access of it to the minds of men. But if he fail in his design here, and truth gets into the mind, then,

2. *He labors to obstruct the operation* of the light; that though it shine into the understanding, it may be imprisoned there, and exert no converting influence upon the will and affections; and this design he promotes,

(1.) By hastening *to quench convictions* and nip them in the bud. Satan knows how dangerous a thing it is, and destructive to his interest, to suffer convictions to continue long; and therefore it is said, "When any one heareth the word of the kingdom, and understandeth it not, then cometh the wicked one and catcheth away that which was sown in his heart." Matt. 13 : 19. Satan is compared in this scripture to the fowls of the air, which pick up the seed before it take root in the earth. The devil is very jealous of this, and therefore labors all he can to destroy the word before it operates upon the heart; which he does sometimes by the cares of the world, and sometimes by vain companions, who extinguish rising convictions. One sinner destroyeth much good.

(2.) No sooner does the god of this world observe the light of truth begin to operate upon the heart, but he obstructs the design by *procrastination* and delay, which delude and destroy convinced souls; he persuades them that if they will alter their course, it will be time enough hereafter, when such troubles in the world are over, if he prevail here, it is a thousand to one but the work fails. James 1 : 13, 14. If the hearer of the word be not a doer, that is, a present doer, while the impressions of it are fresh upon the soul, he does but deceive himself. For it is with the heart as with melted wax: if the seal be applied to it at once, it will receive a fair impression; but if it be let alone for a little while, you can make none at all. It was therefore David's great care and wisdom to set about the work of religion under the first impulse or vigorous motion of his heart and affections. "I made haste, and delayed not to keep thy commandments." Psa. 119: 60. Multitudes of souls have perished by these delays. It is a temptation incident to all under convictions, especially young persons, whom the devil persuades that it were no better than madness in them to deny themselves so much pleasure, and devote their youthful thoughts to such a melancholy subject as religion.

(3.) If all this will not do, but convictions still continue to get ground in the conscience, then he endeavors to fright them out of their convictions, by representing the inward terrors and despair into which they are about to plunge themselves, and that henceforth they must never expect a pleasant day or comfortable hour. Thus does the god of this world blind the minds of them that believe not, both by hindering the access of light to the mind and the influence of it upon the heart.

3. There is yet another policy of Satan to keep souls in darkness, that is, by *the misapplication of truth;* persuading them, that whatever they read or hear of the misery and danger of unregenerate persons does not concern them, but the more profane part of the world ; and by this policy he blinds the minds of moral persons. Thus the Pharisees " trusted in themselves that they were righteous, and despised others." And so the Laodiceans thought themselves rich, and increased with goods ; that is, in a safe and good condition. There are divers things improved by Satan in order to these misapplications of truth.

(1.) The freedom of their lives from the gross pollutions of the world. "All these things have I kept from my youth up." Matt. 19 : 20. A moral course of life is a most effectual blind before many a man's conscience.

(2.) It is the policy of Satan to prevent effectual convictions by convictions that have been ineffectual, and that are vanished away. Thus the troubles that some persons have been under pass for their conversion, though the temper of their heart be the same it was. Their ineffectual troubles are made use of by the devil to blind them to the true knowledge of their condition. These men can speak of the troubles they have had for sin, and the tears they have shed for it ; whereby thorough conviction is effectually prevented.

(3.) *Gifts and knowledge* are improved by Satan against the true knowledge of Jesus Christ and our own state by nature. "Thou art called a Jew, and restest in the law, and makest thy boast of God, and knowest his will, and approvest the things that are more excellent, being instructed out of the law ; and art confident that thou thyself art a guide to the blind." Rom. 2 : 17, 18. And this is the temptation and delusion of intelligent persons, who are so far from being blind in their own esteem, that they account themselves the guides of the blind. Yet who blinder than such men ?

(4.) *External reformation* is improved by Satan against true spiritual reformation, and passes for conversion, though it serves only to strengthen Satan's power in the soul, Matt. 12 : 44 ; and for want of a real change of heart does but increase a man's sin and misery. 2 Pet. 2 : 20. This is the generation that is pure in their own eyes, and yet are not washed from their filthiness. The cleanness of their hands blinds them in discovering the foulness of their hearts.

(5.) The policy of Satan improves *diligence in some duties,* against the conviction of neglect in others : the external duties of religion, as hearing, praying, fasting, against the great internal duties of repenting and believing. "They seek me daily, and delight to know my ways, as a nation that did righteousness and forsook not the ordinance of their God ; they ask of me the ordinances of justice ; they take delight in approaching to God. Wherefore have we fasted, say they, and thou seest not ? Wherefore have we afflicted our souls, and thou takest no knowledge ?" Isaiah 58 : 2, 3. Thus duty is improved against duty, the externals against the internals of religion, and multitudes are blinded this way.

(6.) The policy of Satan improves *zeal against zeal*, and thereby blinds a great part of the world: he allows men to be zealous against a false religion, if thereby he may prevent them from being zealous in the true. He diverts their zeal against their own sins, by directing it against other men's. Thus Paul was once blinded by his zeal for the law. Acts 22 : 3. And many men now satisfy themselves in their zeal against the corruptions of God's worship and the superstitions of others, who never felt the power of true religion upon their own hearts ; a dangerous blind of Satan.

(7.) The policy of Satan improves *the respect* men have for the people of God against their great duty and interest to become such themselves. "Thou hast a name that thou livest, and thou art dead." Rev. 3 : 1. It is enough for many men to obtain acceptance among the saints, though they are not of their number. The good opinion of others confirms their good opinion of themselves.

(8.) The policy of Satan improves soundness of judgment against soundness of heart. An orthodox head against an orthodox heart and life ; dogmatical faith against justifying faith. This was the case of them before-mentioned. Rom. 2 : 18, 19. Men satisfy themselves that they have a sound understanding, though, at the same time, they have a very rotten heart. It is enough for them that their heads are regular, though their hearts and lives be very irregular.

(9.) The policy of Satan blinds us by the blessings of Providence, that we may not discern the want of spiritual blessings ; persuading men that the smiles of Providence in their worldly prosperity are good evidences of the love of God to their souls—not at all discerning how the prosperity of fools destroys them, and that riches are given often to the hurt of the owners thereof.

(10.) The policy of Satan improves false and ungrounded comfort under the word, against the real grounds of comfort arising from the soul's interest in Christ. Thus many men, finding comfort in the promises, are so blinded thereby as never to look after union with Christ, the only solid ground of all comfort. Heb. 6 : 19.

Thus you see how the god of this world blinds the minds of them that believe not, and how the gospel is hid to them that are lost.

CHAPTER XXXV

SATAN'S BLINDING THE CAUSE OF UNBELIEF—CONTINUED

"But if our gospel be hid, it is hid to them that are lost: in whom the god of this world hath blinded the minds of them which believe not, lest the light of the glorious gospel of Christ, who is the image of God, should shine unto them." 2 COR. 4: 3, 4

IN the previous discourse we have drawn from these words the doctrine, that *the understandings of unbelievers are blinded by Satan to their everlasting perdition;* and have shown what blinding the mind, or hiding the gospel from it, is; that the minds of many are thus blinded and the gospel hidden from them; and what policies Satan uses to blind the minds of men, even in the clearest light of the gospel. It remains that I show,

IV. THE DREADFUL NATURE OF THIS JUDGMENT OF GOD UPON THE SOULS OF MEN. There are many judgments of God inflicted upon men, but none are so dreadful as those spiritual judgments which God inflicts immediately upon the soul; and among spiritual judgments, none are more dreadful in their nature and consequences than this of spiritual blindness; which will appear by considering,

1. *The subject of this judgment,* which is the soul, and the principal power of the soul, the understanding. The soul is the most precious part of man, the understanding is the noblest power of the soul; it is to the soul what the eye is to the body, the directive faculty. The loss of the eyes is a sore loss, we lose a great part of our comfort by it. Yet such an affliction is but a trifle to this. If our bodily eyes be blinded, we cannot see the sun; but if our spiritual eye be blinded, we cannot see God, but

wander in the paths of sin. 1 John 2 : 11. We are led blindfold to hell by Satan, as the Syrians were in Samaria. 2 Kings 6 : 19, 20. And our eyes, like theirs, will be opened to see our misery when it is too late. The light of the body is the eye : if therefore thine eye be single, thy whole body shall be full of light. But if thine eye be evil, thy whole body shall be full of darkness. If therefore the light that is in thee be darkness, how great is that darkness. Matt. 6 : 22, 23. By the eye he means the judgment, the understanding, which is the seat for principles, the treasury of the rules of practice, according to which a man's life is formed. If therefore that power of the soul be darkened, how great must that darkness be ; for now the blind lead the blind. The judgment misguides the affections. O what a sad thing that the devil should lead that which leads thee—that he should sit at the helm and steer thy course to damnation ! The blinding of this noble faculty precipitates the soul into the most dangerous courses ; persecution, by this means, seems to be zeal for God. They that persecute you shall think that they do God service. John 16 : 2. Paul once thought verily with himself, that he ought to do many things contrary to the name of Jesus of Nazareth. Acts 26 : 9. He thought he pleased God when he was imprisoning and persecuting his people, as many do at this day ; it will make a man sin conscientiously, which is a very dangerous way of sinning, and difficult to be reclaimed.

2. It is a dreadful judgment, if we consider *the object about which the understanding is blinded*, which is Jesus Christ, and union with him ; regeneration, and its nature and necessity. A man may have knowledge in things natural and moral, but spiritual things are hidden from his eyes. Yea, a man may know spiritual things in a natural way, but he cannot discern them spiritually ; this is a sore judgment, and greatly to be bewailed. "Thou hast hid these things from the wise and prudent, and hast re-

vealed them unto babes." Matt. 11 : 25. Learned men are often ignorant of the things which babes in Christ understand. They are prudent in the management of earthly affairs ; but to save their souls they have no knowledge. They may be able to dispute of every thing investigable by the light of nature ; yea, to defend the doctrines of Christ against his adversaries successfully, and yet be blind in the great mystery of regeneration. The literal knowledge of Jesus Christ shines clearly in our understanding : we are only blinded about the things which should give us saving interest in him, about the effectual application of Christ to our own souls.

3. The dreadful nature of this spiritual blindness farther appears from *the season in which it befalls men,* which is the very time of God's patience, and the only opportunity they have for salvation ; after these opportunities are over, their eyes will be opened to see their misery; but alas, too late. Upon this account Christ shed those tears over Jerusalem, Luke 19 : 42 : "If thou hadst known, even thou, at least in this thy day, the things which belong to thy peace ; but now they are hid from thine eyes"—now the season of grace is gone. Opportunities are the golden spots of time, and there is much time in a short opportunity as there are many pieces of silver in one piece of gold. Time signifies nothing when opportunities are gone; to be blinded in the very season of salvation is the judgment of all judgments, the greatest misery incident to man ; to have our eyes opened when the season of salvation is past, is but an aggravation of misery. They whose eyes are not opened *graciously* in this world to see their disease and the remedy in Christ, shall have their eyes opened *judicially* in the world to come to see their disease, without any remedy. If God open them now, it is by way of prevention ; if they be not opened till then, it will produce desperation.

4. The horrible nature of this judgment farther ap-

pears *from the exceeding difficulty of curing it*, especially in men of excellent natural endowments.   "And some of the Pharisees which were with him heard these words, and said unto him, Are we blind also?   Jesus said unto them, If ye were blind, ye should have no sin : but now ye say, We see ; therefore your sin remaineth," John 9 : 40, 41 ; as if he had said, The pride and conceit of your heart add obstinacy and incurableness to your blindness. These are "the blind people that have eyes."   Isa. 43 : 8. In seeing, they see not.   The conviction of such men is next to an impossibility.

5. The *design and end* of this blindness under the gospel is most dreadful : so says my text, "The god of this world hath blinded the minds of them which believe not, lest the light of the glorious gospel of Christ, who is the image of God, should shine unto them."   Answerable whereunto are those words, "Make the heart of this people fat, and make their ears heavy, aud shut their eyes ; lest they see with their eyes, and hear with their ears, and understand with their heart, and convert, and be healed."   Isaiah 6 : 10.   So that it is plain, this blinding is a prelude to damnation, as the covering of Haman's face was to his destruction.   When the Lord has no purpose of mercy to a man's soul, many occasions of blindness befall him, which Satan improves to his eternal ruin ; among which fatal occasions, blind guides, and scandalous professors are none of the least ; they shall have ministers suitable to their desires, who shall speak smooth things : "If a man walking in the spirit of falsehood do lie, saying, I will prophesy to thee of wine and strong drink, he shall even be the prophet of this people."   Micah 2 : 11.   And the falls of professors shall do the devil not a little service in this fatal design.   "Woe unto the world because of offences."   Matt. 18 : 7.   This shall blind and harden them to purpose.

Thus you see what a dreadful judgment this is, which

cuts off all the present comforts of Christ and religion, takes away restraint from sin, and makes way for final ruin. A far greater judgment it is than the greatest calamity which can befall us in the world. If our names suffer by reproaches, our bodies by painful diseases, our estates by the greatest losses; if God strike every comfort we have in this world dead by affliction; all is nothing, compared with this blinding judgment of God upon the soul. Such afflictions may come from the tender love of God to us, Heb. 12 : 6; but this is the effect of his wrath; they may cleanse away sin, Isa. 27 : 9, but this increases it; they often prove occasions of conversion, Job 36 : 8, 9, but this is the great obstruction to it.

INFERENCE 1. If the unbelieving world be so blinded by the god of this world, *how little should we value its censures and slanders.* Certainly they should move only pity in the soul: if their eyes were opened their mouths would be shut. They would never traduce religion and the sincere profession of it as they do, if Satan had not blinded their minds: they speak evil of the things they know not; their reproaches, which they let fly so freely, are but so many arrows shot by the blind man's bow, which only stick in our clothes, and can do us no hurt, except we thrust them onward by our own discontent to the wounding of our spirits. "I could almost be proud," said Luther, "that I have got an ill name among the worst of men." Beware, Christian, that you give them no occasion to blaspheme the name of your God; and then never trouble yourselves, however they reproach you. Should such men speak well of us, we might suspect ourselves of some iniquity, administering to them the occasion of it.

2. *How absurd and dangerous must it be for Christians to follow the example of the blind world.* Let the blind follow the blind, but let not those whom God has enlightened do so. Christians, let not those lead you who are led blindfold by the devil themselves. The holiness and heaven-

liness of Christians was wont to set the world wondering
that they would not run with them into the same excess
of riot. 1 Pet. 4 : 4. But since God has showed you the
dangerous courses they walk in, it would be the greatest
wonder of all if you s' ould be the companion of such men
and imitate their example. Christian, as humble and lowly
thoughts as thou hast of thyself, I would have thee think
thyself too good to be the associate of such men. If they
will walk with you in the way of holiness, let them come
and welcome ; receive them and be glad of their company;
but beware you walk not in their paths, lest they be a
snare to you. Did they see the end of their way, they
would never walk in it themselves ; why then will you
who do see it walk with them?

3. If this be so, *let Christians be circumspect in their
walk, lest they lay a stumbling-block before the blind.* It is a
great sin to do so in a literal sense. Lev. 19 : 14. And a
far greater to do it in a metaphorical sense. It is the express will of God, "that no man put a stumbling-block or
an occasion to fall in his brother's way." Rom. 15 : 13.
O professors, look to your steps ; the devil desires to make
use of you for such purposes. The sins of thousands,
who make no profession of godliness, will never so fit his
purpose for the blinding of men's eyes as the least failing
of yours will do. The living bird makes the best lure to
draw others into the net : the grossest wickedness of profane sinners passes away in silence, but all the neighborhood will ring with your misconduct. "A righteous man
falling down before the wicked, is as a troubled fountain
and a corrupt spring." Prov. 25 : 26. The scandalous
falls of good men are like a bag of poison cast into the
spring from whence the whole town is supplied with water.
You little know what mischief you do, and how many sinners may thereby fall into hell.

4. *How dangerous is zeal in a wicked man!* It is like a
sword in a blind man's hand, or high mettle in a blind

horse. How much has the church of God suffered on this account, and suffers at this day : the world has ever been full of blind zeal, which, like a hurricane, overturns all that stands in its way, yea, makes a man a conscientious persecutor. I confess it is better for the persecutor if he do it ignorantly, because ignorance leaves him in a capacity for mercy, and sets him a degree lower than' the malicious, enlightened persecutor, 1 Tim. 1 : 13 ; else it were the dreadful case described in Heb. 10 : 38, 39. But yet these are the fierce and dreadful enemies of the church of God. John 16 : 2. Such a man was Paul, a devout persecutor, and such persecution God afterwards suffered to befall himself : "But the Jews stirred up devout and honorable women, and the chief men of the city, and raised persecution against Paul and Barnabas, and expelled them out of their coasts." Acts 13 : 50. An erroneous conscience binds, as well as an informed conscience ; and wherever God gives such men opportunity to vent the rage of their hearts upon his people, they will do it to purpose. With other men Gamaliel's counsel may have influence, and they may be afraid lest they be found fighters against God ; but blind zeal spurs on, and says as Jehu did, "Come, see my zeal for the Lord of hosts." O sinners, be sure of your mark before you discharge your arrows. If you shoot at a wicked man, as you suppose him, and God finds one of his dear children wounded or destroyed, what account will you give to God when you shall come before his judgment-seat?

5. *To those who are still blinded by the god of this world,* to whom the Lord has not given eyes to see their misery in themselves, or their remedy in Christ, so as to make an effectual application of him to their own souls—to all such my counsel is,

Labor to get *a deep sense of the misery* of such a condition ; for till you are awakened by conviction you can never be healed. O that you did but know the difference between common and saving light; the want of this keeps you in darkness: you think, because you know the same things that sanctified men do, there is no difference between their knowledge and yours; and are therefore ready to say to them, as Job to his friends, "Lo, mine eye hath seen all this, mine ear hath heard and understood it: what ye know, the same do I know also; I am not inferior unto you." Job 13:1, 2. But O that you were convinced that your knowledge vastly differs from the knowledge of believers. Though you know the same things that they do, it is a knowledge of another kind and nature. You know spiritual things merely by the light of reason, assisted by the common light of the gospel; they know the same things by spiritual illumination, and in an experimental way. They "have an unction from the Holy One, and know all things." 1 John 2:20. Their knowledge is practical, yours is idle. They are working out their salvation by the light which God has given them. Psalm 111:10. Their knowledge of God and Christ produces the fruits of faith, obedience, and heavenly-mindedness in them: it has no such fruits in you; whatever light there is in your understandings, it makes no alteration in your hearts. Their light brings them to heaven. John 17:3. Yours shall be blown out by death, 1 Cor. 13:8, and you left in eternal darkness, except your eyes be opened seasonably by the anointing of the Holy Ghost. Conviction is a great part of your cure.

Labor also to get *a remedy* for this dangerous disease of your minds: "Awake to righteousness, and sin not; for some have not the knowledge of God: I speak this to your shame." 1 Cor. 15:34. These things give you encouragement, though it is a sore judgment that lies upon you, and difficult to be removed: yet remember Jesus Christ is commissioned to open the blind eyes, Isaiah 42:6, 7; and this excellent Physician advises for his patients, "Anoint thine eyes with eye-salve, that thou mayest see." Rev. 3 : 18. The most enlightened Christians were once as blind in spiritual things as you are, and Christ has cured them. "Ye were sometime darkness, but now are ye light in the Lord." Eph. 5 : 8. Attend therefore on the ordinances of the gospel diligently ; they are God's instruments by which he enlightens the eyes of men's understandings. Acts 26 : 18. And if you would have your eyes opened, allow yourselves time to ponder and consider what you hear. Meditation is a very enlightening duty : above all, cry to the Lord Jesus Christ, as that poor man did, Lord, that mine eyes may be opened, that I may receive my sight. Say, Lord, this is my disease and danger, that in seeing I see not. Others see natural things in a spiritual way, while I see spiritual things only in a natural way. Their light is operative upon their hearts ; mine is but a speculative religion, which brings forth no fruit of holiness. Their knowledge sets them at work in duties of obedience ; mine only leads me to talk of those things which my heart never felt. Lord, open mine eyes and make me to see out of this obscurity : all the light that is in me is but darkness. O Lord, enlighten my darkness, enlighten mine eyes, lest I sleep the sleep of death.

6. Let there be a word of counsel to *such as once were blind, but do now see.*

I beseech you, bless God for the least degree of spiritual illumination. "Truly light is sweet, and a pleasant thing it is for the eyes to behold the sun." Eccles. 11 : 7. But O how sweet is spiritual light ; and what a pleasant thing to behold the Sun of righteousness ! Blessed are your eyes, for they see. God has brought you out of darkness into marvellous light. And marvellous indeed it must be, when you consider how many wise and prudent men are under the power of spiritual darkness, while such babes as you are enlightened. It greatly affected the heart of Christ ; let it affect yours also.

Labor to get a clearer sight of spiritual things every day. For all spiritual light increases like the sun, which shineth more and more unto the perfect day. Prov. 4:18. If a little spiritual light be so comfortable, what would more be? The wisdom of God is manifold wisdom. Eph. 3:10. The best see but little of it. Labor therefore to know spiritual things more extensively and experimentally. Phil. 3:8, 9. Be still increasing in the knowledge of God.

Walk as men whose eyes are opened. Once ye were in darkness, now are ye light in the Lord; walk as children of the light, Eph. 5:8, else your light will but aggravate your sin. Remember how it displeased God, that Solomon's heart was turned from the Lord God of Israel, who appeared to him twice. 1 Kings 11:9. Remember how angry God was with the heathen for abusing the light of nature. Rom. 1:21. How much more evil is it in you to abuse the most precious light that shines in the world; and what mischievous effects the abuse of your light will have upon this blind world. It was a severe rebuke given by an atheist to a good man, who asked him how he could satisfy his conscience to live as he did; nay, rather, said the atheist, I wonder how you can satisfy yourself to live as you do; for did I believe as you do, that there is such a Christ and glory as you believe there are, I would pray and live differently from what you do.

CONCLUSION

And now, reader, in all my discourses of the method of Christ in purchasing the great salvation for us, and the way of the Spirit in applying it to God's elect, thou hast two wonders before thine eyes, either of which may astonish thy soul.

1. *Behold the riches of the mercy of God in preparing such a remedy as this for lost man.* This is that which is called the "great mystery of godliness," 1 Tim. 3 : 16—that mystery which the prophets inquired diligently after, yea, which the angels desire to look into. 1 Pet. 1 : 10, 12. In this glorious mystery of redemption, that manifold wisdom of God, or that wisdom which has such admirable variety in it, is illustriously displayed. Eph. 3 : 10. Yea, the contrivance of our redemption is the most glorious display of divine love that ever was made, or can be made to the children of men; for so the apostle must be understood when he says, God has set forth, or presented his love to man in the most engaging manner, in a way that commends it beyond all comparison to the acceptance of men. Rom. 5 : 8. "This is a faithful saying, and worthy of all acceptation, that Christ Jesus came into the world to save sinners." 1 Tim. 1 : 15. It might be expected that when this glorious mystery should be published by the gospel in the ears of sinners, all eyes should be withdrawn from other objects and fixed with admiration upon Christ, that all hearts should be ravished with these glad tidings, and every man pressing to Christ with the greatest zeal and diligence. But behold, instead thereof,

2. *The desperate wickedness of the world in rejecting the only remedy prepared for them.* This was long since foretold by the prophet. "He is despised, and rejected of men; a man of sorrows, and acquainted with grief: and we hid our faces from him; he was despised, and we esteemed him not." Isa. 53 : 3. His mean appearance, which should have endeared him beyond all estimation to the souls of men, since it was for their sakes that he emptied himself of all his glory, lays him under contempt; he is looked on as the very offcast of men. When his love to man had emptied him of his riches, the wickedness of men loaded him with contempt, and as prophesied

of him, so it was, and at this day is sadly verified all the world over; for the pagan world have no knowledge of him, they are lost in darkness. God has suffered them to walk in their own ways. Acts 14 : 16. The Mahometans who overspread so great a part of the world reject him, and instead of the blessed gospel, which they hiss at with abhorrence, embrace the blasphemous and ridiculous Koran, which they confidently affirm came down from God, calling all Christians infidels. The Jews reject him with abhorrence, and in a blind zeal for Moses, blaspheme him as an impostor. "He came to his own, and his own received him not." John 1 : 11. Nay, the great part of what is called the Christian world reject him; those that are called after his name will not submit to his government. The *nobles* of the world think themselves dishonored by submitting their necks to his yoke. The *sensualists* of the world will not deny their lusts, or forsake their pleasures, for all the treasures of righteousness, life, and peace which his blood has purchased. Worldlings prefer the dross of the world before him; and few among those who profess Christianity love the Lord Jesus in sincerity. The only reason why they are called Christians is, because, by the kindness of Providence, they were born and educated in a country where Christianity is professed.

Now, reader, let me tell thee, that if ever God send forth his law and thine own conscience to arrest thee for thy sins, if thou find thyself dragged away by them towards that prison from whence none return, and that in this unspeakable distress Jesus Christ manifests himself to thy soul, and opens thy heart to receive him, and becomes thy surety with God, and cancels all thy obligations, thou wilt love him at another rate than others do; his blood will run deeper in thine eyes than it doth in the shallow apprehensions of the world; he will be *altogether lovely*, and thou wilt account all things but dung and dross in comparison of the excellence of Jesus Christ thy Lord. To work thy heart to this frame these things are written, which the Lord prosper upon thy soul, by the blessing of his good Spirit upon thee.

Blessed be God for Jesus Christ.